SO-EJH-516

PLUTARCH

ALEXANDER

A Commentary

PLUTARCH
ALEXANDER
A Commentary

J. R. HAMILTON

OXFORD
AT THE CLARENDON PRESS
1969

Oxford University Press, Ely House, London W. 1

GLASGOW NEW YORK TORONTO MELBOURNE WELLINGTON
CAPE TOWN SALISBURY IBADAN NAIROBI LUSAKA ADDIS ABABA
BOMBAY CALCUTTA MADRAS KARACHI LAHORE DACCA
KUALA LUMPUR SINGAPORE HONG KONG TOKYO

PRINTED IN GREAT BRITAIN

TO
ELAINE

PREFACE

I WAS led to begin this Commentary by the surprising discovery that no ancient writer on Alexander, not even the invaluable Arrian, had been provided with an English commentary. (The intervening years have seen the publication of C. Bradford Welles's admirable edition of Diodorus 17 in the Loeb series.) The present work, then, is designed primarily as a contribution to Alexander studies. The references to the ancient sources are meant to be complete; of the extensive modern literature on Alexander I have cited only those books and articles which seemed to me still worth reading. My debt to the biographies of Tarn, Wilcken, and Schachermeyr will be evident, and I have found Tarn's *Sources and Studies* and Berve's second volume indispensable. Nevertheless my greatest stimulus has come from the numerous articles written by Ernst Badian in the last ten years.

Although I have devoted most space to historical matters, I have tried to keep in mind that this is a commentary on Plutarch's *Life*, not a history of Alexander, and to deal adequately with those incidents which attracted the interest of Plutarch as a biographer. It seemed worth while, also, to compare the rhetorical Alexander of the *De Alexandri fortuna* with the Alexander of the *Life*, and to point out the not infrequent passages where the same incident is treated in different ways.

The Introduction owes much to Konrat Ziegler's *RE* article, and was completed before the appearance of R. H. Barrow's *Plutarch and His Times* and A. J. Gossage's chapter on Plutarch in T. A. Dorey's *Latin Biography*. It was written in the conviction that Plutarch's biographies cannot be fully understood without some knowledge of his career and background and of his aims and methods. The section on Plutarch's style, on which much remains to be done, is virtually restricted to the *Alexander*.

The text quoted in the *lemmata*, even where another reading is proposed in the note, is that of Ziegler's revised Teubner edition. Professor Ziegler has put me more deeply in his debt by informing me before publication of those passages where he has adopted a reading different from that of his first edition. I have used the standard English translations of North, 'Dryden', Langhorne, Stewart (Bohn library), and Perrin (Loeb), as well as the German translations of Ax and Ruegg. When I write 'all translators' I mean these.

v

PREFACE

I gladly acknowledge the assistance I have received in writing this book. Professor G. R. Manton encouraged me to undertake it and helped me in the early stages; Dr. C. P. Jones read the Introduction and saved me from a number of errors; Dr. Peter Green is responsible for several interesting suggestions in the Commentary, My debt to Guy Griffith and Ernst Badian extends over many years, a debt which they have now increased by reading the entire work in manuscript and suggesting many improvements. Their criticism has led me to alter or modify my views on many important points, although much remains, I am aware, with which they would disagree.

I am most grateful to the Council of the University of Otago for generously granting me a year's leave of absence which enabled me to complete my manuscript, and to the staff of the Clarendon Press whose care and patience have improved it in many details.

My greatest debt, however, is to my wife not only for her help in compiling the Indexes but much more for her unfailing encouragement and support.

J. R. HAMILTON

Dunedin
6 August 1968

CONTENTS

MAPS

ABBREVIATIONS AND BIBLIOGRAPHY OF SHORT TITLES

Note: Books cited once are not included. References to articles are given in full in the Commentary.

AHR = *American Historical Review*.

AJA = *American Journal of Archaeology*.

AJP = *American Journal of Philology*.

Altheim = F. Altheim, *Weltgeschichte Asiens im griechischen Zeitalter*. 2 vols. Halle, 1947–8.

Ant. Class. = *Antiquité classique*.

BCH = *Bulletin de Correspondance hellénique*.

Bellinger = A. R. Bellinger, *Essays on the Coinage of Alexander the Great*. New York, 1963.

Beloch = K. J. Beloch, *Griechische Geschichte*. Ed. 2. 4 vols. Strassburg–Berlin and Leipzig, 1912–27.

Bengtson = H. Bengtson, *Griechische Geschichte von den Anfängen bis in die römische Kaiserzeit*. Ed. 2. München, 1960.

Berve = H. Berve, *Das Alexanderreich auf prosopographischer Grundlage*. 2 vols. München, 1926.

BIAO = *Bulletin de l'Institut français d'Archéologie orientale*.

Bibl. Or. = *Bibliotheca orientalis*.

BIE = *Bulletin de l'Institut d'Égypte*.

Brown = T. S. Brown, *Onesicritus, A Study in Hellenistic Historiography*. Berkeley–Los Angeles, 1949.

Burn = A. R. Burn, *Alexander the Great and the Hellenistic Empire*. London, 1947.

Bury = J. B. Bury, *A History of Greece*. Ed. 3. London, 1951.

CAF = T. Kock, *Comicorum Atticorum Fragmenta*. 1880–8.

CAH = *The Cambridge Ancient History*.

CHI = *The Cambridge History of India*, vol. 1.

CPhil. = *Classical Philology*.

CQ = *Classical Quarterly*.

CR = *Classical Review*.

Cumont = F. Cumont, *Les Religions orientales dans le paganisme romain*. Ed. 4. Brussels, 1929.

Denniston = J. D. Denniston, *The Greek Particles*. Ed. 2. Oxford, 1954.

Dihle = A. Dihle, *Studien zur griechischen Biographie*. Göttingen, 1956.

Droysen = J. G. Droysen, *Geschichte des Hellenismus*. Ed. 3. Basle, 1952.

Ehrenberg = V. Ehrenberg, *Alexander and the Greeks*. Oxford, 1938.

Etym. Magn. = *Etymologicon Magnum*, ed. T. Gaisford.

ix

F. Gr. Hist. = F. Jacoby, *Die Fragmente der griechischen Historiker.* Berlin–Leiden, 1923–(in progress).

FHG = C. and Th. Müller, *Fragmenta historicorum graecorum.* 5 vols. Paris, 1841–70.

Fränkel = A. Fränkel, *Die Quellen der Alexanderhistoriker.* Breslau, 1883.

Fuller = J. F. C. Fuller, *The Generalship of Alexander the Great.* London, 1958.

Geog. Jour. = *Geographical Journal.*

GHI = M. N. Tod, *Greek Historical Inscriptions.* 2 vols. Oxford, 1946 (vol. 1, ed. 2), 1948 (vol. 2).

Glotz–Cohen = G. Glotz and R. Cohen, *Histoire grecque IV. i.* (in Glotz's *Histoire générale*). Ed. 2. Paris, 1945.

Gomme = A. W. Gomme, *A Historical Commentary on Thucydides* vol. 1. Oxford, 1945.

HA = C. A. Robinson Jnr., *The History of Alexander the Great* 1. Brown University Studies, no. 16. Providence, 1953.

Hammond = N. G. L. Hammond, *A History of Greece to 322 B.C.* Oxford, 1959.

Harv. Stud. = *Harvard Studies in Classical Philology.*

Harv. Theol. Rev. = *Harvard Theological Review.*

Head = B. V. Head, *Historia Numorum.* Ed. 2. Oxford, 1911.

Hoffmann = W. Hoffmann, *Das literarische Porträt Alexanders des Grossen im griechischen und römischen Altertum.* Diss. Leipzig, 1907.

IG² = *Inscriptiones graecae, editio minor.*

Jaeger = W. Jaeger, *Aristotle.* Ed. 2. Oxford, 1948.

Jax Festschrift = 'Natalicium Carolo Jax septuagenario a.d. VII kal. Dec. M.C.M.L.V. oblatum', Pars 1, *Innsbruck Beiträge zur Kulturgeschichte* 3 (1955).

JDAI = *Jahrbuch des deutschen archäologischen Instituts.*

JHS = *Journal of Hellenic Studies.*

JNES = *Journal of Near Eastern Studies.*

JOEAI = *Jahreshefte des Österreichischen archäologischen Instituts.*

JRS = *Journal of Roman Studies.*

Kaerst = J. Kaerst, *Geschichte des Hellenismus.* 2 vols. Leipzig, 1927 (vol. 1, ed. 3), 1926 (vol. 2, ed. 2).

Kornemann = E. Kornemann, *Die Alexandergeschichte des Königs Ptolemaios von Aegypten.* Berlin, 1935.

Kühner–Gerth = R. Kühner and B. Gerth, *Ausführliche Grammatik der griechischen Sprache.* Leverkusen, 1955. References are to the second part (Satzlehre) only.

LSJ = Liddell–Scott–Jones, *A Greek–English Lexicon.* Oxford, 1925–40.

Marrou = H. I. Marrou, *A History of Education in Antiquity* (tr. G. Lamb). London, 1956.

Marsden = E. W. Marsden, *The Campaign of Gaugamela.* Liverpool, 1964.

Mederer = E. Mederer, *Die Alexanderlegenden bei den ältesten Alexanderhistorikern.* Stuttgart, 1936.

Merkelbach = R. Merkelbach, *Die Quellen des griechischen Alexanderroman.* Zetemata 9. München, 1954.

ABBREVIATIONS

Miscellanea Rostagni = *Miscellanea di Studi Alessandrini in Memoria di Augusto Rostagni.* Torino, 1963.

Mnemos. = *Mnemosyne.*

Nilsson = M. P. Nilsson, *Geschichte der griechischen Religion.* 2 vols. München, 1955 (vol. 1, ed. 2), 1950 (vol. 2).

Num. Chron. = *Numismatic Chronicle.*

OCD = *The Oxford Classical Dictionary.*

Olmstead = A. T. Olmstead, *A History of the Persian Empire.* Chicago, 1948.

PACA = *Proceedings of the African Classical Associations.*

Parke–Wormell = H. W. Parke and D. E. W. Wormell, *The Delphic Oracle.* Ed. 2. 2 vols. Oxford, 1956.

Pearson, *LHA* = L. Pearson, *The Lost Histories of Alexander the Great.* New York, 1960.

Phil. = *Philologus.*

Pickard-Cambridge, *Dramatic Festivals* = Sir A. W. Pickard-Cambridge, *The Dramatic Festivals of Athens.* Oxford, 1953.

Pridik = E. Pridik, *De Alexandri epistularum commercio.* Diss. Berlin, 1893.

Proc. Am. Philos. Soc. = *Proceedings of the American Philosophical Society.*

Proc. Camb. Philol. Soc. = *Proceedings of the Cambridge Philological Society.*

Rabe = Inge Rabe, *Quellenkritische Untersuchungen zu Plutarchs Alexander-biographie.* Diss. Hamburg, 1964.

Radet = G. Radet, *Alexandre le Grand.* Ed. 6. Paris, 1950.

RE = Paulys *Real-Encyclopädie der classischen Altertumswissenschaft.* Stuttgart, 1893– .

REA = *Revue des études anciennes.*

REG = *Revue des études grecques.*

Rev. Phil. = *Revue de philologie, de littérature et d'histoire anciennes.*

Rh. Mus. = *Rheinisches Museum.*

Robinson = C. A. Robinson Jnr., *Alexander the Great.* New York, 1947.

RSI = *Rivista Storica Italiana.*

SB Berlin = *Sitzungsberichte der Preussischen Akademie der Wissenschaften, Phil.-hist. Klasse.*

Schachermeyr = F. Schachermeyr, *Alexander der Grosse: Ingenium und Macht.* Graz–Wien, 1949.

Seltman = C. Seltman, *Greek Coins.* Ed. 2. London, 1955.

SIG = *Sylloge inscriptionum graecarum,* ed. W. Dittenberger. Ed. 3. 4 vols. Leipzig, 1915–24.

Smith *EHI* = V. A. Smith, *The Early History of India from 600 B.C. to the Muhammadan Conquest.* Ed. 3. Oxford, 1914.

Stadter = Philip A. Stadter, *Plutarch's Historical Methods.* Cambridge, Mass., 1965.

Strasburger = H. Strasburger, *Ptolemaios und Alexander.* Leipzig, 1934.

Stuart = D. R. Stuart, *Epochs of Greek and Roman Biography.* Berkeley, 1928.

Studies Ehrenberg = *Ancient Society and Institutions,* Studies presented to Victor Ehrenberg on his 75th birthday. Oxford, 1966.

Studies Robinson = *Studies presented to D. M. Robinson*, vol. 2. Washington University Studies, 1953.

TAPA = *Transactions of the American Philological Association.*

Tarn = Sir William Tarn, *Alexander the Great.* 2 vols. Cambridge, 1948.

Tarn, *Bactria* = Sir William Tarn, *The Greeks in Bactria and India.* Ed. 2. Cambridge, 1951.

TGF = A. Nauck, *Tragicorum Graecorum Fragmenta.* Ed. 2. 1889.

Theander = C. Theander, *Plutarch und die Geschichte.* Lund, 1951.

Thomson = J. O. Thomson, *History of Ancient Geography.* Cambridge, 1948.

Trans. Am. Philos. Soc. = *Transactions of the American Philosophical Society.*

UPZ = U. Wilcken, *Urkunden der Ptolemäerzeit*, 1–2. 2. Berlin, 1922–37.

Wilcken = U. Wilcken, *Alexander the Great* (tr. G. C. Richards). London, 1932.

Ziegler = K. Ziegler, *RE* 21 s.v. Plutarchos (2), cols. 636 ff. (1951). Previously published as *Plutarchos von Chaeroneia* (Stuttgart, 1949). The *RE* article contains a few revisions and additions.

Zumetikos = A. Zumetikos, *De Alexandri Olympiadisque epistularum fontibus et reliquiis.* Diss. Berlin, 1894.

INTRODUCTION[1]

I. *Plutarch of Chaeroneia*

Life[2]

PLUTARCH was born about 45[3] in the small town of Chaeroneia in western Boeotia, where Philip had defeated the Greek states in 338 B.C. (*Alex.* 9) and Sulla routed Mithridates' general, Archelaus, in 86 B.C. (*Sull.* 16 ff.). His family, evidently well-to-do,[4] had resided there for generations, and his great-grandfather, Nicarchus, could recall Antony's exactions during the campaign of Actium (*Ant.* 68. 7). His grandfather, Lamprias, a witty and cultured man, survived to appear as a lively conversationalist in the *Quaestiones convivales*.[5] Plutarch never mentions his mother,[6] but his father, probably called Autobulus,[7] figures in several of the dialogues,[8] and Plutarch recalls that when as a young man he had been prominent in an embassy to the Roman governor of Achaea his father gave him the sound advice not to seek to eclipse his fellow-ambassadors in his report to the Council (*Mor.* 816 d). Plutarch had at least two brothers, Timon,[9] to whose character he pays a warm tribute (487 d), and the more versatile Lamprias, whose interests embraced cooking, dancing, etymology, and philosophy, and who was priest at Lebadeia.[10] Plutarch's concern with ethical questions and his passion for study—reinforced by his later philosophical training—surely owed much to his family background.[11]

Plutarch married Timoxena, the daughter of a local magnate,

[1] *Note*: all dates in the Introduction are A.D. unless otherwise indicated. Figures in parentheses refer to sections of the *Moralia*.

[2] Apart from brief notices in Suidas (s.v. Πλούταρχος Χαιρωνεύς) and Eusebius (*Chron. ab. Abr.* 2135 = 119/20 A.D., ed. Schoene 2. 164 ff.) and a few inscriptions (*SIG* 829 a, 843 a, b; cf. ibid. 844 b, 845), we are dependent on Plutarch's own writings.

[3] Plutarch remarks that he was a young man (νέος) when Nero visited Greece in 67 (385 b, 391 e).

[4] We may note that his father kept fine horses (641 f.)

[5] 622 e, 669 c, 738 b.

[6] Perhaps because she died young, as Ziegler 645 suggests.

[7] See Ziegler 643.   [8] 615 e, 641 f, 656 c, 657 e.

[9] Ziegler (*Hermes* 82 (1954), 499–501) argues that Timon was a half-brother of Plutarch; his arguments are not accepted by B. Einarson, *CPhil.* 50 (1955), 253–5.

[10] He is prominent in the *De defectu oraculorum*, the *Quaestiones convivales*, and the *De facie in orbe lunae*; refs. in Ziegler 645. The Lamprias attested as archon at Delphi is probably not Plutarch's brother; see G. Daux, *BCH* 73 (1949), 292.

[11] As R. Flacelière, *Sagesse de Plutarque* (Paris, 1964) 4, has well remarked.

Alexion (701 d), perhaps in the early seventies.[1] The marriage was evidently a happy one; the moving letter of consolation (608 b–612 b) which Plutarch addressed to her on the death of their daughter Timoxena reveals her as a devoted wife and mother and a good housewife. Of her intellectual qualities we know only that she wrote a short treatise on *Love of Ornament* to a certain Aristylla (145 a). They had at least four children apart from Timoxena—Chaeron, who lived only a few years (609 d), Soclarus, who probably died in his teens,[2] and Autobulus and Plutarchus, who both reached manhood. Their interest in philosophy is shown (if it is not a dialogue convention) by their request to their father to explain Plato's teaching on the soul—the result is the *De animae procreatione in Timaeo* (1012 a–1030 c)—and by the prominence of Autobulus in the *Amatorius* (748 e–771 e).

At the age of about twenty Plutarch proceeded to Athens, famous as a 'university city'. There he presumably attended, like other well-to-do young men of his time, the classes of the famous sophists and philosophers, although of his teachers he mentions only the Egyptian philosopher, Ammonius.[3] Plutarch says nothing of his rhetorical studies and later expresses dislike of the excesses of rhetoric (below, p. xxiii), but he undoubtedly received a thorough training, and several of his early rhetorical treatises survive, including two dealing with the *Fortune of Alexander* (Section II, below). He declares his passion for mathematics (387 f), and his writings reveal some knowledge of physics, natural science, and medicine, but it was philosophy that particularly interested him.

In his early life Plutarch doubtless travelled widely, as did most young men of his class, to further his education. Later we know of visits to Tanagra (608 b), Helicon (749 b), Hyampolis in Phocis (660 d), Patrae (629 f), Aedepsus and Chalcis in Euboea (667 c, *Flam.* 16. 5), Eleusis (635 a), and Sparta (*Lyc.* 18. 2, *Ages.* 19. 10 f.). We may be sure that he made many visits to Athens, of which he became an honorary citizen and was enrolled in the tribe Leontis (628 a). He appears to have visited Asia (501 e) and certainly paid a visit early in life to Alexandria. More important were his journeys to Rome and Italy. Plutarch was probably in Rome in the late seventies (973 e ff.),

---

[1] See Ziegler 648, C. P. Jones, *JRS* 56 (1966), 71.

[2] The eldest child was dead when the *Consolatio* was written (609 d). If this was not Soclarus, who reached an age at which he could appreciate poetry (15 a), he must have been a sixth child. Flacelière (*REG* 63 (1950), 302) holds that Autobulus must have been the eldest son, since he bore his grandfather's name, and that the eldest child must have been a girl. But Plutarch's statement (608 c) that 'this daughter (i.e. Timoxena) was born after four sons, when you were longing to bear a daughter' strongly suggests that Timoxena was the *first* daughter.

[3] Ammonius became an Athenian citizen and held the office of *strategos* at least three times. Refs. in Ziegler 651 ff. On Ammonius' career and family see C. P. Jones's important article in *Harv. Stud.* 71 (1967), 205 ff.

and he was certainly there in the latter part of Domitian's reign (*Public.* 15. 3–6; cf. 522 d). He may, of course, have paid other visits to Rome, but the old view (not yet dead) that he spent some fifteen or twenty years there is certainly wrong; the fact that Plutarch never mastered the finer points of Latin, as he himself admits, tends to disprove it.[1] In Rome he made lasting friendships with many distinguished Romans,[2] notably L. Mestrius Florus, the friend of Vespasian (Suet. *Vesp.* 22) to whom Plutarch owed the Roman citizenship and whose *nomen* he adopted (*SIG* 829 a, Μεστρίου Πλουτάρχου; cf. 844 a), and Q. Sosius Senecio, the friend of Trajan and twice consul, to whom he dedicated the *Quaestiones convivales* and (probably) the *Parallel Lives*.[3]

However, a sense of duty, as he tells us (*Dem.* 2. 2), led Plutarch to spend most of his life in his native Chaeroneia, although so small a place could provide neither a good library nor the opportunity for an important political career. There Plutarch founded a school, in which members of his family and his many pupils and friends discussed a variety of philosophical, theological, and scientific problems. These discussions were set down by Plutarch, mainly after 96, in what are loosely but conveniently called his *Moralia* or *Moral Essays*, and during this period he also composed his *Parallel Lives*.[4] In spite of his substantial literary output Plutarch found time to take an active part in the religious and political life of the district.

Despite Plutarch's silence we may reasonably suppose, in view of his standing in the town and his interest in religious matters, that he held a priesthood at Chaeroneia.[5] Certainly he held one of the two life priesthoods of Apollo at Delphi,[6] where during the reigns of Trajan and Hadrian the oracle experienced a considerable revival of prosperity and many new buildings were erected (*RE* 4, 2579 f.). For this revival Plutarch was largely responsible; doubtless he used his influence with Sosius Senecio and other leading Romans to secure imperial favour.[7] At Chaeroneia Plutarch held the office of eponymous

---

[1] *Dem.* 2. 2. For the old view see J. J. Hartman, *de Plutarcho* (Leiden, 1916), 662. Plutarch's difficulties with Latin, however, should not be exaggerated; some of his errors are no worse than Livy's mistranslations of Polybius. In particular, we should be chary of arguing from this admission that Plutarch read hardly any of the Latin authors he cites. The passage explicitly says that he *did*.

[2] For a complete list of Plutarch's Roman friends see Ziegler 687 ff.

[3] See Ziegler 688 f., who, however, wrongly assigns him a third consulship in 102.

[4] On the chronology of Plutarch's writings see esp. Jones, *JRS* (1966) 61 ff.

[5] The fact that the cults were of purely local significance may account for his silence (Ziegler 659).

[6] *SIG* 829 a; cf. *Mor.* 792 f, where λειτουργοῦντα πολλὰς Πυθιάδας probably refers to his priestly office rather than to his position as *epimeletes*. J. Jannoray (*REA* 47 (1945), 257) dates the beginning of his office to between 85 and 90.

[7] In the *De Pythiae oraculis* 29 (*Mor.* 409 c) Theon remarks φιλῶ δὲ τὸν καθηγεμόνα

archon (642 f., 694 a), but he did not hesitate to perform the duties of a minor magistrate (811 b–c). As *epimeletes* of the Amphictyonic League he was responsible for setting up a statue to the emperor Hadrian in the early years of his reign (*SIG* 829 a), and if, as seems likely, Plutarch refers to himself at *Mor.* 785 c, he was a member of the Federal Council of Boeotia (Boeotarch), President of the Pythian Games (*agonothetes*), and enjoyed the privilege of a front seat at meetings of the Amphictyons (*proedria*).[1] There is no reason to question Suidas' statement that Trajan conferred on Plutarch the consular insignia, an honour sometimes granted to distinguished Greeks from the beginning of the second century A.D.,[2] but we need not believe him when he goes on to say that Trajan ordered that no magistrate in *Illyria* should act without Plutarch's approval.[3] Eusebius states, credibly enough, that Hadrian appointed Plutarch in his old age (in 119/20) ἐπιτροπεύειν Ἑλλάδος, by which he probably means that Plutarch became an imperial procurator (*epitropos*).[4]

The exact date of Plutarch's death is unknown, but there is good reason to suppose that he did not live much beyond 120. The omission of his name from Ps.-Lucian's *Macrobioi* suggests that he died before reaching the age of 80, and a piece of evidence, whose importance was first realized by Jones, is almost conclusive. He points out that it is virtually certain that it was as senior priest of Apollo that Plutarch dedicated the statue of Hadrian (*SIG* 829 a) and that when a similar statue was dedicated by the Amphictyons in 125 this was done not by Plutarch but by a certain T. Flavius Aristotimus (*SIG* 835 b). It follows that, unless the Amphictyons had changed their practice in the interval, Plutarch had died and Aristotimus had become senior priest.

Plutarch was honoured, presumably after his death, by the citizens of Delphi and Chaeroneia, who set up a marble herm in accordance

---

ταύτης τῆς πολιτείας γενόμενον ἡμῖν καὶ τὰ πλεῖστα τούτων ἐκφροντίζοντα καὶ παρασκευάζοντα. This is generally, and rightly, taken to refer to Plutarch; so (most recently) Jones, *JRS* (1966), 63 ff., who rejects Flacelière's view (*Rev. Phil.* 8 (1934), 56 ff. and subsequently) that Hadrian is referred to and that this passage supports a date after 125 for Plutarch's death.

[1] Ziegler 660 agrees that Plutarch refers to himself in this passage, although at 657 he doubts whether Plutarch was Boeotarch.

[2] See A. Stein, *Der römische Ritterstand* (München, 1927) 246 ff., 274 f. The honour did not confer membership of the senate.

[3] Some scholars take Illyria to be a mere slip for Achaea, since until Diocletian the governor of Illyria had no jurisdiction over Achaea. Even so the statement is doubtful. We might, however, read 'Chaeroneia' for 'Illyria'. K. Latte (ap. Ziegler 658, n. 1) is sceptical of the whole matter, including the grant of consular insignia and Eusebius' statement (below).

[4] So E. Groag, *Die römischen Reichsbeamten von Achaia* (1939) 145–7, and H. G. Pflaum, *Les Carrières procuratoriennes équestres* 3 (1961), 1071. Groag suggests that the work was done by Plutarch's staff or alternatively that the office was honorary.

with a decree of the Amphictyons (*SIG* 843 a). His family continued to reside in Chaeroneia until at least the middle of the third century (*SIG* 845), and more than one of his descendants shared his interest in philosophy (*SIG* 844, 845).

The Political and Cultural Background

The 'freedom' of the Greeks proclaimed by Nero at Corinth in November 67 was soon revoked by Vespasian.[1] Apart from this brief interlude (and the years 15–44 when it was under imperial jurisdiction) Greece had since 27 B.C. been a senatorial province governed by a proconsul of praetorian rank stationed at Corinth.

This fact dominated Plutarch's political outlook.[2] The Greek statesman, he writes, should always remember not only that he governs free men but also that he is a subject in a state ruled by Caesar's proconsul, whose power is supreme (813 d, 824 e). Plutarch's undoubted patriotism[3] did not blind him to the fact that the age of a free Greece had gone beyond recall; when he writes of the great figures of the past, of Pericles or Phocion or Demosthenes, he does not dream that the situation of the fifth and fourth centuries B.C. can be restored. Intelligent men, he holds, should admit the weakness of Greece,[4] they should make the best of it and live in peace and concord (825 a). Plutarch lists (824 c) the greatest benefits a city can enjoy: peace, freedom, good crops, a large population, and concord. Of these peace is assured by Roman rule,[5] the emperors have given the people as much liberty as is good for them, plenty and abundance of men must be prayed for: the major task facing a magistrate is the prevention of *stasis*. Indeed Plutarch lays great stress on the need to avoid a situation which will bring about Roman intervention. Magistrates who urge the people to emulate the warlike achievements of their ancestors harm their country and expose themselves to the danger of execution or exile; the glories of Marathon, Plataea, and the Eurymedon are topics

---

[1] Nero's speech: *SIG* 814; cf. *Flam.* 12, Suet. *Nero* 11. Freedom revoked: Suet. *Vesp.* 8. 4.

[2] As expressed in his *An seni res publica gerenda sit?* (783 a–97 f) and, especially, his *Praecepta gerendae rei publicae* (798 a–825 f).

[3] Nero bestowed freedom upon 'the best of peoples and the one most loved by the gods' (568 a).

[4] At *Mor.* 414 a Plutarch writes that Greece can put only 3,000 hoplites into the field. It is impossible to believe that this represents all the men of military age, and J. A. O. Larsen, *An Economic Survey of Ancient Rome* 4 (1938), 481 f., suggests that Plutarch means those who had received training as ephebes. If so, there must have been a considerable decline in the number of the wealthy; but there still remained a small group with enough money to travel and to lead a life of leisure.

[5] Magistrates no longer have the opportunity to wage wars, overthrow tyrants, or conclude military alliances (805 a).

best left to the sophists.[1] On the other hand he deprecates excessive dependence on the Romans; too often magistrates refer every decision, great or small, to the Roman authorities. What Greeks should aim at in his view is a proper balance between unbecoming subservience and dangerous independence.

The leading Romans, Plutarch maintains, were very eager to assist their friends in their political endeavours, and it was the duty of a patriotic Greek to co-operate with them; by this means the advancement of Greece could best be secured.[2] This advice clearly reflects Plutarch's own experience, and the results of such co-operation are evident in the revival of Delphi (above). Plutarch correctly assesses the Roman attitude. The emperors sought good government in the provinces—there was, after all, no profit in bad—but above all they sought stability. This they obtained not by military force, or even by the threat of military force (even the neighbouring province of Macedonia had no garrison), but by their support of the leading Greeks in the various cities. This patron–client relationship, of advantage to both sides, was no less vigorous under the Principate than it had been under the Republic,[3] and Roman intervention was seldom required except when the financial distress of the cities led to the sending of *correctores*.[4] In his *Praecepta* Plutarch defends the democratic ideal and clearly regards himself as living in a democracy; but it was a democracy, as he was well aware, very different from that of fifth-century Athens. The cities were ruled by the Councils, whose members were drawn from the small number of wealthy citizens, men like Plutarch himself.[5] Even if Plutarch does not exaggerate the importance of public opinion, as we may suspect, the assemblies evidently possessed little importance, and we hear little of them.

Despite his admiration for Roman society and his consciousness of Rome's achievements, Plutarch has no time for those Greeks who seek 'gainful commissions and the administration of provinces', i.e. for those who embark upon a career in the imperial civil service and turn their back on domestic affairs.[6] His outlook was national (or 'provincial') rather than imperial, and he felt that such men were lost to

---

[1] See Lucian, *Master of Rhetoric*, ch. 18.   [2] 776 a–779 c, 814 c–d.

[3] See esp. G. W. Bowersock, *Augustus and the Greek World* (Oxford, 1965), ch. 1 and pp. 143 ff., and for the Republic E. Badian, *Foreign Clientelae* (Oxford, 1957).

[4] On these officials see A. N. Sherwin-White, *The Letters of Pliny* (Oxford, 1966), on *Ep.* 8. 24. The earliest of them appears to have been Maximus in the first decade of the second century; see Pliny, ad loc.

[5] See A. H. M. Jones, *The Greek City* (Oxford, 1940) 129 f., 170; T. Renoirte, *Les Conseils politiques de Plutarque* (Louvain, 1951).

[6] 814 d. Although they were regularly employed among the Greek-speaking peoples; see Bowersock, op. cit. 147.

neglect Plato's metaphysics, although it appears from the *De animae procreatione in Timaeo* that he did not always understand them. But it is no accident that the *Republic* and *Laws* are largely drawn upon; Plutarch was doubtless attracted by Plato's view that the philosopher should concern himself with the good of the state and its citizens. For he had no patience with philosophers who sought to live in an 'ivory tower', as his criticism of the Epicureans shows (below). On some questions Plutarch did not accept Plato's views. In the *Amatorius*, for instance, he refuses to concede that homosexual love is superior to that between man and woman,[1] while in the *De audiendis poetis* he adopts Aristotle's position that moral improvement should be sought through the charm of poetry in preference to Plato's prohibition of its teaching. But in most fundamental matters Plutarch sided with his master. He agreed with him that the gods were everlasting and the source of all good in the world, and he severely criticizes the Stoics for holding that only Zeus was immortal; they are 'more godless than the Epicureans',[2] who maintained that the gods did not concern themselves with the affairs of men. Even if, like Plato, he sometimes writes of 'God', he was a firm believer in the traditional Greek pantheon; nevertheless, while rejecting the wilder orgiastic cults, he tended to equate non-Greek deities with their Greek counterparts. Like all serious thinkers Plutarch was deeply concerned with the problem of evil which, in a world governed by beneficent gods, so often appeared to triumph. The solution he found in the old view that there existed *daimones*, beings intermediate between gods and men, who were responsible for the existence of evil in the world.[3] As a Platonist and an initiate into the mysteries of Dionysus, Plutarch naturally held fast to a belief in the immortality of the individual soul and rejected the views of the Stoics and the Epicureans that it perishes at death or soon after.

Indeed Plutarch often attacks Stoic teachings, although he scarcely less often accepts them. For example, myths which showed the gods behaving in a fashion opposed to traditional Greek morality he interpreted, like them, in an allegorical manner. To the Epicureans he is consistently hostile: indeed his attitude closely resembles Cicero's. Not only are their religious views attacked, but they come under fire for holding that virtue is not worth having if unaccompanied by pleasure. But perhaps their worst fault in Plutarch's eyes was that they advocated withdrawal from public life. The Epicureans, he complains,[4]

---

[1] For Plutarch's enlightened views on women see Stadter 5 ff.

[2] *De comm. notit. adv. Stoicos* 32 = *Mor.* 1075 e.

[3] On *daimones* see J. Oakesmith, *The Religion of Plutarch* (London, 1902), ch. 6–8, and esp. G. Soury, *La Démonologie de Plutarque* (Paris, 1942). On Plutarch's religious views in general see Nilsson 2. 402 ff. (with full bibliography).

[4] *Adv. Coloten* 33 = *Mor.* 1126 e–f.

Greece. The local magistrate, in his view, had a real and important contribution to make to the life of Greece, to maintain the proper relation between the local administration and the central authority. The acceptance of an imperial procuratorship in his later years does not indicate a change of heart. An imperial request might be difficult to refuse, and in any case he was working in Greece; nor need his post have interfered to any great extent with his writing or with his civil and religious duties at Chaeroneia and Delphi. Plutarch's political outlook was clearsighted and realistic, even if it was perhaps easier for him than for some of his contemporaries to accept this rather restricted political horizon. He had no consuming political ambitions, and despite his conviction that a man ought to play his part in political life it is likely that he felt he could make a greater contribution to Greece as an educator.

Plutarch's 'school' at Chaeroneia was organized, predictably, on the pattern of the Academy, and instruction was given by means of formal lectures, dialogues, and symposia. A great variety of topics (ethical, political, scientific, theological, and psychological) was discussed, but the greatest importance was attached to ethics—for Plutarch, as for the majority of his contemporaries, the most essential part of philosophy.

Even Plutarch's admirers have seldom failed to remark that he was not an original thinker with original theories of his own to propound. Tucker[1] puts it thus: 'To his generation he served as a milch-cow of practical philosophy on the ethical side. He browsed on literature and thought, secreted the most valuable constituents, and yielded the cream to his readers or hearers.' He is representative of contemporary culture, not in advance of it, and as such his writings are valuable evidence for that culture. The extent of Plutarch's reading in philosophy, as in other subjects, is impressive. He was evidently familiar with the writings of many of the pre-Socratics,[2] and had a thorough knowledge of the teachings of the four major schools—the Academy, the Peripatetic, the Stoic, and the Epicurean. Although he did not adhere consistently to the tenets of any one school—like that other great humanist, Cicero, he was an eclectic and, like him, he often asserts the right of the philosopher to withhold assent—he probably thought of himself as a Platonist. Certainly for him the 'divine' Plato was the supreme philosopher (cf. 90 c, 700 b), and quotations from his works appear in most of Plutarch's writings, some 650 times in all.[3] Clearly the *Moralia* owe much to the dialogues of Plato, although Plutarch normally eschews the Socratic dialectic, and the use of myth is inspired by Plato. At the close of the *De sera numinis vindicta*, for example, the myth of Er is obviously his model. Nor did Plutarch

---

[1] T. G. Tucker, *Selected Essays of Plutarch* (Oxford, 1913) 15.
[2] See Ziegler 767 f., 919 f.   [3] Details in Ziegler 749 ff.

have produced no one who has advanced human society; they fail to be of service to the state but enjoy the benefits in the cities. In the same way the early Stoics, especially Chrysippus, are found guilty of writing at length about political activity and then taking no part in politics. They have deserted their homeland to devote themselves to philosophy, and for all their talk they lead a life no better than that of the Epicureans.[1] For Plutarch the prime task of the philosopher was to lead himself, his pupils and friends, and those who after he became famous sought his aid, to *arete* and to the happiness which depends upon it. This *arete* manifested itself in right conduct, and man should not be concerned only with his own soul but should strive, as a duty, to benefit his fellow-citizens by engaging in political activity.

For readers of the *Parallel Lives* Plutarch's attitude to the passions is of particular importance.[2] These are not, as the Stoics maintained, to be eradicated; on the contrary, they are necessary, for without them reason would be condemned to inactivity like a steersman when the wind drops. Practical reason (*phronesis*) should regulate them so that a mean between excess and lack of passion is achieved. It is significant for Plutarch's portrait of Alexander that τὸ θυμοειδές (which is prominent in his character) is part of the irrational part of the soul and that anger, according to Plutarch, is the worst of passions. It destroys any society; it is not noble or manly, but attacks particularly the weak—women, the sick, and the elderly. To control anger is true bravery, and it is the function of philosophy to prepare the soul to meet storms of anger.

Rhetoric[3]

Since the fourth century B.C. philosophers and rhetoricians had been engaged in a constant struggle for supremacy, a struggle in which, surprising as it may seem to us, the rhetoricians had gained the upper hand. In Plutarch's day the practice of rhetoric offered to the ambitious young man the most rewarding career, and the most gifted pupils became sophists. Indeed, as Sandbach remarks,[4] 'something like a passion for eloquence seems to have possessed the Greek-speaking world'. This is the movement known as the Second Sophistic, represented for us mainly by Plutarch's contemporary Dion of Prusa (until his conversion to philosophy), and afterwards by Aristides and Lucian.

Although sophists might appear as advocates in the law-courts or

---

[1] *De Stoicorum repugnantiis* 2 = *Mor.* 1033 c.

[2] See especially the short treatises *De virtute morali* (440 c–452 d) and *De cohibenda ira* (452 d–464 d).

[3] See especially Marrou 194 ff., 210; A. and M. Croiset, *Hist. de la litt. grecque*, 5. 556 ff.　　　　　　　　　　　　　　　　　　　[4] *CAH* 11. 681.

act as counsellors in local politics the greatest fame and the greatest rewards were to be won by epideictic speeches. It was in these display-pieces that the sophist could best exhibit his powers of expression and his ability to improvise. This talent was the result of a long and arduous training, of which two aspects must be emphasized here in view of the theory that the majority of Plutarch's citations in the *Parallel Lives* are second-hand (see below, p. xliii). The rhetorician was expected to read (and to continue reading) widely, if not deeply, particularly in the historians and orators. This reading provided him with a vast store of *exempla* with which to embellish his oratory. In particular, he had to know thoroughly the political history of Greece in the period from Solon to the death of Alexander.[1] To enable him to use these *exempla* when required the sophist had to have a prodigious memory, and to this end his memory was developed systematically. The student began by repeating a story dictated by his teacher and ended by offering proof or refutation of the facts of some assumed case (*controversiae*) or discussing the merits of some particular course of action (*suasoriae*).[2] In these exercises, since the student had to speak without notes, memory was of prime importance, and at all stages of his course he was obliged to practise constantly. Even when he was a famous sophist, Herodes Atticus declaimed daily. What results such training might produce may be seen in the remarks of the elder Seneca in the introduction to his *Controversiae* (1. 2): there he recalls that in his youth he could repeat 2,000 names, said once, in the same order, and could recite in reverse order over 200 verses spoken by his fellow-students. Indeed, the *Controversiae* were apparently written from memory.[3] There is no reason to suppose that Plutarch's memory was markedly inferior.

If in many respects Plutarch was representative of his age, this is not true of his attitude to rhetoric; for he came down strongly on the side of philosophy and several times (48 d, 80 a, 999 e–f) asserts the superiority of philosophic to sophistic education. It was not that he was hostile to artistic speech—in the *Praecepta* (801 e) he tells the young Menemachos that it is the duty of a statesman to make use of rhetoric[4] —but character ($\mathring{\eta}\theta os$), formed by philosophic training and expressed in words, is for him more important than rhetoric; it is the $\delta\eta\mu\iota\nu\rho\gamma\grave{o}s$ $\pi\epsilon\iota\theta\sigma\upsilon s$. Rhetoric, on the other hand, is its tool ($\mathring{o}\rho\gamma\alpha\nu\sigma\nu$), indispensable

---

[1] In Philostratus' *Lives of the Sophists* there is no theme in Greek history later than 326 B.C.

[2] For details see S. F. Bonner, *Roman Declamation* (Liverpool, 1949).

[3] In the sixteenth and seventeenth centuries the Jesuits paid the greatest attention to the training of the memory. 'A top-notch pupil would volunteer to repeat a page of poetry after reading it only once; another would offer to repeat two pages' (Gilbert Highet, *The Art of Teaching* (London, 1951), 131).

[4] Cf. *Mor.* 243 a, 743 d, 745 c.

as a means to an end, but not to be pursued as an end in itself.[1] Many rhetoricians, however, appear to have concerned themselves little with the truth of what they said, but to have paid excessive attention to the way in which they said it. This applies both to their matter and their delivery. They quite intoxicated their hearers, modulating, smoothing, and intoning their voices (41 d), and Plutarch complains of their 'paltry thought, empty phrases, affected bearing', their 'elaborate and pretentious diction', their 'dainty, flowery words and theatrical matter' which is 'fodder for drones who play the sophist' (40 c–41 e). The word 'theatrical' recurs:[2] 'The speech of a statesman', he writes (802 e), 'should not be theatrical, as if he were making a harangue composed, like a garland, of curious and florid words, nor should it consist of over-subtle arguments and periods exactly framed by rule and compass.'[3] Here speaks the mature Plutarch, who has outgrown his early rhetorical training and has come to despise the rhetorical excesses which he himself once practised. 'Over-subtle arguments and periods exactly framed by rule and compass' might well describe his speeches *De Alexandri fortuna*.

11. *The Speeches* De Alexandri Magni fortuna aut virtute[4]

In default of a detailed commentary a brief summary of these two speeches may perhaps serve two purposes: to provide an example of first-century rhetoric, and to allow comparison of the achievement of Plutarch as a rhetorician and as a biographer.

De Alexandri fortuna 1

(1) Plutarch announces that he is going to reply on behalf of Philosophy (or rather of Alexander) to Fortune, who has claimed Alexander as her work. In fact Alexander succeeded against great odds and at great cost with the support of the virtues of forethought, endurance, courage, and moderation (*sophrosyne*). (2) Other kings (Darius, Sardanapalus, Ochus, Artaxerxes) owed their position to Fortune, but Alexander had to fight for his victories. His many wounds (ten instances given) show Fortune's malice. So far from favouring Alexander, she was actively hostile, especially at the Malli town where she

---

[1] *Mor.* 33 f; cf. *Per.* 8, *Fab.* 1, *Cat. Min.* 4.
[2] In Plutarch, a term of censure; see the Commentary, n. to 75. 5.
[3] See also his criticism of Isocrates at *Mor.* 350 d ff.
[4] There is no external evidence for the date of these two speeches, but they are generally regarded, together with Plutarch's other rhetorical works, as among his *Jugendschriften*; cf. Schmid–Stählin, *Gesch. d. gr. Litt.* 2. 1. 486, 491; Ziegler 716 f. The effort of J. E. Powell, *JHS* 59 (1939), 235 f., to prove that they reveal knowledge of the *Life* is quite unsuccessful.

shut him in with unknown barbarians and almost brought him to an ignoble end. (3) Even before the campaign began Alexander had to deal with troubles in Greece (Thebes, Athens), Macedonia (Amyntas, the sons of Aeropus), Illyria, and Scythia. His treasury was empty, he was in debt, and his forces were small (various estimates); nevertheless he formed the idea of ruling all men. (4) Despite his meagre (material) resources this was no rash or headstrong plan, for Philosophy had given him greater resources than any other king; indeed he owed more to Aristotle than to Philip. Because he wrote nothing and did not teach in the Academy or the Lyceum men reject the statement that his real equipment (*ephodion*) was Philosophy, although in deference to Homer they accept the view that the *Iliad* and the *Odyssey* were his *ephodion*. Yet other philosophers (Pythagoras, Socrates, Arcesilaus, Carneades) wrote nothing, although they were not busy, like Alexander, civilizing the barbarians, and still we account them eminent philosophers because of their utterances, their way of life, and their teachings. Judged by the same criteria Alexander too will be seen to be a philosopher.

[The remainder of the speech is devoted to proving the thesis that Alexander was not only *a* philosopher but *the greatest* of philosophers. His teachings are treated in chapters 5–9 (init.), his sayings in 9–10, and his deeds in 11–12.]

(5) Whereas the pupils of Socrates and Plato (Critias, Alcibiades, Cleitophon), who at least spoke Greek, rejected his teaching, Alexander taught the barbarians not to kill their fathers or marry their mothers, but to worship Greek gods, to bury their dead instead of eating them, and to read Greek literature. While Plato wrote a *Republic* (*Πολιτεία*) which no one used, Alexander founded more than seventy cities (*πόλεις*) and introduced Greek institutions. Few men read Plato's *Laws*, but countless men used (and still use) Alexander's laws. Since they enjoy the blessings of civilization, those whom Alexander conquered are more fortunate than those who escaped, and if philosophers pride themselves upon civilizing individuals Alexander should be considered the greatest of philosophers for civilizing whole peoples. (6) Zeno wrote a celebrated *Republic* advocating that all men should consider themselves citizens of a single commonwealth, but this was only a philosopher's dream; Alexander realized it. He rejected Aristotle's advice to act as a *leader* towards the Greeks and as a *master* towards the barbarians, and believing that he had a divine mission to control and reconcile all men, either by persuasion or by force, he 'mixed their lives and customs, their marriages and ways of life as in a "loving-cup"', and made the difference between Greeks and barbarians one of virtue and vice. (7) Demaratus of Corinth wept to think that past generations of Greeks were deprived of the joy of seeing

Alexander sitting on the throne of Darius. Yet this was due to Fortune; how much more desirable would it have been to see the marriages at Susa of Greeks and Macedonians to Persian women? This was the proper way to link Europe to Asia, not, as Xerxes did, to build a bridge of boats. (8) Alexander's adoption of a mixed Persian and Macedonian dress was designed to win over the conquered peoples and to create one united people. To have retained the Macedonian dress would have been silly and indeed childish, when he could by a slight change win their affection for Macedonian rule. He was no brigand who regarded Asia as mere booty, as Hannibal did Italy, and had he not died so soon all men would now look to a single law as to a common light. (9) The purpose of the expedition—to create concord, peace, unity among all men—shows Alexander a philosopher.

The characters of kings are revealed by their *sayings*. Those of Antigonus, Dionysius (the elder), and Sardanapalus reveal, respectively, injustice, impiety, and love of pleasure; those of Alexander, if one subtracts his diadem, his noble birth, and Ammon, might have been uttered by Socrates or Plato or Pythagoras. The inscriptions under his busts and statues and his reported remark, 'I am the son of Zeus', are poetic extravagance and flattery. His *genuine* utterances (Olympic Games, Philip's wound) reveal the mind of a philosopher rising above the weaknesses of the body. (10) Alexander's favourite Homeric line was 'A goodly king and a mighty warrior', which he took as a text for himself, and his rejection at Troy of the offer of Paris' lyre reveals his philosophic outlook. It is revealed also in his attitude to philosophers (Aristotle, Anaxarchus, Pyrrho, Xenocrates, Onesicritus) and in his remark, after meeting Diogenes at Corinth: 'If I were not Alexander, I would be Diogenes.' By this he did not mean 'If I were not king' or 'If I were not rich and an Argead' but 'If I were not carrying out my civilizing mission, I would be emulating the *frugalitas* of Diogenes'. Alexander too had to 'change the stamp of the common currency' and put the impress of a Greek *politeia* on barbarian material.

(11) Alexander's *actions* reveal not chance and warlike violence, but the bravery and justice, the moderation and gentleness of one acting with sober and wise reason. They confirm the Stoic *dictum* that in whatever the Wise Man does he acts with every virtue. Alexander exhibited valour with humanity, gentleness with courage, generosity with economy, and so on and so on. . . . Consider his treatment of Porus, his marriage to Roxane, his treatment of the dead Darius, his trust in Hephaestion; if these actions do not reveal the philosopher, what actions do? (12) Contrast the actions of recognized philosophers. Socrates allowed Alcibiades to sleep with him, but Alexander furiously rebuked Philoxenus for offering to send him a beautiful boy. We admire

Xenocrates for refusing an offer of fifty talents from Alexander; should we not admire Alexander for offering them? Even under fire Alexander repeatedly remarked that he needed wealth to reward such men. This shows him a philosopher, for the judgements of ordinary men are confounded by imminent danger whereas philosophy renders those of philosophers strong against danger. . . . (here our manuscript of the speech breaks off).

De Alexandri fortuna 2

(1) Plutarch begins by saying that he omitted yesterday to mention the great number of artists who flourished during the reign of Alexander. This was due to the king, in whom they found a discriminating critic and patron and who, unlike other kings (Dionysius, Alexander of Pherae, Archelaus, Ateas the Scythian), encouraged them. (2) He concentrated on being a great warrior and honoured artists without envy. He refused to intervene in the contest between the tragedians Athenodorus and Thettalus (ch. 29), he rewarded the comic actor Lycon (ch. 29), and set up a statue to Aristonicus the harper, who fell in battle. In his reign lived Apelles the painter, whose 'bearer of the thunderbolt' was inimitable, and Lysippus the sculptor, who alone was allowed to sculpt Alexander since he alone preserved Alexander's character and *arete* (ch. 4). But Alexander refused the offer of Stasicrates to transform Mount Athos into a gigantic likeness of himself (ch. 72); the Caucasus, the Tanais, and the Caspian, he said, would be his memorials.

(3) Had this memorial been completed it would not have been due to Fortune any more than the works of Apelles and Lysippus; much less is a great man, indeed the greatest, the product of Fortune. To those who do not know how to use them the gifts of Fortune are a danger and a proof of their weakness; without *arete* everything else is useless, as we may see by comparing the lives of Semiramis and Sardanapalus. Fortune bestowed no greater gifts (arms, money, etc.) on Alexander than on other kings, but she could not make Arrhidaeus great, or Amasis, or Ochus, or Oarses, or Tigranes, or Nicomedes of Bithynia. (4) Fortune owes much to the rule of Alexander, since in him she was seen to be unconquered, noble, and so on. Leosthenes compared Alexander's army after his death to the Cyclops after his blinding, stretching out his hands uncertainly. We may perhaps better compare it, says Plutarch, to a dead body after the soul has departed; Perdiccas, Meleager, Seleucus, and Antigonus gave it a fitful existence, but it eventually decayed and put forth unworthy leaders like maggots. Alexander himself indicated as much when he reminded Hephaestion, quarrelling with Craterus, that he had no power without him (ch. 47). Take away the *arete* of the conqueror, and he is utterly

insignificant; as poor craftsmen, who put huge bases under small statues, emphasize their smallness, so Fortune, when she elevates a wretched creature, displays his instability. (5) Greatness consists in the *use*, not the possession, of good things. Even infants inherit kingdoms, as Charillus and Arrhidaeus (a virtual child), whom Meleager set on Alexander's throne although he was only a 'mute character'. Even a woman or child can give another wealth, power, etc. (as Bagoas gave Oarses and Darius the Persian throne), but to support and use great power requires *arete* and *nous*. Alexander, whom men accuse of drunkenness, was not intoxicated by power, as others were who could not bear even a little (Cleitus, Demetrius, Lysimachus, Clearchus the tyrant of Heracleia, Dionysius II, and Dionysius I). Some called themselves Euergetai, Kallinikoi, Soteres, Megaloi, in spite of their lusts, their dicing, and their constant feasting. (6) But Alexander breakfasted at dawn, sitting, and dined towards evening; he drank (only) when sacrificing to the gods and diced (only) with Medius when he had a fever. He married Roxane for love and Stateira for reasons of state. Towards Persian women he displayed great self-control ('he passed by those whom he saw more than those whom he did not'), and though in other matters most humane he treated beauty cavalierly. He would not hear a word about the great beauty of Darius' wife, and grieved so much at her death that his motives were misconstrued by Darius, who thought that Alexander's victory was due to Fortune (i.e. that he did not possess *arete*). When he learned the truth, he prayed that in the event of his defeat Alexander, and no one else, might sit upon the throne of Cyrus, i.e. he called the gods to witness that he adopted Alexander (ch. 30). (7) This is the way in which *arete* conquers. We may ascribe to Fortune Alexander's military successes, but moderation, self-control, superiority to pleasure and desire are not due to Fortune, and it was these that defeated Darius. In battle Tarrias, son of Deinomenes, Antigenes, and Philotas were invincible, but against pleasure, women, and money they were no better than slaves. Philotas boasted that Alexander owed everything to him, but although Alexander knew of this through Antigone he did not reveal his suspicions for seven years; yet men say he was a drunkard, had no self-control, and communicated everything to Hephaestion (as the episode of Olympias' letter is supposed to prove). (8) Even if Alexander became great through Fortune, he is greater because he used Fortune well. The more men praise his Fortune, the more they praise his *arete*.

But he did not gain the throne of Cyrus because of a horse's neigh, like Darius, nor because of the favour of a woman, like Xerxes. Fortune made others king, as she brought Aigon to the throne of Argos or Abdalonymus to that of Paphos, (9) but Alexander faced every danger and toil. He enjoyed *no* good Fortune either at the hands of man or

Nature. Fortune should depart to Antiochus, son of Seleucus, or Artaxerxes or Ptolemy Philadelphos, who were proclaimed king when their fathers were alive. But Alexander was wounded from head to foot (eight instances). (10) Fortune did well to make Alexander great by exposing every part of his body to wounds! She did not save him from serious injury, as Athena did Menelaus. In fact, Alexander suffered more at the hand of Fortune than any other king. Yet despite her persistence she found Alexander, like Hercules, invincible. But for Alexander's great spirit, derived from his *arete*, he would have given up in the face of sieges, pursuits, countless revolts, and all the other difficulties. He would have tired of cutting off the hydra heads which grew again in fresh wars. (11) Fortune almost made men doubt that Alexander was the son of Ammon; for no son of a god, except Hercules, was called upon to perform such laborious tasks. But whereas one evil man imposed on Hercules the task of capturing lions to prevent him punishing Antaeus and putting an end to the murders of Busiris, *arete* imposed on Alexander the divine task of bringing all men under one rule, a desire which he had from childhood, as his questions to the Persian envoys showed (ch. 5). When Alexander was about to begin his expedition Fortune dragged him back by contriving wars with the Triballians and Illyrians, with Thebes and Athens, wars against fellow-Greeks that could bring him no glory. His financial resources were meagre, but he distributed his property and revenues to his Companions, of whom Perdiccas alone refused to accept them (ch. 15). (12) What hopes did Alexander take with him to Asia? Not an army and navy as large as Xerxes', but an army whose members vied with each other in *doxa* and *arete*. In himself he had great hopes; piety towards the gods, loyalty towards his friends, *frugalitas*, *continentia*, and so on. God formed Alexander's nature out of all the virtues—the spirit of Cyrus, the moderation of Agesilaus, the wisdom of Themistocles, etc., etc. He was more temperate than Agamemnon, more generous than Achilles, more pious than Diomedes, more missed by his relatives than Odysseus. (13) Solon, Miltiades, and Aristeides were great because of *arete*, not Fortune; yet if Alexander is compared to them he surpasses Solon's *seisachtheia* by paying his soldiers' debts, Pericles' use of tribute to adorn the Acropolis with temples by sending the wealth of the East to erect temples in Greece, and Brasidas' celebrated dash along the seashore to Methone by his leap into the Malli town, like Apollo landing on earth. Fortune's malice shut Alexander up in an insignificant village in which he could win no glory in death, as Pelopidas and Epaminondas did, and prevented his soldiers from entering. After Alexander was wounded, *arete* engendered in him courage, and in his companions strength and zeal. Limnaios, Ptolemy, and Leonnatus defended Alexander because of their love of Alexander's *arete*. A spectator would have said that it was a struggle between *arete* and Fortune. The speech ends with a description of Alexander's wound and a contrast between Alexander's courage and the despair of his followers.

Before examining the speeches we should perhaps ask whether in writing these speeches Plutarch was merely displaying his rhetorical talents or whether, as several distinguished scholars have held, he had in mind a more serious purpose.[1] Hirzel (*Der Dialog* 2. 78) and Tarn (*AJP* (1939) 56; *Alex.* 2. 296), impressed by the portrait of 'the philosopher in action' which Plutarch develops in the first speech, both consider that he was seeking to refute the charges made against Alexander's character by the philosophical schools (see below, pp. lx ff.). Hirzel thinks that Plutarch had in mind the Cynics and Stoics, while Tarn would add the Peripatetics.[2] Several considerations tell against this view. First, Alexander is contrasted favourably not only with philosophers of the Cynic, Stoic, and Peripatetic schools, but also with Plato and especially with Socrates (1. 4, 5, 9, 12); indeed, he is superior to *all* philosophers. The only philosophers, moreover, who are spoken of favourably are the Cynics Antisthenes and Crates (2. 3) and the Stoic Zeno (1. 6). It may be argued that to show Alexander as the supreme philosopher is one form of defence, but it should not be overlooked that 'the philosopher in action' occupies only a portion (although admittedly a major portion) of the first speech, while it is hardly mentioned in the second. Again when we bear in mind the full title of the speeches, *De A. M. fortuna aut virtute*, we can see that this portion is consistent with the main theme. Since the philosopher is the embodiment of virtue, the proof that Alexander was a philosopher constitutes proof of his *arete* and contributes to a solution of the *tyche–arete* problem. The attempt to prove Alexander a philosopher is not the chief aim of the speeches, but a means to an end. Nor are we compelled to believe that Plutarch is answering the criticisms of the philosophers; by his time these criticisms were commonplaces of the schools of rhetoric (see below, p. lxi).

In the most recent substantial discussion of the speeches[3] Wardman

[1] I merely mention the suggestions of Eicke (*Veterum philosophorum qualia fuerint de A. M. iudicia* (1909) 53 ff.) that in praising Alexander for his *continentia* Plutarch was dropping a hint to Trajan, who was supposed to be addicted to *amor*, and of Hirzel (*Der Dialog* (Leipzig, 1895) 2. 81) that by laying stress on deeds rather than words Plutarch was consoling Trajan for his defective education. They are 'too esoteric to be credible' (so Wardman, *CQ*, n.s. 5 (1955), 99, of Eicke's view), and in addition it is difficult to credit that these highly rhetorical speeches were written when Plutarch was over 50.

[2] Tarn (*AJP* 60 (1939), 56, n. 86) doubts whether the speech is Plutarch's work. But there is no reason to doubt its authenticity, although Sandbach (*CQ* 33 (1939), 196, n. 3) may be right in thinking that it is an earlier work revised later.

[3] A. E. Wardman, *CQ*, n.s. 5 (1955), 96–107.

has maintained that they are developed from two antitheses: *logos–ergon* and *tyche–arete*. The former theme is directed against earlier philosophical treatment of Alexander by the Stoics and Peripatetics, but is not apparently a serious defence of Alexander.[1] Plutarch's treatment of the second antithesis, Wardman suggests, is to be considered together with the *De Romanorum fortuna*. We can then see that 'Plutarch is viewing the whole of history as a trend towards world unity. Unity was accomplished by Rome, but—*this seems to be the implication* [my italics] —was also the object of Greek history and Alexander's campaigns.' Plutarch's view, he argues, was that the Romans had succeeded because they possessed both Fortune and *arete*, while Alexander had the *arete* but lacked the Fortune necessary to succeed. This is to take Plutarch, particularly the young Plutarch, much too seriously as a political thinker and as a philosopher. His insistence in the *De Alexandri fortuna* on Fortune hampering Alexander[2] is adequately explained by rhetorical practice,[3] and the implication that Alexander's campaigns were a trend towards world unity is far from obvious. Moreover, the *De Romanorum fortuna* is unfinished (and perhaps in the process of revision), and if, as Wardman believes, the speech did not contain a portion in favour of *arete*, it must follow that Plutarch argued that Rome's success was due primarily to Fortune and that, just as in the first speech *De Alexandri fortuna*, Plutarch replies to a speech in favour of Fortune,[4] so in the *De Romanorum fortuna* his opponent argued in favour of *arete* and he put the case for Fortune.

A strong reason for considering these speeches rhetorical exercises is the perfection of Alexander. This is best explained not by the admiration of the youthful Plutarch[5] but by the maxim of the rhetorical schools that one should not rest content with refuting one's opponents, but should seek to prove the exact opposite. So there is no hint of criticism: Alexander is the embodiment of all the virtues. Moreover, a serious defence of Alexander would surely require that Plutarch should deal with such topics as the execution of Philotas, the murder of Cleitus, Callisthenes and the Pages' conspiracy, and *proskynesis*. Yet of these vital topics we hear not a whisper! Philotas is mentioned—but

---

[1] At any rate Wardman (p. 99) claims that his explanation offers a middle way between Tarn's view and the view that Plutarch has no serious purpose.

[2] The advantage claimed by Wardman for his view is that it helps to explain this.

[3] Indeed it might well be argued that in the (lost) first speech Fortune has claimed Alexander as her handiwork and that in the second Philosophy counters by (*inter alia*) charging Fortune with actually obstructing him.

[4] Wardman (100, n. 5) believes, against most scholars, that the opening words, οὗτος ὁ τῆς Τύχης λόγος, are simply 'a dramatic way of stating the view against which Plutarch is to argue'.

[5] Tarn (*AJP* 60 (1939), 56) thinks that the first speech was written 'in a white heat of passion' to defend Alexander's reputation; so also 2. 296.

only to show that Alexander did not reveal his suspicions of him even to Hephaestion for seven years (!).

It seems most probable that the obvious view is the correct one, that the two speeches are 'epideictic display-pieces', devoid of any serious purpose.[1] The wide reading expected of the rhetorician is evident not only from the many authors cited in the speeches but still more from the references to a large number of events in Greek and Persian (and even Roman) history. The orator was required to *display* his knowledge; hence the speeches contain many more incidents outside the reign of Alexander than does the *Life*. Many of these were no doubt commonplaces of the rhetorical schools, as e.g. the references to Xerxes (1. 7, 2. 12), but many must derive from Plutarch's recollection of his own reading; perhaps the references to Tigranes and Nicomedes come into this category. For a serious exercise the student must have been required to undertake a course of reading, amounting almost to research in our sense.

We can see to some extent how Plutarch has used his material to develop his thesis. Since Onesicritus (fr. 17) described Alexander as 'the philosopher in arms', the idea of him as 'the philosopher in action' may well be taken from him; perhaps also the statements that the *Iliad* was Alexander's *ephodion* and that he owed more to Aristotle than to Philip. At any rate both statements occur in chapter 8 of the *Life* in the same context. But the *development* of this conception of Alexander, the comparison with Pythagoras, Socrates, and other philosophers, and the somewhat forced parallelism between Plato's *Republic* and *Laws* and Alexander's city-foundations and his laws are best attributed to Plutarch himself. In his portrait of the 'cosmopolitan' Alexander (1. 6–9) Plutarch makes use of quite disparate pieces of information and combines them, not unskilfully, into a consistent whole. From Eratosthenes he derives Alexander's adoption of a mixed Persian–Macedonian dress and probably also the division between Greeks and barbarians according to virtue and vice. In both cases Plutarch has adapted his material. In the *Life*, which we may reasonably suppose represents his considered judgement on Alexander, Plutarch writes (ch. 45. 1) that either Alexander wished to win over the barbarians by adopting elements of native costume or else was seeking to promote the introduction of *proskynesis*; in the speech (1. 8) his adoption of this mixed dress is a measure to forward his universal commonwealth. Again, in the speech (1. 6) Alexander instructs all men to make the division between Greeks and barbarians a division between virtue and vice; yet we know from Strabo (1. 4. 9) that this was a remark made

---

[1] The phrase is Badian's (*Historia* 7 (1958), 436). This view is argued at length by Hoffmann 87–96.

about him by Eratosthenes. Plutarch has quite simply attributed it to Alexander; for there is no reason to suppose that he ever uttered it or ever held the view expressed in it. At the beginning of ch. 9 Plutarch states that Alexander's goal *from the start of his expedition* was to create *in all men ὁμόνοιαν καὶ εἰρήνην καὶ κοινωνίαν*. Now in Arrian's description of the banquet at Opis (7. 11. 9) Alexander is said to have prayed for ὁμόνοιάν τε καὶ κοινωνίαν τῆς ἀρχῆς Μακεδόσι καὶ Πέρσαις. The similarity of expression suggests that Plutarch borrows, perhaps unconsciously, from Arrian's source.[1] In fact, Alexander's prayer, not uttered until 324, was limited to concord and partnership in rule between Macedonians and Persians (Iranians); it had nothing to do with a world commonwealth.[2] The splendid picture of the loving-cup (1. 6), too, may be a rhetorical device suggested to Plutarch by the banquet and his interpretation of it. The marriages at Susa, where ninety leading Macedonians married women of the Persian nobility, were part of Alexander's 'policy of fusion'.[3] Of this Plutarch was well aware; nevertheless this incident also is adapted to his thesis of 'Alexander the cosmopolitan'.

This adaptation of material by Plutarch can be illustrated by numerous less important examples. Alexander's remark after his meeting with Diogenes at Corinth, which in the *Life* (ch. 14) is used, reasonably enough, to show his reverence for philosophers, is developed in a quite ridiculous fashion into an expression of 'Alexander the civilizer' (1. 10). We can see, too, how Plutarch used this same remark in a different context in a completely different way. At *Mor.* 782 a–b (= *Ad principem ineruditum* 6) it is interpreted to mean that Alexander was vexed at his own position and power, because they were an obstacle to the virtue for which he could find no time. He envied the moral invincibility of Diogenes, although by the practice of philosophy he might have secured the moral character of a Diogenes while still retaining the position of an Alexander. A similarly strained interpretation is put on the incident in which Alexander questions the Persian ambassadors, which in the *Life* (ch. 5) illustrates his charm and seriousness of purpose. In the *Moralia* (2. 11) his questions show the desire he felt *from childhood* to create a universal commonwealth. His reply to those who urged him to compete in the Olympic Games (1. 9) is supposed to prove him a philosopher, while in the *Life* (ch. 4) it is properly used to show that he did not desire every kind of *doxa*. Finally his extended pursuit of the Scythians across the River Tanais while suffering from dysentery reveals in the *Life* (ch. 45) his

---

[1] That Ptolemy was Arrian's source is probable; see Tarn 2. 290 ff., Badian, op. cit. 429.

[2] See esp. Badian, op. cit. 428 ff., 432 ff.

[3] On this policy see esp. H. Berve, *Klio* 31 (1938), 135–68.

indifference to hardship; in the *Moralia* (2. 9) it is one of many illustrations of the malice of Fortune.

These differences between the *Life* and the speeches, the list of which could be greatly extended, enable us to see the manner in which Plutarch, as a rhetorician, adapted and interpreted his material in the interests of his thesis. It follows that we cannot accept his *interpretation* of any event without confirmatory evidence, although we are justified in placing the *facts* in the speeches on the same level as those in the *Life*. We may, for example, place just as much (or as little) reliance on his statement that Alexander refused to compete at the Olympic Games as we do on Alexander's rejoinder to the wounded Philip (1. 9). We need not, and cannot, take these speeches seriously as representing Plutarch's view of Alexander. Indeed, it would need much faith to believe that at any period in his life Plutarch thought that Alexander was as perfect as he is portrayed. As Badian well remarks,[1] the difference between the speeches and the *Life* is not to be explained by Plutarch's additional reading or by his greater maturity, but by the difference between rhetoric and biography.

III. *The* Parallel Lives[2]

Although many of Plutarch's other biographies have perished,[3] the whole series of twenty-three pairs of *Parallel Lives* has survived with the exception of the (probable) first pair, Epaminondas and Scipio.[4] In this series Plutarch compares a distinguished Greek with his Roman counterpart, as he compares Alexander with Caesar.

Choice of Heroes

This was based, as Erbse has convincingly demonstrated,[5] not only on the qualities which he considered the two men to share, although this was probably the decisive factor,[6] but also on the similarities in their careers; for, since Plutarch subscribed to the Peripatetic view of

---

[1] *Historia* 7 (1958), 437. Cf. T. S. Brown, *Historia* 16 (1967), 360.

[2] On this section D. A. Russell, 'On Reading Plutarch's *Lives*', *Greece and Rome* 13 (1966), 139 ff., is valuable. See also his articles on the *Coriolanus* and the *Alcibiades* in *JRS* 53 (1963), 21 ff., and *Proc. Camb. Philol. Soc.*, N.S. 12 (1966), 37 ff.

[3] For details of these, see Ziegler 895 ff. The extant *Lives* of Aratus, Artaxerxes, Galba, and Otho do not form part of the *Parallel Lives*.

[4] Ziegler 895 f. considers that this was Scipio Africanus Maior. However K. Herbert, 'The Identity of Plutarch's lost *Scipio*', *AJP* 78 (1957), 83 ff., has argued persuasively in favour of Scipio Aemilianus.

[5] In his important article, *Hermes* 84 (1956), 398–424, at p. 400.

[6] Plutarch (*Sert.* 1. 3–10) is scornful of previous writers who compared men on the basis of mere coincidence in their careers, as e.g., the two Scipios were compared because the elder had defeated the Carthaginians and the younger had destroyed Carthage.

character as manifesting itself in action (see below, pp. xxxviii–ix), their reactions to similar (or nearly similar) circumstances afforded an opportunity to compare their characters. Since Alexander and Caesar were the outstanding figures in the ancient world it might appear obvious (or indeed inevitable) that Plutarch would select them for comparison,[1] but it is evident that he discerned in them many common qualities. In particular, both appear greatly influenced by ambition and concerned with their reputation;[2] both are extremely generous (especially to their fellow-soldiers) and chivalrous towards their defeated enemies;[3] both display self-control;[4] finally, both later reveal certain tyrannical qualities.[5]

Each pair of *Lives* is normally followed by a summary comparison (*synkrisis*), which serves especially to set out the *differences* between the heroes, but in the case of the *Alexander–Caesar* this is absent.[6]

Chronology of the Lives

We do not know when Plutarch began writing the *Parallel Lives*, but Jones's suggestion[7] that 'Sosius' consulate in 99 furnished an occasion for Plutarch to dedicate the new undertaking to him' is attractive. Plutarch himself gives only one direct indication of the dates of composition: at *Sull.* 21. 8 he remarks that weapons were still being found in the marshes near Orchomenos 'almost 200 years' after Sulla's victory (in 86 B.C.). From this we should probably conclude only that the pair *Lysander–Sulla* was written within the decade 100–110. Recently, however, Jones has pointed out that those *Lives* in which Sosius Senecio is addressed (either directly or by the use of the second person

---

[1] Velleius (2. 41. 1) had already compared them briefly. They are later compared at length by Appian (*BCiv.* 2. 149 ff.) and by Julian (*Conv.* 320 a–325 c). Nevertheless the comparison of Alexander with Scipio (the elder) was common (Gellius, *NA* 7. 8); it had been made as early as the middle of the 2nd century by C. Acilius (Livy 35. 14. 7; cf. Plut. *Flam.* 21, Appian, *Syr.* 10, Lucian, *Ver. Hist.* 2. 9). Varro had compared him with Pompey (ap. Pliny, *HN* 7. 95), as had Pompey himself (cf. his *cognomen Magnus*) and his contemporaries; see Sallust, *Hist.* 3. 88.

[2] *Alex.* 4. 8, 5. 5–6, 13. 4, 42. 4; *Caes.* 5. 8–9, 10. 9, 11. 3–6, 17. 1, 22. 6, 54. 4, 58. 4–5, 69. 1.

[3] Generous: *Alex.* 39, 42. 5; *Caes.* 12. 4, 15. 4, 17. 1, 57. 8. Chivalrous: *Alex.* 21. 1–5, 43. 5–7, 59. 1–5, 60. 14–15; *Caes.* 15. 4, 18. 5, 34. 7–8, 48. 3–4, 54. 4.

[4] *Alex.* 21–23; *Caes.* 17

[5] *Alex.* 48–55; *Caes.* 4. 8, 57. 2–3, 60. 1 and 4, 61. 1.

[6] For this view, which shows the limitations of Plutarch's scheme, see Erbse, *Hermes* 84 (1956), 406. He maintains that the *synkrisis* was an essential complement to the narrative of the two *Lives*; for a less favourable view of its importance see Ziegler 909 f. The *synkrisis* is absent also in the *Phocion–Cato Minor*, the *Pyrrhus–Marius*, and the *Themistocles–Camillus*, in Erbse's view because in the first instance the similarities and in the latter two the differences were too great. The more general view is that the *synkriseis* were written and are missing.

[7] *JRS* 56 (1966), 70.

pronoun) must precede his death, which occurred almost certainly before 116.[1]

From indications in the *Lives* we can reconstruct in outline their *relative* chronology. Plutarch's statements (*Dem.* 3. 1, *Per.* 2. 5, *Dion* 2. 7) enable us to place the pair *Demosthenes–Cicero* in the fifth position, the *Pericles–Fabius* in the tenth, and the *Dion–Brutus* in the twelfth. In many *Lives* (although not in the *Alexander*) there are references to other *Lives* as either completed or, rarely, as in prospect. Unfortunately (on the assumption that the references are original) some of them contradict each other: in the *Caesar* (62. 8, 68. 7), for example, Plutarch indicates that the *Brutus* is complete, while in the *Brutus* (9. 9) he refers to the *Caesar* in similar terms.[2] Those scholars who investigated the problem in the nineteenth century[3] came to the conclusion that some of the references were not made by Plutarch but were marginal notes which had found their way into the text, and found a solution in the removal of the offending references.[4] In 1907, however, Mewaldt[5] put forward the hypothesis that the references were all genuine, that Plutarch worked on a number of *Lives* simultaneously and published them in groups, e.g. the *Theseus–Romulus, Lycurgus–Numa*, and *Themistocles–Camillus*, and as a second group the *Dion–Brutus, Aemilius–Timoleon*, and *Alexander–Caesar*. But in 1929 Stoltz, in an exhaustive study of the subject, rejected Mewaldt's solution and returned to the older view, deleting the references at *Dion* 58. 10, *Brutus* 9. 9, and *Camillus* 33. 10.[6] Stoltz found the method of working suggested by Mewaldt hard to credit, for while much of the material for the *Brutus* would be relevant to the *Caesar* and that of the *Dion* to some extent relevant to the *Timoleon*, the material for the *Aemilius* and the *Alexander* would have no relevance to any of the other

---

[1] Jones, op. cit. 69 f. The *Lives* are *Dem.–Cic., Thes.–Rom., Dion–Brut., Aem.–Tim., Agis–Cleom.–Gracchi.*

[2] Similarly while *Dion* 58. 10 cites the *Timoleon, Timoleon* 13. 10 and 33. 4 cite the *Dion*, and while *Camillus* 33. 10 cites the *Romulus* and *Theseus* 1. 4 and *Romulus* 21. 1 cite the *Numa, Numa* 12. 13 cites the *Camillus*.

[3] Details in Ziegler 899 ff.

[4] The possibility that some of the references may have been added subsequently by Plutarch has been somewhat hastily rejected on the grounds that since the *Lives* were written in extreme old age (certainly not true of all) Plutarch would have had no time to make a *revision*, and that a revision would have eliminated the many inaccuracies and contradictions. But we need not envisage anything so elaborate as a second edition (see Ziegler 901), and this solution remains a real possibility.

[5] J. Mewaldt, *Hermes* 42 (1907), 564–78. His solution is favoured by Stadter 32, n. 1 and by Flacelière (most recently in *Plutarque Vies I*, xxv–xxvi). Jones adopts his scheme, but holds that the *Lycurgus–Numa* must have been published before the *Theseus–Romulus* (see below, p. xxxvi).

[6] C. Stoltz, *Zur relativen Chronologie der Parallelbiographien Plutarchs* (Lund, 1929). He is followed by Ziegler 901 ff., and (implicitly) by C. Theander, *Eranos* 56 (1958), 12–20.

Lives in the group. He further maintained that the pair *Theseus–Romulus* must be among the last of the *Lives*, whereas, in view of the references to the *Lysander* in the *Pericles* (22) and to the *Lycurgus* in the *Lysander* (17), the other pairs in this suggested group must precede the *Pericles–Fabius*, the tenth pair. Proof of the (late) position of the *Theseus–Romulus* he found in Plutarch's statement in the introduction to the *Theseus* (1. 2) that he is going to deal with the mythical period 'after passing through the periods accessible to probability in which history based on fact can find a footing'.[1] In Stoltz's view this must mean that Plutarch has dealt with all (or nearly all) the *Lives*; but surely Plutarch merely means that in the *Lycurgus–Numa* he has reached the limits of the historical period, without implying anything about the number of *Lives* already completed.[2] When Plutarch goes on to say (1. 4) that he thought he might reasonably go back to Romulus, being brought by his history so near to his time τὸν περὶ Λυκούργου τοῦ νομοθέτου καὶ Νομᾶ τοῦ βασιλέως λόγον ἐκδόντες, one would naturally conclude that the *Lycurgus–Numa* had already been published.[3] Mewaldt (572) and Flacelière (*REG* 61 (1948), 68 f.), however, hold that the two pairs were published simultaneously and that the preface to the *Theseus* is a preface to both pairs; they therefore translate ἐκδόντες as 'publishing'. But it is very doubtful whether the aorist participle can bear this meaning. Flacelière (loc. cit.) adduces a further argument. If the *Lycurgus–Numa* had already been published, he maintains, then Plutarch must have considered Lycurgus and Numa to be historical personages, for the *Lives* of Theseus and Romulus mark in this respect an innovation which is underlined in the preface; but this, he considers, is just what Plutarch did not do. As proof he points to his statements at the beginning of the *Lycurgus* and the *Numa*, that: 'It is impossible to affirm anything about Lycurgus which is not doubtful' and 'Opinions differ very greatly about the time when Numa lived.' A brief examination of the *Lives* in question will, in fact, prove exactly the opposite. In the *Theseus* Plutarch is clearly dealing with myth, not history;[4] in the *Lycurgus* and the *Numa*, on the other hand, he is dealing with history and the statements of historians. At *Lycurgus* 1. 1 he writes

---

[1] τὸν ἐφικτὸν εἰκότι λόγῳ καὶ βάσιμον ἱστορίᾳ πραγμάτων ἐχομένῃ χρόνον διελθόντι. . . .

[2] We should perhaps conclude that the *Lycurgus–Numa* immediately preceded the *Theseus–Romulus*; so Jones, *JRS* 56 (1966), 67, and W. Bühler, *Maia* 14 (1962), 281.

[3] Especially as at *Romulus* 21. 1 Plutarch refers to the *Numa* as written (γέγραπται).

[4] At 1. 5 he remarks 'Let us hope that *Fable* may, in what shall follow, so submit to the purifying process of *Reason* as to take on the appearance of *History*' (ὄψιν ἱστορίας). Cf. 2. 3—both Theseus and Romulus are said to have fallen foul of their fellow-citizens, 'if among the traditions that appear least fabulous there is any that helps to discover the truth'.

that 'Even the establishment of his laws and his constitution is variously reported *by historians*' and at 1. 7 'Although *history* is so disputed'.[1] So in the *Numa* the 'opinions which differ very greatly' are those of *historians*. It seems reasonable, then, to conclude that the *Theseus–Romulus* was written after the publication of the *Lycurgus–Numa*. If this is so, Mewaldt's thesis must be considered improbable.

Nevertheless whether we accept Stoltz's views or those of Mewaldt there is little doubt about the majority of the *Lives* which composed the first dozen pairs. There is general agreement that the missing pair, *Epaminondas–Scipio*, was composed first, and the fifth, tenth, and twelfth pairs are known (above, p. xxxv). The *Cimon–Lucullus*, the *Lysander–Sulla*, and the *Pelopidas–Marcellus* must be included in the first ten pairs,[2] together with the *Lycurgus–Numa* and the *Themistocles–Camillus*.[3] Thus eight of the first ten pairs are settled. The two vacant places may be allotted to the *Sertorius–Eumenes* and the *Theseus–Romulus*, and either the *Solon–Publicola* or the *Philopoemen–Flamininus* may fill the eleventh position.[4]

If Mewaldt's theory is correct, the *Alexander–Caesar* and the *Aemilius–Timoleon* must have occupied the thirteenth and fourteenth (or fourteenth and thirteenth) positions immediately after the *Dion–Brutus*, and since Sosius Senecio is referred to in the *Aemilius* and the *Dion* we may date the *Alexander* (?some years) before 116.[5] If it is not correct, as seems probable, the position of the *Alexander–Caesar* within the series cannot be precisely determined; all that we can say *for certain* is that it was not later than the eighteenth pair. Nevertheless it would seem likely that it was published between 110 and 115.

Plutarch's Biographical Aims and Methods

Plutarch is preoccupied with the *character* of his heroes. At the beginning of the *Timoleon* he tells us that he began writing at the request of others but continued for his own sake, 'the virtues of these great men serving me as a sort of looking-glass in which I may see how to adjust and adorn my own life'. His method, he says, is by the study of history and the familiarity acquired in writing to habituate his memory to receive and retain images of the best and worthiest characters. By turning his thoughts to view these noble examples he is enabled to free

---

[1] ἡ . . . πραγματεία διαφόρους ἔσχηκε ἱστορίας; cf. 1. 7, οὕτω πεπλανημένης τῆς ἱστορίας. . . .

[2] The *Cimon* and the *Lysander* are referred to in the *Pericles* (9; 22), and the *Marcellus* in the *Fabius* (19; 22).

[3] The *Lycurgus* is cited in the *Lysander* (17) and the *Camillus* in the *Numa* (9; 12).

[4] See Jones's table, p. 68. Ziegler is in agreement except that (following Stoltz) he excludes the *Theseus–Romulus*.

[5] For the relevance of the mention of Sosius Senecio see above, pp. xxxiv–v.

himself from any ignoble or vicious impressions.[1] Even bad examples may have their use. For Plutarch includes the *Lives* of Demetrius and Antonius not for variety or for the amusement of his readers, but because knowledge of the bad may encourage men to imitate the better lives (*Demetr.* 1).

The clearest statement of Plutarch's aims is contained in the first chapter of the *Alexander*. There he states plainly that he is not a historian, but a biographer; hence he will not attempt to include all the famous deeds of Alexander and Caesar.[2] It is the insignificant action, the casual remark or jest that affords the clearest insight into *character*, and so he will concentrate, as a painter does, on those features which reveal this. So, in the introduction to the *Nicias*, he disclaims any intention of rivalling Thucydides, as Timaeus had foolishly tried to do, and distinguishes between τὴν ἄχρηστον ἱστορίαν and τὴν πρὸς κατανόησιν ἤθους καὶ τρόπου (χρήσιμον ἱστορίαν). He means, of course, not that history is 'useless', but that certain facts which would be relevant to history do not concern him as a biographer.[3] Moreover, as Gomme observes,[4] Plutarch was not a biographer in the fullest sense, but an essayist; his *Parallel Lives* are moral essays—a complement to the *Moralia*—concerned with the hero's character, not with his place in history.

Plutarch repeatedly states his intention of illustrating the character (ἦθος) of his subject through his actions (πράξεις), including in the case of an orator his speeches.[5] The terminology is Peripatetic.[6] The nature (φύσις) of a man is a basic and unchanging element in his character, which is not only revealed by his actions but is formed by habitual or repeated action and by his reactions to events. Education (παιδεία) and philosophy (λόγος), too, play an important part in the formation of character. For example, since the character of the elder Brutus was

---

[1] Moral good is a practical stimulus; it is no sooner seen than it inspires an impulse to practise (*Per.* 2. 4–5).

[2] As he observes in the *Galba* (2. 3) it is the task of ἡ πραγματικὴ ἱστορία to provide a detailed record of events.

[3] For the correct interpretation of this passage see Gomme 77, n. 2; Theander 32, n. 1, 49; Ziegler 910, n. 1, and for this sense of ἄχρηστος cf. *Dion* 21, *Tim.* 15. But Plutarch does not always exclude the stuff of history; at *Fab.* 16, for example, he includes a detailed description of Carthaginian tactics, which is quite irrelevant to Fabius' character and which he attributes to those who wrote τὰς διεξοδικὰς ἱστορίας; cf. *Aem.* 8–9 (Antigonid history), *Cam.* 15–16 (Gauls).

[4] pp. 54, 55.

[5] See *Dem.* 11. 7 and the other passages cited by F. Leo, *Die griechisch-römische Biographie* (Leipzig, 1901) 184 ff.

[6] See Leo 188 ff., and esp. Dihle 60 ff. Cf. Erbse, *Hermes* 84 (1956), 400, n. 1. This may be evidence for the prominent part played by the Peripatetics in biographical writing, but it does not mean that Plutarch used Peripatetic sources in the *Alexander*.

harsh by nature and was not 'softened' by philosophy he came to grief and killed his son; whereas the younger Brutus was a harmonious blend of action and reflection because of education and philosophy (*Brutus* 1. 2).[1] It is sometimes said that the development of character was unknown to ancient writers. This statement requires modification: a person's nature (φύσις) did not change, but character (ἦθος) might alter. So in ch. 52. 7 Plutarch writes that Anaxarchus made Alexander's character 'more conceited and lawless'.[2]

In general, in composing his biographies, Plutarch relates his hero's career from birth to death in chronological order. But he allows himself a good deal of scope, and the precise arrangement and the amount of space allotted to each topic depends on whether the hero is predominantly an orator, a politician, or a military man, and on the amount of material available to him.[3] The *Alexander* provides a good example of his practice. After the introductory chapter, Plutarch begins with a reference to Alexander's ancestry (brief presumably because it was well known), then mentions his parents' marriage, and deals at length (and rather sceptically) with the prophecies concerning the unborn Alexander. His birth is then dated, and various prophecies of his future greatness are mentioned (2–3). Next Plutarch treats of his physical appearance, his character as a boy and his early education (4–5). The breaking of Bucephalas is allotted a full chapter (6), and in chapter 7 Plutarch relates how Aristotle was summoned to educate the young Alexander, and deduces the content of his teaching from the letters. Alexander's education is treated in two parts principally because of the importance of Aristotle's influence; this is underlined by the digression on Alexander's interest in medicine, literature, and philosophy, which he owes to Aristotle. We then hear of Alexander's activities during Philip's reign, the domestic troubles caused by Philip's marriage to Cleopatra and Alexander's attempt to ally himself with the Carian dynast, Pixodarus, and finally of Philip's murder (9–10). The next four chapters (11–14) relate Alexander's campaigns in Illyria and Greece (with a digression on his treatment of Timocleia (12)), and his preparations for the Persian expedition. This begins with the crossing of the Hellespont (15), and henceforth Alexander's

---

[1] On the need for education and philosophy cf. *Tim.* 6; yet the Stoic philosophy might be dangerous to certain natures (*Cleom.* 2. 6). Compare also *Mar.* 2 and *Them.* 2. 7, where Themistocles is said often to have taken the worse course because he lacked λόγος καὶ παιδεία.

[2] The clearest example of a change of character occurs in the *Demetrius*: see Dihle 76 ff., who has a good discussion of the difference between ancient and modern character-drawing. Note Plutarch's remarks at *Sert.* 10, esp. paras. 5 ff., a passage not discussed by Dihle. See also Russell, *Greece and Rome* 13 (1966), 144 ff., who notes (p. 147, n. 2) that Plutarch's terminology is not always consistent.   [3] See the examples collected by Leo 184 f.

deeds are recounted in chronological order up to his death. The final chapter (77) discusses the story that he was poisoned and breaks off in the middle of an anecdote about his successor.

As is customary, the narrative is interrupted at various points by digressions, where a number of anecdotes are assembled out of chronological order to illuminate certain aspects of Alexander's character. Apart from those in chapters 8 and 12 (above), his treatment of the captive Persian women is followed by a discussion of his continence and subsequently of his self-control and habits (21. 5–23). Similarly the visit to Siwah is followed by a chapter (28) examining Alexander's attitude to his own divinity, and the burning of the palace at Persepolis occasions the longest digression (39–42. 4), illustrating the king's generosity and his loyalty to and care for his friends. Much briefer digressions occur at 45. 4–6, where Alexander's valour is demonstrated, and at 47. 5–12, where his measures to further his 'policy of fusion' are described. The German scholar Adolf Weizsäcker coined the terms 'Chronographisch' and 'Eidologisch' to describe the two elements in Plutarch's work.[1] These are useful to the historian who is attempting to date events, but the distinction is misleading to the extent that the illustration of character is not confined to the 'Eidology'. The narrative also is designed to bring out the character of the hero.

The portrait of Alexander is built up in several different ways, for Plutarch is too good an artist to rely on any single method. In view of his aims it is hardly surprising to find that the amount of space devoted to military operations, even in the case of so famous a leader as Alexander, is small. In the descriptions of the major battles interest is concentrated on the person of Alexander, and little effort is made to elucidate the topography or tactics involved. It is safe to say that we could not understand any of the battles from Plutarch's narrative. Although Gaugamela with its preliminaries occupies three chapters (31–3), the main stress is laid on Alexander's confidence before and during the battle, which Parmenio's request for aid serves to heighten. The actual fighting is disposed of in less than a chapter, in which the two kings are the protagonists. At Issus the battle itself is described in a single sentence (20. 8), which reveals how Alexander took advantage of Fortune's favour, and the actual fighting against Porus is allotted only two sentences (60. 10–11). The comparatively lengthy description of the operations at the Granicus (16. 1–14) is to be explained by the prominence of Alexander and his *aristeia* against Spithridates and Rhoesaces. The episode at the Malli town is fully treated, as we would

---

[1] In his *Untersuchungen über Plutarchs biographische Technik* (Berlin, 1931). For his refinements on these basic terms and criticism of them see Ziegler 907 f.

expect, but the pursuit of Darius (42–3) serves merely to introduce Alexander's refusal of water, showing his ἐγκράτεια and μεγαλοψυχία, and the request of the dying Darius to Polystratus to reward Alexander for his ἐπιείκεια. The fierce and prolonged fighting in Bactria and Sogdiana is represented only by a series of episodes (45. 5–6; 58), showing the king's valour and daring and his φιλανθρωπία. The account of the siege of Tyre (24. 5–25. 3) well illustrates Plutarch's technique: we have a few words at the beginning and end about the military operations, but the bulk of the narrative is taken up with Alexander's dreams and the episodes involving Lysimachus and Aristander, which show the king's loyalty to his friends.

Apart from the major military operations Plutarch could hardly fail to include many well-known incidents such as the Gordian knot (18), the founding of Alexandria and the expedition to Siwah (26–7), and the visit of the Amazon queen (46). Nor could he avoid mentioning the 'conspiracies' of Philotas and the royal pages and the murder of Cleitus (49–55). Elsewhere he had more freedom of choice, and his *selection* of anecdotes, from which the narrative is built up, shows us how he intended to portray the character of Alexander. A number of themes, some dealt with more systematically in the digressions, recur. We see, for instance, his ἐγκράτεια and σωφροσύνη in his treatment of women, Timocleia (12), and the Persian captives (21; 30), while the same qualities are attributed to him when he refuses the water in the desert (42. 7–10). His meetings with the Nysaean envoys (58. 7–9), Taxiles (59), and Porus (60. 14–15) all serve to bring out his generosity towards his enemies, both those who submitted and those defeated in battle. The expedition against the Arabs and his order to alter the calendar during the siege of Tyre (24–5) demonstrate his loyalty to his companions, while his trust in them is exemplified by the dramatic scene with his doctor, Philip (19). A less attractive side of Alexander's character appears in his superstitious belief in the series of omens in ch. 73 and his treatment of Cassander (74). The vast majority of anecdotes are relevant to Plutarch's main theme, the character of Alexander, but in a few cases, e.g. the purple of Hermione and the storing of Danube and Nile water in the Persian treasury (36. 2–4), information seems to be included simply because it interested Plutarch.

Although Plutarch generally allows his portrait of Alexander to emerge through his narrative of great events and the numerous anecdotes, he often comments in his own person on many of the most important aspects of his character, especially in the digressions to link or to introduce the anecdotes. In ch. 28, for example, Plutarch's remarks make it clear that in his view Alexander did not believe in his divinity but used other people's belief in it as a political device, and in ch. 23 he states his opinion that Alexander was not addicted to drink. Plutarch's technique can be seen most clearly in the 'great digression' (39–42. 4). He begins by stating that Alexander was extremely generous and that his generosity increased with his increasing means; this is shown by numerous examples. Plutarch goes on to illustrate the luxury of the king's followers (40), adding the comment that Alexander reproved them 'gently and philosophically'. He then relates that by exposing himself to danger Alexander tried to reform them, but that they were so devoted to luxury that they abused him (41). At first, Plutarch remarks, Alexander reacted 'gently', saying that to endure abuse when doing good was a king's duty, but finally (42. 4) became furious and was cruel and implacable, because he valued reputation (*doxa*) above life itself. Earlier (4. 8, 5. 5) the biographer has commented on and exemplified Alexander's love of reputation, although not from every kind of activity. Plutarch's own views are clearly expressed at 20. 7 and 26. 14, Alexander's superiority to Fortune and his invincibility due to his spirited nature (τὸ θυμοειδές), already deduced from his bodily heat (4. 7). Towards the end of Alexander's life Plutarch himself attests his suspicion and despondency (74. 1), and his addiction to superstition (75. 1–2). It is likely, too, that the alternative reasons given for Alexander's generous treatment of Athens (13. 2), for his adoption of a mixed dress (45. 1), and for his slowness to take action against Philotas (49. 2) are Plutarch's own comment.

Finally Alexander's character is revealed directly by what he himself says and, less often, by what others say of him. His desire for the right kind of *doxa* is shown by his remarks that he would run at the Olympic Games if his opponents were all kings (4. 10), and that Philip would leave him nothing to accomplish (5. 4). His philosophic nature is illustrated by the famous remark 'If I were not Alexander, I would be Diogenes' (14. 5), and by his statement that he was indebted to Philip for life but to Aristotle for the good life (8. 4). His attitude to luxury is brought out by his comment on Darius' tent after Issus (20. 13), while his confidence is stressed by the celebrated reply to Parmenio, who advocated a night attack at Gaugamela, 'I do not steal victory' (31. 12), and perhaps also by his remark to him at 29. 8. His seriousness of character in childhood moves the Persian envoys to comment (5. 3), and his future greatness is foreshadowed when Philip says to him 'Macedonia is not large enough for you' (6. 8). The deserter Amyntas assures Darius that he need not worry about Alexander running away (20. 3); the eunuch tells Darius of Alexander's ἐγκράτεια καὶ μεγαλοψυχία (30. 11), and Darius' dying words emphasize his ἐπιείκεια (43. 4).

Plutarch's artistry consists largely in the way in which he skilfully employs these different methods of illustrating character in combination. Direct statement is confirmed by anecdote, and the major events are related in such a fashion that attention is concentrated on the person of Alexander and the biographer's conception of him gradually emerges through the narrative.

Plutarch's Historical Methods

In the *Moralia* and the *Lives* Plutarch cites no fewer than 150 historians (in the wider sense), including forty who wrote in Latin.[1] Despite this, or perhaps rather because of it, a highly sceptical view of the extent of Plutarch's historical reading prevailed for much of this century. For example, Busolt and Beloch in their standard histories held that Plutarch obtained most of his information at second hand.[2] The most obvious way of settling the question, the analysis of individual *Lives*, was by no means neglected but, unfortunately, produced widely differing and sometimes contradictory results.[3] In fact, it is rarely possible by source analysis to *prove* that one author has consulted another directly and not through an intermediary.[4]

Two doubts influenced those who favoured the theory that Plutarch used intermediate sources: first, how could he find time, while writing as much as he did, to read all the authors he cites, and secondly, if he could find time, was it conceivable that his library at Chaeroneia contained all these works, many of them far from common? The first difficulty has perhaps been exaggerated. Despite the claims of a busy public life the elder Pliny had written over 100 books before his death at the age of 55, an age when Plutarch had just begun to write his *Parallel Lives*.[5] The second difficulty, apparently more substantial when we consider the writer's isolation at Chaeroneia,[6] vanishes if we agree with Gomme[7] that Plutarch did not write surrounded by

[1] Ziegler 911; for details of authors cited in the *Lives* see Index I to vol. 4. 2 of his Teubner edition (1939).

[2] The most extreme view was advanced by Eduard Meyer in his *Forschungen zur alten Geschichte* (Halle, 1899); he asserted (2. 65, 67) that in his *Parallel Lives* Plutarch did not *use* (although he had *read*) even the 'classics' (Herodotus, Thucydides, Xenophon) at first hand, but depended on biographers such as Hermippus; even Hermippus, he claimed (2. 69), was known to Plutarch only through an intermediary. This view was demolished by Gomme (below, n. 7) and may be considered dead.

[3] For work on the *Lives* between 1909 and 1934 see A. Hauser in Bursian's *Jahresbericht* 251 (1936), 35–86, and from 1934 to 1952 A. Garzetti, 'Plutarco e le sue "Vite Parallele"' in *RSI* 65 (1953), 76–104, esp. 79 ff.

[4] See the forthright remarks of Fergus Millar, *A Study of Cassius Dio* (Oxford, 1964) viii.

[5] For his career see A. N. Sherwin-White, *The Letters of Pliny* (Oxford, 1966), 219–21.

[6] This should not be exaggerated; Athens was not too distant, and Plutarch doubtless made many visits. There must also have been a library at Delphi, and we should probably reckon on his receiving gifts of books from his many friends.

[7] A. W. Gomme, *A Historical Commentary on Thucydides* 1 (Oxford, 1945), 54–84,

books, but relied to a great extent on his excellent memory and for the rest consulted his notes of books he had previously read. Gomme pointed, in particular, to Plutarch's wide reading[1] and to his statements that he had read various authors.[2]

What little we know of the methods of ancient writers supports Gomme's view. In a letter to Baebius Macer (*Ep.* 3. 5) the younger Pliny describes (§ 10) how his uncle worked: 'A book was read aloud while he made notes and extracts, as he did with every book he read.' It is not surprising to hear (§ 17) that his uncle left him '160 volumes of notes, written in a tiny hand on both sides of the page, so that these 160 volumes were equivalent to many more'.[3] Plutarch tells us (*Mor.* 457 d) that Minucius Fundanus made collections of material on various subjects, and we probably possess two such collections of his own in the *Regum et imperatorum apophthegmata* and the *Apophthegmata Laconica* (172 a–242 d).[4] We have no means of telling how detailed Plutarch's notes were, but we are probably safe to conclude that he relied mostly on his trained memory.[5] The assumption that he was writing from memory best explains the many errors of detail in the *Lives*. At *Them.* 12. 8, for example, Panaetius commands a trireme from *Tenedos*, while in Herodotus (8. 82), an author whom Plutarch had certainly read, he commands a *Tenian* trireme. In the same *Life* (15. 3) Lycomedes, an Athenian tricrarch, is said to have made a dedication from the first Persian vessel captured at *Salamis*; yet from Herod. 8. 11 we know that he captured this vessel at *Artemisium*.[6]

a *locus classicus* on the subject; see esp. 54 ff., 78 ff. In 1865 H. Peter, *Die Quellen Plutarchs in den Biographien der Römer* (Halle), had taken a similar view; so, more recently, R. Zimmermann, *Rh. Mus.* 79 (1930), 55–64.

[1] For the extent of his reading see esp. Ziegler 914–28, *Die Quellen der Bildung Plutarchs*, and W. C. Helmbold and E. N. O'Neill, *Plutarch's Quotations* (Philadelphia, 1959).

[2] *Alex.* 4 (Aristoxenus); *Mor.* 422 e (Phanias); *Ages.* 19; *Mor.* 514 c (Ephorus); cf. *Mor.* 1093 c, from which it is clear that he had read Eudoxus, Aristotle, and Aristoxenus.

[3] Even at dinner he took rapid notes (§ 11), and while being rubbed down, after bathing, he had a book read to him or dictated notes (§ 14). Cassius Dio also made notes for the whole of his Roman history before arranging his material and writing it up; see Millar, op. cit. 32.

[4] On these see Ziegler 863–7, Gomme 78, n. 1. Ziegler considers that, since the corresponding portions of the *Lives* are more detailed, the former collection was not made by Plutarch; but I do not see why Plutarch may not have combined other material with it while at work on the *Lives*. Both collections were probably *based* on existing collections and published after Plutarch's death. At *Mor.* 464 f Plutarch refers to his note-books (ὑπομνήματα).

[5] See above, p. xxii, for the benefits of rhetorical training. Zimmermann, op. cit. 61 f., who refers to Seneca, thinks that Plutarch used *hardly any* notes. I find this difficult to believe.

[6] There is no lack of examples. For those in the *Alexander* see the notes to 16. 15 and 67. 3, for those in the *Coriolanus* see D. A. Russell, *JRS* 53 (1963), 22.

Recent studies have confirmed that Plutarch worked in this way. In 1951 Theander examined his use of some sixteen Greek authors and proved beyond reasonable doubt that Plutarch had read these authors. He pointed out that Plutarch quotes *verbatim* and in particular criticizes authors or compares one with another in such a way that it is apparent that he had read them.[1] Several times, too, Plutarch indicates his use of an intermediate source, especially Hermippus, who is cited six times in this way.[2] This, Theander rightly claimed, must mean that he had read the more recent author. Unfortunately Theander's study, inevitably, does not embrace the many obscure writers cited by Plutarch. Argument in future is likely to concern itself not with whether Plutarch habitually used *Mittelquellen*—this is settled[3]—but with what proportion of the authors cited he knew at first hand.

Ziegler, who had already rejected the idea that Plutarch always used second-hand material, attempted to draw up a table showing which authors Plutarch had certainly read, which he had probably read, and which he knew only through an intermediary.[4] Using as a criterion the number and spread of the citations, he concluded that rather more than half fell into the last category. But his criterion is evidently too simple, since it ignores the scope of an author's work, which Plutarch might have no occasion to consult except in one or two *Lives*;[5] moreover the results of the most recent investigation suggest that Ziegler was somewhat too cautious.

It has generally been thought (see Ziegler 859) that in the *Mulierum Virtutes* (242 e–63 c), twenty-seven little-known stories illustrating the

---

[1] Theander 42 ff. Quotations: Ephorus (*De Herod. mal.* 5), Charon of Lampsacus (ibid. 20, 24). Alexander's letters are quoted at *Alex.* 22. 5, cf. 47. 3, 60. 1. 11. Criticism: below, pp. xlvii f. Comparisons: Ephorus, Timaeus, Anaximenes (*Praecepta* 6); Ephorus, Timaeus, Philistus (*Dion* 36); Thucydides, Philistus, Timaeus (*Nic.* 1); Thucydides and Theopompus (*De Herod. mal.* 1).

See also E. Meinhardt, *Perikles bei Plutarch* (Frankfurt, 1957) 9–16, who adds the absence of any reference by Plutarch to a biographical source; which is not perhaps decisive. H. Erbse, *Hermes* 84 (1956), 420 ff., argues that Plutarch must have read widely in the available literature in order to discern the qualities in his heroes which enabled him to pair them satisfactorily.

[2] Op. cit. 54 ff.

[3] See the remarks of K. Büchner, *Gnomon* 32 (1960), 307. It is particularly encouraging that Flacelière adopts this point of view in his Budé edition of the *Lives*. However, M. Gelzer (*Gnomon* 36 (1964), 658 ff.) believes that the *Cicero* was based on an existing biography, while H. Homeyer (*Klio* 41 (1963), 145 ff.) still adheres to the theory of *Mittelquellen*; for her views on the *Alexander* see below, pp. l–lii.

[4] Rather *two* tables (912 f., 924 f.), for they do not coincide. e.g. Charon is doubtful 924 but second-hand 913, Phanias doubtful 925 but certain 912, Stesimbrotus certain 912 but doubtful 924.

[5] e.g. Charon of Lampsacus, who wrote a *Persica* and a *Chronicle of Lampsacus*. He is, in fact, quoted in the *De Herod. mal.* 20, 24 (verbatim), in the *Mul. Virt.* 18, and at *Them.* 27.

heroic qualities of women, Plutarch and Polyaenus (who relates nineteen of them) used a common source, an existing anthology. Stadter, however, has proved that Polyaenus used Plutarch, who made his own selection, and has made it almost certain, by a detailed study of the individual stories, that Plutarch had read the writers he mentions.[1] Some of these are well known, but the majority are local historians. If Plutarch had read these, it is reasonable to conclude that he had also read at least the majority of the authors he cites elsewhere. This may be true even of much of the anecdotic material and the citations from the comic writers, which Büchner and Ziegler believe to be second-hand; but we must agree with Büchner that in many cases it is difficult or impossible to distinguish first-hand from second-hand material.[2]

Statements that 'no one took the duties of a historian more seriously than Plutarch' or that 'within their chronological limits the *Lives* provide a universal history of the Greco-Roman world' can excite only incredulity.[3] Plutarch himself does not claim so much (*Alex.* 1), and he made no attempt to provide the historical background to his heroes' actions or to explain the origins and long-term effects of their policies.[4] His reliance on memory is excessive, he is indifferent to detail, and, more important, he imposes his own interpretation of his hero's character on the narrative at the expense of the facts.[5] Nevertheless it would be wrong to conclude that Plutarch was credulous or even uncritical. Gomme[6] lists three main weaknesses: lack of insight into the political conditions of the classical age, indifference to chronology, and inability to value his authorities. About the first there can be no dispute. As for the second, it is disconcerting to find that Plutarch (*Sol.* 27) accepts the tradition that Solon met Croesus despite 'the so-called canons of chronology' because the meeting accords with his view of Solon's character.[7] Yet he could use the archon lists to prove that Aristeides was archon in 489/8 B.C. (*Arist.* 5),

---

[1] Plutarch's statement that he is avoiding the best-known stories does not perhaps absolutely rule out the possibility that Plutarch is selecting from an anthology, but Stadter's points (pp. 126, 136), that 18 of the 27 stories are known only through Plutarch and that he had already used local historians to refute Herodotus in the *De Herod. mal.*, make his conclusion very probable.

[2] Büchner loc. cit., Ziegler 914.

[3] R. Hirzel, *Plutarch* (Leipzig, 1912) 48, 63. Theander (82), however, cites the former statement with approval.

[4] Gomme 54 f. See, however, for exceptions p. xxxviii, n. 3 above.

[5] The last point is admirably illustrated by Russell (*JRS* 53 (1963), 21 ff.) in his analysis of the *Coriolanus*.　　　　　　　　　　　　　　　　　　　　[6] p. 58.

[7] At *Per.* 10 Plutarch rejects Idomeneus' statement that Pericles murdered Ephialtes because of envy and jealousy, since such an act is not consonant with his character. He adds, however, that Aristotle attributed the murder to Ephialtes' oligarchic enemies.

and at *Them.* 2. 5 he refutes Stesimbrotus' statement that Themistocles was a pupil of Anaxagoras and Melissus by pointing out that Anaxagoras was a friend of Pericles, against whom Melissus commanded the Samian forces in 440/39.

About Gomme's third point I feel less sure. It may be true that Plutarch 'had no *scientific* appreciation of the difference between first-hand and second- or third-hand authorities', but it must be emphasized that he sought, where possible, to use contemporary or near-contemporary sources. It is significant that the *Themistocles* is based primarily on Herodotus and Thucydides, and that he followed Hieronymus of Cardia in the Hellenistic *Lives*, and Timaeus (? and Theopompus) in the *Timoleon*. So in the *Dion* (31. 2, 35. 6) the versions of Timonides and Philistus, who were contemporary with the events, are preferred to that of Timaeus.[1] Again, in the *Alexander* (see next section) his main authorities were men who had all (except Cleitarchus) accompanied Alexander. Note, too, his use of contemporary documents: in the *Solon* the poems of Solon, in the *Alexander* the king's letters (used in preference to other sources), and in the *Dion* the letters of Plato.[2] In the *Lives* of Cicero and Demosthenes he made considerable use of their speeches and in the *Demosthenes* of those of Aeschines as well.

Herodotus (7. 152) expressly states that he need not be thought to believe every statement he makes; Plutarch makes no such disclaimer, but we have no right to suppose that he would have vouched for the truth of every detail in the *Lives*. He often sets out variant views without comment,[3] as Herodotus had done, but frequently criticizes his authorities. His criticism is based to some extent on his knowledge of the character of their writings,[4] but he did not rely only on this knowledge. The dramatic descriptions of Alexander's passage along the Pamphylian coast (17. 6) and of his death (75. 5) are refuted in the one case by the evidence of the king's letter[5] and in the other by Aristobulus' statement.

---

[1] At *Cim.* 4 Plutarch expressly notes that Stesimbrotus was a contemporary of Cimon.

[2] W. H. Porter, *Dion* (Dublin, 1952), rightly maintains that Plutarch consulted the Platonic epistles directly.
If Plutarch had not the critical equipment to determine the authenticity of these letters, we have not progressed much further.

[3] See, e.g., *Alex.* 18. 3–4, 33. 10, 38. 8, 55. 9, 61. 1, 65. 2–4.

[4] He distrusts the 'tragic' element in Duris (see esp. *Alc.* 32. 2 = fr. 70, *Eum.* 1 = fr. 53) and Phylarchus (esp. *Them.* 32. 4 = fr. 76); he is aware that Ctesias was inclined to the fabulous and the dramatic (*Artox.* 6. 9 = fr. 29), that Timaeus was justly nicknamed '*Epitimaeus*' (esp. *Nic.* 1 = T. 18, *Dion* 36 = fr. 154), and that Theopompus dispensed blame more readily than praise (*Lys.* 30. 2 = fr. 333; cf. *Them.* 19. 1 = fr. 85, *Ages.* 33. 1 = fr. 323).

[5] For the use of the letters in this way see also 20. 9, 27. 8, and 46. 5 (doubtfully).

Plutarch was well aware not only that the passage of time rendered the discovery of the truth difficult but also that contemporary historians might be swayed by hostility or by partiality (*Per.* 13. 16). At *Aratus* 38 he comments that Phylarchus' version would not be worthy of credit were it not supported by Polybius; for Phylarchus was an enthusiastic admirer of Cleomenes and constantly wrote like an advocate. Similarly he rejects (*Per.* 28. 3) Duris' allegations of Pericles' cruelty to the Samian captives, not only because Thucydides, Ephorus, and Aristotle say nothing of it, but also because it was likely that Duris would exaggerate the misfortunes of his fellow countrymen to blacken the Athenian character.[1] Plutarch makes much use of the *argumentum ex silentio*: at *Alc.* 32. 2, for example, he rejects Duris' version of Alcibiades' return to Athens in 408 because of the silence of Theopompus, Ephorus, and Xenophon;[2] typically, he adds the comment, based on his reading (? or misreading) of Alcibiades' character, that he would not have been likely to act in this way at this time.[3]

Perhaps the passage which best illustrates the merits and limitations of Plutarch's criticism is *Aristeides* 1. Demetrius of Phaleron had maintained that Aristeides was well-to-do: he had been chosen archon by lot, he had been ostracized, and he had set up a choregic monument. The last argument Plutarch counters by adducing the epigraphic evidence of Panaetius, which is conclusive; yet he does not regard this point as settled, and has indeed prefaced Panaetius' evidence with a quite inconclusive suggestion of his own. Against the other points made by Demetrius he shows that not all those ostracized were members of noble houses, and cites Idomeneus for the fact that Aristeides was *elected* archon. Plutarch's faults are clear: he does not appreciate the value of the epigraphic evidence, and he does not trouble to consult Aristotle's *Constitution of Athens*, which he had certainly read,[4] but relies on his recollection of a statement by Idomeneus, an author whom he criticizes elsewhere.[5] Yet he deserves credit for the clarity with which he sets out the arguments of Demetrius and Panaetius, and for his wide reading which provided this knowledge.

[1] Gomme (59) notes his failure to ask what value Duris had for fifth-century history; but may he not have assumed that Duris, as a Samian, had access to local information? Nor am I persuaded that Plutarch here thinks that the silence of Ephorus had the same value as that of Thucydides.

For Plutarch's appreciation of Ctesias' bias in favour of Clearchus and the Spartans see *Artox.* 13. 7 = fr. 23.

[2] See also *Cic.* 49. 3 and *Phoc.* 4. 1–2, where he adds acutely that if Phocion had been of low birth he would not have attended the Academy or have indulged in aristocratic pursuits from his earliest years.

[3] At *Dem.* 13. 1, 18. 3, and 21. 2 he quarrels with Theopompus' reading of Demosthenes' character.

[4] See esp. Stadter 130 f.

[5] *Arist.* 10. 7, *Phoc.* 4. 1, and esp. *Per.* 10. 7 (see p. xlvi, n. 7).

Plutarch's criticism contains much good sense, but it is easy to overvalue it; certainly it is too much to say, as Theander (78) does, that 'he became a historian almost against his will'. Nevertheless, Theander is right, particularly in view of the opinions sometimes expressed by his detractors, to emphasize Plutarch's curiosity about monuments (including portraits), topography, and ancient customs,[1] and his use of collections of documents.[2]

iv. *The Sources of the* Alexander

In the *Alexander*, apart from the letters written by or to Alexander which are mentioned over thirty times, Plutarch names no fewer than twenty-four authorities. Of these he cites Aristobulus (15. 2; 16. 15; 18. 4; 21. 9; 46. 2; 75. 6), Chares (20. 9; 24. 14; 46. 2; 54. 4; 55. 9; 70. 2), and Onesicritus (8. 2; 15. 2; 46. 1; 60. 6; 61. 1; 65. 2) six times, Callisthenes (27. 4; 33. 1; 33. 10) three times, and Eratosthenes (3. 3; 31. 5), Duris (15. 2; 46. 2), and the Ephemerides or Royal Journal (23. 4; 76. 1) twice each. The following writers are mentioned once each:[3] Antigenes, Anticleides, Aristoxenus (4. 4), Cleitarchus, Dinon (36. 4), Hegesias (3. 6), Hecataeus of Eretria, Heracleides (26. 3), Hermippus (54. 1), Ister, Philip of Chalcis, Philip of Theangela, Philon, Polycleitus, Ptolemy, Sotion (61. 3), and Theophrastus (4. 5).

Not all scholars believe that Plutarch had read all these authors. An extreme view is advanced by J. E. Powell (*JHS* 59 (1939), 229 ff.), who, observing certain similarities between his narrative and that of Arrian, concluded that both writers used a large variorum source-book and that Plutarch supplemented this from a collection of spurious letters.[4] Tarn (2. 306 ff.) made a brief but effective rejoinder to Powell; he pointed out *inter alia* that there are no precedents for the kind of volume envisaged by him, which would have to contain the whole of Ptolemy's history; and, we may add, a great deal besides. Recently Inge Rabe[5] has examined in detail the passages in Arrian

---

[1] Theander 2–32 and *Eranos* 57 (1959), 99–131 (on his use of oral information). On portraits see the Commentary, n. to 4. 1.

[2] Theander 78 ff. He points to the references to Craterus' collection of decrees at *Arist.* 10. 19. 26, *Cimon* 13, *Them.* 10, *Nic.* 12, *Dem.* 27; to the list of Pythian victors and the *hypomnemata* of the Delphians at *Sol.* 11, and to the *anagraphai Laconicai* at *Ages.* 19.

[3] Authors to whom no reference is given are all mentioned at 46. 1–2.

[4] Powell was, essentially, reviving the theory of A. Schoene, to whom he refers at 238, n. 6; this had been refuted at length by Fränkel 30–92, and was firmly rejected by Schwartz (*RE* 2, 1238).

[5] In her excellent doctoral dissertation, *Quellenkritische Untersuchungen zu Plutarchs Alexanderbiographie* (Hamburg, 1964), 42–125.

INTRODUCTION

and Plutarch on which Powell relies, and has demonstrated beyond question that in *no* case is the theory of a common source tenable.

The view advanced by Helene Homeyer,[1] that for the *Alexander* Plutarch used Eratosthenes and Duris, in whom the remaining authorities were already incorporated, needs more discussion. First, however, we should note Plutarch's statement in the introduction to the *Alexander*, that he does not propose to narrate *all* the famous exploits of Alexander and Caesar but to deal with only some of them, in summary fashion for the most part. This *ought* to mean, one would think, that he is selecting from a mass of material. Secondly, although Plutarch names twenty-four writers in the *Alexander*, this number is deceptive; for no fewer than seventeen are cited once only, ten of these at 46. 1–2 (the Amazon story).[2] This does not, of course, prove that Plutarch did not use these authors elsewhere, but in fact only Cleitarchus may have been used extensively (see below, p. li). The other seven who are cited once[3] are referred to only for isolated incidents, and it is highly probable that all these references derive from Plutarch's own reading. Even Powell (p. 230) concedes that a few of them may be recollections from earlier reading; he instances Hegesias. This is certainly the case at 4. 4–5, where Plutarch combines Aristoxenus' statement that Alexander had a 'sweet smell' with Theophrastus' theory.[4]

Finally, if it can be shown that Plutarch consulted any of the major primary sources directly Miss Homeyer's theory collapses. For those who believe that he had before him a collection of Alexander's letters, and did not find them in his sources, Fränkel long ago established that Plutarch consulted Onesicritus directly. For he remarked (p. 135) that in the middle of the letter describing the battle at the Hydaspes (ch. 60) there occurs a quotation from Onesicritus. Obviously, if it is a genuine letter, Alexander cannot have included it, and it is surely inconceivable that a forger would have been so stupid as to insert it. Miss Homeyer, however, thinks that Plutarch found the extracts from the letters in his sources. Her position is not, I think, tenable. She remarks that they are cited 'nur oberflächlich', and it is self-evident that they are not quoted in full. But if they *were* contained in his sources, they must have been reported in full; for the manner in which Plutarch writes at 17. 8 strongly suggests that *he* is summarizing the letter, and

[1] *Klio* 41 (1963), 145–57, esp. 154, n. 2. Schachermeyr 135 also considers that Plutarch used *Mittelquellen*.

[2] For the view that some at least of these references may derive from a monograph on the subject, perhaps by Ister, see 46. 1 nn.

[3] Aristoxenus, Dinon, Hegesias, Heracleides, Hermippus, Sotion, Theophrastus.

[4] See n. ad loc. We may compare ch. 35. 10 ff., where Plutarch adduces two separate pieces of information in support of one view of the origin of naphtha. The whole of this passage is beyond question his own work.

1

conclusive proof is furnished at 46. 3, where he writes that Alexander seems to support those writers who say that the Amazon story is fiction. 'For', he continues, 'when writing in detail to Antipater, Alexander says that the Scythian offered him his daughter's hand, but makes no mention of the Amazon.' Evidently Plutarch had the whole letter before him, and it is very difficult to credit that Duris or Eratosthenes transcribed it (or any of the others) in full. The matter is settled, in my opinion, by Powell's observation (230 f.) that 'the quiet naïveté with which again and again he takes credit to himself for making use of the letters for the first time is the best proof that he used them directly'. Powell points out that the majority of the citations occur in the digressions on character, which must be Plutarch's own work.

There can be no doubt that the source of Plutarch's information in ch. 12 (the Timocleia episode) is Aristobulus, who is cited for the story at *Mor.* 1093 c.[1] A comparison with *Mor.* 259 d–260 d (= *Mul. Virt.* 24), where the incident is described in greater detail but with no significant difference, makes it evident that Plutarch is himself summarizing Aristobulus' version.[2] It is significant, as Rabe (pp. 130 f.) saw, that the episode is not even referred to by any other author.[3] Plutarch, therefore, was familiar with the works of Onesicritus and Aristobulus. That he had read Callisthenes and Chares cannot be demonstrated, but may reasonably be assumed.

Yet it is difficult to suppose that all the information contained in the *Alexander* was derived from these four authors, and it is likely that Plutarch used another source or sources. The most probable candidate is Cleitarchus; there are many incidents in the latter part of the *Life* where Plutarch's narrative is similar to that of the 'vulgate',[4] and in some of them at least Plutarch cannot be following Aristobulus (whose version, known from Arrian, was different), while it is unlikely that Chares and Onesicritus dealt with all the incidents. In particular, Plutarch gives Cleitarchus' version of the burning of Persepolis (ch. 38) and of the *komos* in Carmania (ch. 67), while at ch. 75. 5 he rejects his account of Alexander's death. It remains possible that Plutarch found this information in a later writer, perhaps Duris, as Miss Homeyer suggests, but while this possibility cannot be absolutely ruled out it seems to me much more probable that Plutarch consulted Cleitarchus directly.[5] It would be surprising, in view of his marked

---

[1] Stadter (113, n. 291) rightly rejects attempts to connect the story with Cleitarchus because of its 'un-Aristobulian colouring'.

[2] For full (and excellent) analyses see Stadter 112 ff., Rabe 126 ff.

[3] Except Polyaenus (8. 40), whose version derives from Plutarch (above, p. xlvi).

[4] Diodorus 17, Curtius, and Justin's *Epitome* of Trogus; see Tarn 2. 1.

[5] We know little of Duris' account of Alexander's reign, but apart from the two citations (15. 2, 46. 2) there is nothing to suggest that Plutarch is using his history. Moreover, although he cites Duris 11 times in the *Lives*, he had a poor opinion of

preference for primary sources (above, p. xlvii) and of the popularity of Cleitarchus in the late Republic and early Empire, if Plutarch had *not* read his book.

We cannot hope to assign every statement to its source,[1] but if we consider the character of the works of the contemporary sources and of Cleitarchus, as revealed by their extant fragments, some progress is possible.[2] We may reasonably suppose that where Alexander's divine sonship is mentioned or where he seeks to win over the Greeks (as at 34. 2) Callisthenes is his source; Onesicritus will have supplied information about Alexander's education and shown him as the 'philosopher in action', while Chares may be responsible for incidents concerning the court and Aristobulus for personal details. Plutarch's sources may also be surmised from the similarity of his narrative to that of the other extant sources. *Close* correspondence with Strabo may indicate that he is using Aristobulus or Onesicritus, and, in particular, resemblance to Arrian may show use of Aristobulus, and to the 'vulgate' use of Cleitarchus. Unfortunately this criterion is difficult to apply, especially in the first part of the *Life*, since all the historians drew on Callisthenes' account. Even after Callisthenes' history ceased the situation is complicated, as Cleitarchus used Onesicritus and Aristobulus used Cleitarchus.[3] Finally, in one or two instances Plutarch relates the same incidents in the *Moralia* and there names his source.

Using these criteria we may tentatively assign the following passages to their sources[4]—citations are marked with an asterisk:

Callisthenes: 17. 6; 26–7. 7*;[5] 30. 2–14 (cf. Arr. 4. 20. 1–3, Curt. 4. 10. 25–34); 31. 8–14; 32–3* (cited at 33. 1, 33. 10).[6]

Aristobulus: 4. 1 (cf. Arr. 1. 16. 4); 11 (for § 12 cf. Arr. 1. 9. 10); 12 (cited at *Mor.* 1093 c); 13. 1–2 (cf. *Dem.* 23. 3 ff.); 14. 8–9 (cf. Arr. 1. 11. 2); 15. 2*; 16* (cited at 16. 15; cf. Arr. 1. 16. 4, 7); 18. 2–4*; 20. 1–3 (cf. Arr. 2. 6. 3 ff., 2. 7. 1 ff.); 21. 9*; 23. 1 (cf. Arr. 7. 29. 4); 29. 7–9 (cf. Arr. 2. 25. 1–3); 31. 6–7 (cf. Arr. 6. 11. 4 ff.); 38. 8

him; see esp. *Per.* 28, where he comments that his narrative was usually untruthful, and on *Alc.* 32 and *Eum.* 1 see p. xlvii and n. 4.

[1] See Tarn's remarks at 2. 296.

[2] For a brief account of their writings see pp. liii ff.

[3] For this view of their relationship see pp. liv f.

[4] A longer list will be found in Fränkel 327 f. I have omitted many of the instances he gives as the evidence seems insufficient for any decision.

In several instances (26. 2, 27. 8, 30. 14, 60. 12; cf. 31. 6, 61. 1, 77. 5) Plutarch evidently found substantially the same version in different authors and might have found it difficult to say whose version he finally presented; cf. Welles, *Diodorus*, vol. 8 (Loeb ed.), p. 10.

[5] Callisthenes is cited at 27. 4, but much of these chapters is Plutarch's combination of various sources.

[6] Although 32. 8–12 *may* derive from Chares.

(cf. Arr. 3. 18. 11); 42. 5 (cf. Arr. 3. 19. 5); 45. 5–6 (cf. Arr. 3. 30. 11, esp. the form Orexartes); 46. 2*; 57. 5–9 (cf. Arr. 4. 15. 7, Strabo 11. 518); 63. 2–14 (cf. *Mor.* 341 c, Arr. 6. 9. 1 ff.); 75. 6*.

Chares: 6 (cf. Gell. *NA* 5. 2); 20. 9*; 20. 13; 24. 10–14*; 46. 2*; 50–1 (cf. Berve 2. 207, n. 1); 54. 4–6*; 55. 1 ff.; 55. 9*; 70. 2*; 70. 3–6.

Onesicritus: 5. 7–8; 8. 2*; 15. 2*; 22. 7–10; 25. 6–8; 26. 1–2 (cf. 8. 2); 46. 1*; 59. 1–5 (cf. Strabo 15. 698); 60. 6*; 60. 12–16; 61. 1–2*; 62 (except §§ 4, 9); 65. 2*.

Cleitarchus: 37. 1–2 (cf. Curt. 5. 4. 10 ff., Diod. 68. 5); 38. 1–7 (cf. Curt. 5. 7. 2 ff., Diod. 72); 39. 2 (cf. Curt. 4. 9. 24 ff.); 43. 3–4 (cf. Curt. 5. 13. 24, Justin 11. 15. 7 ff.); 46. 1*; 49 (cf. Curt. 6. 7. 1 ff., Diod. 79); 57. 1–2 (cf. Curt. 6. 6. 14 ff.); 66. 4–7; 67. 1–7 (cf. Curt. 9. 10. 24–8, Diod. 106. 1); 75. 3–5.

Theophrastus: 35. 15 (cf. *Mor.* 648 d).

Ctesias: 69. 1 (see n. ad loc.).

Plutarch's Main Sources[1]

Callisthenes

(Jacoby no. 124. Robinson 45–77. Pearson 22–49. See also T. S. Brown, 'Callisthenes and Alexander', *AJP* 70 (1949), 225–48.)

Callisthenes accompanied Aristotle, his great-uncle, from Atarneus to Macedonia in 343/2, and must have known Alexander well, although he was too old to have been his fellow-pupil, as later tradition asserted (Berve 2. 191). He probably owed the invitation to join Alexander's staff (see 53. 1 n.) as much to his connection with Aristotle as to his reputation as a historian, although by 334 he had composed an encomium on Hermeias, a work on the Sacred War, and a ten-book *History of Greece* (387–357), and had co-operated with Aristotle in compiling a list of Pythian victors (see *GHI* 2. 187).

His task was evidently to produce for Greek consumption an account of Alexander's progress which would conciliate Greek public opinion, and it seems a necessary assumption that he sent his work back to Greece in instalments. He clearly understood what was required (*pace* Pearson 23), and wrote as Alexander wished him to write; the unfavourable portrait of Parmenio is his work (see 33. 10 n.). That his motives were 'patriotic' and that he hoped for

[1] The fragments are collected in F. Jacoby, *Die Fragmente der griechischen Historiker* 2B (Berlin, 1927) with a commentary in 2D; they are translated by C. A. Robinson Jr., *The History of Alexander the Great* 1 (Providence, 1953). The best commentary on these authors is L. Pearson, *The Lost Histories of Alexander the Great* (*Amer. Phil. Ass.* 1960); see Badian's important review in *Gnomon* 33 (1961), 660–7.

a 'national regeneration' through Alexander, as Schachermeyr (127) maintains, cannot be proved or disproved. Later writers criticized him for his 'flattery' of Alexander, and his 'Exploits of Alexander' was to some extent at least a rhetorical encomium of the king. Of the dozen extant fragments the most important (14(*a*)) describes the visit to Siwah. From this we can see that Alexander was cast in *heroic* mould; the motive for the expedition was rivalry with his ancestors, Perseus and Heracles, and Alexander receives divine aid from two ravens. Even a rainstorm is the work of Zeus (see 27. 2 n.). Callisthenes was responsible for spreading the story that Alexander was the son of *Zeus* (cf. 33. 1, Alexander's prayer at Gaugamela)—which is not the same thing as making him a god (see esp. Badian, *Gnomon* 33 (1961), 661). The passage of Mount Climax (17. 8) is treated in similar fashion, and thunder at Sardes and Gordium is probably to be interpreted as an example of divine approval (see Pearson 36–8, 39). Callisthenes also dealt with Homeric sites in Asia Minor in order to emphasize Alexander's heroic ancestry, as Pearson (39–45) has well demonstrated. He was familiar with the terrain from his stay at Atarneus and was said to have collaborated in a recension of Homer (see 26. 2 n.). His account of the battle of Issus is severely, and in the main justly, criticized by Polybius (12. 17–22); his account of Gaugamela seems to have been no better, if we may judge by the versions of Plutarch (32–3) and Curtius—although they, admittedly, may be partly to blame.

Aristobulus

(Jacoby no. 139. Robinson 205–43. Pearson 150–87. See also G. Wirth, 'Anmerkungen zur Arrianbiographie', *Historia* 13 (1964), 213 ff.)

Aristobulus is called 'a man of Cassandreia', which means that he settled there after its foundation in 316, but he may have been a Phocian by birth (see Pearson, *AJP* 73 (1952), 71 ff.). He did not hold any military command, so far as is known, but was entrusted with various commissions, such as the restoration of Cyrus' tomb (69. 3), which suggest that he was an engineer or an architect.

Arrian selected him, together with Ptolemy, as the chief source for his *Anabasis* and evidently considered him a reliable authority, while Strabo used his book extensively in his account of India. Modern views of his abilities vary. The really important question (see Pearson 152 ff.) is whether he was a primary authority, writing before Ptolemy and Cleitarchus, or whether he drew on their works and was (in part) a secondary writer. The prevailing view, that Cleitarchus wrote towards the end of the fourth century, has been challenged by Tarn (2. 16 ff.) and, more effectively, by Pearson (226 ff.), who favour a date after 280, but it still appears to me to be more probable.[1] If this is so, Cleitarchus is clearly earlier than Aristobulus, who, it is agreed, wrote not earlier than 295 B.C.[2]

It seems certain on any view that Aristobulus did not indulge in rhetoric or exaggeration and did not aim at sensation. He is, for example, much more reticent than Onesicritus about the marvels of India, and did not relate the visit of the Amazon queen (46) or the *komos* in Carmania (67). He described accurately what he had seen, e.g. the tomb of Cyrus (see Pearson 180 f.) and the Gymnosophists at Taxila (fr. 41), and displayed 'a vivid interest in geography and natural history'. On the other hand, his portrait of Alexander appears to have been uniformly, and suspiciously, favourable.[3] He had little to say about the 'conspiracy' of Philotas (fr. 22), while Cleitus deserved what he got (fr. 29) and the pages implicated Callisthenes (fr. 31). For all these events Plutarch preferred more detailed (and better) sources. But he no doubt welcomed Aristobulus' statement (surely false) that Alexander was not a heavy drinker (fr. 62; cf. fr. 59), and relates from Aristobulus the various anecdotes—Timocleia (ch. 12), Darius' women-folk after Issus and Barsine (ch. 21)—which show Alexander's self-control and generosity to captive women.

For major events, such as the expedition to Siwah and the battle of Gaugamela (and doubtless those of the Granicus and Issus as well) Plutarch preferred Callisthenes, although he was impressed enough to adopt Aristobulus' argument that the battle took place at Gaugamela and not at Arbela. In the events described in ch. 73 (Peithagoras and the man who sat on the king's throne) Plutarch rejected Aristobulus' version, perhaps because it did not square with his view that by this time Alexander had fallen victim to superstition. In fact, after Gaugamela there is little that can be positively attributed to Aristobulus, except Alexander's exploit at the Malli town (ch. 63).

Chares

(Jacoby no. 125. Robinson 77–86. Pearson 50–61.)

We know nothing of his life except that he was a native of Mytilene and was appointed Chamberlain (εἰσαγγελεύς), presumably in 330

[1] See my article in *Historia* 10 (1961), 448–59, and Rabe 8–40. Badian, *PACA* 8 (1965), 5 ff. argues against a late date for Cleitarchus but leaves the question of priority open. Cf. D. Kienast, *Historia* 14 (1965), 185 (Cleitarchus writing before Megasthenes).

[2] See, e.g., Tarn 2. 42, Pearson 152, Jacoby 509. Whether he wrote earlier than Ptolemy is disputed; Jacoby 499 and Strasburger 15 f. think it probable that he did not, but Tarn and Pearson hold the opposite view. Tarn considers that they wrote independently, but Pearson 172 argues that at Arr. 5. 14. 4 ff. Ptolemy is criticizing Aristobulus; this is very debatable, see *PACA* 4 (1961), 19, n. 24. In fact, there is no evidence for a late date for Ptolemy and he may have written much earlier; see Badian, *Gnomon* 665 f., and cf. Pearson's remarks (193).

[3] For ancient views of him as a *kolax* see Jacoby T. 4–5.

after the death of Darius. His *Stories of Alexander* (so, rightly, Pearson 51), in at least ten books, was read by Aristobulus, Duris, and probably Cleitarchus (see *F.Gr. Hist.* 2D, 433). The majority of the nineteen fragments (all but two preserved by Plutarch and Athenaeus) are unimportant, and his only contribution to military history is the story that at Issus Darius was wounded by Alexander! Tarn (2. 70) concludes that 'one or two passages apart, like the *proskynesis* affair (which he presumably saw), the fragments only exhibit a trifler, immersed in court ceremonies and dinners, the minutiae of his office'. This is not unfair, and Schachermeyr (131) clearly goes too far in calling his book 'one of the three great works (the others are those of Ptolemy and Aristobulus) of the Alexander period'. Nevertheless, Chares is a valuable witness for events at court—the Susa weddings (fr. 4), the refusal of Callisthenes to drink unmixed wine (fr. 13), the *proskynesis* affair (ch. 54), and (almost certainly) the murder of Cleitus (ch. 50–1)—all the more valuable as Ptolemy (and Aristobulus) practised what Badian (*Gnomon* 33 (1961), 666) has aptly called 'a highly selective and purposeful reserve'. Chares seems to have been interested in description rather than character (Pearson 61), but if we may judge from his version of Callisthenes' death (55. 9), in which he seems to attempt to exculpate Alexander, his verdict on Alexander is unlikely to have been unfavourable.

Onesicritus

(Jacoby no. 134. Robinson 149–66. Pearson 83–111. See also T. S. Brown, *Onesicritus*.)

Onesicritus was a native of the town of Astypalaea on Cos; see the works cited in *Historia* 10 (1961), 457, n. 68. Otherwise we know only that he studied under Diogenes (65. 2) and that, as he became chief steersman of Alexander's fleet, he must have been an experienced sailor (see 66. 3 n.).

Whether he had a connection with Aegina is disputed. Suidas (s.v. *Φίλισκος Αἰγινήτης*) registers a Philiscus of Aegina who was one of Alexander's teachers, while Diogenes Laertius (6. 75–6) mentions 'a certain Onesicritus' of Aegina (*'Ονησίκριτόν τινα*) who sent his son, Philiscus, to study under Diogenes and later joined him as a student. It has, therefore, been suggested that Suidas' Philiscus was the father of the historian and had the same name as his grandson. However, Strasburger (*RE* 18, 460 f.) and Jacoby (*F.Gr.Hist.* 2D, 469) reject the identification, since Onesicritus was too famous to be referred to as 'a certain O.', and, as he had two grown-up sons before he joined Alexander, he would have been too old to play the part he did in the expedition. Nevertheless, in view of the rarity of the name (see Strasburger *RE* 18, 461), it is tempting to conclude that Onesicritus was a relative of Alexander's teacher, since this would explain how he obtained his information about the young Alexander. That he possessed such information is a necessary deduction from the title of his book, which Diogenes Laertius (6. 84) gives as πῶς Ἀλέξανδρος ἤχθη and compares with the *Cyropaideia* of Xenophon.[1]

The comparison with the *Cyropaideia* is significant. Xenophon had depicted Cyrus as 'the shepherd of mankind', and in Onesicritus' book Alexander evidently appeared in Cynic fashion as 'the philosopher in arms', who had a mission to civilize the world; see Strabo 15. 1. 64 (= fr. 17 (a)). The idea is prominent in the first speech *De Alex. fort.* (see above, p. xxiv), but in the *Life*, although Alexander is devoted to philosophy and literature, it is largely absent. As a biographer Plutarch naturally was not interested in the strange customs and peculiarities of geography and natural history with which the extant fragments are mostly concerned, although it is probable that Onescritus was his source for much of chapters 59–62. There is no indication that Onesicritus was concerned with military matters or with political events. Presumably the charge of flattery which is levelled at him (see T. 7) means that he 'played down' the more unpleasant aspects of Alexander's character and his crimes, such as the murders of Cleitus and Parmenio.

Tarn (2. 35) justly describes his book as 'a professed romance' written by a professional seaman who made no claim to write history.[2] The evident attraction (and danger) of the work lay in the skilful blending of fact and fiction, as in the visit of the Amazon queen. Plutarch seems to have made little use of Onesicritus except in the early part of the *Life* (this can be demonstrated only for ch. 8 and ch. 15) and for India. For Onesicritus' influence on later writers see Strasburger, *RE* 18, 466 f.

Cleitarchus

(Jacoby no. 137. Robinson 171–83. Pearson 212–42. See also T. S. Brown, *Clitarchus, AJP* 71 (1950), 134–55.)

Nothing is known of his life except that he was the son of the historian Dinon and worked in Alexandria. He wrote apparently only a *History of Alexander* in at least twelve books, probably towards the end of the fourth century (on the date see above, p. liv). He was widely read in the late Republic and early Empire, but was adversely criticized both as a historian and a stylist (see Pearson 212 f.).

As Cleitarchus did not accompany Alexander's expedition he was

---

[1] Pearson's suggestion (87 ff.), that the title should be altered to πῶς Ἀλ. ⟨ἀν⟩ήχθη and Παιδείαν Κύρου corrected to Ἀνάβασιν Κ., has been generally rejected. His alternative suggestion (89), that πῶς Ἀ. ἤχθη may be the opening words of Onesicritus' book, has much to be said for it. For the date of the book see n. to 46. 4.

[2] See also G. T. Griffith, *CR*, N.S. 1 (1951), 169 ff., reviewing Brown.

dependent on earlier writers, Callisthenes (in the early part of his book), Onesicritus, Nearchus, and Polycleitus, and on oral information from the soldiers, mainly Greek, who had served with Alexander and Darius. The thirty-six extant fragments tell us little about his portrait of Alexander, and a much better idea can be gained from the seventeenth book of Diodorus.[1]

Hoffmann (26 ff.) and Jacoby (*RE* 11, 641) held that Cleitarchus wrote an unalloyed panegyric of Alexander, and it is undeniable that the prevailing tone of the work is favourable. In the first chapter of Diodorus (1. 3–4) Alexander is said to have surpassed the achievements of all kings from the beginning of time, and to have acquired a reputation rivalling that of the heroes and demi-gods of old. In fact, Alexander displays all the characteristics of a *hero*. He strives to rival Heracles (85. 2) and struggles with a river like Achilles (97. 3). His opponents are all brave, not only Darius (6. 1–2) and the Persians, but the Tyrians and Porus as well. Great stress is laid on his bravery (*passim*) and on his desire for glory (e.g. 42. 6, 78. 3, 85. 2, 93. 4). He decides (or intends to decide) by his own exertions the battles and sieges (examples in Tarn 2. 66, Hoffmann 27). Moreover, as Tarn (loc. cit.) has demonstrated, Alexander possesses also the stock virtues of a Hellenistic monarch, φιλανθρωπία, μεγαλοψυχία, and so on; see especially the treatment of the captive Persian women (37–8) and captured cities (22. 5, 24. 1).

Nevertheless, although Alexander was in the main portrayed favourably, Tarn has shown conclusively that he was at times depicted as cruel and possessed by anger.[2] In particular, Alexander frequently indulges in massacres (Tarn 2. 67), and cheats or resorts to trickery. But these examples do not prove that Cleitarchus was hostile to Alexander; they are rather to be seen as highly sensational stories, in some cases at least exaggerating what actually happened.[3] Similarly, when in ch. 77 Alexander adopts Persian customs, including a harem

[1] The close harmony at many points between Diodorus and Curtius makes it certain that they depend on a common source; see Schwartz's list in *RE* 4, 1873 f., which, however, requires to be used with caution as by no means all his instances are valid. That this source was Cleitarchus is shown by the similarities between his fragments and Diodorus. Jacoby (*RE* 11, 631) and Pearson 217 believe that Diodorus used him directly, but Welles (Loeb ed., p. 10) and M. J. Fontana (*Kokalos* 1 (1955), 155 ff.) have given good reasons for thinking that Diodorus used an intermediary (their suggestions of Trogus and Duris are not convincing). Tarn's attempt to prove that Diodorus used a variety of sources, esp. Aristobulus and Cleitarchus and a 'Mercenaries' source', has been refuted by Strasburger, *Bibl. Or.* 9 (1952), 202 ff.; cf. Pearson 241, n. 123. Against a *written* 'Mercenaries' source' see Pearson 78 ff., P. A. Brunt, *CQ*, N.S. 12 (1962), 141 ff.

[2] These two aspects are not irreconcilable, as Tarn held; they are the light and shade of the rhetorical Cleitarchan portrait and do not indicate two *sources*.

[3] See Brown, *AJP*, 154 f.

of 365 concubines (which may even be true—see Welles's note ad loc.), the tone is not hostile, since Diodorus remarks that Alexander used these customs sparingly to avoid offending the Macedonians. Nevertheless, Alexander's detractors might eagerly seize on this material and present it in a hostile way.

Cleitarchus does not appear to have influenced Plutarch's view of Alexander to any great extent. Plutarch adopts a number of picturesque anecdotes from his book, e.g. the Lycian guide (37. 1–2), Erigyius' single combat (39. 2), the *komoi* at Persepolis and in Carmania (38, 67), the death of Darius (43. 3), and the burning of the Macedonian baggage (57. 1–2). On the other hand, he rejects the view that Alexandria was founded *after* the visit to Siwah (26. 8), the Amazon story (46), and, more important, the 'cup of Heracles' (75. 5) and the poisoning of Alexander (77), while he does not mention Alexander's visit to the Persian captives (see 21. 2 n.). The most important borrowings are the story of the 'conspiracy' of Philotas (49), and the anecdotes in ch. 73 which show the king a prey to superstition. These may have determined, to some degree, Plutarch's view of Alexander's last months.

The Letters of Alexander

In the course of the *Life* Plutarch refers to or quotes from more than thirty letters written by Alexander or his correspondents. It is clear from the manner in which some of them are introduced (see above, pp. l–li) that Plutarch found many of them in a collection.[1] Some, e.g. those contained in chapters 19, 29, and 34, he probably found in his historical source. All these letters he evidently believed to be genuine and used in preference to his other sources, as we can see most clearly in chapter 60.

The authenticity of these letters has often been disputed, especially by J. Kaerst (*Phil.* 51 (1892), 602 ff.) and Pearson (*Historia* 3 (1954/5), 444 ff.), and just as often asserted, notably by E. Pridik, *De Alex. epistularum commercio* (Berlin, 1893), and A. Zumetikos, *De Alex. Olympiadisque epist. fontibus et reliquiis* (Berlin, 1894). Both sides claimed too much. Kaerst and Pearson showed that for various reasons forgery was rife in the Hellenistic age, but they failed to prove their contention that all the letters in Plutarch were not genuine. Authentic letters certainly existed; see esp. Strabo 9. 2. 18, where the engineer Crates

---

[1] Since seven letters are written to Antipater and one by him to Alexander, while those cited at 17. 8 and 60. 1 (which have no addressee) may have been written to him, it is possible that there was a separate collection of Antipater's letters. If it was published in the reign of Antigonus Gonatas, Antipater's grandson, the letters would not have been available to the first generation of Alexander-historians; see *PACA* 4 (1961), 11.

writes to Alexander about the drainage operations at Lake Copais. Here forgery is surely out of the question.[1] On the other hand, Pridik and Zumetikos tended to assume that the letters were genuine because the information contained in them tallied with the evidence of Ptolemy and Aristobulus, without considering the possibility, acutely remarked by Pearson, that a forger might have used this evidence to provide verisimilitude.

The truth is that in the majority of cases no decision is possible. Many letters, e.g. those cited in chapters 39–42, cannot be tested by independent evidence and are referred to so briefly that nothing whatsoever can usefully be said about them. Others, such as those mentioned at 20. 9, 27. 8, 46. 3, 57. 8, and 71. 8, cannot be proved genuine, but there seems no obvious reason why they should not be. In the case of those in 17. 8, 47. 3, and 55. 7 it can at least be shown that many of the arguments directed against them are not valid. Finally those quoted at 28. 2 and 60. 1 ff. have strong claims to be considered genuine, and the authenticity of the letter to the generals (55. 6) can hardly be doubted.[2]

Philosophers and Rhetoricians

As Plutarch was not only widely read in the historical literature on Alexander, but must also have been familiar with the views of Peripatetic and Stoic philosophers and of the rhetorical schools, these views may properly be included among his sources.

Theophrastus' judgement on Alexander was certainly unfavourable. In his *Callisthenes or about Grief* he described him (in Cicero's words) as a man 'summa potentia summaque fortuna sed ignarum quem ad modum rebus secundis uti conveniret',[3] and a later Peripatetic, Hieronymus of Rhodes, cites him for the statement that Alexander was semi-impotent.[4] Until recently it has been generally held that Theophrastus created a 'Peripatetic portrait' of Alexander as a man who was well educated by Aristotle but was corrupted by success and became a cruel tyrant.[5] This view has now been refuted by Badian (*CQ*, N.S. 8 (1958), 144 ff.), who shows the weakness of the evidence in its favour and points out that the title indicates that the work dealt only incidentally with Alexander, and by E. Mensching (*Historia* 12

---

[1] Private letters (e.g. to Olympias) must have been much more difficult to obtain, and the possibility of forgery in their case is higher.

[2] For an examination of all the letters see *PACA* 4 (1961), 9–20.

[3] *Tusc. Disp.* 3. 10. 21. Cf. *Ad Att.* 13. 28. 2–3, where Cicero writes that Aristotle's pupil, after he became king, became haughty, cruel, and uncontrolled (*immoderatus*).

[4] Ap. Athenaeum 435 a = fr. 38 (Wehrli); see Tarn 2. 320.

[5] See Tarn 2. 100 f., who maintains (incredibly) that this portrait was first *written down* by Curtius.

(1963), 274 ff.), who shows that, of the Peripatetics contemporary with Alexander, Aristoxenus was favourable to him and that none, apart from Theophrastus, is known to have written unfavourably of him. Among the extant fragments of Peripatetic writers there are few references to Alexander,[1] and the members of the school evidently exhibited greater independence of judgement than did the Stoics.

The Stoics regarded Alexander as spoiled by τῦφος, by delusions of grandeur as we might say, and they blamed his teacher Leonidas for not knocking it out of him; see J. Stroux, *Phil.* 88 (1933), 222 ff. This attitude is attested by Diogenes of Babylon in the first half of the second century B.C., but is doubtless older; it is repeated by Panaetius (ap. Cic. *Off.* 1. 26. 90), who compares Philip and Alexander and concludes that the father possessed *facilitas et humanitas* and was therefore *magnus*, whereas Alexander was often *tumidissimus*.[2]

By imperial times the criticisms of the philosophical and rhetorical schools are virtually indistinguishable.[3] They can be seen most clearly in Livy's well-known digression in Book 9 (ch. 17–19), in many passages of the younger Seneca, and in Lucan's attack on Alexander (10. 20 ff.). After depreciating Alexander's opponents and commenting on his drunken progress through India, Livy goes on (18. 1–5) to describe, in a manner reminiscent of Theophrastus, how he was corrupted by success, 'secundis rebus quarum nemo intolerantior fuit', and exhibited the characteristic features of τῦφος. He arrogantly adopted Persian dress, attempted to introduce *proskynesis*, murdered his friends 'inter vinum et epulas', and aspired to divinity. Finally Livy mentions his desire for drink, which increased daily, and his anger ('trux et perfervida ira'). In short, Livy asserts, his character virtually changed. Elsewhere he alludes to Alexander's unbroken *felicitas* (18. 8) and to his *temeritas* (18. 18).

Almost all these charges can be paralleled in Seneca's writings. Alexander is often described as 'vesanus adulescens',[4] and his *feritas*, particularly in connection with the murder of Cleitus, is a favourite topic.[5] Unlike the Stoic *sapiens*, Alexander failed to control his passions (*Ep.* 113. 29, where the deaths of Cleitus and Hephaestion are mentioned), his drunkenness leads to Cleitus' death and to his own (*Ep.* 83. 19, 23), and instead of *virtus* he enjoys *felix temeritas* (*Ben.* 1. 13. 3, 7. 3. 1; cf. Lucan 10. 21). He has an inexhaustible desire for fame

---

[1] See the Register to F. Wehrli, *Die Schule des Aristoteles* in Heft 10; one of these, Ariston of Ceos (fr. 13. IV), shows Alexander in a favourable light.

[2] Adopting Stroux's convincing emendation (op. cit. 236 f.) of the MSS. *turpissimus. Tumor animi* = τῦφος; cf. Tarn 2. 123, n. 1.

[3] See Hoffmann 53, n. 4, for the close parallels in the writings of the younger Seneca and the *Suasoriae* of his father.

[4] *Ben.* 1. 13. 1, 2. 16. 1; *Ep.* 91. 17, 94. 62. Cf. Lucan 10. 20, 42–*vesanus rex*.

[5] *Clem.* 1. 25. 1; *Ira* 3. 17. 1, 23. 1; *Ep.* 94. 62.

and possessions (*Ben.* 7. 2. 5 f.; *Q Nat.* 5. 18. 10), and is addicted to
τῦφος (*Ben.* 5. 6. 1, 'homo super mensuram humanae superbiae
tumens'; cf. 2. 16. 2, '*tumidissimum* animal').

v. *The Character and Value of the* Alexander

In the *Life* little emphasis is laid on Fortune, since it would be useless for illustrating character.[1] Fortune prevents serious consequences
at Philip's wedding (9. 9) and luckily (κατὰ τύχην) Alexander lands
on his feet when he jumps into the Malli town (63. 3), but although
Fortune helps Alexander at Issus his generalship is the decisive factor
in his victory (20. 7), while at 26. 14 Fortune yields to his assaults and
at 58. 2 he strives to overcome Fortune by his daring. Plutarch's outlook is revealed most clearly at 17. 6, where he remarks sarcastically
that many writers wrote bombastically that the sea retired before
Alexander 'by some heaven-sent good fortune', and proceeds to refute them by citing a letter of Alexander.

In general the *Life* is apologetic in tone. Plutarch does not deny that
Alexander spent a long time drinking after dinner, but he cites
Aristobulus for the view that he did so only for the sake of conversation (23. 1, 6). Yet this is difficult to reconcile with his subsequent
statement (23. 7) that the influence of drink made him unpleasant and
boastful and ready to listen to flatterers, and is indeed incompatible
with his own view (4. 7) that the king was ποτικός. He devotes a whole
chapter (28) to the refutation of the Stoic charge that by believing
that he was divine Alexander displayed τῦφος. It was only a political
device, concludes Plutarch, for his own ends; Alexander himself was
not deluded (οὐδὲν τετυφωμένος). Alexander's *temeritas* is defended: the
risks he takes in battle are incurred to encourage his followers (40. 4).
Nor is he sunk in luxury: his own habits are frugal (22. 7 ff., 23. 9)
and he sets a limit to expenditure on banquets (23. 10). On the
contrary, it is his friends who display extravagance (τρυφή), and it is
the abuse which they heap on him when he attempts to remonstrate
with them that makes him cruel (40–42. 4).

Plutarch, of course, had to tackle the question of Alexander's
responsibility for the deaths of Philotas and Parmenio, Cleitus and
Callisthenes. Here again he tends to be unduly charitable.[2] Before
relating the story of Cleitus' murder (which was widely criticized as an
example of unbridled passion; above, p. lxi) Plutarch tries, not un-
reasonably, to mitigate Alexander's crime; it was not deliberate

[1] Perhaps also Plutarch implicitly answers the criticism that *continuous* good fortune spoilt Alexander.
[2] This tendency is not confined to the *Alexander*. Cf. *Cim.* 2 (where the parallel
with the portrait-painter recurs).

murder, but due to a mischance (δυστυχίᾳ τινι). In the case of Philotas the real culprits are his enemies, who seize the opportunity to convince the king that Philotas must be the instigator of the plot. So, after the fiasco of the *proskynesis* when Callisthenes has mortally offended the king, his enemies' accusations are believed (55. 3). Plutarch makes no explicit comment on the death of Parmenio, but his comments about Parmenio's services to Philip and Alexander and the deaths of his sons may imply reproach.

Indeed criticism is not absent from the *Life*, a fact which distinguishes it sharply from the speeches. Alexander is no paragon, but a real figure of flesh and blood (see Wardman, *CQ*, N.S. 5 (1955), 101). Alexander is twice described as 'cruel (fearsome) and implacable' (42. 4, 57. 3), and Callisthenes is said (54. 3) to have saved him from a great disgrace by refusing to perform *proskynesis*. Alexander's reaction to Hephaestion's death is stigmatized as 'utterly unreasonable' and his expedition against the Cossaeans is described as a consolation for his grief (72. 3–4), while he plans a monument for Hephaestion that is much stranger than Stasicrates' grandiose plans for Mount Athos (72. 8). His massacre of the Indian mercenaries is 'a kind of stain' on his otherwise unblemished record as a commander (59. 7).[1] Almost all Plutarch's criticisms occur in the last part of the *Life*, for he recognized a deterioration in Alexander's character—see esp. 52. 7, where Anaxarchus is blamed—although, unlike Curtius (6. 2. 1 ff., 6. 6. 1 ff.), he does not date this precisely. But Alexander's action in delegating the decision about the fate of Thebes to those allies who were present is surely criticized by the use of the verb καλλωπισαμένου (11. 11). This suggests that Alexander sought to evade responsibility, and the criticism is perhaps due to Plutarch's sympathy for Thebes (Wardman, loc. cit.).

Again, when the army mutinies at the Hydaspes Alexander shuts himself up in his tent like Achilles through 'despondency and anger'. In fact, anger is the chief defect in Alexander's character. He is enraged with Philotas for failing to introduce Dimnus (49. 7), with Antigenes for his deceit (70. 4), and with Cassander for mocking a Persian performing *proskynesis* (74. 3), while in the Cleitus affair anger is mentioned three times.[2] The reason for this is that, as Wardman (esp. 102 ff.) has shown, Plutarch sees Alexander as θυμοειδής;[3]

---

[1] Tarn 2. 300 notes that Plutarch has already recorded without blinking Alexander's order to massacre the prisoners at Persepolis; it is, however, fair to say that immediately before this statement there is a lacuna in the text which may have contained some justification of Alexander's action.

[2] 50. 2, ὀργήν; 51. 1, παροξυνθείς; 51. 10, εὐθὺς ἀφῆκεν ὁ θυμὸς αὐτόν; cf. 10. 6 and 16. 14.

[3] The idea is evidently not Plutarch's own. In the *Moralia* (339 f) he relates how Alexander did not reveal his suspicions of Philotas for *seven* years—οὐκ ἐν

this means (in Peripatetic terms) that he is both subject to fits of anger and endowed with 'spirit', which is responsible for his ambition. However, Wardman is mistaken in thinking that Plutarch regarded Alexander as 'the spirited man' (ὁ θυμοειδής), and attempted to explain his whole life in terms of this quality, as Peripatetic biographers such as Aristoxenus and Satyrus (see Dihle 70 f., 104 ff.) had attempted to generalize from a single quality. The Alexander of Plutarch is a many-sided character.

The value of Plutarch's biographies to the historian depends partly on the amount of other material available,[1] and the value of the *Alexander* is enhanced by 'the regrettably inadequate documentation' of the expedition. All our extant sources are late, and only Justin is complete. Particularly unfortunate are the loss of the first two books of Curtius (as well as lacunae in the tenth book) and the great lacuna in Diodorus, which deprives us (as the Table of Contents shows) of his version of Cleitus' murder, the conspiracy of the pages, the arrest and death of Callisthenes, and Alexander's marriage to Roxane. In Arrian too there is a substantial lacuna in the last book.

Our first debt, then, is the preservation of material from primary sources. Much of the information is trivial, e.g. the fact that Alexander made the customary payment on entering Pasargadae (69. 1) or that he sent part of the spoils to Croton (34. 3). Other items are more important; we may mention the proclamation of Alexander as 'king of Asia' after Gaugamela, his letter to the Greeks (34. 1–2), and the length of his stay in Persepolis (37. 6). In particular Plutarch, most commendably, cites an extract from a letter of Alexander to the Athenians which runs counter to his thesis that Alexander did not believe in his divinity (28. 2). If this is genuine (see n. ad loc.), it throws much light on the state of the king's mind towards the end of his life, and supports the view that in 324 Alexander issued a 'request' to the Greek cities to worship him as a god.[2] Even if the statements of the writers cited by Plutarch are not true, they may enable us to see the tendencies of their work; to take one important example, the citations from Callisthenes in ch. 33 reveal his bias against Parmenio.

Much of what Plutarch tells us about Alexander's early life is to be

οἴνῳ ποτε . . . ἐξέφηνεν ὁ μεθύων, οὐ δι' ὀργὴν ὁ θυμοειδής! Plutarch is clearly using the word ironically to refute someone, presumably a Stoic, who had said that Alexander *was* θυμοειδής.

[1] The *Gracchi*, e.g., is of greater value to us than the *Cicero*, partly at least because for the Ciceronian period we have, relatively speaking, a mass of material while for the Gracchan period Plutarch's *Life* and Appian's *Civil War* are the only substantial literary sources.

[2] Many scholars, however, do not believe this; see, e.g., J. P. V. D. Balsdon, *Historia* 1 (1950), 363 ff., E. Bickerman, *Athenaeum* 41 (1963), 70 ff. But, in favour, P. A. Brunt, *Greece and Rome* 12 (1965), 210 f.

found nowhere else, and its authenticity cannot be checked. There is, however, no reason to doubt that Olympias was a savage and passionate woman—her later career confirms this—or that she was a devotee of ecstatic rites. It would also be excessively sceptical not to believe that Alexander was devoted to Greek culture,[1] although his passion for philosophy may well be exaggerated. The ninth and tenth chapters are particularly valuable; but for Plutarch we should know little of Alexander's relations with Philip and the atmosphere in the royal palace. Alexander's reaction to his father's marriage, and the Pixodarus affair (for which Plutarch is our sole authority), throw much-needed light on the vital years 338–336.

It would be idle to complain that Plutarch tells us practically nothing of events in Greece during Alexander's expedition; the same criticism might legitimately be made of Arrian's book, a professed history, and the dominance of Alexander provides some excuse. But even as a biography of Alexander the *Life* is inadequate. Little is said of his great military achievements (see above, pp. xl f.), or of that hotly debated question, his future plans (see 68. 1 n.), while the wider aspects of his policies are ignored. We are told nothing of the administration of the Empire,[2] or of the significance of the Susa weddings. Plutarch is interested only in Alexander the man.

Plutarch's portrait of Alexander contains a good deal of truth. We need not hesitate to credit his generosity or his chivalry towards women: his treatment of Timocleia (12) and Darius' wife and mother (21) is surely historical. Nor should we question his care for his followers (41), even if Plutarch's instances may not all be genuine. The 'philosopher in arms' (see p. xxxi) has disappeared, which is all to the good; but we may suspect that Alexander was less of a philosopher than Plutarch in the *Life* would have us believe (see esp. 27. 10 n.). Certainly the treatment of his enemies, for example Taxiles (59. 1–5) and Porus (60. 14–15), was largely motivated by policy. Plutarch appreciates that the adoption of a mixed dress (45) and the training of the 30,000 young Persians (47, 71), although not apparently the attempt to introduce *proskynesis* (54), are part of the 'policy of fusion'; he is aware too of the opposition that these measures aroused among the Macedonians, although he seems to think that this opposition was soon overcome because of respect for Alexander's *arete*. He does not deny the deterioration in Alexander's character (see p. lxiii), which certainly took place,[3] although his attempt to explain this in terms of Alexander's love for *doxa* (42. 4) is not convincing. Again, even if

---

[1] See 4. 1, 11; 7–8; 11. 12; 26. 1; 29. 1–3.

[2] On this see Badian, *Greece and Rome* 12 (1965), 166 ff.

[3] Even Tarn 2. 97 admits this—'no one need deny that the Alexander of 324 was not the Alexander of 334'.

Plutarch is too ready to excuse Alexander (see pp. lxii–iii), what he says about the part played by the 'flatterers' may not be altogether wide of the mark. That Alexander became increasingly addicted to superstition towards the end of his life may in general be true, although Plutarch's narrative is clearly influenced by his own attitude to superstition (see 75. 1 n.) and the picture is doubtless overdrawn. On the other hand Plutarch failed to understand the essentially 'heroic' character of Macedonian society and of Alexander himself. He did not realize just how savage and ruthless Alexander could be, if he felt his position was in any way threatened. This ruthlessness was in no way due to a deterioration in Alexander's character; at the very beginning of his reign he had removed all possible rivals.[1]

Plutarch makes his greatest contribution to our knowledge of Alexander in chapters 48–55. His accounts of Cleitus' murder and the *proskynesis* affair are accepted by almost all scholars, and we owe to him the vivid portraits of Philotas, Cleitus, and Callisthenes which help to fill in the background and bring them to life. We are enabled to see something of the conflicts in the entourage of Alexander, the jealousies between the philosophers and the *literati*, and between high-ranking Macedonians.[2] Plutarch, it is true, does not appear to have appreciated all the implications of the information he gives, but from this material a critical modern historian can create a truer portrait of Alexander.

vi. *The Style of Plutarch*[3]

Plutarch was largely unaffected by the prevailing Atticism.[4] This movement—an ostensible return to the style of the classical Attic writers—had arisen about the middle of the first century B.C. as a reaction against the bombast of the Asiatic orators. But the Atticists were more successful in imitating the vocabulary and syntax of the Attic writers than in recapturing their simplicity. More important, in their efforts to reproduce the classical Attic style they sought to cut out everything which had come into the literary language during Helle-

---

[1] It is the appreciation of this fact that distinguishes the work of Badian (see esp. his articles in *TAPA* (1960) and *JHS* (1961)) and Schachermeyr (see Welles' review in *AJA* (1951), 433–6).

[2] A subject on which Arrian's authorities were significantly reticent; cf. however Arr. 7. 13. 1, where (after a lacuna) the reconciliation between Hephaestion and Eumenes is mentioned.

[3] See in general Ziegler 931 ff., and for the style of the *Marius* T. F. Carney, *JHS* 80 (1960), 24–31.

[4] On Atticism see Marrou 200 f., and esp. A. Lesky, *A History of Greek Literature* (London, 1966), 829 ff. W. Schmid's four volumes, *Der Atticismus* (Stuttgart, 1896), are a mine of information on the usage of the Atticists; they also contain much useful material on Plutarch, esp. on his vocabulary.

nistic times, and to confine themselves to authorized Attic material. While Plutarch, then, doubtless sympathized with their dislike of bombast,[1] he was not prepared to cut himself off from the living language. For him style was less important than subject-matter.[2] Its function was to render the thought more vivid and persuasive; it must not obtrude or obstruct. Hence he did not join in their search for rare Attic words and expressions nor did he coin new words on anything like the same scale.[3] His vocabulary and syntax are basically those of the literary Koine, which itself contains a large Attic element. Particularly revealing is his use of the optative, which he employs roughly as often as Strabo and Philo but only about one-fifth as often as Plato.[4] His use of negatives also follows the practice of the Koine, μή being used not only in conditional clauses but in clauses expressing time, cause, or any attendant circumstance. Admittedly his vocabulary is much more extensive than that of other writers of the Koine and includes many common Attic words not used by them. Whether this is conscious archaizing or the result of his wide reading in Attic writers, especially Plato, is debatable.

The most striking feature of his style is the strict avoidance of hiatus, leading at times to an awkward distortion of the normal order of words.[5] Less obvious is his use of certain prose rhythms at the end of the sentence, particularly the double trochee, the cretic plus trochee, and the hypodochmius.[6]

Plutarch makes limited use of tropes. Chiasmus is seldom employed and in some cases, e.g. 31. 13, 45. 3, 51. 4, is perhaps due to the desire to avoid hiatus. Asyndeton, on the other hand, is relatively frequent at the beginning of the sentence, especially with ταῦτα. Asyndeton within the sentence is occasionally combined most effectively with repetition, as at 23. 2 οὐκ οἶνος ἐκεῖνον, οὐχ ὕπνος, οὐ παιδιά τις, οὐ γάμος, οὐ θέα . . . ἐπέσχε; cf. 67. 4. His similes are in general unremarkable,[7] as, for example, the comparison of the Tyrian Apollo to

[1] For Plutarch's attitude see the Commentary at 3. 6, 17. 6.

[2] See the revealing passage in his essay *On the Student At Lectures* (*Mor.* 42 d), where Plutarch criticizes those students who do not concern themselves with the subject-matter but demand a 'pure Attic style' from the lecturer.

[3] For the coinages of the Atticists see Schmid 4. 685 ff. In the *Alexander* the following words *may* have been coined by Plutarch: φιλαναγνώστης (8. 2), ἰδιόστολος (34. 3), εὐροεῖν (53. 3). Moreover χαίτη (16. 7), ἀσύμβολος (26. 3), and πλαίσιον (67. 2) are not previously attested in the meanings used by Plutarch.

[4] So Ziegler 932. A. Meillet, *Aperçu d'une histoire de la langue grecque*[3] (Paris, 1930), 276, gives higher figures for Philo and Strabo.

[5] For details of permitted hiatus see Ziegler 932 ff. A. J. Kronenberg, *Mnemos.* 5 (1937), 311, n. 2, adds that Plutarch allows hiatus after proper names and forms of θεός.

[6] See Sandbach's table of frequencies in *CQ* 33 (1939), 197.

[7] Some may derive from his sources: certainly the comparison of the shape of

a deserter (24. 7) and Alexander after Cleitus' murder to a slave (52. 5).
More effectively, the confused hubbub from the Persian camp before
Gaugamela is likened to the sound of a vast ocean (31. 10), and the
beautiful Persian women ignored by Alexander to lifeless statues (21.
11). The stage provides two similes: some writers described Alexander's death as 'the closing scene of a great drama' (75. 5), and the
weak-minded Arrhidaeus is a mere 'mute character' (77. 7). Perhaps
the most vivid is the comparison of the Macedonians after Issus to
hunting-dogs on the scent of Persian wealth, which is enhanced by the
use of the epic verb ἀνιχνεύειν (24. 3).[1] Metaphors are infrequent but
effective, occurring at critical points in the narrative.[2] Philip's domestic troubles affect the kingdom (9. 5), and at his death (11. 2) he
leaves a kingdom as disturbed as the sea (σάλος). The same sea metaphor describes the state of the Empire on Alexander's return from
India (68. 3), and at Gaugamela the ebb and flow of the battle is
likened to the surge of the sea and to the recurrence of an illness (32.
5).[3] Alexander allows himself to be 'ridden' by his flatterers (23. 7),
and later opens his ears to Philotas' enemies (49. 10), a passage
doubtless intended to recall 42. 2, where the king is said (literally) to
have covered one of his ears when the prosecutor was speaking.
Finally, the resentment of the discharged Macedonian veterans is
cleverly evoked by their scornful reference to the young Persians as
'war-dancers' (71. 3).[4]

Plutarch has a remarkable power of visualizing a scene and a keen
sense of dramatic effect. This is admirably illustrated by the scene
between Alexander and his doctor Philip (which he himself describes
as θαυμαστὴν καὶ θεατρικήν), where the effect is enhanced by the use of
the tragic verb θεοκλυτεῖν, and by his account of the breaking of
Bucephalas (ch. 6).[5] In the main Plutarch's narrative is simple and
vivid, but the brevity which he praised in others escapes him. He is
discursive by nature (some might say long-winded), and he has
a habit of using two words where one would do; words of similar
form are often chosen, e.g. 48. 1, φιλόδωρος δὲ καὶ φιλέταιρος, 72. 6,
διατύπωσιν . . . διαμόρφωσιν. Stylistically the *Alexander* is not, I think,

Alexandria to that of a *chlamys* (26. 8, where see n.), and probably Alexander compared to a lion sated with blood (13. 2).

[1] Evidently Plutarch's own borrowing, as probably βρύχημα at 51. 10.

[2] For the use of metaphor to indicate the unity of lengthy passages and for cross-
reference see Carney, op. cit., 24 f.

[3] σάλος is very frequently used by Plutarch with reference to political disturbance
(see n. to 32. 5). For other medical metaphors see (e.g.) *Num.* 8. 2, *Cam.* 9. 3, *Caes.*
28. 6.

[4] Other metaphors occur at 11. 11, 21. 10, 22. 9, 33. 8, 35. 8, 49. 9, 51. 2.

[5] Cf. also ch. 12 (Timocleia); 16. 6–8 (battle of the Granicus); 9. 5 (Alexander's brawl with Philip); 67. 2–6 (*komos* in Carmania).

one of the best *Lives*; Plutarch deals with many episodes in summary fashion, as he promised in the introduction (1. 1), because of the mass of material. His expansive style requires space and is seen to greatest advantage in extended passages, as in his account of the murder of Cleitus.[1] His sentences sometimes extend to a considerable length and tend to straggle, but are seldom difficult to follow. A good example is 40. 1–2, a sentence of some fourteen lines; Plutarch begins with a temporal clause followed by four result clauses (the last with a dependent participle), then comes the main verb (qualified by two adverbs), a participle with dependent infinitive, and two causal clauses each followed by a noun clause (both with dependent participle), the second of which is subdivided by μέν . . . δέ. Despite the length and complexity of the sentence, the meaning is perfectly clear.[2]

Yet such sentences are the exception. In style, as in subject-matter, Plutarch sought variety,[3] for he was well aware of the dangers of being tedious. Indeed, we may apply to Plutarch himself his remark about Homer (*Mor.* 504 d): 'He continually avoids the tendency to surfeit which threatens talk of every kind, carrying his hearers from one story to another, and relieving their satiety by his constant freshness.'

---

[1] See also ch. 30. 2–13 (Darius and the eunuch), and esp. *Cam.* 10 (the schoolmaster of Falerii).

[2] For similarly lengthy and involved sentences see *Caes.* 28. 2–4, 58. 4–7.

[3] See D. A. Russell's perceptive remarks in *Proc. Camb. Philol. Soc.*, N.S. 12 (1966), 37 ff., esp. 47. Compare also Plutarch's habit of avoiding continuous exposition by digression in the philosophical works; see Sandbach, *CQ* 34 (1940), 21.

COMMENTARY

I. *Introduction to the* Lives *of Alexander and Caesar. Plutarch explains and justifies his selection of material.*

1. ὑφ' οὗ κατελύθη Πομπήϊος: Plutarch distinguishes C. Iulius Caesar from Augustus, who is called simply ὁ Καῖσαρ (e.g. *Alex.* 69. 9; *Per.* I. I); cf. *Num.* 19, Καίσαρος τοῦ καταγωνισαμένου Πομπήϊον. At *Brut.* I. 4, where it is clear from the context who is meant, Julius is called ὁ Καῖσαρ. Similarly Plutarch distinguishes Mark Antony as Ἀντωνίου τοῦ αὐτοκράτορος (*Demetr.* I), and Scipio Africanus as Σκηπίωνος τοῦ καταπολεμήσαντος Ἀννίβαν (*Ti. Gracch.* I); for Fabius Maximus (Cunctator) see *Per.* 2. 5 (cited below).

καταλύειν is the regular term for the overthrow of an established form of government or, less frequently, of a person in authority: cf. *Caes.* 28. I, Καίσαρι δὲ πάλαι μὲν ἐδέδοκτο καταλύειν Πομπήϊον, ὥσπερ ἀμέλει κἀκείνῳ τοῦτον; cf. *Sull.* 6. 9, *Per.* 6. 3, *et saepe.*

ἐν τούτῳ τῷ βιβλίῳ: Plutarch generally calls a unit of two *Parallel Lives* a βιβλίον, as at *Dem.* 3. I, *Demetr.* I. 7, and *Per.* 2. 5, τοῦτο τὸ βιβλίον δέκατον συντετάχαμεν, τὸν Περικλέους βίον καὶ τὸν Φαβίου Μαξίμου τοῦ διαπολεμήσαντος πρὸς Ἀννίβαν περιέχον. At *Dion* I. I he calls it γραφή, at *Dion* 2. 7 λόγος.

ἐὰν μὴ πάντα ... ἀπαγγέλλωμεν: 'if I do not relate all their great deeds or deal exhaustively with any one of them'. ἐξειργασμένως means 'exhaustively, in detail' rather than 'accurately' (so LSJ).

ἐπιτέμνοντες: 'in summary fashion'; cf. *Artox.* II. I, ἡ δὲ Κτησίου διήγησις, ὡς ἐπιτεμόντι πολλὰ συντόμως ἀπαγγεῖλαι, τοιαύτη τίς ἐστι.

μὴ συκοφαντεῖν: 'not to complain'. For the non-technical sense of the word cf. Plato, *Rep.* 341 b.

2. οὔτε γὰρ ἱστορίας γράφομεν ...: See the Introduction, page xxxviii.

οὔτε ... πάντως: 'not always'.

ἔμφασιν ἤθους ἐποίησε: 'reveals the character'—a gnomic aorist. For Plutarch's preoccupation with the character of his heroes see the Introduction, pages xxxvii f.

3. ὥσπερ οὖν οἱ ζωγράφοι ...: 'And so, just as a painter seeks to obtain a likeness of his subject by concentrating on the face and the expression of the eyes by which the character is revealed and pays little attention to the rest of his person, I must be allowed to penetrate to what reveals the soul of my subject and through this to portray the life of each, leaving others to describe their great exploits.'

For the comparison of the painter and the biographer see also *Cim.* 2. 3.

τῶν περὶ τὴν ὄψιν εἰδῶν: By a common post-classical usage περί+ accus. is equivalent to the genitive. τὴν ὄψιν = τὰς ὄψεις, 'the eyes'— a poetic usage common in Plutarch; see the Index to Holden's *Pericles*.

οἷς ἐμφαίνεται τὸ ἦθος: cf. *Cim.* 2. 2, εἰκόνα δὲ πολὺ καλλίονα νομίζοντες εἶναι τῆς τὸ σῶμα καὶ τὸ πρόσωπον ἀπομιμουμένης τὴν τὸ ἦθος καὶ τὸν τρόπον ἐμφανίζουσαν, ἀναληψόμεθα τῇ γραφῇ τῶν παραλλήλων βίων τὰς πράξεις τοῦ ἀνδρός; [Aristotle] *Phgn.* 806ᵃ30, τὰ ἤθη τὰ ἐπὶ τοῦ προσώπου ἐμφαινόμενα. See also ch. 4. 1.

II–III. *The parents of Alexander and the circumstances attending his birth.*

1. πρὸς πατρὸς ... Νεοπτολέμου: 'was a descendant of Heracles *through* Caranus on his father's side, on his mother's a descendant of Aeacus *through* Neoptolemus'. Cf. Arr. 1. 11. 8, Diod. 17. 1. 5, Livy 45. 9.

Caranus is unknown to Herodotus (8. 137 ff.), who begins with Perdiccas. He appears first in Theopompus (see the table in *F. Gr. Hist.* 2D. 401–2) and is evidently an artistic creation designed to link the Macedonian and Argive dynasties.

Neoptolemus (also called Pyrrhus), the son of Achilles, was driven off course while returning from Troy and landed in Molossia, where he founded the dynasty of the Πυρριάδαι. Cf. *Pyrrh.* 1; Pausanias 1. 11. 1 (with table in Frazer's edition); Hesychius, s.v. Πυρριάδαι; Tzetzes, *ad Lycophron* 1439; Strabo 13. 1. 27 (594).

2. ἐν Σαμοθράκῃ: The main centre of the worship of the Cabiri, deities of a chthonian character, who promoted fertility and protected sailors. Their worship involved initiation—Herod. 2. 51 ὅστις δὲ τὰ Καβείρων ὄργια μεμύηται, τὰ Σαμοθρήικες ἐπιτελέουσι παραλαβόντες παρὰ Πελασγῶν, οὗτος ὡνὴρ οἶδε τὸ λέγω. Cf. Ar. *Pax* 277—but little is known of their content. For further detail see *OCD*, s.v. Cabiri (Guthrie); *RE* 10. 1399–1450, esp. 1423 ff. (Kern).

μειράκιον ὤν: Philip was born in 382, and was a hostage in Thebes from 368 until 365 (Diod. 15. 67. 4, 16. 2. 2; Justin 6. 9. 6, 7. 5. 1 f.). The initiation presumably took place between 365 and 361, since the upper limit for a μειράκιον was 21 (see Hippocrates, cited by LSJ, s.v.). For Plutarch's use of the word, which bears out Hippocrates' statement, see W. H. Porter on *Arat.* 4. 1. His description of Marius as a μειράκιον at Numantia in 134 (*Mar.* 3. 4), when he would be about 23, is due to the fact that Marius was doing his first military service, normally performed earlier.

ὀρφανῆς γονέων: On the death of her father Neoptolemus, Arybbas became her guardian. See esp. Justin 7. 6. 10 ff.

ἐρασθῆναι: Doubtless policy and affection went hand in hand, as with Alexander (see ch. 47. 7). Philip hoped to strengthen his position in Epirus and to make the Molossians dependent on him (Satyrus, *FHG* iii, fr. 5). Arybbas for his part probably hoped to extend his power beyond Molossia. Cf. Justin, loc. cit.

τὸν ἀδελφὸν αὐτῆς Ἀρύββαν: Really her uncle; see the stemma below. Hence the emendations πατράδελφον (Anon.) and ἀδελφὸν τοῦ πατρὸς αὐτῆς (Xylander). But the error may be due to Plutarch.

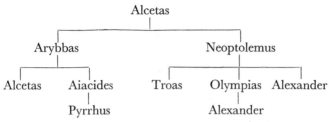

Between 351 and 349 Arybbas became a virtual vassal of Philip, who eventually (343–342) drove him from his kingdom and gave it to Olympias' brother, Alexander. Arybbas found refuge at Athens, where he and his sons were granted citizenship (see *GHI* 2. 173). He probably died in exile (Treves, *AJP* 63 (1942), 129 ff.). On Philip's relations with Molossia see further N. G. L. Hammond, *Epirus* (Oxford, 1967), 517, 533 f., 545, 557 ff.

3. τῆς νυκτός, . . . θάλαμον: The bride was led veiled to the bridal-chamber, which the bridegroom then closed (κατακλάζειν τὴν νύμφην): see Gow on Theocritus 15. 77, where the proverb ἐνδοῖ πᾶσαι, ὁ τὰν νυὸν εἶπ' ἀποκλάξας is quoted. Before the door of the chamber the epithalamium (see Theocritus 18, with *scholia*) was sung by a chorus of maidens. According to Pollux 3. 42 the door was guarded by the 'best man'.

4. ὁ δὲ Φίλιππος . . .: 'To a Greek reader this should recall the dream of the mother of Pericles, as told by Herodotus (6. 131)—that she gave birth to a lion' (Pearson, *LHA* 11). For the incident cf. *Per.* 3. 3. It may be significant that Alexander's ancestors, Heracles and Achilles, were called 'lion-hearted'; cf., e.g., Homer, *Il.* 5. 639, *Od.* 11. 267 (Heracles); Hesiod, *Theog.* 1007 (Achilles). The lion was, of course, a symbol of courage and nobility (Arist. *Pol.* 1338ᵇ19, *Hist. An.* I. 1. 488ᵇ16), and of royal power (Herod. 5. 92 β 3, where see How and Wells's note). Plutarch's source may be Ephorus, who is cited by Tertullian (*De Anima* 46 = *F.Gr.Hist.* no. 70, fr. 217) as his authority.

5. ὑφορωμένων τὴν ὄψιν: 'viewed the vision with suspicion (or apprehension)'; cf. *Sull.* 7. 6, ὑφεωρῶντο δὴ στάσιν οἱ τερατοσκόποι; *Nic.* 6, 1. The story is probably unhistorical; it is difficult to credit that any seer cast aspersions of this nature on Olympias within six months of her marriage. When she and Philip were later estranged, this sort of thing could safely be invented.

Ἀρίστανδρος ὁ Τελμησσεύς: Berve no. 117. The Telmissians of Lycia were noted for their skill in interpreting prodigies (Herod. 1. 78; Arr. 2. 3. 3) and Aristander is called 'peritissimus vatum' (Curt. 4. 2. 14; cf. 5. 4. 1; Arr. 3. 2. 2). He accompanied Alexander to Asia and prophesied before almost all the important events. Only once (Curt. 5. 4. 1) is he recorded to have failed. At the R. Tanais he is reported to have refused to change his prophecy to suit Alexander (Arr. 4. 4. 3), and was proved right by events. After the death of Cleitus in 327 he is not heard of again. Fränkel, 171 ff., and C. A. Robinson, *AJP* 50 (1929), 195 ff., attribute the disappearance of Aristander from our sources to the death of Callisthenes, who, they contend, is responsible for all mentions of the seer. Robinson maintains in particular that Aristander's opposition to Alexander at the Tanais implies powerful backing from Callisthenes and others. Their arguments are hardly conclusive, and as Aristander must have been an old man in 327 it is more reasonable to suppose that he died a natural death soon after.

καὶ κύειν: Castiglioni (*Gnomon* 13 (1937), 136) rightly objects to Ziegler's proposal to delete these words, on the grounds that the climax would be destroyed and that the parenthesis renders the repetition necessary.

θυμοειδῆ: See ch. 4. 7.

6. ὤφθη δέ ποτε: For a detailed examination of chs. 2. 6–3. 4 see Egon Braun in *JOEAI* 39 (1952), 139–45. It is perfectly conceivable that Philip may have seen such an incident as Plutarch describes; Cicero (*De div.* 2. 135) mentions a pet snake kept by Olympias. Later writers (see Pease ad loc.) developed the incident. Justin (9. 5. 9; 11. 11. 3–6) regards the admission by Olympias that Alexander's father was an enormous snake as the cause of her divorce by Philip ('velut stupri compertam') when he married Cleopatra (see ch. 9. 6). Justin (11. 11. 3–6) also connects the incident with Alexander's divine birth (so Lucian *Alex.* 7) and alleges that Alexander suborned the priests of Ammon to salute him as the god's son (see ch. 26). Among modern writers Tarn (2. 353–4) and Wilcken (see esp. *SB Berlin* 1928, 589) hold that the stories are subsequent to Alexander's visit to Siwah and originate from it; Radet (*REA* 28 (1926), 223–5; *Mélanges Bidez* 780; *Alex.* 11 ff.) and A. Gitti (*Quando nacque in Alessandro Magno l'idea della filiazione divina* (Bari, 1951)), however, believe that they circulated in Macedonia during Alexander's youth and that Alexander's belief in his divine sonship antedated his arrival in Egypt. It is not impossible that a woman like Olympias may have believed that the god (Dionysus) in the shape of a snake (cf. Eur. *Bacch.* 1017–18) was the father of Alexander and perhaps even said so. Callisthenes' remark (ap. Arr. 4. 10. 2) about 'Olympias' lies regarding Alexander's birth' gives some support to this view (Gitti, op. cit. 18), and the existence of such a story, which Olympias' many enemies would exploit, might help to explain the point of Attalus' exhortation (ch. 9. 7) that people should pray for a legitimate heir from Philip and Cleopatra. But even granted all this, Alexander's belief in a divine father is scarcely proved. Despite the widespread knowledge of Ammon in Greece by this time (see C. J. Classen, *Historia* 8 (1959), 349 ff.), it is most improbable that the snake would have been connected with *Ammon* before Alexander's visit to Siwah (ch. 26). The snake surely would be taken to be Dionysus.

τὴν ὁμιλίαν . . . ἀφοσιούμενον: 'refused to associate with her'; for this meaning of the verb cf. ch. 3. 4 and *Num.* 6. 1, τοιούτοις λόγοις ἀφοσιουμένου τὴν βασιλείαν.

7. τῇδε: In Macedonia. On the Dionysiac cult in Macedonia see W. Vollgraff, *BCH* 51 (1927), 433 ff.

πᾶσαι μέν: answered by ἡ δ' Ὀλυμπιάς (§ 9).

Κλώδωνές τε καὶ Μιμαλλόνες: The former name is the older, if we can believe Polyaenus 4. 1 —perhaps from Callimachus (see Pfeiffer on fr. 503).

8. τὸ θρησκεύειν ὄνομα . . . ἱερουργίαις: 'The name "thrēskeuein" came to be applied to violent and extravagant rites.' Both words imply excess; cf. LSJ, s.v. κατακορής, esp. the medical writers and Plut. *Mor.* 140 d. On the derivation of θρησκεία see *Etym. Magn.* 455. 10.

9. ἡ δ' Ὀλυμπιάς: For her addiction to Dionysiac rites see Athenaeus 14. 659 f. (though the letter from Olympias to Alexander may not be genuine); 13. 560 f. (= Duris, *F. Gr. Hist.* no. 76, fr. 52).

κατοχάς, . . . ἐνθουσιασμούς: 'divine possession . . . divine inspiration'. For the meaning of the words see *Mor.* 758 e, ὡς γὰρ ἔμπνουν τὸ πνεύματος πληρωθὲν ἔμφρον δὲ τὸ φρονήσεως, οὗτος ὁ τοιοῦτος σάλος

5

ψυχῆς ἐνθουσιασμὸς ὠνόμασται μετοχῇ καὶ κοινωνίᾳ θειοτέρας δυνάμεως. ἐνθουσιασμοῦ δὲ τὸ μαντικὸν ἐξ Ἀπόλλωνος ἐπινοίας καὶ κατοχῆς, τὸ δὲ βακχεῖον ἐκ Διονύσου. . . .

ὄφεις μεγάλους: On snake-handling see esp. E. R. Dodds, *Harv. Theol. Rev.* 33 (1940), 155 ff.; *The Greeks and the Irrational*, Appendix I; and the Introduction to his edition of Euripides' *Bacchae*. Dodds, however, argues (*Harv. Theol. Rev.* 171 ff.) that Euripides' description is based primarily on the cult of Sabazius, the oriental counterpart of Dionysus, in Athens. For his cult at Athens in Alexander's time see Dem. *De cor.* 259–60, ἐν δὲ ταῖς ἡμέραις τοὺς καλοὺς θιάσους ἄγων διὰ τῶν ὁδῶν, τοὺς ἐστεφανωμένους τῷ μαράθῳ καὶ τῇ λεύκῃ, τοὺς ὄφεις τοὺς παρείας θλίβων καὶ ὑπὲρ τῆς κεφαλῆς αἰωρῶν.

λίκνων: Baskets sacred to Dionysus, carried on the head at his festivals.

III.

1. οὐ μὴν ἀλλά: i.e. despite the explanation just given, which would account for the presence of the snake. Plutarch evidently gives little credence to the first version (2. 6).

τὸ φάσμα: i.e. ὃ ὤφθη, ὃ εἶδε: So correctly Langhorne and Ruegg. North, Dryden, Perrin, and Ax all wrongly translate 'dream, vision'. But the ὄναρ of 2. 4 has been interpreted by Aristander (2. 5); see E. Braun, *JOEAI* 39 (1952), 143, n. 25. Philip wants to know the significance of the snake in Olympias' bed.

πέμψαντι Χαίρωνα: Parke–Wormell, i. 240, are doubtless correct in regarding this story as legendary, dating 'at least after Alexander's visit to Ammon'. Nothing is known of Chaeron.

2. ἀποβαλεῖν: Ax, Ruegg, North, and Langhorne regard this as an *aorist* infinitive, dependent on λέγουσι; but it is future, part of the priestess's words (depending on a verb of saying implied in κελεύοντος): so Perrin, Stewart, and Parke–Wormell, loc. cit. Philip was struck in the eye by an arrow at Methone in 354 (Diod. 16. 34. 5; cf. Callisthenes. fr. 57, Theopompus fr. 52, and Duris fr. 36, where see Jacoby's note); for the date see Bengtson 302, n. 4.

Ἄμμωνι: see ch. 26.

3. Ἐρατοσθένης: of Cyrene; 'The Admirable Crichton' of ancient learning, called by his enemies βῆτα, 'second-rate'. On his dates, perhaps 296–214, see *F. Gr. Hist.* 2D. 704. After a lengthy stay in Athens he succeeded Apollonius Rhodius *c.* 246 as head of the library at Alexandria. His best work, of the highest quality, was in geography and his Γεωγραφικά was used extensively by Strabo (Thomson, 158–

66). His other works included mathematics, astronomy, twelve books on comedy, and, most important, a comprehensive chronological history, in which he attempted to fix the dates of all events, both literary and historical (Jacoby ad loc.). His fragments are collected in *F. Gr. Hist.* no. 241; the origin of the three (28–30) dealing with Alexander cannot be determined. Oddly enough, in view of this passage, Eratosthenes is reported to have held that all the 'divinity stuff' (τὸ θεῖον) in the Alexander historians had been invented to please Alexander (Arr. 5. 3. 1; Strabo 15. 1. 7–8 (688)).

περὶ τὴν τέκνωσιν: 'the secret of his birth'; see ch. 28 for this sense of τέκνωσις. γενέσεως refers to his divine parentage.

4. ἀφοσιοῦσθαι: 'repudiated'; cf. ch. 2. 7.

διαβάλλων πρός: 'making H. jealous of me, setting H. at variance with me', rather than 'slandering me to H.' (Perrin).

5. δ' οὖν: 'at any rate'. Whatever the truth of the preceding statements may be, this at least is certain. See Denniston, 464. Plutarch is properly sceptical.

ἱσταμένου . . . ἕκτῃ: i.e. about 20 July 356. This date is generally accepted and is probably correct. According to Aristobulus (ap. Arr. 7. 28. 1) Alexander was 32 years and 8 months old at the time of his death; as this occurred on 10 June 323 (see 75. 9 n.), this would put his birth in October 356. But the contradiction is only apparent, due to Aristobulus accepting the *official* accession date, October 336, instead of the actual date in June (see 11. 1 n.). The Olympic Games were held in July or August and the last day of the Games coincided with the full moon. If in odd Olympiads the Games were held in July and in even Olympiads in August, as Beloch (1. 2. 139 f.) maintained (this seems likely—see R. Sealey, *CR* N.s. 10 (1960), 185 f.), in 356 (Ol. 106) the Games will have ended on 28 August. Parmenio's victory probably took place in August (see 3. 8 n.). The synchronism is, therefore, very approximate.

For a list of Attic months with their Macedonian equivalents see Bischoff, *RE* 10. 1586–7, and for details of the Athenian calendar see on 25. 2.

ὁ . . . νεώς: There were several successive temples of Artemis at Ephesus (*RE* 5. 2807 ff.); the temple mentioned here was set on fire by Herostratus to win a name for himself; see Strabo 14. 641, and further *RE* 8. 1145–6. The fire is attested by Arist. *Meteor.* 371ᵃ30, and Cicero (*De div.* 1. 47, *De nat. deor.* 2. 69); cf. Solinus 40. 4.

6. Ἡγησίας ὁ Μάγνης: A native of Magnesia on the Sipylus; for his date (? between 300 and 250) see Pearson, *LHA* 247. His fragments, including three from his *History of Alexander*, are collected in *F. Gr. Hist.* no. 142. Hegesias is the chief representative of one type of 'Asiatic' style (Cic. *Brut.* 325), with short jerky sentences and unnatural word order (see esp. fr. 5), which Cicero severely criticizes (*Brut.* 286, *Or.* 226). See further W. R. Roberts, *Dionysius of Halicarnassus on Literary Composition* (London, 1910), 52–5. Cicero (*De nat. deor.* 2. 69) attributes this remark to Timaeus—'concinneque(!), ut multa, Timaeus'. Plaumann (*RE* 8. 1146) thinks that Cicero has carelessly added this detail from Hegesias to Timaeus' account. If both authors did tell this story the question of priority can hardly be decided, since little is known of the dates of Timaeus' work. See most recently T. S. Brown, *Timaeus of Tauromenium* (Berkeley, 1958), 1–20.

ὑπὸ ψυχρίας: For ψυχρία (more usually ψυχρότης) = Lat. *frigus*, a well-known fault of style, the *locus classicus* is Arist. *Rhet.* 1405ᵇ35. It means either 'tameness, flatness' or 'tastelessness, affectation' (as here); cf. W. R. Roberts's edition of *Demetrius On Style* (Cambridge, 1902), 114 ff. Plutarch, mocking the tasteless rhetoric of Hegesias, plays on the literal meaning of ψυχρόν, as Aristophanes, *Ach.* 138 ff., and Horace, *Sat.* 2. 5. 41, had done before him.

ἀσχολουμένης . . . μαίωσιν: 'being busy delivering Alexander'. Jacoby (*F. Gr. Hist.* 2B, 807) attributes the remainder of the chapter to Hegesias. There seems no good reason to credit him with more than the remark about Artemis (τὸ μαίωσιν).

7. τῶν μάγων: cf. Cicero, *De div.* 1. 47, 'clamitasse magos pestem ac perniciem Asiae proxima nocte natam'. The μάγοι were a priestly class taken over by the Achaemenids from the Medes. Without them no sacrifice could take place (Herod. 1. 132), and they were frequently called on to interpret dreams (Herod. 1. 107, 108, 120, etc.). They also guarded the royal tombs (e.g. that of Cyrus—Arr. 6. 29. 7) and tended the sacred fire. But their presence in *Ephesus* is very suspect. As Cicero does not mention Ephesus, Plutarch may be responsible for its insertion.

8. ἄρτι Ποτείδαιαν ᾑρηκότι: Philip captured Pydna early in 356, and proceeded with the help of the Olynthians to take Potidaea, which he handed over to them. The Athenians then formed an alliance with the kings of Thrace, Paeonia, and Illyria against Philip (Diod. 16. 22. 3). The decree accepting the alliance was proposed on 26 July (see *GHI* 2. 157) and Parmenio attacked the kings while they were still collecting their forces. It is doubtless his victory over them that is referred to here; this probably occurred in August.

ἵππῳ κέλητι: 'a race-horse'. The horse race was one of the chief events at the Olympic Games, and many of Pindar's odes are addressed to victors in this race. Plutarch (*Mor.* 105 a) speaks of a victory in the chariot race, but the correctness of the present passage is proved by a new issue of silver coins by Philip. These show on the reverse a naked boy rider, with the victor's fillet round his head, holding a palm-branch (see Seltman, 200 and Pl. XLVI, nos. 11–14; G. F. Hill, *Historical Greek Coins* (London, 1906), no. 44, pp. 80 ff.). On Philip's early coinage see A. B. West, *Num. Chron.* (1923), 169 ff.

τρισὶ νίκαις: Potidaea, Illyria, and Olympia.

9. ἀνίκητον: See on ch. 14. 6, and cf. *Mor.* 782 b (cited on 52. 9).

IV. *Alexander's physical appearance. His bodily heat perhaps responsible for his love of drink and his spirit. His dislike of athletic pursuits.*

1. οἱ Λυσίππειοι: Lysippus of Sicyon, who was active in the second half of the fourth century, is mentioned by Cicero (*De orat.* 3. 7. 26) as one of the great masters of Greek sculpture, together with Myron and Polycleitus. His work marked a turning-point in Greek sculpture, with its realism (cf. Quint. *Inst.* 12. 10. 9), its use of depth, and the introduction of more slender figures with smaller heads. He is said to have produced some 1,500 sculptures, but no original is extant; copies of his portraits of the king are generally admitted to exist in the Louvre (The 'Azara herm'), and elsewhere. He is said to have made portraits of Alexander from early boyhood (Pliny, *NH* 34, 63), and on Alexander's accession became court sculptor. On his 'group portraits' see chs. 15 and 40.

The passages in classical authors relating to Lysippus are collected and translated in F. P. Johnson, *Lysippus* (1927), Appendix I, who also discusses the portraits of Alexander attributed to Lysippus (pp. 213–29). For a comprehensive examination of the portraits of Alexander see M. Bieber, *Alexander the Great in Greek and Roman Art* (Chicago, 1964); she also deals in detail with Lysippus in her *Sculpture of the Hellenistic Age*, rev. ed. (New York, 1962). On Plutarch's interest in physiognomy see E. C. Evans, *TAPA* 72 (1941), 104–5, and esp. A. E. Wardman, *CQ* n.s. 17 (1967), 415 ff.

ὑφ' οὗ μόνου . . .: cf. *Mor.* 335 a–c: διὸ καὶ μόνον Ἀλέξανδρος ἐκέλευε Λύσιππον εἰκόνας αὐτοῦ δημιουργεῖν. μόνος γὰρ οὗτος, ὡς ἔοικε, κατεμήνυε τῷ χαλκῷ τὸ ἦθος αὐτοῦ καὶ συνεξέφερε τῇ μορφῇ τὴν ἀρετήν. οἱ δ' ἄλλοι τὴν ἀποστροφὴν τοῦ τραχήλου καὶ τῶν ὀμμάτων τὴν διάχυσιν καὶ ὑγρότητα μιμεῖσθαι θέλοντες οὐ διεφύλαττον αὐτοῦ τὸ ἀρρενωπὸν καὶ λεοντῶδες; *Arr.* 1. 16. 4, Ἀλεξάνδρου κελεύσαντος Λύσιππον ποιῆσαι ὅσπερ καὶ Ἀλέξανδρον μόνος προκριθεὶς ἐποίει; Cicero, *ad Fam.* 5. 12. 7. Although

Pliny (*NH* 7. 125) and Horace (*Epist.* 2. 1. 239) talk of an 'edictum', Alexander was certainly represented by other artists; perhaps he did not 'sit' for them or give them commissions. πλάττεσθαι is opposed to γράφεσθαι, as sculpture to painting.

2. πολλοὶ τῶν διαδόχων: *Mor.* 53 c, Alexander's συνηθεῖς imitated Alexander's ἔγκλισιν τοῦ τραχήλου καὶ τὴν ἐν τῷ διαλέγεσθαι τραχύτητα (ταχύτητα, some manuscripts) τῆς φωνῆς; *Pyrrh.* 8. 2, the Macedonians thought that Pyrrhus alone resembled Alexander in appearance and action, τῶν μὲν ἄλλων βασιλέων ἐν πορφύραις καὶ δορυφόροις καὶ κλίσει τραχήλου καὶ τῷ μεῖζον διαλέγεσθαι. These other kings included Demetrius—see *Demetr.* 41–2.

τήν τ' ἀνάτασιν . . .: Bieber, *Proc. Am. Philos. Soc.* 93 (1949), 383, points out that this means that the neck is stretched and bent to the left while the head is turned to Alexander's right, as in the small bronze figure in the Louvre (Johnson, op. cit., Plate 47; Bieber, op. cit., Fig. 18). In the later head from Alexandria in the British Museum the direction of head and neck is reversed, though it perhaps shows best the 'melting gaze' (τὴν ὑγρότητα τῶν ὀμμάτων).

3. Ἀπελλῆς: of Colophon near Ephesus. He was generally considered the greatest of Greek painters, excelling all in χάρις, 'grace' or 'charm'; cf. Quint. *Inst.* 12. 10. 6 (see R. G. Austin ad loc.). This quality was no doubt present in his most famous work, the *Venus Anadyomene*, which Augustus dedicated in the temple of Caesar at Rome (Pliny, *NH* 35. 91). Apelles is known to have been at Philip's court *c.* 340, and he became the court painter. Plutarch refers to the famous painting of Alexander holding a thunderbolt, executed for the temple of Artemis at Ephesus at a fee of 20 talents (Pliny, *NH* 35. 92). It was noted for the perspective treatment of the hand and thunderbolt, a technique to be seen on the Neison gem in Leningrad (Furtwängler, *Die antiken Gemmen*, I (Leipzig–Berlin, 1900), Pl. 32, no. 11). However, this is probably not a copy of Apelles' picture, but the work of an unknown artist in Alexander's entourage (W. B. Kaiser, *JDAI* 77 (1962), 234–5, 239). Lysippus, who sculpted Alexander with a lance, as a man, found fault with Apelles for depicting Alexander with the attributes of divinity (*Mor.* 360 d). This, however, was probably done with the full approval of the king (see on ch. 28 and Kaiser, op. cit. 237–8).

⟨αὐ⟩τὸν κεραυνοφόρον: Coraes' emendation is unnecessary. At *Mor.* 335 a Plutarch writes ὁ μὲν ἔγραψε τὸν κεραυνοφόρον. He surely means *the famous* (portrait of A. as a) wielder of the thunderbolt.

οὐκ ἐμιμήσατο . . .: 'failed to reproduce his complexion, and made it too dark and swarthy. For he was fair, as they say, and his fairness inclined to red, about his breast particularly.' φαιός is 'dark-complexioned', neither μέλας nor λευκός; πίνος is used of the natural grease in wool or the patina on bronze statues. For λευκός (= fair, pale) see Dodds on Eur. *Bacch.* 457. Perhaps his secret varnishing process (Pliny, *NH* 35. 97) was responsible for the darkish colour of the flesh. A. P. Laurie, *Greek and Roman Methods of Painting* (Cambridge, 1910), 33 ff., suggests that it was a thin glaze of bitumen.

4. ἐν ὑπομνήμασιν Ἀριστοξενείοις: See F. Wehrli, *Die Schule des Aristoteles*, Heft 2 (Basel, 1945), for a full collection of the fragments of Aristoxenus, with commentary; this is no. 132. Aristoxenus, born at Tarentum between 375 and 360, came to Athens and eventually joined the school of Aristotle, but was disappointed in his expectation that he would succeed him. He is known particularly for his writings on harmonics and rhythm (Mountford in *OCD*), but occupies a prominent position in the history of biography (Stuart, 129 ff.). Fragments of his Lives of the philosophers remain. The extant fragments of his ὑπομνήματα (nos. 128–39) are extremely varied, and for the most part unimportant. Wehrli assigns to Aristoxenus the following two sentences as well (to Θεόφραστος), but A. E. Wardman, *CQ* n.s. 5 (1955), 102–3, and E. Mensching, *Historia* 12 (1963), 274–6, correctly restrict his contribution to the first sentence. With the whole passage cf. *Mor.* 623 e–f.

Fragrance is frequently associated with divinity (see, e.g., *Hymn. Hom. Dem.* 277 f., Eur. *Hipp.* 1392, Verg. *Aen.* 1. 403, Ovid, *Fast.* 5. 375), and Mensching (275) is surely correct in suggesting that Alexander's εὐωδία is a sign of his superhuman quality. But did Aristoxenus think of him as a god or as a hero? Mensching inclines to the latter view but, as E. Lohmeyer, *Vom göttlichen Wohlgeruch* (*SB Heidelberg* 1919, Abh. 9), on whom he relies, mentions only gods in this connection, he does not venture to assert this. It is clear, however, from the very similar passage at *Mor.* 421 b, φθεγγομένου δὲ τὸν τόπον εὐωδία κατεῖχε τοῦ στόματος ἥδιστον ἀποπνέοντος, that such fragrance could be thought to emanate from a lesser being. Cf. also Aesch. *PV* 115. We should probably conclude that Aristoxenus wrote of Alexander as a hero.

ἀνέγνωμεν: 'I have read'. This means what it says; Plutarch is *not* using an intermediate source (see esp. Theander 59–60). Ziegler, 912, is over-cautious.

5. ὡς οἴεται Θεόφραστος: Theophrastus of Eresos in Lesbos (372/69–288/5) joined Aristotle between 348 and 345, became his favourite pupil, and succeeded him in 323 as head of the Lyceum. He was the author of standard works on botany (*History of Plants, Causes of Plants*) and on the history of philosophy, but is best known for his *Characters*, portraits of types reminiscent of Aristotle's *Nicomachean Ethics*. He was one of Plutarch's chief sources for scientific information, cited some 50 times (Ziegler, 922). Theophrastus is the source for the following two sentences as well. Wehrli and Mensching refer to *Caus. Plant.* 6. 16. 2 ff. and 6. 18. 3, and *De odor.* 3 for the theory of εὐωδία, but Plutarch may have in mind especially *Caus. Plant.* 6. 14. 8, εὐοσμότερα δὲ καὶ ἡδίω καὶ ὅλα καὶ κατὰ μέρος ἐν τοῖς εὔπνοις καὶ ξηροῖς τόποις ἀφηρημένου τοῦ ὑδατώδους καὶ τοῦ καταλοίπου πεπεμμένου μᾶλλον . . . σημεῖον δὲ καὶ τὸ ἐν ταῖς θερμοτέραις χώραις πλείω γίνεσθαι καὶ μᾶλλον τὰ εὔοσμα.

The theory of Theophrastus is applied to the statement of Aristoxenus by Plutarch himself, as is shown by ἴσως and ὡς ἔοικε (so Wardman, 102). Mensching (275, n. 7) unplausibly supposes that the combination was made by Plutarch's source.

Wardman (102–3) draws attention to the importance of this passage for Plutarch's view of Alexander—'Plutarch suggests that εὐωδία is simply one case of Alexander's θερμότης; the fact of φύσις is given an explanation in terms of φύσις. This in turn serves to portray Alexander's whole character; it makes him prone to drink (though this is just one tendency) and makes him also θυμοειδής.' On Wardman's view that 'τὸ θυμοειδές is the key to Alexander in the *Life*' see the Introduction, p. lxiv.

6. ὥσπερ ὕλην κτλ.: 'like a source of corruption lying on the surface of bodies'.

8. σωφροσύνη: At 21. 11 Alexander's σωφροσύνη (coupled with ἐγκρατεία) is instanced in his disregard of the Persian captive women. It occurs in the same connection at 30. 10.

φιλοτιμία κτλ.: 'his ambition kept his spirit serious and lofty in advance of his years'. Alexander's ambition is mentioned again at 5. 6, 7. 7, and 34. 2 (φιλοτιμούμενος); cf. 16. 17.

μεγαλόψυχον: Alexander's μεγαλοψυχία is coupled with ἐγκρατεία at 30. 11, and at 42. 10. For other references to this and similar words see F. Pfister, *Historia* 13 (1964), 69–70.

9. δόξαν: Alexander's desire for δόξα is a recurrent theme in the *Life*; cf. 5. 5, 13. 4, 42. 4.

σοφιστικῶς καλλωπιζόμενος: 'preening himself on his eloquence like a sophist'. In Plutarch σοφιστής is always derogatory; cf. Introduction, p. xxiii.

τὰς ἐν Ὀλυμπίᾳ νίκας κτλ.: In 348 Philip destroyed Olynthus and replaced its coinage with gold staters bearing a head of Apollo on the obverse and on the reverse a two-horse chariot: G. F. Hill, *Historical Greek Coins* (London, 1906), nos. 43, 80–3; Seltman, 201 and Pl. XLVII, 2–4. For the enormous popularity of these 'Philippeioi', their subsequent use in Italy, and their adaptation and imitation in Gaul and Britain see Seltman, 215 n., and C. H. V. Sutherland, *Art in Coinage* (London, 1955), 72–3.

10. τῶν περὶ αὐτὸν ἀποπειρωμένων: In the *Moralia* (179 d) Philip himself exhorts Alexander to compete. Cf. *Mor.* 331 b, where Alexander's refusal proves him a philosopher.

11. ἀλλοτρίως ἔχων: Well illustrated in the anecdote in the *Moralia* (180 a)—ἐν δὲ τῇ Μιλήτῳ πολλοὺς ἀνδρίαντας ἀθλητῶν θεασάμενος Ὀλύμπια καὶ Πύθια νενικηκότων, "καὶ ποῦ τὰ τηλικαῦτα," ἔφη, "ἦν σώματα, ὅτε οἱ βάρβαροι ὑμῶν τὴν πόλιν ἐπολιόρκουν;" In ch. 34 Alexander honours the athlete Phayllus, not for his victories but for his part in the defeat of Xerxes.

πλείστους . . . ἀγῶνας: After the first arrival of artists in Egypt we hear of frequent gymnastic and musical competitions, esp. the former (e.g. Arr. 3. 6. 1, 4. 4. 1, 5. 3. 6). Of τραγῳδοί we know Athenodorus and Thessalus (ch. 29), while Chares (fr. 4), in his detailed description of the marriage feast at Susa, mentions αὐληταί, κιθαρῳδοί and ῥαψῳδοί (further details in Berve 1. 75, 89). The only athlete we know of is Dioxippus (Berve, no. 284), who had been victorious in the pancration at the Olympic Games; Pliny, *NH* 35. 139; *Mor.* 521 b; Diod. 17. 100. 2, 101.

v. *Illustrations of Alexander's ambitious nature (1–6). His early life (7–8).*

1. ἀποδημοῦντος Φιλίππου: A. Momigliano (*Filippo il Macedone* (Firenze, 1934), 139, n. 1) dates the embassy to 341 and associates it with the Hermeias episode, while F. R. Wüst (*Phil. II. v. Mak. u. Griechenland* (München, 1938), 89, n. 2) puts it in 340 during Philip's absence at Byzantium. Schachermeyr (499, n. 25) connects it with the supposed Persian alliance with Philip, dated to the summer of 343 by Wüst, loc. cit. But even if such an alliance existed—the only (doubtful) evidence is Arr. 2. 14. 2—the date assigned to it is quite arbitrary. If the episode really occurred—P. Treves (*Athenaeum* 14 (1936), 199) regards it as an invention designed to show Alexander's heroic anti-Persian spirit from his earliest years—it cannot be dated, since embassies might come at any time. παιδικόν might suggest a date in the early forties.

2. ἐρώτημα παιδικόν: According to *Mor.* 342 b–c he did not ask about the golden vine, the hanging gardens, or the king's dress, but about the Persian army and the roads leading to Persia.

3. δεινότητα: probably 'shrewdness, cunning', as at Dem. *De cor.* 144, ὅση δεινότης ἦν ἐν τῷ Φιλίππῳ θεάσεσθε; although it is often used of the power of oratory; cf. ch. 4. 9, λόγου τε δεινότητι and *Mor.* 343 a (of Pericles). North so takes it here.

ὁρμὴν καὶ μεγαλοπραγμοσύνην: 'his son's eager disposition to do great things' (Perrin). μεγαλοπραγμοσύνη when applied to Alcibiades (*Alc.* 6. 4, 38. 6) is not altogether favourable.

4. ὁσάκις γοῦν: cf. *Mor.* 179 d.

7. πολλοὶ μὲν οὖν: For a list of A's teachers, including Leonidas and Aristotle, see Ps.-Call. 1. 13. 4. Cf. Iul. Val. 1. 7. See Berve 1. 4.

τροφεῖς καὶ παιδαγωγοί: In inscriptions of the second century B.C. τροφεὺς βασιλέως means 'royal tutor'. A παιδαγωγός was a kind of male nurse, very low in the social scale; hence the comment about Leonidas.

Λεωνίδας: Berve no. 469. Chief of the teachers of Alexander. Examples of his αὐστηρὸν ἦθος are given in chs. 22 and 25. Despite his character he was blamed by the Stoics for not knocking the τῦφος out of Alexander (Diogenes Babylonius ap. Quint. *Inst.* 1. 1. 9; Clem. Alex. *Paedagogus* 1. 7; Jerome, *Ep.* 52). For the Stoic view of Alexander see the Introduction, pp. lxi ff. Stroux suggests that Onesicritus may be Plutarch's source regarding Leonidas.

καθηγητής: applied by Plutarch to his teacher Ammonius (*Mor.* 70 e, etc.). ? 'Professor'.

8. Λυσίμαχος: Berve no. 481. See chs. 24 (Chares) and 55 (?Chares). The source of the present passage is probably Chares also—so Pearson, *LHA* 57. The tone of all the passages is distinctly hostile—*contra* Pearson, loc. cit., who holds that at 55. 1 Lysimachus the Bodyguard is meant.

ὑποποιούμενος: 'assuming, claiming (falsely)'; cf. *Caes.* 41. 3, Φαώνιος ('Cato's Ape') δὲ τὴν Κάτωνος παρρησίαν ὑποποιούμενος μανικῶς.

Φοίνικα: Homer, *Il.* 9. 168 f.; cf. Plato *Rep.* 390 e, where Phoenix is called the παιδαγωγός of Achilles. Ziegler also compares Dio Chrys. 2. 14–16.

vi. *How Alexander tamed Bucephalas.*

In 'Bucephalas and His Legend' (*AJP* 51 (1930), 1–21) A. R. Anderson deals very fully with the name Bucephalas, his origin, his age, and the manner of his death, and traces the development of the legend concerning him. He translates the whole of this chapter. See also Burn, 18–21.

1. Φιλονίκου: of Pharsalus (Pliny, *NH* 8. 154, cited below).

τὸν Βουκεφάλαν: The name of a famous breed of Thessalian horses, branded on the shoulder with the sign of an ox's head (so *Etym. Magn.* 207, 50 ff.); Alexander's horse became Bucephalas *par excellence*. The horse was probably not called Bucephalas because of a white blaze in the shape of an ox on his forehead (so Burn), although Arr. 5. 19. 5 gives both versions. The correctness of the former version is supported by the practice of calling horses bearing the brands ϙ (Koppa) and Σ (San) κοππατίας and σαμφόρας respectively. (See V. Ehrenberg, *People of Aristophanes*[2], 138; Starkie on Ar. *Nub.*, p. 315). On the fame of Thessalian horses see W. Ridgeway, *Origin and Influence of the Thoroughbred Horse* (Cambridge, 1905), 300; J. K. Anderson, *Ancient Greek Horsemanship* (Berkeley, 1961), 20 ff.

ὤνιον: Diod. 17. 76. 6 (? from Cleitarchus using Chares, *F. Gr. Hist.* 2D. 437) says he was given as a gift by Demaratus of Corinth. We may suppose that Demaratus paid the 13 talents to Philonices and gave the horse as a gift to Philip—so Gell. *NA* 5. 2 (= Chares, fr. 18), 'emptum Chares scripsit talentis tredecim et regi Philippo donatum'. Kaerst's doubts (*RE* 3. 995) seem unjustified.

τρισκαίδεκα ταλάντων: So Gellius (above). Pliny, *NH* 8. 154, has 'XVI talentis ex Philonici Pharsalii grege emptum'; but this should certainly be emended to XIII.

The price is unparalleled. The next highest recorded is 100,000 sesterces (*c.* 4 talents) paid by Dolabella for the famous horse of Cn. Seius (Gell. *NA* 3. 9). An average price was perhaps 12 minae (Lys. 8. 10, Ar. *Nub.* 21 ff.); Isaeus (5. 43) mentions 3 minae.

2. κατεξανιστάμενος: 'rearing'.

3. περιπαθοῦντος: A very strong word; cf. *Sol.* 6. 6, τὸν μὲν ὁρμῆσαι παίειν τὴν κεφαλὴν καὶ τἆλλα ποιεῖν καὶ λέγειν, ἃ συμβαίνει τοῖς περιπαθοῦσιν.

6. περιέβη: The emendations ἀνέβη (Anon.) and περιανέβη (Palmerius) are unnecessary. Photius, 395 b, reads περιέβη. See also *Alex.* 33. 9; *Aem.* 19; *Pyrrh.* 11; cf. *Mor.* 213 e, κάλαμον π., and Diodorus 17. 88, who uses π. of the riders of elephants.

7. περιλαβών: 'drawing the reins and bridle from left to right' (Ziegler, *Rh. Mus.* 84 (1935), 369–70); 'gently feeling his mouth' (Burn).

προσανέστειλεν: 'checked him': cf. Aelian, *VH* 12. 64, ἀνέστειλε δὲ τὴν ὁρμὴν τοῦ Περδίκκα ὁ Πτολεμαῖος; 'held in hand' (Anderson).

ἀφεικότα τὴν ἀπειλήν: Not 'was rid of the fear that beset him' (Perrin, Anderson), but 'was free of all rebelliousness' (Dryden), 'had ceased to rear' (R. M. Jones, *CPhil.* 15 (1920), 400).

ἀφείς: I retain the manuscript reading (read also by Zonaras, p. 286, 12) with hesitation, as there appears to be no exact parallel to this use of ἀφίημι. At *Phil.* 6, τὸν μὲν ἵππον ἀφῆκεν . . . αὐτὸς δὲ πέζος . . . διελαύνεται, the verb clearly means 'sent away'. Coraes' emendation ἐφείς is not justified by *Arist.* 14, Μαρδόνιος . . . τὴν ἵππον ἀθρόαν αὐτοῖς ἐφείς, 'launching all his cavalry against them'; cf., however, Plato, *Protag.* 338 a. If emendation is required, ἀνείς is attractive in view of Soph. *El.* 721, δεξιὸν δ' ἀνείς σειραῖον ἵππον and Xen. *De Eq. Mag.* 3. 2, εἰς τάχος ἀνιέναι τοὺς ἵππους.

ἐδίωκεν: 'Bene habet. Haud raro Plut. hoc vocabulum usurpat pro *urgere cursum,* laxatis frenis equum in cursum effundere' (Reiske).

8. ὦ παῖ κτλ.: Anderson (op. cit. 17) sees in this remark the beginning of the prophecy that the rider of Bucephalas would rule the world (Ps.-Call. I. 15, 17).

VII. *Aristotle becomes Alexander's teacher.*

2. μουσικήν: i.e. reading, simple arithmetic, and music (see Haarhoff, *OCD* s.v.).

τὰ ἐγκύκλια: Sc. παιδεύματα: lit. 'ordinary, everyday'. Used of a 'general education' before professional studies, not of 'encyclopaedic' education. Although the content varied, it generally included the 'seven liberal arts', i.e. grammar, rhetoric, dialectic (the *Trivium*), together with geometry, arithmetic, astronomy, and the theory of music (the *Quadrivium*). Plutarch (*Mor.* 7 c) holds that a young gentleman should have a smattering of the other so-called ἐγκύκλια παιδεύματα, but that philosophy should be the staple. See further Marrou, 176–7, 406–7.

κατάρτισιν: But κατάρτυσιν may be what Plutarch wrote. LSJ cite no other example of κατάρτισις = 'training, discipline', whereas κατάρτυσις occurs with παιδεία at *Them.* 2, and the verb καταρτύω is used several times in this sense, e.g. *Mor.* 38 d, κ. τὴν φύσιν, Soph. *Ant.* 478, σμίκρῳ χαλινῷ δ' οἶδα τοὺς θυμουμένους ἵππους καταρτυθέντας (with Jebb's note); the occurrence of χαλινῷ is significant in view of χαλινῶν in the fragment cited in the next line; cf. Plato, *Laws,* 808 d.

πολλῶν χαλινῶν . . .: *TGF* fr. 785. For the combination of the same metaphors see also *Mor.* 33 f, 369 c, 966 f.

ἐνδοξότατον καὶ λογιώτατον: Plutarch presents the traditional but un-historical view of Aristotle. After Plato's death in 348 Aristotle had gone with Xenocrates to Asia Minor, where at Assos, the gift of Hermeias, tyrant of Atarneus, he established what amounted to an offshoot of the Academy. In 345 Aristotle moved to Mytilene in

Lesbos, where he was teaching in 343/2 when Philip invited him to Macedon. Aristotle was not yet the outstanding philosopher he later became, and Jaeger, 105 ff., esp. 120, has made it almost certain that Aristotle owed his invitation to political reasons; for he was the son-in-law of Hermeias, with whom Philip concluded an agreement in 342 or 341 and whose kingdom was to serve as a bridge-head in the invasion of Persia which Philip planned; for further refs. see P. Merlan, *Historia* 3 (1954/5), 61, n. 1, who accepts Jaeger's view. Schachermeyr (499, n. 27), however, has rightly warned against too one-sided a view; certainly Philip must have been satisfied of Aristotle's abilities. For his father's connection with the court see on ch. 8. 1.

διδασκάλια: = διδακτρα, reward for teaching (cf. Theocritus 8. 86). On the form of the word cf. *Mor.* 189 e, 213 e, 217 d, *Lyc.* 13, *Pel.* 15, *Ages.* 26 (all of the same event).

3. τὴν ... πόλιν: Stagirus (later Stagira) in the Chalidian peninsula (on its location, Gomme on Thuc. 4. 88. 2) was founded in 655/4 from Andros and Chalcis. Its unimportance in the fifth century is reflected in its payment of only 1,000 drachmae to the Delian League. It was destroyed by Philip in 350 (Diod. 16. 52. 9—under 349/8: but see Bengtson, 306, n. 3).

ἀποκατέστησε: The part played by Aristotle in the restoration is frequently mentioned: *Mor.* 1126 f.; Dio Chr. 2. 79, 47. 9; Ael. *VH* 3. 17, 12. 54; etc. The restoration is attributed to Alexander at the end of Aristotle's life by Val. Max. 5. 6, ext. 5; cf. Pliny, *NH* 7. 109 and Diog. Laert. 5. 4 (who, however, seems to place this during Aristotle's stay at Pella). Perhaps Alexander interceded with Philip.

4. σχολὴν καὶ διατριβὴν ἀπέδειξε: 'assigned the sanctuary of the Nymphs as a school and place of instruction'. **Μίεζαν:** In the district of Emathia (*RE* 15. 1548 f. (Lenk)).

5. ἔοικε: This is Plutarch's own view, based on the two letters following. There is no independent evidence (cf. Merlan, *Historia* 3 (1954/5), 73, n. 2).

There is little direct evidence for the content of Aristotle's teaching. Merlan, however, argues (op. cit. 60–81) that Isocrates' letter to Alexander (*Ep.* 5) is genuine, and that eristics played a prominent part in Alexander's education; he finds confirmation in the episode described at ch. 53. 3 ff. and in Alexander's reference to σοφίσματα at 73. 5. He holds that there is no reason to suppose that Alexander did not receive the normal Academic teaching.

Aristotle's influence on Alexander may be traced in the king's general interest in philosophy, as evinced by the number of philosophers who accompanied him (see chs. 8 and 17, and Berve 1. 65 ff.), in scientific inquiry, esp. geography (see Schachermeyr, 72—rather speculative), botany, and zoology (Pliny, *NH* 8. 44; cf. Jaeger, 330), and in medicine (cf. ch. 8. 1). To Aristotle Alexander clearly owed his veneration for Homer and Pindar, whose house and descendants he spared in the destruction of Thebes (ch. 13), and indeed his interest in literature generally (ch. 8). But to attribute to Aristotle, as Schachermeyr (70) does, the origin of Alexander's famous πόθος (for which see Ehrenberg, 52 ff.), is quite unconvincing. His πόθος is in any case much exaggerated in the sources; see, e.g., Arr. 1. 3. 5, where Alexander has a 'longing' to cross the Danube—surely no irrational impulse!

Aristotle wrote a work on monarchy (περὶ βασιλείας) and a dialogue (?) entitled Ἀλέξανδρος ἢ ὑπὲρ ἀποίκων (or ἀποικιῶν). Plutarch (*Mor.* 329 b = fr. 658R³ = Ross, *Frag. Sel.* (Oxford, 1955), p. 63) records also that Aristotle counselled (συνεβούλευεν) Alexander to treat the Greeks ἡγεμονικῶς, like friends and relations, but the barbarians δεσποτικῶς, like animals or plants.

It is generally agreed that the περὶ βασιλείας was an early work written perhaps for Alexander's accession (Jaeger, 259, n. 3, 311; Badian, *Historia* 7 (1958), 442) or even earlier (Ehrenberg, 85); unfortunately we know nothing of its content. Ross (op. cit. 62) assigns to it the fragment (647R³) in which Aristotle remarks that philosophy is a positive handicap to a ruler, but that he should listen to philosophic councillors; this is 'mere conjecture' (Merlan, 74, n. 1), and Jaeger (86) thinks it part of a work written with reference to a particular situation during Alexander's campaign.

The general opinion is that the dialogue ὑπὲρ ἀποίκων (-ιῶν) was written after 327, perhaps as late as 324, as a protest against Alexander's methods of colonization in Asia (most fully argued by Ehrenberg, 85 ff., to whom Schachermeyr (524, n. 269) refers). Ehrenberg lays particular (? undue) stress on the use of ὑπέρ in the title—the only instance of ὑπέρ in the list of Aristotle's writings in Diog. Laert. 5. 22 ff.—contending that it is not simply equivalent to περί, but means 'on behalf of'; he believes with most scholars that fr. 658 belongs to this work. Recently Badian (442, n. 71) has argued for an early date. He makes the capital point that according to Ammonius, a fifth-century philosopher (cited Ross, *Frag. Sel.* pp. 61–2), this work was written at the request of Alexander; if this is true the strained relations between the two men after 327 make a late date unlikely; he would therefore connect it with the foundation of Alexandropolis (cf. ch. 10) in 340. It is worth noting that Jaeger (24, 318), noting the title Ἀλέξανδρος, had already assigned it to a period when the relations between Alexander and Aristotle were unbroken, i.e. *before* 327, although he too considered it a protest against Alexander's racial policy.

He points out also that this dialogue is (on his dating) exceptional in that all other dialogues, it is generally held, were written early. In opposition to most scholars (see Ehrenberg, 85, n. 1), Jaeger (259, n. 2) thinks that fr. 658 comes from a letter (he offers no suggestion about its date). Badian (442 f.) also considers it part of a letter; he points to Plutarch's use of συνεβούλευεν and to Cicero's description (*Ad Att.* 12. 40. 2) of a letter of Aristotle to Alexander as συμβουλευτικός. He sees in this fragment the same attitude towards barbarians as in Book 1 of the *Politics* before (as he holds) Aristotle's views had been modified, and would therefore date it to the time of Alexander's accession. Barker (*CAH* 6. 532) also thinks it early but considers it, less probably, a fragment of the περὶ βασιλείας.

τῶν ἀπορρήτων κτλ.: 'secret and more profound'.

οἱ ἄνδρες: 'those philosophers', i.e. the Peripatetics.

ἀκροατικὰς καὶ ἐποπτικάς: Gellius 20. 5. 1 ff. contrasts ἀκροατικά with ἐξωτερικά; he defines the former as those 'in quibus philosophia remotior subtiliorque agitabatur quaeque ad naturae contemplationes disceptationesve dialecticas pertinebant'. Cf. also Cicero, *De fin.* 5. 5. 12; *Ad Att.* 4. 16. 2, and for ἐποπτικαί see *Mor.* 382 d. In the morning Aristotle discussed the more abstruse subjects, i.e. logic and metaphysics, with a select audience, and in the evening expounded rhetoric and politics to a larger audience. For a thorough discussion of the question (with full documentation) see I. Düring, *Aristotle in the Ancient Biographical Tradition* (Göteborg, 1957), 426 ff., and for proof that ancient philosophers did not have secret doctrines, G. Boas, 'Ancient Testimony to Secret Doctrines', *The Philosophical Review* 62 (1953), 79–92 (cited by Düring, 440).

6. εἰς Ἀσίαν διαβεβηκώς: Gellius (20. 5. 7) is more precise: (cum) ea tempestate armis exercitum(?–am) omnem prope Asiam teneret (sc. Alexander) regemque ipsum Darium proeliis et victoriis urgeret . . .

ἧς ἀντίγραφόν ἐστιν: Gellius (20. 5. 11–12) reproduces the (same) text of this letter and Aristotle's reply (which Plutarch paraphrases) from the book of Andronicus of Rhodes, a philosopher of the Ciceronian age (see Ross in *OCD*). These letters are rightly considered to be forgeries—see esp. Pridik, no. 49 (pp. 90–1); Zumetikos, 67–70 (with full bibliography of earlier work) and Kaerst, *Phil.* 51 (1892), 613 ff.; all rely chiefly on Zeller's arguments (2⁴. 2. 24, 120 ff.) that the view expressed in the letters that the acroatic writings were to be kept secret is unfounded and that they were not published by Aristotle; see also Düring, op. cit. 286. Kaerst also notes the tendency in this letter, and in others which he discusses, e.g. Gellius 9. 3, to exalt the lover of philosophy above the monarch.

ἡ περὶ τὰ φυσικὰ πραγματεία: Ziegler adopts Xylander's emendation of the MSS. μετὰ τὰ φυσικά, but this reading is confirmed by the sixth-century commentator, Simplicius (*In Phys.*, *CIAG* 9, p. 8. 30). After citing the two letters, Simplicius writes Πλούταρχος δ' ὁ Χαιρωνεὺς ἐν τῷ Ἀλεξάνδρου βίῳ ἐπὶ τῇ ἐκδόσει τῆς Μετὰ τὰ φυσικὰ ταῦτα γεγράφθαι φησιν. The name 'Metaphysics' probably originates with Andronicus (W. D. Ross, *Aristotle* ed. 5 (London, 1949), 13).

9. ὑπόδειγμα τοῖς πεπαιδευμένοις: 'a memorandum for those already trained therein' (Perrin). Cf. Gellius (20. 5. 12), ξυνετοὶ γάρ εἰσιν μόνοις τοῖς ἡμῶν ἀκούσασιν.

VIII. *Alexander's love of Medicine, Literature, and Philosophy.*

1. δοκεῖ: Like ἔοικε (7. 5), an inference drawn by Plutarch.

καὶ τὸ φιλιατρεῖν: 'love of medicine *as well as* of philosophy'. For Aristotle's interest in medicine see Jaeger, 336. His father Nicomachus had been the personal physician of the Macedonian king, Amyntas II.

προστρίψασθαι: 'imparted, communicated to'. In later Greek this is the usual meaning of the verb; it may have a good sense (as here and *Pomp.* 55) or, more frequently, a bad one, e.g. *Mor.* 89 f, Θεμιστοκλεῖ Παυσανίας μηδὲν ἀδικοῦντι προσετρίψατο τὴν ὑποψίαν τῆς προδοσίας διὰ τὸ χρῆσθαι φίλῳ.

θεωρίαν: in its post-classical sense of theory as opposed to practice (cf. Polyb. 1. 5. 3).

ἐκ τῶν ἐπιστολῶν: In ch. 41.

2. ἀρετῆς ἐφόδιον: ἐφόδιον is literally something that helps one on the road, e.g., in ch. 15, money and provisions; at Arist. *Rhet.* 1411ᵃ12 τὰ ἐφόδια τοῦ πολέμου are 'the sinews' of war. At *Mor.* 327 f Alexander's real ἐφόδιον is his philosophic teaching! See also Pearson, *LHA* 91.

τὴν μὲν Ἰλιάδα κτλ.: For the casket see ch. 26, 1–2; cf. Strabo 13. 1. 27 (594), Pliny, *NH* 7. 108, Dio Chr. *Or.* 2, Ath. 12. 537 d.

Strabo (loc. cit.) mentions 'the recension (διόρθωσις) of the casket' which, he says, was done by Alexander himself with Callisthenes and Anaxarchus; he does not mention Aristotle—*pace* Tarn 2. 436, n. 2. W. Leaf, *Strabo on the Troad* (Cambridge, 1923), 150, thinks that the discrepancy of the two versions condemns the whole story, and that the 'Recension of the Casket' amounted to no more than the marking of a few passages. He points also to Aristotle's careless citation of Homer in his extant works. But Aristotle wrote on *Homeric Problems* (in six (?) books of a philological character) and Jaeger (328) even regards Aristotle as 'the creator of philology'. On the other hand, it is difficult to believe that Callisthenes and Anaxarchus collaborated in such an enterprise, in view of their relations (see ch. 52) ; Strabo, however, may mean that *first* Callisthenes and *then* Anaxarchus made the recension—probably not detailed in any case.

ὡς Ὀνησίκριτος ἱστόρηκε: Fr. 38.

3. Ἅρπαλον: Berve no. 143. One of Alexander's boyhood friends, banished in 337 (ch. 10) but recalled on Philip's death. Unfit for active service, he was put (?in 334) in charge of the war-chest (ὁ ἐπὶ τῶν χρημάτων). In the autumn of 333 he fled to Megara, possibly through pique at being superseded (so Badian, *Historia* 9 (1960), 245 f.), but in 331 rejoined Alexander at Tyre and resumed his former position (Arr. 3. 6. 4 ff.). After the financial reorganization of 331 (see Berve 1. 314 ff.) he was put in charge of the finances of the central satrapies at Ecbatana and later at Babylon. It is probable that he exercised an overriding control over the other financial superintendents (Cleomenes in Egypt, Philoxenus in Asia Minor, and Menes, who succeeded Coeranus, in Phoenicia)—so Tarn 1. 128–9; Berve, loc. cit.; Wilcken, 254. Schachermeyr, 214, 417, regards this as unproven. At Babylon he lived in regal splendour and bestowed large sums on the Greek courtesans Pythonice (Berve no. 676) and Glycera (Berve no. 231) ; on Python's satyr-drama *Agen*, which deals with this episode in Harpalus' life, see B. Snell, *Scenes From Greek Drama* (Berkeley, 1964), 99 ff., with H. Lloyd-Jones' criticisms in *Gnomon* 38 (1966), 16 f. When Alexander returned from India he fled to Athens (spring 324) with 6,000 mercenaries and 5,000 talents. For the view that his flight was connected with the fate of Cleander and the satraps see Badian, *JHS* 81 (1961), 22–4. He failed, despite lavish expenditure, to persuade the Athenians to embark on war and when his extradition was demanded fled to Crete ; there he was killed by one of his officers.

Φιλίστου: A native of Syracuse, Philistus helped Dionysius I to become tyrant, commanded his navy and governed Syracuse. He wrote a history of Sicily in at least twelve books, in which he imitated Thucydides. See Barber in *OCD*; *RE* 19. 2409–29 (Laqueur). T. S. Brown (*Historia* 16 (1967), 359 ff.) offers some interesting, if unprovable, suggestions about Alexander's choice of books.

Εὐριπίδου: On Alexander's knowledge of Euripides see 51. 8 n. I see no reason to agree with Brown (op. cit. 361 f.) that Alexander asked only for Euripides, and that Plutarch added Sophocles and Aeschylus.

Τελέστου καὶ Φιλοξένου: Telestes of Selinus, one of the most famous dithyrambic poets, was victorious at Athens in 402/1. For the (scanty) extant frags. see Edmonds, *Lyra Graeca*, 3. 272 ff. Philoxenus of Cythera wrote at the court of Dionysius I. He was noted for the introduction of 'new' music. Fragments in Edmonds, op. cit. 3. 382–99. Perhaps

best remembered for his criticism of Dionysius' poetry which he described as 'pitiful' (οἰκτρά), Diod. 15. 6.
On both see C. M. Bowra in *OCD* s.vv.

4. δι' ἐκεῖνον μὲν ζῶν κτλ.: The phrase is reminiscent of Aristotle's remark about the state, γινομένη μὲν τοῦ ζῆν ἕνεκεν, οὖσα δὲ τοῦ εὖ ζῆν (*Pol.* 1. 1. 8); cf. also Arist. *Protrepticus* fr. B 53 (Düring). 'ἐκεῖνον redit ad posterius, patrem, τοῦτον ad prius, Aristotelem' (Reiske): For a similar inversion of the normal order see ch. 45. 2.

ὕστερον ὑποπτότερον ἔσχεν: See chs. 55, 74. Plutarch deduces their ἀλλοτριότης from the events described in these chapters.

5. Ἀνάξαρχον: See on ch. 28.

Ξενοκράτει: of Chalcedon, head of the Academy since 339. He refused an invitation to accompany Alexander (*Mor.* 1043 d), but wrote four books περὶ βασιλείας (a theoretical exposition of the duties of a king according to Academic principles) which he dedicated and sent to Alexander (*Mor.* 1126 d). See Berve no. 576. This incident is frequently mentioned: *Mor.* 181 e, 331 e, 333 b; Suidas, s.v. Ξενοκράτης; Val. Max. 4. 3, ext. 3; Diog. Laert. 4. 8; Cic. *Tusc. Disp.* 5. 91. In the last three versions Xenocrates accepts 30 minae, 'ne aspernari regis liberalitatem videretur' (Cicero).

Δάνδαμις καὶ Καλανός: See chs. 65, 69.

IX. *Alexander as regent. The battle of Chaeroneia. Disputes in the royal household culminating in Alexander's withdrawal to Illyria after Philip's marriage to Cleopatra. His restoration through the good offices of Demaratus.*

1. Φιλίππου δὲ στρατεύοντος κτλ.: in 340, following his failure to capture Perinthus, largely because of the support given by the Persian satraps and the Byzantines; see Diod. 16. 76. 3, 77. 2–3, with Welles's notes in the Loeb edition.

κύριος . . . τῆς σφραγῖδος: Master of the Royal Seal and therefore regent of Macedonia. For the view that Antipater and Parmenio were both away campaigning with Philip see Schachermeyr 499, n. 35, who cites Theopompus, *F. Gr. Hist.* no. 115, fr. 217. His evidence is not decisive and more probably Antipater remained with Alexander, as Isocrates (*Ep.* 4) suggests. On his death-bed Alexander handed his ring to Perdiccas, who was thereby acknowledged as regent (Diod. 17. 117. 3; 18. 2. 4). The seal-ring would be used to sign all official correspondence.

Ἀλεξανδρόπολιν: Steph. Byz. s.v. Ἀλεξάνδρειαι (3). It was, as

Plutarch's συμμίκτους implies, a military colony (which could be settled by a subject) which later attributed itself, possibly with truth, to Alexander and took his name (Tarn 2. 248–9). To have founded a *city* (πόλις) bearing his name would have been an act of rebellion by Alexander. As Philip and Alexander were still on good terms it is quite credible that Alexander was acting with his father's approval, and imitating the founding of Philippopolis in Thrace two years earlier: on Philippopolis see Theopompus, fr. 110 (with Jacoby's note); cf. Diod. 16. 71. 1–2.

Philip was perhaps trying to consolidate Alexander's position as crown prince; note the prominent position assigned to Alexander in the Battle of Chaeroneia (below).

Μαίδων: One of the most powerful Thracian tribes, on the upper Strymon, separated by Mt. Kerkine from the Paeonians (Thuc. 2. 98). The Maedi were repeatedly at war with the Macedonian kings and were later allies of Rome against Macedon. Finally subdued by Rome in 29 B.C.

2. Χαιρωνείᾳ: The famous battle fought on the 7th of Metageitnion (*Cam.* 19), probably 2 August 338. Diod. 16. 86 provides our only detailed account of the battle; Alexander supported by several experienced generals commanded the Macedonian left; for his part in the action see §§ 3–4, τοῦ Ἀλεξάνδρου φιλοτιμουμένου τῷ πατρὶ τὴν ἰδίαν ἀνδραγαθίαν ἐνδείξασθαι καὶ φιλοτιμίας ὑπερβολὴν οὐκ ἀπολείποντος. Diod. confirms that the breakthrough was first made on Alexander's wing. On the topography of the area and the tactics of the battle see esp. N. G. L. Hammond, *Klio* (1938), 186–218, and W. K. Pritchett, *AJA* 62 (1958), 307–11, with plates 80–1.

τῷ ἱερῷ λόχῳ: A picked corps of 300 men, formed in 378 and maintained at public expense; traditionally organized as pairs of lovers, they played a large part in the Theban victories at Tegyra (375) and Leuctra (371), where they acted as shock troops: see H. W. Parke in *OCD*, s.v. Sacred Band. The discovery of 254 skeletons in 7 rows has confirmed the statement of Pausanias (9. 40. 10) and Strabo (9. 414) that the famous Lion Monument surmounted a common grave of the Thebans; there can be little doubt that the dead of the Sacred Band were buried here; see Pritchett op. cit. 310–11, who rejects Hammond's contention (218) that the monument marks the position of the dead on the Macedonian right.

3. ἐδείκνυτο: Plutarch had certainly seen 'Alexander's oak'; see Theander 19–20.

τὸ πολυάνδριον: On its discovery by Soteriades see Pritchett, op.cit.308; it contained fourth-century vases and the points of Macedonian *sarissae*.

5. τοὺς γάμους: A list of Philip's 'wives' in Athenaeus 13. 557 c; cf. Beloch 3. 2. 68–73 (with table). They were all political connections and were 'married' only for the duration of a campaign.

δυσζήλου καὶ βαρυθύμου: 'exceedingly jealous and resentful'—both very derogatory. The former is coupled with φιλόφθονον (*Mor.* 91 b) and βασκανόν (*Mor.* 471 a), the latter is used of Carthage, πόλιν ἄνωθεν ἐχθρὰν καὶ βαρύθυμον (*Cat. Mai.* 26, 3).

6. ἐκφανεστάτην: sc. αἰτίαν, or perhaps better διαφοράν.

ἐν τοῖς Κλεοπάτρας γάμοις: Athenaeus 13. 557 d–e, (560 c); Pausanias 8. 7. 7; Arr. 3. 6. 5; Justin 9. 5. 9; 9. 7. 2–6. Arrian (loc. cit.) calls Cleopatra Eurydice, which Berve (no. 434) suggests may have been her name before marriage (cf. Tarn 2. 262, n. 1). She was later murdered by Olympias (see ch. 10. 8). The marriage with the high-born Cleopatra threatened Alexander's succession (see Schachermeyr 79–80 and especially Badian, 'The Death of Philip II', *Phoenix* 17 (1963), 244 ff.; cf. Tarn 2. 261, n. 3).

7. γνήσιον . . . διάδοχον: Gitti (op. cit. 17) holds that this refers to Olympias and the snake—perhaps rightly; see ch. 2. 6. But Attalus also implies that this marriage was intended to produce an heir of pure Macedonian blood. Despite Plutarch's statement that this was a love match, it is possible that Philip was acting at the behest of an influential group of nobles, headed by Attalus and his father-in-law Parmenio, who were not prepared to accept the son of the barbarian Olympias as Philip's successor; see *Greece and Rome* 12 (1965), 120.

10. οὗτος μέντοι: Both words are bitterly sarcastic; on μέντοι see the examples in Denniston, 399, esp. Ar. *Nub.* 1338.

11. διέτριβεν: 'resided, stayed'. For this meaning LSJ cite only two papyri; but cf. *C. Gracch.* 19. 1; *Sull.* 11. 1; *Them.* 23. 1.

12. Δημάρατος: Berve no. 253; *RE* 4. 2705 (Kirchner). He had been Corinthian ambassador to Syracuse in 345 (*Tim.* 21, 24, 27) and was one of the leaders of the Macedonian party at Corinth (Dem. *De cor.* 295) and ξένος of the Macedonian royal family (*Mor.* 329 d; cf. ch. 37. 7, πατρῷον φίλον). He fought as a Companion at the Granicus (Arr. 1. 15. 6). For his presence at Susa see 37. 7, and for his death 56. 2.

14. συμφρονήσας: 'coming to his senses', as in chs. 71 and 73. It may also mean 'conspire with' (ch. 11. 6), or 'become aware of, understand' with a relative clause (ch. 60. 9), an accusative (*Nic.* 19), or a participle (*Nic.* 23). (See Holden's discussion at *Them.* 28. 2.)

x. *The affair of Pixodarus (1–5). The murder of Philip and its aftermath (6–8).* On this chapter Badian, *Phoenix* 17 (1963), 244 ff., is fundamental.

1. **Πιξώδαρος:** On the form of the name see Ziegler, *Rh. Mus.* 84 (1935), 370. The youngest of the five children of Hecatomnos (Beloch 3. 2. 145), he had in 340 driven out his sister Ada (see ch. 22) who retired to Alinda, where she maintained herself until the arrival of Alexander (334). The troubles in Persia following the death of King Ochos in 338 had encouraged Pixodarus to embark on an independent policy and he naturally approached Philip whose intention of invading Asia was already known. Seeing the troubles in the Macedonian court he withdrew his offer and returned to his former allegiance. He married his daughter to Orontobates, who became joint satrap with him and at his death (? spring 334) succeeded him (Diod. 16. 74. 2).

Ἀρριδαίῳ: Younger than Alexander, and half-witted (see ch. 77. 7). That Alexander could suppose that Philip intended to replace him with the weak-minded Arrhidaeus shows conclusively how precarious he felt his position to be and the hollowness of his reconciliation with his father. For his date of birth see C. Ehrhardt, *CQ*, 1967, 297.

Ἀριστόκριτον: Perhaps the tragic actor who was present at the wedding-feast in Susa in 324 (Berve no. 125).

τῆς μητρός: Olympias was still in Epirus, where she remained until Philip's death. Her part in the affair may well be due to a hostile source.

εἰσοικειοῦντος: ἅπ. λεγ. Cf. Thuc. 3. 65, οἰκειοῦν ἐς τὴν ξυγγένειαν.

2. **Θεσσαλόν:** The head of a troupe of actors (*Mor.* 334 d–f), victorious at the Dionysia in 347 and 340 (*IG* 2², 2318, 2320) and for the second time at the Lenaea in 347 (*IG* 2², 2325). He took part in the tragic contest at Tyre (ch. 29), and probably joined Alexander in Egypt— ἧκον δὲ αὐτῷ οἱ ἀμφὶ ταῦτα τεχνῖται ἐκ τῆς Ἑλλάδος οἱ δοκιμώτατοι (Arr. 3. 1. 4).

On the importance of actors in political negotiations at this period and their organization into guilds see A. W. Pickard-Cambridge's fascinating chapter, 'The Artists of Dionysus' in *Dramatic Festivals*, 286 ff.

3. **αἰσθόμενος † ὄντα:** No satisfactory solution has yet been found for this crux. νοσοῦντα (Kronenberg, *Mnemos.* (1927), 72) is palaeographically excellent, but there is no reason to suppose Alexander was ill (and would a sick man have been so treated?). All that can reasonably be said is that ὄντα appears to be the end of a participle and that δωμάτιον must be A.'s room. There may be a substantial lacuna

25

before ὄντα, and a finite verb (e.g. εἰσῄει) may have been lost before (or after) εἰς τὸ δ. The general sense of the passage may be rendered thus: 'Philip, perceiving that A. . . ., [entered] his room, taking as a witness (παραλαβών) Philotas, the son of Parmenio, one of A.'s friends and contemporaries . . .'.

Φιλώταν: See ch. 48. It may have been Philotas who informed the king of Alexander's action. There is no other evidence that he was a friend of Alexander and his father was now the son-in-law of his bitter enemy, Attalus. It is significant that Alexander's friends were exiled, but not Philotas.

Καρὸς ἀνθρώπου: 'a *mere* Carian' (Stewart). For criticism of this version see Badian, 245, who points out that the explanation given here is refuted by the fact that Philip treated Alexander's action as high treason. This is shown by the treatment of Thessalus and A.'s friends.

4. ἀναπέμψωσιν: 'refer to a higher authority', as at *Phoc.* 33, *Mor.* 714 c, and often in the gospels.

Ἅρπαλον: ch. 8. 3.

Νέαρχον: Berve no. 544; Pearson, *LHA* 112–49. Fragments and Testimonia in *F. Gr. Hist.* no. 133; translated *HA* 100–49.

A native of Crete, he later settled in Amphipolis and called himself a Macedonian. He was honoured (perhaps *c.* 336) by the people of Delphi with προξενία and the usual privileges; the reason for this is unknown (see *GHI* 2. 182). In 334 he was appointed governor of Lycia and Pamphylia and later held a command in the hypaspists. But it was as a naval officer and author that he won fame. Appointed to command the entire fleet in 326 during its voyage down the Hydaspes, he was sent by Alexander to find a sea-route from India to Persia and to obtain exact information about the sea-coast (Arr. *Ind.* 20. 2 ff.). Between 320 and 310 (Berve 2. 272) he wrote a (?) Παράπλους τῆς Ἰνδικῆς possibly in reply to Onesicritus' book (*F. Gr. Hist.* 2D, 446; Brown, 106), commencing with the building of the fleet on the Hydaspes and ending probably with an account of Alexander's plans for the Arabian expedition. It was used extensively by Arrian in his *Indike*, by the geographers Strabo and Eratosthenes, and by Cleitarchus.

Ἐρίγυιον: Berve no. 302. A native of Mytilene, he commanded the allied cavalry in the three great battles and, after their discharge, was put in charge of part of the mercenary cavalry. He was appointed to the Companions and entrusted with important independent commands; his best-known exploit was the killing, in single combat, of the Persian leader Satibarzanes (Arr. 3. 28. 2 f., Curt. 7. 4. 33 ff.).

For his part in the arrest of Philotas see Curt. 6. 8. 17. The cause of his death in 327 is unknown.

Πτολεμαῖον: Berve no. 668. A distant connection of the royal house through his mother. He was one of Alexander's ἑταῖροι, but held no independent command until 331 (Arr. 3. 18. 9). After he became a bodyguard in 330 (Arr. 3. 27. 5) he was employed extensively in command of detachments, e.g. in the capture of Bessus (43. 6 n.); but, although he distinguished himself on the march to India, he was never one of Alexander's leading generals. On the death of Alexander he chose Egypt as his satrapy, and played a cautious but shrewd part in the wars of the Successors. He took the title of king in 305 and founded the Ptolemaic dynasty. Subsequently he wrote a *History of Alexander*, which Arrian used as his main source; for the time of writing see Introduction, page lv, n. 1.

The fragments and testimonia in *F. Gr. Hist.* no. 138; trans. *HA* 183 ff. Of earlier work on the *History* H. Strasburger, *Ptolemaios und Alexander* (Leipzig, 1934), retains its value. See more recently Tarn 2 (Index s.v.); Pearson, *LHA* 188 ff. (with Badian's remarks in *Gnomon* 33 (1961), 665 f.); *RE* 23, 2467 ff. (Wirth); C. B. Welles, 'The Reliability of Ptolemy as a Historian', *Miscellanea Rostagni* 101 ff.

ἐκ Μακεδονίας μετέστησεν: In placing the exile of Alexander's companions at a time 'when A. had incurred Philip's suspicion after his marriage to Cleopatra', Arr. (3. 6. 5) does not contradict Plutarch. He mentions the episode in a brief flashback to introduce Harpalus and explain concisely who he was. He naturally does not relate the Pixodarus' affair, but gives merely a general indication of time, sufficient for his purpose.

Arrian adds to the list of those exiled Laomedon, the brother of Erigyios (Berve no. 464).

6. ἐπεὶ δὲ Παυσανίας: Diod. 16. 93–4 (the main account); Arist. *Pol.* 1311ᵇ2; Justin 9. 6. 4–7. 14; *POxy.* 1798. See also Berve 2. 309.

Pausanias (no. 614) had when a youth ('primis pubertatis annis', Justin 9. 6. 5) *c.* 344 been grossly outraged by Attalus and, failing to obtain satisfaction from Philip, had stabbed the king to death at the wedding of Philip's daughter, Cleopatra, to Alexander of Epirus in 336. He was probably killed by Alexander's bodyguards, not crucified (presumably after a formal trial), as stated by the writer of *POxy.* 1798. See Welles on Diod. 16. 95. 4. Plutarch, as is evident from his mention of (the other) Cleopatra, wrongly regards the outrage as recent. Diodorus and Aristotle assign a purely personal motive to the crime, but it is not credible that after eight years Pausanias decided without prompting to kill Philip. The official version made the three Lyncestian princes responsible; later Alexander accused Darius of boasting that he had bribed Pausanias to murder Philip (Arr. 2. 14. 5). For a refutation of these accounts and convincing arguments that Alexander was implicated in the murder see Badian, *Phoenix* 17 (1963), 244 ff. Plutarch does not refer to the Lyncestians or the Persian king, since he is interested in the event only in so far as it affects Alexander. Berve 2. 285 ff., and Kaerst 1. 318 think it at least possible that Olympias was guilty; but as she was still in Epirus she cannot have been directly concerned.

7. προενέγκασθαι: 'cited'. Cf. Diod. 14. 109, 16. 92, ποιήματα; *Mor.* 622 a, στίχους = *versus recitare.*

τὸ . . . ἰαμβεῖον: *Med.* 288, where Euripides alludes to Creon, Jason and Creusa. Alexander means Attalus, Philip, and Cleopatra.

8. τοὺς συναιτίους: So Diod. 17. 2. 1; Justin, 11. 2. 1. The Lyncestians Heromenes and Arrhabaeus were executed without trial (cf. Arr. 1. 25. 1). The former king, Amyntas III, disappears—murdered by Alexander (Justin 12. 6. 14). Attalus was assassinated in Asia Minor on Alexander's orders. He is said, probably correctly, to have been intriguing with the Athenians and later to have attempted to prove his loyalty by sending Alexander a letter he had received from Demosthenes; cf. *Dem.* 23. 2 (cited on ch. 11. 6), Diod. 17. 2. 3 f., 5. 1.

ἀναζητήσας: 'searching out', unclassical in this sense. Cf. ch. 42. 1, *Arat.* 40. 2.

τὴν Κλεοπάτραν: Philip's wife, not her own daughter. Justin (9. 7. 12) says that Cleopatra was forced to hang herself after seeing her infant daughter murdered in her arms. According to Pausanias (8. 7. 7) they were both roasted over a brazier.

XI. *Alexander deals with revolutionary movements among the Greeks and the neighbouring barbarians. The destruction of Thebes. (336–335 B.C.).*

1. ἔτη γεγονὼς εἴκοσι: So Aristobulus (Arr. 7. 28. 1), Justin 11. 1. 9; Arr. 1. 1. 1, says *about* 20. As Philip was probably killed in June 336 (see Welles on Diod. 16. 94. 3 (Loeb ed.)), Alexander was a little under 20 at his accession. For his date of birth, see ch. 3. 5.

τὴν βασιλείαν . . . ἔχουσαν: Justin 11. 1. 5 ff.; *Mor.* 327 c (very rhetorical). Alexander's wish (see ch. 5. 6) has been fulfilled.

2. οὔτε τὴν Ἑλλάδα κρατήσας: For the situation in Greece see, e.g., Tarn 1. 4–5; Wilcken, 64 ff. (based on Diod. 17. 3). Plutarch concentrates, rightly in view of his aims, on Alexander's determination; he omits entirely Alexander's first expedition to Greece in 336, when he secured successively recognition from the Thessalian League as τάγος, from the Amphictyones as ἡγεμών and from the συνέδριον of the Corinthian League as ἡγεμών and στρατηγὸς αὐτοκράτωρ: see Diod. 17. 3–4 (much abbreviated), Arr. 1. 1. 1–3.

4. αὐτὸς ἀπ᾽ ἐναντίων λογισμῶν …: We need not doubt that Alexander, typically, disregarded the advice of his advisers (? Antipater chiefly), although Plutarch is concerned to stress Alexander's boldness and strategic grasp.

ἐπιβησομένων: ἐπιθησομένων (Solanus); but cf. *Arist.* 18, 3; *Arat.* 38, 4.

5. τὰ βαρβαρικὰ … κινήματα: Arr. 1. 1. 4 ff.; Diod. 17. 8. 1 ff.; Strabo 7. 301 (citing Ptolemy); cf. Curt. 6. 3. 2, 9. 6. 20. Alexander's object was to secure his rear in view of the impending invasion of Asia. For his strategy, Fuller, 219 ff., Burn, 63, Wilcken, 67; his route, Schachermeyr, 92–3 and notes 46, 47; Fuller, 220; the effects of his campaign, Wilcken, 69—'it was almost 50 years before the Celts invaded Macedonia and Greece'.

Σύρμον ἐνίκησε: Arr. 1. 2. The Triballi were situated in modern Bulgaria, and were being driven towards Macedonia by the pressure of the Celts (*RE* s.v. *Τριβαλλοί* (Polaschek)). Aristophanes (*Av.* 1520 ff.) caricatures their barbarity.

τὸν Ἴστρον: Alexander actually crossed the river and defeated the Getae (Arr. 1. 4. 3 ff.).

6. Θηβαίους δ᾽ ἀφεστάναι: Arr. 1. 7–8; Diod. 17. 8. 2 ff.; Justin 11. 2. 7 ff. (very confused); *Dem.* 23. 2; Polyaenus 4. 3. 12. On the versions of Arr. and Diod. see *F. Gr. Hist.* 2D, 486—on Cleitarchus fr. 1.

διὰ Πυλῶν: Thermopylae, the Gates of Greece: cf. Herod. 7. 201; Arr. 1. 7. 5. For their importance in 352 see, e.g., Dem. 4. 16 f., Diod. 16. 38. 1 f.

Δημοσθένει … ἀποκαλοῦντι: cf. *Dem.* 23. 2, καὶ τὸ βῆμα κατεῖχεν ὁ Δ., καὶ πρὸς τοὺς ἐν Ἀσίᾳ στρατηγοὺς τοῦ βασιλέως ἔγραφε, τὸν ἐκεῖθεν ἐπεγείρων πόλεμον Ἀλεξάνδρῳ, παῖδα καὶ Μαργίτην ἀποκαλῶν αὐτόν. That Demosthenes referred to Alexander as Margites is confirmed by Aeschines 3. 160, ἐπωνυμίαν δ᾽ Ἀλεξάνδρῳ Μαργίτην ἐτίθετο. Margites was the hero of a satirical poem of the same name attributed to Homer. He had never grown up mentally and the word came to be used as a synonym for 'an imbecile'. Probably Demosthenes sneers at Alexander's desire to rival Achilles, whereas (it is suggested) he resembles the silly hero of the *Margites.* ἀποκαλοῦντι, 'calling contemptuously', as at ch. 48. 5, Φιλώτας Ἀ. μειράκιον ἀπεκάλει. The word may have a good sense, e.g. *Sull.* 34. 2, σωτῆρα καὶ πατέρα τὸν Σ. ἀποκαλοῦντες. For both senses, *Caes.* 61. 9–10.

7. προσμείξας: 'approaching', not 'attacking' (as Wyttenbach); cf. *Tim.* 12. 5 (T.) ἤκουσεν ἄρτι προσμιγνύναι τὸν ῾Ικέτην τῷ πολιχνίῳ (where neither commander had entered the village).

ἐξῆτει Φοίνικα καὶ Προθύτην: Nothing further is known of these men. Berve (nos. 809, 661), following A. Schaefer, *Demosthenes u. seine Zeit* ed. 2 (Leipzig, 1887) 3. 117, n. 2, regards the story as fiction designed to exculpate Alexander and points out that neither Arr. nor Diod. mentions such a demand. But neither gives a detailed account of the preliminaries to the attack, and Alexander certainly waited for some time to see if the Thebans would surrender. Ziegler (*RE* 23. 978 f.) accepts Plutarch's version and suggests that βοιωταρχοῦντες ἔστιν οἵ (Arr. 1. 7. 11) may include the two men. Berve (locc. citt.), rather inconsistently, accepts them as leaders of the anti-Macedonian faction.

8. Φιλώταν καὶ Ἀντίπατρον: Schaefer (loc. cit.) and Berve (nos. 808, 94) again reject Plutarch's version, largely on the ground that Antipater was not at Thebes. But this objection is not decisive; Philotas is known from Diod. 17. 8. 7 to have been the Macedonian commander in the Cadmeia; Antipater may then be taken to be his second-in-command (not otherwise known), or, if we hold that the famous Antipater is meant, we may suppose that he is mentioned as the leading Macedonian general. The demand is obviously not meant seriously. Cf. the Theban proclamation mentioned at Diod. 17. 9. 5.

10. τὴν Καδμείαν: The citadel of Thebes, in which (as at Corinth and Chalcis) Philip had established a garrison after Chaeroneia (Diod. 16. 87. 3).

11. καλλωπισαμένου: Plutarch indicates by the use of this verb that Alexander was guilty of deception; cf. *Caes.* 28. 7, where the same word is used of Pompey's feigned reluctance to become dictator. Plutarch is clearly correct, since Alexander could have resisted the demands of the allies. No doubt he wished, as Plutarch says, to frighten the rest of the Greeks into obedience, which he did (Arr. 1. 10. 1 f.).

Φωκεῖς καὶ Πλαταιεῖς: Arr. (1. 8. 8) mentions them as serving with Alexander. Diod. (17. 13. 5) gives Thespians, Plataeans, and Orchomenians, and Justin (11. 3. 8) adds the Phocians. Diod. (17. 14. 1) says the decision was entrusted to the κοινὸν συνέδριον, but it is clear from Arr. 1. 9. 9 that only the allies who had taken part in the attack are meant. Nevertheless Diodorus is probably technically correct. Alexander must (surely) have called out the members of the League to deal with the rebels *against the League* (not against himself); he now handed over the rebels to the loyal members for judgement. In view of Thebes' record (Arr. 1. 9. 7, Diod. 17. 14. 2) and the hatred of her opponents, however, the decision could not be doubtful. The responsibility is Alexander's.

12. ὑπεξελόμενος: Arr. 1. 9. 9–10 says that all the survivors, including women and children, were sold πλὴν ἱερέων τε καὶ ἱερειῶν καὶ ὅσοι ξένοι Φιλίππου ἢ Ἀλεξάνδρου ἢ ὅσοι πρόξενοι Μακεδόνων ἐγένοντο. Aelian (*VH* 13. 7) points out that Philip had been a hostage in Thebes in his youth (see Diod. 16. 2. 2 ff.).

Arrian adds (as a λόγος) that Pindar's house and descendants were spared because of Alexander's reverence for Pindar. Instinsky, *Historia*, 10 (1961), 248, however, while not denying this, has drawn attention to the statement of Dio Chr. (2. 33), ignored by historians, that they were saved because Pindar had composed an encomium of Alexander I (see frags. 106 a, b (Bowra)). He points out that the obligation entailed by this εὐεργεσία passed to the king's descendants. He remarks also that the others spared (priests, ξένοι) were 'under the protection of the Gods'. This neglects τοὺς ὑπεναντιωθέντας τοῖς ψηφισαμένοις τὴν ἀπόστασιν.

περὶ τρισμυρίους γενομένους: So Diod. 17. 14. 1, Aelian, loc. cit., who also give 6,000 Thebans killed. Tarn (1. 7, n. 2), however, regards the figure of 30,000 as conventional, referring to the figures for the Tyrian captives. Reckoning the price of slaves at this time as 3 to 4 minae, he calculates on the basis of the 440 talents realized by their sale (Diod. 17. 14. 4) that they numbered only about 7,500. But although Arr. (2. 24. 5) gives 30,000 captives at Tyre, Diod. (17. 46. 4) gives 13,000, and there is no evidence for the price of slaves at this time (Welles on Diod. 17. 14. 4).

As the entire surviving population was enslaved, there seems no reason to doubt the figure of 30,000.

XII. *The Episode of Timocleia.*

Plutarch tells the story again at *Mor.* 259 d–260 d (= *Mulierum Virtutes* 24) in greater detail and from a different point of view. At *Mor.* 1093 c it is expressly attributed to Aristobulus (fr. 2), who is evidently the source here; see Introd. p. li and the works of Stadter and Rabe. Polyaenus (8. 40) follows Plutarch (with some errors); see Stadter, ch. 2.

1. ὁ δὲ ἡγεμών: Wrongly called Θρᾷξ by Plutarch, and Θρᾷξ ἵππαρχος by Polyaenus. This is a mere slip on the part of Plutarch, who is not concerned with the details of the story and who tells us in the same passage that he was a Macedonian called Alexander (ὁμώνυμος ἦν τοῦ βασιλέως), and commanded a troop of Thracian cavalry (ἦρχε δὲ Θρᾳκίου τινος ἴλης). For their presence (later) in Alexander's army, see Berve I. 134.

Τιμοκλείας: The sister of Theagenes, who commanded the phalanx at Chaeroneia and was killed there (*Mor.* 259 d; cf. Dinarchus 1. 74).

3. **ἀνήχθη**: 'was brought up as a prisoner', LSJ 1. 11. Cf. *Luc.* 12. 5, ἐν δὲ τοῖς ἁλοῦσιν ἀνήχθη καὶ Μάριος; Arr. 4. 22. 2.

XIII. *Alexander and Athens. He repents of his treatment of Thebes.*

1. **Ἀθηναίοις δὲ διηλλάγη**: For the details see Arr. 1. 10. 2 ff., Diod. 17. 15, *Dem.* 23. 3 ff., *Phoc.* 17. 2 ff., Justin 11. 4. 9 ff., Suidas, s.v. Ἀντίπατρος.

The Athenians had sent the Thebans a quantity of arms and on the motion of Demosthenes had voted to assist them, but had taken no action (Diod. 17. 8. 5 f.). Alexander demanded the surrender of either eight or ten of the leading Athenian statesmen—details in Arr., Plut. *Dem.* (cf. *Phoc.*), Suidas; they are discussed by Jacoby at *F. Gr. Hist.* no. 76, fr. 39, and Berve 1. 240, 2. 377—but on the appeal of Phocion and Demades he withdrew the demand. Charidemus alone was exiled, and went to the Persian court (Arr., Diod., Justin, locc. citt.).

Nevertheless it is clear that several others left Athens at this time. Ephialtes (Berve no. 329) and Thrasybulus (Berve no. 378) are found fighting on the Persian side at Halicarnassus (Diod. 17. 25. 6) while Chares (Berve no. 819) was at Sigeium in 334 (Arr. 1. 12. 1) and two years later surrendered Mytilene to the Macedonian admiral Hegelochus (Arr. 3. 2. 6, Curt. 4. 5. 22).

τὴν τῶν μυστηρίων ἑορτήν: The Eleusinian mysteries, held from 15th to 23rd Boedromion (Sept./Oct.).

ὑπὸ πένθους: Arr. (loc. cit.) is nearer the mark—τὰ μὲν μυστήρια ἐκπλαγέντες ἐξέλιπον. The Athenians brought in their possessions from the country, expecting to have to stand a siege.

τοῖς καταφυγοῦσιν: Despite the order of the *koinon synedrion* that no Greek city should shelter a Theban (Diod. 17. 14. 3).

2. **ἀλλ' εἴτε μεστὸς ὤν** . . .: For the simile cf. *Dem.* 23. 5 (Demades receives bribes to intercede with Alexander) εἴτε τῇ φιλίᾳ πιστεύων εἴτε προσδοκῶν μεστὸν εὑρήσειν ὥσπερ λέοντα φόνου κεκορεσμένον. The reasons given by Plutarch for Alexander's clemency throw an interesting light on his own psychology, but do not adequately explain Alexander's conduct. Although Alexander may well have admired Athens, considerations of policy will have weighed heavily with him.

It would have been rash of him to embark on a siege which might prove long and difficult, for the Athenians had naval superiority and with the sea open to them might hope for effective support from Persia. After Chaeroneia Philip had thought it prudent to make peace with Athens, even though he had 2,000 Athenian prisoners in his hands. The Greek states were cowed for the moment, but they were by no means friendly to Macedon. Moreover the situation in Athens did not require force, since the pro-Macedonian faction was in power, while the campaign in Asia, where Parmenio had suffered a number of reverses during 335, required his urgent attention.

προσέχειν ἐκέλευσε: cf. Plut. *Phoc.* 17. 8, where Alexander makes this statement after listening to Phocion's advice to make war on Persia, rather than attack Athens. The remark is suspect; Droysen 1. 96, n. 24.

3. ὕστερον μέντοι: We hear (Arr. 2. 15. 2 ff.) of the release of the Theban ambassadors to Darius captured after Issus, although the Athenian and Spartan envoys were detained. So Plutarch (*Mor.* 181 b) relates that Alexander set free the Theban mercenaries, but kept the Athenian and Thessalian. Nevertheless Thebes was not rebuilt during Alexander's lifetime.

4. τὸ περὶ Κλεῖτον ἔργον: See chs. 50 ff.

τὴν . . . ἀποδειλίασιν: Ch. 62.

εἰς μῆνιν ἀνῆγε Διονύσου: For this see Arr. 4. 8. 2 (a λόγος), and 4. 9. 5 where some of the seers give the wrath of Dionysus as the cause of the tragedy. At Curt. 8. 2. 6 Alexander thinks of this reason himself.

XIV. *Alexander meets Diogenes. He visits Delphi. Orpheus' statue sweats.*

1. εἰς τὸν Ἰσθμόν: i.e. at Corinth, during Alexander's *first* visit to Greece in 336 (before the events described in ch. 11. 5, which took place in 335)—Arr. 1. 1. 2; Diod. 17. 4. 9.

ἡγεμὼν ἀνηγορεύθη: Plutarch uses ἡγεμών in a non-technical sense, 'was proclaimed leader'. The office of ἡγεμών, the federal general elected for life by the delegates of the Greek states, is to be distinguished from the στρατηγὸς αὐτοκράτωρ (the ἡγεμών in his military aspect, Kaerst 1. 553, n. 1) appointed for a particular campaign. In 337 Philip was appointed ἡγεμών and *at a later meeting* in the same year was chosen στρατηγὸς αὐτοκράτωρ for the campaign against Persia. Certainly Alexander must have been appointed ἡγεμών before his appointment as στρατηγὸς αὐτοκράτωρ, whether this took place at the same meeting or not: see Wilcken 64 ff.

On the Corinthian League see esp. Wilcken 43 ff., Kaerst 1. 530 ff.; *GHI* 2. 177. For an up-to-date bibliography, Bengtson, 316, n. 3: *add* J. A. O. Larsen, *Representative Government in Greek and Roman History* (Berkeley, 1955), esp. 49, 52; T. T. B. Ryder, *Koine Eirene* (Oxford, 1965), 102 ff., 150 ff.

2. Διογένην τὸν Σινωπέα: The famous Cynic (ὁ κύων), born at Sinope on the Black Sea, who was exiled and came to Athens. He spent most of his life there, but also visited Corinth. The story of their meeting is doubtless a fiction, one of the many legends which grew up around Diogenes: Arr. (7. 2. 1) gives it only as a λόγος. It was a famous anecdote: Plutarch tells it three times elsewhere (*Mor.* 331 ff, 605 d, 782 a), and Berve (2. 417, n. 3) lists no fewer than 22 references. Diogenes always gets the better of Alexander, who sometimes appears as the Great King, an obvious anachronism. Elsewhere (Diog. Laert. 6. 79) Diogenes is said to have died on the same day as Alexander, although his death is probably to be placed somewhat later.

On the legends surrounding Diogenes see K. von Fritz, *Philologus Supplementband*, 1926, Heft 3 (p. 27 for this incident); cf. D. R. Dudley, *A History of Cynicism* (London, 1937), ch. 2; Brown 24–38, esp. 28.

3. ἐν τῷ Κρανείῳ: One of the pleasantest suburbs of Corinth, to the east of the city, where there was a grave of Diogenes near the city gate (*RE* 11, 1571).

4. διέβλεψεν εἰς τὸν Ἀλέξανδρον: 'looked A. straight in the face'. For the compound see Burnet on Plato *Phaedo* 86 b.

6. ἦλθεν εἰς Δελφούς: This anecdote is generally considered to be fiction, but Tarn (2. 338 ff.) has argued vigorously that it is historical. He bases his case on Diod. 17. 93. 4, where Alexander is said to have been called ἀνίκητος by the Pythia, and on a Delphic inscription (*SIG* 251 H) recording the gift late in 336 of 150 'Philips' to the treasurers of the temple. He is probably correct in thinking the donor to be Alexander, who will have visited Delphi on his way home from Corinth. If this is correct, his visit was doubtless included in the records of the priests; but it is difficult to credit that Plutarch found the Pythia's words recorded there. As Tarn himself admits (2. 346), no oracle was given to Alexander. No great weight need be given to Diodorus' unsupported statement; it is probable that his source was Cleitarchus (? from Onesicritus; see on ch. 62. 2). It is more likely that the story was invented after Alexander's death 'to provide a proper sanction for the traditional epithet' (Parke–Wormell 1. 240, who see in the anecdote about Philomelus (Diod. 16. 25. 3, 27. 1) the model for it—1. 231, n. 21). Berve (*Gnomon* 5 (1929), 376, n. 2) is probably correct in seeing the origin of the title in a proposal by Demosthenes to erect in

324 at Athens a statue of Alexander as θεὸς ἀνίκητος. The text of the passage (Hypereides *Adv. Dem.* 32. 4) is mutilated and the adjective depends on restoration but is accepted by G. Colin in the Budé edition and by A. D. Nock (*Harv. Stud.* 41 (1930), 2, n. 1).

κατὰ τύχην ἡμερῶν ἀποφράδων οὐσῶν: This statement is the only evidence for the occurrence of *dies nefasti* at Delphi. It has been held (by W. R. Halliday, *The Greek Questions of Plutarch* (Oxford, 1928), 61 ff.; cf. Tarn 2. 338, n. 2) to show that for most of Greek history consultation of the oracle was possible every day except for a few *dies nefasti* and for the period from mid-November to mid-February when the oracle was closed. But Plutarch merely says that it happened to be a *dies nefastus* when Alexander arrived, without implying anything about the frequency of these days. Halliday's view is ruled out by Plutarch's statement at *Mor.* 292 e, ὀψὲ γὰρ ἀνείθησαν αἱ κατὰ μῆνα μαντεῖαι τοῖς δεομένοις, πρότερον δ' ἅπαξ ἐθεμίστευεν ἡ Πυθία τοῦ ἐνιαυτοῦ, 'For it was only lately that oracular answers were given to enquirers every month (i.e. *once* every month, as *Mor.* 398 a makes clear); formerly the Pythia gave answers only once a year.' H. W. Parke (*CQ* 37 (1943), 19 ff.) points out that by using πρότερον Plutarch clearly envisages only annual and monthly consultation. Whether the change had taken place by Alexander's time is uncertain. Parke (loc. cit.), holding that ὀψέ was used by Plutarch's authorities, Anaxandrides and Callisthenes (*F. Gr. Hist.* no. 124, fr. 49), believes that it occurred during the First Sacred War (*c.* 590 B.C.). But it is at least as likely that ὀψέ and πρότερον are Plutarch's own words and that annual consultation was still in operation in 336. In times of crisis (as, e.g., in 480) extraordinary consultations may have been possible, and by the middle of the fourth century a system of giving oracles by lot was in operation at Delphi; for this see P. Amandry in *BCH* 63 (1939), 183 ff., and on the whole matter the same writer's *La mantique apollinienne à Delphes* (Paris, 1950), 32 ff., 81 ff., and Parke–Wormell 1. 17 ff.

τὴν πρόμαντιν: The Pythia, the representative of the God and the oracle of his prophecies.

7. βίᾳ . . . εἷλκεν: Hardly 'He took her arm and said "O, come along"', as Tarn 2. 346, n. 1; to say that 'any display of real force is out of the question' for Alexander misjudges his character.

8. τὸ . . . ξόανον: Arr. (1. 11. 2) relates the incident in very similar fashion, perhaps following Aristobulus (Strasburger 23). For the phenomenon of sweating statues see A. S. Pease on Cicero *De div.* 1. 98 (p. 271). Theophrastus (*Hist. Plant.* 5. 9. 8) explains that it is due to condensation (cf. Arist. *De plant.* 822ᵃ31). Sweating statues and other supernatural happenings are related by Diod. (17. 10. 4) on Alexander's arrival at Thebes.

περὶ Λείβηθρα: A city and district in Macedonian Pieria at the foot of Olympus. It was connected in myth with Orpheus (Pausanias 9. 30. 9 ff.).

9. Ἀρίστανδρος: See on ch. 2. 5. In the Romance (Ps.-Call. 1. 42. 6 f.; Iul. Val. 1. 46) the legendary seer Melampus has replaced him.

xv. *Alexander's resources at the beginning of the expedition. His visit to Troy.*

1. τῆς δὲ στρατιᾶς τὸ πλῆθος: The totals given by the various writers range from 30,000 to 43,000 for infantry, and for cavalry from 4,000 to 5,500: see the tables in Berve 1. 177, P. A. Brunt, *JHS* 83 (1963), 46. Diod. (17. 17. 4) gives a detailed list of units totalling 32,000 and 5,100; these agree with Arrian's figures and should be accepted. The higher figures for infantry given by Anaximenes (43,000) and Callisthenes (40,000) are best explained by the assumption that they include the 10,000 men sent to Asia under Parmenio in 336 (so G. T. Griffith, *Mercenaries of the Hellenistic World* (Cambridge, 1935), 13 and n. 3; Brunt, op. cit. 32 ff.). For other (less probable) views see Jacoby on Anaximenes (*F. Gr. Hist.* 2A no. 72), fr. 29. But it is by no means certain (*pace* Brunt, op. cit. 34 ff.) that they all remained to hold Abydos and joined Alexander's forces in 334. They are not included in his calculations by Marsden 24 ff., who reconciles Arrian's totals for Alexander's forces at Gaugamela, 40,000 infantry and 7,000 cavalry, by allowing for losses of 1,000 up to that point and garrisons (excluding Egypt) of about the same number. Alexander, he holds, will have withdrawn every available man for the battle. However, all calculations are to be received with caution since 'the tally of losses and garrisons is quite inaccurate or incomplete' (Brunt 34) and we have no reason to suppose that all reinforcements are recorded.

On Alexander's troops see Berve 1. 103 ff. Tarn 2. 135 ff.; cf. Marsden 65 ff. On his mercenary troops see Griffith 12 ff. On the Macedonian cavalry see Brunt 27 ff.

2. ἐφόδιον δέ . . .: Bellinger 36 ff. inclines to discount the statements of Aristobulus and Duris, and Seltman 207 thinks that Onesicritus exaggerates in order to show how well Alexander surmounted his financial difficulties. But in his speech at Opis Alexander is reported to have said that he had found less than 60 talents in the treasury at his accession, that Philip owed 500 talents, and that he had had to borrow 800 talents (Arr. 7. 9. 6, Curt. 10. 2. 24, both based *in this*

particular on Ptolemy; see Tarn 2. 296). Even if the mines at Pangaeus produced 1,000 talents annually (Diod. 16. 8. 6), Philip's outlay on the army was very large, and it is entirely credible that he was in debt at his death; see Griffith, *Greece and Rome* 12 (1965), 127. There is no doubt that Alexander was very short of money until he captured the Persian treasure at Damascus. He disbanded his fleet in the first year of the war, partly at least through lack of funds (Arr. 1. 20. 1, Diod. 17. 22. 5), and imposed contributions (*syntaxeis*) on Priene (*GHI* 2. 184 f.; on these inscriptions see Badian, *Studies . . . Ehrenberg*, 47 ff.) and presumably other cities. His need of money explains also his harsh treatment of Aspendus (Arr. 1. 26–7; see Badian, *Greece and Rome* 12 (1965), 167), and possibly his sale of the Theban captives (ch. 11. 12).

For details of Alexander's finances see Berve 1. 302 ff. and, especially, Bellinger 35 ff.

3. τῶν ἑταίρων: The Companions 'formed a pool on which Alexander drew for satraps, generals, and men to command on some special occasion or to fill some new office'. (Tarn 2. 138.) Among them were several Greeks, but only one Oriental (see 43. 7), so far as is known. For details see Berve 1. 30–7, with a list of known Companions on p. 31; *add* (in view of *Mor.* 340 d) Abdalonymus (Berve no. 1).

They are described by the Greek writers as ἑταῖροι, the correct form always used by Arrian, or as φίλοι, the Hellenistic term preferred by Diodorus; see Berve 1. 30, nn. 3, 4; Welles, *Diodorus*, 14, n. 1. Plutarch regularly calls them ἑταῖροι (see 19. 6, 20. 12, 29. 7, 31. 10, 43. 7, 45. 3, 76. 8), but occasionally φίλοι (certainly only at 34. 1 and 39. 7; cf. 67. 3, 70. 1). The present instance well illustrates Plutarch's indifference to terminology; here he uses the technical term ἑταῖροι, but at § 5 he calls the same men φίλοι (cf. 19. 5–6 where φίλων and ἑταίρων are probably the same men).

συνοικίας πρόσοδον: 'the revenue of some hamlet' (Dryden); *vici proventum* (Reiske). For this meaning of συνοικία cf. Polyb. 16. 11. 1 (Philip retreats) πορθῶν τὰ φρούρια καὶ τὰς κατὰ τὴν χώραν συνοικίας. The more common meaning, 'tenement', seems less appropriate.

ἀπονεῖμαι τῷ μὲν ἀγρόν: cf. Justin 11. 5. 5, patrimonium omne suum, quod in Macedonia Europaque habebat, amicis dividit, sibi *Asiam* sufficere praefatus'.

The story that Alexander distributed all his property (or even τὰ πλεῖστα) is obviously a romantic exaggeration; 'King's land does not vanish from Macedonian history' (Tarn 1. 14; cf. Bellinger 37 f.). But there is no reason to doubt that Alexander made lavish gifts to his officers (Kaerst 1. 334; Berve 1. 224): a gift to Ptolemy the Bodyguard is attested by *SIG* 332.

5. ἔνιοι τὸ αὐτὸ ἐποίησαν: *contra Mor.* 342 d, μόνος δὲ Περδίκκας οὐδὲν ἔλαβε διδόντος.

7. τὸν Ἑλλήσποντον διεπέρασεν: Arr. 1. 11. 6 ff.; Diod. 17. 17. 1 ff.; Justin 11. 5. 12; Aelian *VH* 12. 7.
    Alexander left Parmenio to see to the transport of the bulk of the troops from Sestos to Abydos while he sailed with sixty ships from Elaeon to the Achaean harbour near Troy. On Alexander's actions in the Troad see esp. H. U. Instinsky, *Alexander der Große am Hellespont* (Godesberg, 1949), with Walbank's comments in *JHS* 70 (1950), 79 ff.

ἀναβὰς δ' εἰς Ἴλιον: Diodorus (17. 17. 3, 18. 1) distinguishes between offerings (ἐναγίσματα) to Achilles, Ajax, and the other heroes in the Troad (cf. Justin), and a sacrifice (θυσία) to Athena after leaving there. Arr. (1. 11. 7) mentions a sacrifice to Zeus, Athena, and Herakles where A. landed, and at Ilium sacrifices to Athena and to Priam, in order that he might not be angry with the race of Neoptolemus (cf. ch. 2. 1). Wilcken 84 holds that 'this excursion to Ilium gives us a profound insight into the romantic soul of the young king'. We should remember, however, that Alexander was well aware of the value of propaganda, as Callisthenes' dispatches show.

8. ἐστεφάνωσε: Arrian (in a λόγος) and Aelian relate also that Hephaestion crowned the tomb of Patroclus, signifying that his relationship to Alexander was similar to that of Patroclus to Achilles.

ἀλειψάμενος λίπα: All English translators (punctuating after λίπα) take Plutarch to mean that Alexander anointed Achilles' *stele*; for this practice see Pausanias 10. 24. 6 (with Frazer's note). But the middle ἀλειψάμενος indicates that Alexander anointed himself (so Ax, Ruegg), or ἀλείφειν seems *always* to be used transitively; punctuate, therefore, after στήλην. For the practice of athletes of anointing themselves with oil and exercising naked see Thuc. 1. 6, Marrou 126 f.

μακαρίσας αὐτόν: cf. Arr. 1. 12. 1 (a λόγος).

9. Ἀλεξάνδρου λύραν: i.e. Paris; cf. *Mor.* 331 d, τὴν Πάριδος λύραν. **τὰ κλέα καὶ τὰς πράξεις**: cf. Homer *Il.* 9. 189.

XVI. *The Battle of the R. Granicus.*

The battle is described by Arr. 1. 13–16 and Diodorus 17. 18. 4–21. 6; cf. Justin 11. 6. 10–13. For an excellent modern analysis, Fuller 147 ff. It is clear from a comparison with Arrian's account that Plutarch uses Aristobulus; see Brunt, *JHS* 83 (1963), 27, n. 3.

1. μεγάλην δύναμιν: 20,000 cavalry and almost as many (Gk. mercenary) infantry (Arr. 1. 14. 4); 10,000 cavalry and 100,000 infantry (Diod. 17. 19. 4 f.); 600,000 troops (Justin 11. 6. 11)! Tarn 1. 16 and Schachermeyr 140 f. (with notes 84 f.) rightly think Arrian's figure for the mercenaries too high and Schachermeyr adopts Diodorus' 10,000; Fuller (loc. cit.) points out that the Persian force was clearly inferior to Alexander's. Oddly the Persian cavalry were drawn up in *front* of the infantry. Tarn (loc. cit.) holds that the object of the Persians was to kill Alexander, but Fuller (149) attributes the unusual formation to military etiquette.

τοῦ Γρανικοῦ: For the topography see Fuller loc. cit.; W. Leaf, *Strabo on the Troad* (Cambridge, 1923), 71 f.

μάχεσθαι μὲν ἴσως . . .: A difficult passage which the English translators gloss over. τῆς(Ziegler) seems necessary: 'to fight *at the same time* for the entry (into Asia) and for the empire.' (So Ax, Ruegg). Castiglioni, *Gnomon* 13 (1937), 140, assumes more extensive corruption; he proposes εἰσόδου καὶ ⟨διακινδυνεύειν ἐξ⟩ ἀρχῆς, but probably unnecessarily.

2. Δαισίου: Corresponding to the Attic Thargelion (May/June). Cf. *Cam.* 19. 7. At *Arat.* 53, 5 it is wrongly equated with Anthesterion (Feb./Mar.); see W. H. Porter, ad loc. This prohibition was probably connected with the need to get in the harvest at this time. See the entry in the *Etym. Magn.*, p. 252, l. 29: ΔΑΙΣΙΟΣ: μὴν παρὰ Μακεδόσιν. Ἑρμηνεύται σιτογόνος.

3. Παρμενίωνος: In Arr. (1. 13. 2 ff.) Parmenio advises crossing at dawn before the enemy (who, he thinks, will encamp at some distance from the river) can oppose them. Fuller 149 misunderstands Parmenio's advice; there is no suggestion that the enemy will run away. In Diod. (17. 19. 3) Alexander does cross at dawn without opposition (see Welles ad loc.). Alexander realized the propaganda value of forcing a crossing in the teeth of Persian opposition. With his superiority in numbers, he had no doubts of the outcome.

ἀποκινδυνεύειν: 'fight *decisive* battle' cf. Thuc. 7. 81; *Alex.* 17. 3, περὶ τῶν ὅλων; *Sull.* 29. 4, περὶ τῶν ἐσχάτων; comp. *Ages./Pomp.* 4, περὶ τῶν μεγίστων.

αἰσχύνεσθαι τὸν Ἑλλήσποντον: In Arrian (1. 13. 6 f.—from Aristobulus) Alexander remarks that he should feel ashamed (αἰσχύνομαι) if, after crossing the Hellespont, he should be held up by the Granicus.
  For a list of occasions on which Alexander rejects Parmenio's advice see 33. 10 n.

σὺν ἴλαις ἱππέων τρισκαίδεκα: The eight squadrons of the Companion cavalry, the four squadrons of scouts (πρόδρομοι) and the Paeonians, as is clear from Arr. 1. 14. 6 f.

For the πρόδρομοι, sometimes called σαρισσοφόροι, see Berve 1. 129 f., Brunt, op. cit. 27 f.; Tarn 2. 157 f. They were probably Macedonian— so Berve and Brunt. Tarn (followed by Marsden 71 ff.) thinks they were Thracian.

4. παραφέροντος: 'that swept men off their feet'. For the verb see Holden on *Tim.* 28, 5 and add Diod. 18. 35. 1, ἐξεδέχετο τοὺς παραφερομένους ('carried away') ὑπὸ τοῦ ποταμοῦ.

5. ἐμφὺς τῇ διαβάσει: lit. 'clinging to'. A favourite verb with Plutarch, used both literally and metaphorically; see Holden on *Them.* 9. 3, *Nic.* 9. 1.

7. ἦν δὲ τῇ πέλτῃ . . . θαυμαστόν: This helmet, or a very similar one, is shown on the silver decadrachm issued in ?324 to commemorate Alexander's victory over the Indian king, Porus (ch. 60). There Alexander wears a helmet with a crest, or plume (χαίτη), between two very large feathers.

For these coins see Seltman 213 f., and Pl. 49 nos. 6, 7; Bellinger 27, and Pl. 1. 13; and in particular W. B. Kaiser, *JDAI* 77 (1962), 227 ff., esp. 232 f. Kaiser rightly emphasizes the realism of the coins.

ὑποπτυχίδα: 'the joint of the breastplate'.

8. Ῥοισάκου: Berve no. 687. In 344 satrap of Ionia and Lydia; succeeded by his brother Spithridates (Diod. 17. 20. 1). His later position is unknown. Beloch, 3. 2. 137, thinks the Rhoesaces mentioned here is the *son* of the satrap, but for no good reason.

Σπιθριδάτου: Berve no. 715. Diod. (loc. cit.) wrongly calls him a son-in-law of Darius, no doubt through confusion with Mithridates, who has just been killed (Arr. 1. 15. 7). At *Mor.* 326 f Plutarch refers to Mithridates and Spithridates.

The incident is variously reported. According to Arr. (1. 15. 7 ff.) Rhoesaces strikes Alexander on the helmet with a cleaver (κοπίς) and Alexander kills him with his (unbroken) lance. In Diod. (17. 20. 3 ff.) Spithridates attacks first and is killed by Alexander with his lance, already broken on Spithridates' breastplate. Rhoesaces rides up and deals Alexander a blow on his helmet; Cleitus cuts off his arm (as in Arrian).

ἐκκλίνας: 'dodging'; cf. *Mor.* 584 d, ἐν μὲν γὰρ ταῖς μάχαις τὸν εὖ βάλλοντα τῶν πολεμίων ἐκκλιτέον.

οὕτως: For the emendation see Ziegler, *Rh. Mus.* 84 (1935), 370 f.

9. ὑποστήσας: The precise meaning of the verb is uncertain. 'intellige ἀναστήσας' (Ziegler), (?) following Reiske: 'videtur esse calcari compunctum equum adigere, ut in crura postica nonnihil assurgat. ὑπό in compositis saepe minuit significatum. στῆσαι equum est adigere, ut quantum potest maximam ad proceritatem, paene perpendicularem, sese attollat.' For the meaning 'stop', see Xen. *An.* 4. 1. 14, τοὺς στρατιώτας; Polyb. 1. 50. 6, τὴν ναῦν.

συνεξαναστάς: 'una cum equo assurgente' (Reiske).

10. τὴν πτέρυγα: 'the broad edge' of the scimitar. For the incident cf. also *Mor.* 327 a, 341 c.

11. ἐπαιρόμενον: With the manuscript text we must understand πληγήν with ἑτέραν; Ziegler suggests its insertion after πάλιν. But there is no exact parallel to ἐπαίρομαι πληγήν; the verb governs the weapon used, e.g. *Caes.* 39. 7, τὴν μάχαιραν; cf. *Mor.* 185 b. There is much to be said for Bryan's proposal to insert εἰς before ἑτέραν; or perhaps better πρός (easily lost after κοπίδος). The particle often occurs in third position, e.g. 16. 12. ἐπαιρόμενον would then mean 'raising himself up'.

Κλεῖτος ὁ μέλας: Berve no. 427. So-called to distinguish him from Cleitus 'The White', the infantry commander (Berve no. 428). He was the brother of Alexander's nurse, Lanike, and a man of great bravery. He commanded the Royal Squadron of the Companion cavalry from the beginning and took part in the three great battles. In 330 he and Hephaestion were appointed joint commanders of the cavalry, and in 328/7 (winter) he was designated satrap of Bactria and Sogdiana (Curt. 8. 1. 19), but did not live to take up the position. On his murder by Alexander see chapters 50 f.

12. συνῆγον αἱ πεζαὶ δυνάμεις: Since *all* the infantry on the Persian side were Greek mercenaries (Arr. 1. 14. 4), Bryan would emend αἱ πεζαί to αἱ Περσικαί or insert Περσῶν after πεζαί. But probably no change is required. Plutarch has failed to realize that the Persians had no foot-soldiers apart from the mercenaries. The subject of ὑπέστησαν (= resisted) is, of course, the Persian infantry.

13. ᾔτουν τὰ πιστά: 'they asked for terms'.

14. θυμῷ μᾶλλον ἢ λογισμῷ: Alexander's object was to discourage mercenaries from taking service with the Persians. Plutarch, characteristically, takes the charitable view that it was not due to policy, but to anger. Arr. (1. 16. 2) confirms the massacre.

15. πεζοὶ μὲν δισμύριοι: 2,000 of the (20,000) Greeks survived, and over 1,000 cavalry perished (Arr. 1. 16. 2); Diodorus gives the Persian losses as over 10,000 infantry and not less than 2,000 cavalry with over 20,000 prisoners. Fuller 154 points out that the chief Persian loss was in commanders; see Arr. 1. 16. 3.

τῶν δὲ περὶ τὸν Ἀ.: About 25 Companions fell in the first attack and in addition more than 60 of the rest of the cavalry and 30 infantry perished (Arr. 1. 16. 4). Justin (11. 6. 12) has CXX equites (? to be emended to VXX), novem pedites. Either Aristobulus (fr. 5) gives the official version and ignores other losses or Plutarch disregards them.

16. τούτων: Plutarch is misleading or incorrect; statues of the 25 Companions only were set up at Dium in Macedonia (Arr. 1. 16. 4; Berve 2. 242 wrongly includes the infantry). As Aristobulus, living not far away, must be presumed to have known the truth, the mistake is doubtless Plutarch's. This famous group (see F. P. Johnson, *Lysippos* (1927), 224) was removed to Rome by Metellus Macedonicus after the Macedonian defeat in 148 B.C. (Vell. 1. 11. 4; Pliny *NH* 34. 64).

17. κοινούμενος δὲ τὴν νίκην: This was a diplomatic gesture to the Greeks (Wilcken 88). Although only the Greek cavalry had been engaged and the victory was in substance a Macedonian one, Alexander stresses his position as ἡγεμών of the Corinthian League. The Spartans are explicitly excluded; they had refused to send delegates to the congress at Corinth in 337 and were not members of the League; for their relations with Philip after Chaeroneia, see C. Roebuck, *CPhil.* (43) 1948, 86 ff. The surviving Greek mercenaries were sent to hard labour in Macedonia for contravening the resolution of the League by assisting Persia (Arr. 1. 16. 6).

According to Arrian (1. 16. 7) the inscription (which he gives in identical words) was attached to the 300 panoplies sent to Athena of Athens. He does not mention any other spoils. Plutarch's text is sound; see Ziegler, *Rh. Mus.* 84 (1935), 371.

XVII. *The conquest of coastal Asia Minor. Portents in Lycia and Pamphylia.*

After capturing Zeleia Alexander sent Parmenio to capture the important fortress of Dascylium while he marched south and accepted the surrender of Sardis. Marching south west he reached the coast at Ephesus. In Caria he detached Parmenio (who had rejoined him) to occupy Phrygia, and proceeded in midwinter along the southern coast of Asia Minor as far as Pisidia. There he turned north and rejoined Parmenio in his winter-quarters at Gordium.

Arr 1. 17–29; Diod. 17. 21. 7–22. 5, 23. 4–27. 6; Justin 11. 6. 14 f.

1. μεγάλην ... μεταβολήν: So Justin 11. 6. 14, post victoriam maior pars Asiae (sc. Minoris) ad eum defecit. For the effect of the battle see

Tarn 1. 17 ff., Wilcken 90 ff. Plutarch, who is not interested in the historical facts as such but only in Alexander's personal development, very much underestimates the Persian resistance; for this see especially Arr. 2. 1. 1 and ch. 18. 5 n. Plutarch does not mention the suppression of oligarchies and the establishment of democracies (Arr. 1. 18. 2) until 34. 2.

καὶ Σάρδεις: 'even Sardes', despite the strength of its fortress (for which see Arr. 1. 17. 5; Diod. 17. 21. 7). The seat of the Lydian satrapy, it was surrendered by its Persian commander without a fight, as were Ephesus, Magnesia, and Tralles.

πρόσχημα: probably 'bulwark'; cf. Caes. 25. 5, ἀφειστήκει μὲν οὖν πόλλα φῦλα, πρόσχημα δ' ἦσαν Ἀρβέρνοι καὶ Καρνουντῖνοι; Cam. 2 (of Veii). It may also mean 'pride, ornament', as at Herod. 5. 28, Polyb. 3. 15. 3.

2. Ἁλικαρνασσός: The capital and largest city of Caria, and the main Persian naval base commanding the southern approach to the Aegean. The defence, conducted with great skill by Memnon, is described at length by Arrian (1. 20. 2–23. 6) and Diodorus (17. 23. 4–27. 6), who perhaps uses information derived ultimately from the besieged (so Kaerst 1. 354, n. 1; Schachermeyr 505, n. 94; Tarn's theory of a *written* mercenary source (2. 71 ff.) I regard as demolished by Brunt, *CQ* N.S. 12 (1962), 141 ff.). Two of the three citadels held out for twelve months after the city was taken.

On the siege see esp. Fuller 200 ff.

Μίλητος: As at Halicarnassus the resistance was due to the presence of a large body of mercenaries.

For Alexander's route from Miletus to Phrygia see Freya Stark, *JHS* 78 (1958), 102 ff.

3. οἷον ἐνασκήσας καὶ ῥώσας αὐτόν: For ἐνασκεῖν LSJ cite only this example; see, however, Polyb. 1. 63. 9. For ῥώσας αὐτόν cf. 19. 4, Cam. 37. 3.

4. τῆς Λυκίας: Arrian merely mentions the capture of Xanthus.

αὐτομάτως: 'the word is used of phenomena for which there is no visible cause' (Gow on Theocritus 21. 27; see the whole note).

5. ἀνακαθήρασθαι: 'clear up'; cf. Caes. 58. 10; Ant. 9. 9, τὰ περιόντα τοῦ πολέμου ἀ.

μέχρι τῆς Φοινίκης καὶ Κιλικίας: Freya Stark, op. cit. 114, n. 23 suggests that Plutarch means 'the town of Phoenice (mod. Finike) and Cilicia'. I share Gomme's doubts (ad loc.), although, admittedly, the *order* of names is odd, especially as Plutarch was not ignorant of these countries. It is misleading to talk of Plutarch's source here: he is writing on the basis of his reading in several authors. He is in essence correct. Alexander had decided to clear the sea-coast of all possible Persian bases, i.e. he had in mind *at this time* the elimination of Phoenicia including Tyre. Issus was an interruption not contemplated by Alexander; the decisive conflict with Darius was to come after the Persian fleet had been neutralized. Plutarch does *not* say that Alexander actually cleared up the sea-coast, as some translators imply; ἠπείγετο denotes intention.

6. πολλοῖς . . . τῶν ἱστορικῶν: Callisthenes (*F. Gr. Hist.* no. 124, fr. 31) is generally thought to say that the sea did προσκύνησις to Alexander. See, however, Pearson, *LHA*, 36 ff. who points out that the remark may be due to the Scholiast. See also Badian's remarks (*Gnomon* 33 (1961), 661). Brown, *AJP* 83 (1962), 200, suggests that Callisthenes may have had in mind Xen. *An.* 1. 4. 18; ἐδόκει δὴ θεῖον εἶναι καὶ σαφῶς ὑποχωρῆσαι τὸν ποταμὸν Κύρῳ ὡς βασιλεύσοντι; but this would scarcely be a happy augury for Alexander. Other references in Josephus *AJ* 2. 348, ὑπεχώρησε τὸ Παμφύλιον πέλαγος . . . τοῦ θεοῦ θελήσαντος, καὶ τοῦτο πάντες ὁμολογοῦσιν οἱ τὰς Ἀλεξάνδρου πράξεις συγγραψάμενοι; Appian *BCiv.* 2. 622, τὸν Παμφύλιον κόλπον . . . διέτρεχε δαιμονίως, καὶ τὸ πέλαγος αὐτῷ τοῦ δαίμονος κατέχοντος, ἔστε παρέλθοι; Anonymous (Frag. Sabb.), *F. Gr. Hist.* 151, fr. 1 § 2, αἰφνίδιον δὲ θαυμάσιόν τι καὶ θειῶδες αὐτῷ συνέβη; Arr. 1. 26. 2 (the north winds provided a passage) οὐκ ἄνευ τοῦ θείου, ὡς αὐτός τε καὶ οἱ ἀμφ' αὐτὸν ἐξηγοῦντο; Strabo 14. 3. 9 (666), τὸ πλέον ἐπιτρέπων τῇ τύχῃ; cf. Seneca *Suas.* 1. 11.

ὑπόθεσις γραφικὴ . . . ὄγκον: 'a subject that permitted striking and bombastic treatment'. For ὄγκος cf. *Mor.* 79 b, ὁ Αἰσχύλου ὄγκος; although it is sometimes favourable in meaning. ἐκπλήττειν = *percellere animos.*

The mature Plutarch censures the extravagant rhetoric which he once practised, e.g. in the speeches *De Alex. fortuna*; cf. 3. 6 n.

σπανίως δέ ποτε: 'and only occasionally revealed beneath the cliffs and ravines of the mountain-side glimpses of tracks (πάτους) that were narrow and exposed to the wind (προσεχεῖς)'. The manuscript readings πάγους and προσηχεῖς can hardly be defended. At Homer *Od.* 5. 411 the former clearly means 'reefs', and elsewhere, e.g. *Cat. Mai.* 13. 2, it appears to mean 'cliffs'. προσηχής is not attested elsewhere, although the verb occurs at ch. 31. 11, where it means 're-echo'. Ziegler proposes προσάντεις ('steep'), but προσεχεῖς (frequent in Strabo in this sense, e.g. 5. 3. 6, 5. 4. 4) is a simpler correction.

7. δηλοῖ δὲ καὶ Μένανδρος: Menander, born in Athens in 342/1, was the 'star' of the New Comedy. For an appreciation of his work see T. B. L. Webster, *Studies in Menander* ed. 2 (Manchester, 1960), and E. W. Handley's edition of the *Dyskolos* (Methuen, 1965), the first complete play to be preserved. Since the *editio princeps* of the *Dyskolos* in 1959 considerable fragments of the *Sikyonios* and the *Misoumenos* have been published; see, e.g., *CR* N.S. 16 (1966), 294 ff. For this fragment see *CAF* 3. 240 and Menander ed. Koerte (Teubner, 1953), 2. 236 (no. 751). It cannot be doubted that this quotation derives from Plutarch's own reading which is probably responsible for the historical references to Alexander as well; see the Introduction, pp. xliii ff.

8. ἐν ταῖς ἐπιστολαῖς: On Alexander's letters see the Introduction, pp. lix f. For detailed discussion of this letter see *PACA* 4 (1961), 12. It cannot be said to conflict with Arrian (1. 26. 2), οὐκ ἄνευ τοῦ θείου, since Alexander need not have mentioned the incident esp. if he was writing to a sceptical Macedonian baron (? Antipater). By διελθεῖν Alexander must have meant the coast passage, not the road, the Climax. Plutarch is summarizing.

ὁδοποιῆσαι: 'made a road'; for the verb, cf. *Sull.* 28. 9; Arr. 1. 26. 1. The road is the so-called Climax or Ladder, not the mountain, as Strabo 14. 3. 9 (666) has it. For a description, based on autopsy, see Freya Stark, *JHS* 78 (1958), 117 f., *Geog. Jour.* 122 (1956), 298 f., with photograph opposite p. 302. διό in the following sentence shows that this was the reason for his delay in Phaselis. For his visit cf. Arr. 1. 24. 5 f.

9. Θεοδέκτου: He came to Athens and was initially a rhetor, but became famous for his tragedies with which he won 8 victories, 7 of them at the Greater Dionysia. It is generally held on the basis of Suidas' notice that he was a pupil of Aristotle and knew Alexander personally. His death at the age of 41 is put in 334 or a little earlier (so Pickard-Cambridge in *OCD*; Ernst Diehl in *RE* (Zweite Reihe) 5. 2. 1722 ff.). Capps, *AJP* 21 (1900), 38 ff., however, rightly holds, on the basis of *IG* 2². 2325, that Theodectes' first victory is to be placed in 365 or 368. His birth, therefore, may be dated *c.* 390 and his death *c.* 349. Alexander will have 'learned to esteem the man and his works through the poet's friend and collaborator, Aristotle. This is the meaning of ὁμιλία in Plutarch's reference to Alexander's act of homage' (Capps, op. cit. 41). F. Solmsen, *Hermes* 67 (1932), 144 ff. and Berve 2. 419 take the same view. See also T.B.L. Webster, *Hermes* 82 (1954), 303.

κειμένην: Castiglioni (*Gnomon* 13 (1937), 140) would retain the compound ἀνακειμένην, for which cf. *Public.* 19. 8, the only example of the verb in this sense in Plutarch. But the simple verb is more common, and is strongly supported by *Mar*. 2. 1, Μαρίου λιθίνην εἰκόνα κειμένην ἐν Ραβέννῃ; *Caes.* 66. 1, Πομπηΐου μὲν εἰκόνα κειμένην ἔχων.

ἀποδιδοὺς ἐν παιδιᾷ: Transposed by Ziegler to avoid hiatus. Castiglioni (loc. cit.) suggests μετὰ παιδιᾶς ἀποδιδούς.

XVIII. *Conquest of Pisidia and Phrygia. The Gordian Knot. Conquest of Paphlagonia and Cappadocia. Death of Memnon. Approach of Darius encouraged by an omen.*

After leaving Phaselis Alexander advanced to Side (Arr. 1. 26. 4 f.), then turned north to Aspendus (Arr. 1. 27. 1 ff.).

1. Πισιδῶν τοὺς ἀντιστάντας: esp. Termessus and Sagalassus (Arr. 1. 27. 5–28. 8).

Φρυγίαν ἐχειροῦτο: He entered Phrygia by L. Ascania and in 5 days reached Celaenae, which surrendered.

§§ 2–4. *The Gordian Knot.*

Sources: Arr. 2. 3; Curt. 3. 1. 14 ff.; Justin 11. 7. 3 ff.; cf. Aelian *NA* 13. 1; Scholiast on Eur. *Hipp.* 671 ed. Schwartz. (Diodorus does not refer to the incident).

2. Γόρδιον πόλιν: on the R. Sangarius (Arr. 1. 29. 5; Curt. 3. 1. 12), where Parmenio rejoined him and where reinforcements from Greece met him.

ἑστίαν: probably 'capital' rather than 'home' (Perrin); cf. Polyb. 5. 58. 4, ἑ. τῆς δυναστείας; Diod. 4. 19, ἑ. καὶ μητρόπολις.

Μίδου: According to Arrian Midas was chosen king by the Phrygians in fulfilment of an oracle; the other tradition (Justin and (?) Curtius) says it was his father Gordius.

τὴν θρυλουμένην ἅμαξαν: The waggon on which Midas and his parents entered the city. All sources agree that it belonged to Gordius. It was placed in the temple of Zeus Basileus on the Acropolis.

φλοιῷ κρανείας: 'with bark of cornel wood' (so Arrian).

βασιλεῖ . . . τῆς οἰκουμένης: All other sources are explicit that the person untying the knot would become King of Asia (i.e. the Persian Empire, Tarn 2. 309, n. 3): ἄρξαι τῆς Ἀσίας (Arr.); *Asiae* potiturum (Curt.); *tota Asia* regnaturum (Just.); cf. Schol. Eur. The use of the word οἰκουμένη may be due to Plutarch; it is doubtful whether it meant 'the inhabited world' in Alexander's day, Tarn 2. 79, n. 5.

Schachermeyr 161 suggests, perhaps rightly, that Callisthenes changed the original prophecy which referred merely to the kingship of Phrygia.

3. τυφλὰς ... ἀρχάς: 'hidden ends'. Cf. *Galb.* 18, τυφλὸν κίνημα (of a revolution).

δι' ἀλλήλων ... ὑποφερομένων: 'were intertwined many times in crooked coils' (Perrin). Both σκολιός (Callim. *Del.* 311) and ἑλιγμός (Herod. 2. 148) are used of the Cretan labyrinth.

διατεμεῖν ... τὸ σύναμμα: This version is given by Justin, Curtius, and Arrian (in a λόγος). It is assigned originally to Cleitarchus by Jacoby, *F. Gr. Hist.* 2D 511 (on Arist. fr. 7) and Mederer 10; Tarn 2. 262 ff. thinks it due to the malevolence of the Stoics; Schachermeyr 161 f. credits it to Callisthenes, from whom Cleitarchus took it. For his use of Callisthenes elsewhere see, for example, Jacoby on Call. fr. 36–37.

4. Ἀριστόβουλος δέ: *F. Gr. Hist.* no. 139, fr. 7, cited also by Arr. 2. 3. 7. Tarn loc. cit. holds that Aristobulus preserves the correct version, since the sword version makes Alexander cheat and lie to heaven, while Ptolemy, who does not mention the incident, would have given this version if it were true. But in Aristobulus' version too Alexander cheats, admittedly a little less blatantly, and Ptolemy evidently considered the incident too trifling to mention. We must agree with Pearson, *LHA* 157, that 'no one can really hope to know what actually happened at Gordium any more than one can say what song the Sirens sang'. The effect of the incident on Alexander, despite his sacrifice to the gods (Arr. 2. 3. 8), was probably nil (so Schachermeyr 162). For the view that it determined Alexander to conquer the Persian Empire, see E. A. Fredricksmeyer, *CPhil.* 56 (1961), 160 ff., who gives an interesting account of the Macedonian tradition deriving Midas from Macedonia.

τὸν ἔστορα: 'the wooden peg' (through the pole); cf. Arr. loc. cit., ὃς ἦν τύλος διαβεβλημένος διὰ τοῦ ῥυμοῦ διαμπάξ; Homer *Il.* 24. 272.

τὸ ζυγόδεσμον: 'the band', for fastening the yoke to the pole.

5. Παφλαγόνας τε καὶ Καππαδόκας: Arr. 2. 4. 1 f. At Ancyra Alexander received an embassy of Paphlagonians, who submitted and begged him not to enter their country. They were 'attributed' to Calas, satrap of Phrygia. Alexander received the surrender of the Cappadocians on both sides of the R. Halys, appointed Sabictas satrap and hurried on to the Cilician Gates, which he took without a struggle.

τὴν Μέμνονος ... τελευτήν: Berve no. 497. A native of Rhodes, brother of Mentor and brother-in-law of Artabazus. After the latter's unsuccessful revolt (353 B.C.) he fled with him (? ultimately) to Macedonia and remained there, until recalled in 342 through Mentor's influence with the Greek King. He does not appear to have succeeded his brother as supreme commander over the West coast of Asia Minor, but only to have been given this position after his brilliant defence of Halicarnassus (Diod. 17. 29. 1, στρατηγὸς τοῦ παντὸς πολέμου; cf. Arr. 2. 1. 1). In 336 he operated with success against Parmenio and Attalus (Polyaenus 5. 44. 4 f.; Diod. 17. 7. 3, 8–10), but failed (? or did not try, Fuller 89) to prevent Alexander's crossing. In 334 he had advocated a 'scorched earth' policy and carrying the war into Greece (Arr. 1. 12. 9; Diod. 17. 18. 2 ff.; Curt. 3. 4. 3). Tarn 1. 16 doubts this without justification; see Wilcken 84, Kaerst 1. 359, Burn, *JHS* 72 (1952), 84. The rejection of his plan by the Persian leaders led to the disaster of the Granicus. After his appointment as supreme commander he took Chios and most of the cities of Lesbos and at the time of his death (spring 333) was besieging Mytilene (Diod. 17. 31. 3–4; Arr. 2. 1. 1); for his plans (similar to those proposed in 334) see esp. Burn loc. cit.

Tarn 1. 22 regards his capacity as unproved and doubts whether Memnon's death meant much to Alexander. Wilcken's judgement (97)—'His death at this moment was the greatest stroke of luck in Alexander's life.'—may be exaggerated; but cf. Arr. 2. 1. 3, who regards it as 'the severest blow *during this period* to the hopes of Persia'. Diod. 17. 31. 3 mentions Alexander's relief.

6. ἐκ Σούσων κατέβαινε: On Memnon's death Darius gave up his plan to carry the war into Greece and, failing to find a suitable successor, was compelled to take the field in person (Curt. 3. 2. 1 ff.; Diod. 17. 30–31).

ἑξήκοντα ... μυριάδας: So Arr. 2. 8. 8, and *POxy.* 1798, fr. 44 col. 2. 2/3. Diod. 17. 31. 2 and Justin 11. 9. 1 give 400,000 infantry and 100,000 cavalry. Curtius (3. 2. 1) gives details of units totalling 250,000 infantry (including 30,000 Greek mercenaries) and 62,200 cavalry. These figures are, of course, impossible. The true figures, which doubtless became known to the Macedonians, were suppressed for propaganda reasons (Tarn 1. 25, Marsden 31 ff.). Marsden (5, n. 2) estimates the Persian force at Issus at between 40,000 and 50,000 men, but his reasons are not entirely convincing.

τινος ὀνείρου: In Curtius (3. 3. 2 ff.) Darius' vision differs slightly: 'castra Alexandri magno ignis fulgore collucere ei visa sunt, et paulo post Alexander adduci ad ipsum in eo vestis habitu, quo ipse factus rex fuisset, equo deinde per Babylona vectus subito cum ipso equo oculis esse subductus.' (factus rex was supplied by Hedicke from § 6, 'quoniam in eo habitu Darius fuisset, cum appellatus est rex').

πρὸς χάριν ἐξηγοῦντο: ὡς ἔοικεν shows that Plutarch is giving his own view of the interpretations in the light of the result of the campaign. According to Curtius (loc. cit.) some of the seers predicted that Alexander would conquer the Persian Empire, others that Darius would be victorious.

7. ἀστάνδης: 'a royal courier': ἀστάνδαι, οἱ ἐκ διαδοχῆς γραμματοφόροι (Suidas); so Eustathius *ad Od.* p. 1854, 28. Hesychius calls them ἡμεροδρόμοι or κράββατοι or ἄγγελοι. At *Mor.* 326 e, Plutarch calls Darius δοῦλος καὶ ἀστάνδης (cf. *Mor.* 340 c); Aelian *VH* 12. 43 also calls him a slave. He was in fact a grand-nephew of Artaxerxes I, though not a member of the ruling house (Diod. 17. 5. 3 ff.; Justin 10. 3. 3 ff.; Strabo 15. 3. 24).

XIX. *Alexander's illness cured by Philip. His trust in his friend revealed.*

1. καταγνοὺς δειλίαν Ἀλεξάνδρου: Despite the advice of Amyntas (see ch. 20. 1).

2. διὰ νόσον: Arr. (2. 4. 7) gives both versions, assigning the former (ὑπὸ καμάτου) specifically to Aristobulus (fr. 8). Curtius (3. 5. 1 f.), Justin (11. 8. 3 ff.) and apparently Diod. (17. 31. 4)—see *RE* 2, 1243—give the latter version. Alexander had ridden hard to save Tarsus (Arr. 2. 4. 5 f.) and would undoubtedly be weary; this does not, of course, exclude the possibility that Alexander caught a chill in the Cydnus.

τοῦ Κύδνου: The Cydnus rises in Mt. Taurus and flows through Tarsus. It was noted for the coldness of its waters.

καταπαγέντι: With καί, καταπαγέντι will apply to Alexander, 'having got a chill' (perhaps supported by Curt. and Justin locc. citt.); with the manuscript reading it applies to the Cydnus, 'whose waters were icy'.

4. Φίλιππος ὁ Ἀκαρνάν: Berve no. 788. He had been with Alexander since boyhood, and was friend as well as doctor (Curt. 3. 6. 1). He is mentioned again only at Gaza (Curt. 4. 6. 17) and the feast of Medius in 323 (Ps.-Call. 3. 31). Berve suggests that he may have remained in the Middle East. It is perhaps more likely that the reference in Ps.-Call. is false and that he died during the campaign. The incident is described by Plutarch in order to show Alexander's trust in his friends, but there is no reason to doubt the story which is given by all our extant authorities.

παραβαλλόμενος: 'risking his life'. Cf. 40. 4; *Caes.* 37. 7, ἀλλ' οὗτος παραβάλλεται, καθάπερ οὐ διώκων πολεμίους, ἀλλὰ φεύγων.

ἐπεχείρησε φαρμακείᾳ: 'prepared a medicine' (Perrin).

5. Παρμενίων ἔπεμψεν ἐπιστολήν: This incident has sometimes been ignored, e.g. by Wilcken, or doubted, e.g. by Pridik 119 f. He favours Thirlwall's view (*History of Greece*, 6. 174) that it is a doublet of the attempted bribery of Alexander the Lyncestian (Arr. 1. 25. 1), on the ground that Parmenio was with Alexander at Tarsus; for Arrian (2. 5. 1), after describing the incident, writes ἐκ δὲ τούτου Παρμενίωνα μὲν πέμπει ἐπὶ τὰς ἄλλας πύλας . . . But Schachermeyr (170; 507, n. 113) is probably correct in regarding ἐκ τούτου as a loose connecting phrase and in supposing that Parmenio was sent on at the beginning of Alexander's illness; cf. Burn 104 f. Justin (11. 8. 5) oddly says that Parmenio was in Cappadocia.

ἐπὶ δωρεαῖς . . . θυγατρός: Curt. 3. 6. 4, 1,000 talents and marriage with Darius' sister; Iul. Val. 2. 24, part of his realm and marriage with his sister; Justin 11. 8. 6, pecunia ingens. Arrian merely says that Philip was bribed and Diodorus omits all reference to it.

6. ἐπέδωκεν: 'handed over'. For the compound (post-classical in this sense) see *Caes.* 65. 4, ἔνιοι δέ φασιν ἄλλον ἐπιδοῦναι τὸ βιβλίον τοῦτο; *Mor.* 202 f, 207 b.

7. τοῦ μὲν ἀναγινώσκοντος κτλ.: So Arrian and Justin. Curtius (3. 6. 9) says that Alexander drank, then handed the letter (which he had received 2 days before) to Philip.

διακεχυμένῳ: 'by his radiant, beaming countenance'. Plutarch is very fond of διαχέομαι and its derivatives; see Holden on *Dem.* 25. 3.

8. θεοκλυτοῦντος: A tragic word. For the phrase cf. *Ages.* 33. 8, τάς τε χεῖρας ὀρεγόντων καὶ θεοκλυτούντων.

None of the other versions gives this detail: οὐ γὰρ ἐκπλαγῆναι, Arr. 2. 4. 10; ut securum (sc. Philippum) conspexit, Justin 11. 8. 9; plus indignationis quam pavoris ostendit, Curt. 3. 6. 10. It is probably due to Plutarch.

10. ῥαΐσας: 'having recovered'; a necessary emendation of the commoner ῥώσας. For ῥαΐζω cf. Plato *Rep.* 462 d; *Dem.* 1. 13; *Demetr.* 48.

xx. *The Battle of Issus.*

1. Ἀμύντας: The son of Antiochus; Berve no 58. Arr. (1. 17. 9) says that he fled from Macedonia because of dislike and fear of Alexander. Berve (ad loc.) suggests that he was afraid because of his friendship with Amyntas (Berve no. 61), the former king, who had been put to death on Alexander's accession. Burn 76 (? relying on Curt. 3. 11. 18, praetor hic Alexandri fuerat) conjectures, perhaps correctly, that he was one of Parmenio's corps commanders sent to Asia in 336 who had deserted because of the fate of Attalus. After the Battle of the Granicus he fled from Ephesus to Darius, allegedly bringing a letter from Alexander the Lyncestian (Arr. 1. 25. 3). He commanded Greek mercenaries at Issus, and escaped with 4,000 of them to Tripolis; from there he went to Cyprus and Egypt, where he met his death (Arr. 2. 13. 2 f.; Curt. 4. 1. 27 ff.; Diod. 17. 48. 2 ff.).

On his advice to Darius see Arr. 2. 6. 3 ff., esp. 5 f. Curt. (3. 8. 1) attributes this advice to Thymondas, the commander of the Greek mercenaries.

4. οὐκ ἔπειθεν: The opposition came from the Persian nobles, who feared that he was trying to betray the Persian cause (Arr. 2. 6. 5 ff.; Curt. 3. 8. 3 ff.). They were doubtless jealous of the Greeks and failed to appreciate the soundness of his advice. They were always opposed to the surrender of territory (cf. the opposition to Memnon at the Granicus), perhaps because of the revenues which they would lose.

εἰς Κιλικίαν: Darius had encamped at Sochoi, south-east of the Amanus mountains, where the wide plains would give his numerical superiority, esp. in cavalry, full scope, to await Alexander. When he failed to arrive because of his illness, Darius decided to march against him in Cilicia. He moved north and crossed the Amanus mountains by the Amanic Gates (Arr. 2. 7. 1), also called the Bogtche Pass or Toprak Kalessi; then he turned south to Issus, where he massacred Alexander's sick. Meanwhile Alexander, learning at Mallus of Darius' presence at Sochoi, had left Cilicia by the coast road. He proceeded past Issus, the R. Pinarus and the Pillar of Jonah to Myriandros, intending to march on Sochoi through the Beilan Pass (Syrian Gates). At Myriandros he was informed that the Persian army was in his rear. After verifying this, he marched northward to meet Darius who had unwisely moved south to take up a position in the narrow plain along the north bank of the R. Pinarus.

Arrian's account (2. 6. 1–7. 2) is clear and detailed. For modern accounts see esp. Wilcken 99 ff.; Schachermeyr 169 ff. (with map on p. 139); Fuller 97 ff. (with map 7 on p. 155).

5. διαμαρτόντες ἀλλήλων: Plutarch perhaps thinks of the two armies passing close to each other. In fact, Darius' route lay 30 miles or so to the east of the coastal road with the Amanus mountains between.

τῇ συντυχίᾳ: 'opportunity, good fortune' rather than simply 'occurrence'. For this sense of the word, cf. Thuc. 1. 33, γενήσεται δὲ ὑμῖν πειθομένοις καλὴ ἡ ξυντυχία κατὰ πολλὰ τῆς ἡμετέρας χρείας; *Ti. Gracch.* 6. 2, ἡσθέντες οὖν οἱ Νομαντῖνοι τῇ συντυχίᾳ τῆς χρείας. . . . **τὴν προτέραν . . . στρατοπεδείαν:** 'to recover his former position' lit. encampment. Sochoi is meant. In fact, Darius was bent on pursuing Alexander, whose return he did not anticipate.

ἐξελίξαι: Generally = ἀναπτύσσειν, 'deploy'; here 'extricate'.

6. πρὸς τῆς ὀλιγότητος . . . θέσιν: 'which favoured Alexander's small force'. For the battle of Issus see Arr. 2. 8–11; Diod. 17. 33–4; Curt. 3. 9–11; Justin 11. 9. 1 ff.; Polyb. 12. 17–22 (= Callisthenes fr. 35) in P. Pédech's edition (Paris, 1961). Of modern accounts see esp. Fuller 155 ff. For Alexander's aims at Issus, Marsden 1 ff.

8. οὐ παρέσχε κύκλωσιν: Alexander gave Parmenio on the left strict orders not to edge away from the sea, since the Persians seemed likely to overlap the Macedonian line (Arr. 2. 8. 4). The Macedonian right did not extend right up to the mountain ridge and here Alexander posted cavalry, archers, and the invaluable Agrianians at an angle to face the Persians in the mountain-valleys (Arr. 2. 9. 2).

ὑπερβαλών: 'outflanking', though LSJ cite only the middle in this sense. For the manœuvre, Arr. 2. 9. 4.

κατὰ κέρας: 'in flank' (Arr. 2. 11. 1). 'Alexander's plan of battle was much the same as that of his adversary; it was, while Parmenio held back the Persian right, to hurl his Companion cavalry at the Cardaces on the left of Darius' Greek mercenaries, break through them and then take the mercenaries in flank and rear' (Fuller 160).

τρωθῆναι . . . τὸν μηρόν: The wound is historical; see Arr. 2. 12. 1; Diod. 17. 34. 5; Curt. 3. 11. 10; Justin 11. 9. 9. It was sustained when Alexander was endeavouring to reach Darius. For his desire to capture or kill Darius, Marsden 4.

9. Χάρης φησίν: *F. Gr. Hist.* no. 125, fr. 6. On the tendency (κολακεία) to depict Alexander as engaging in single combat, W. B. Kaiser, *JDAI* 77 (1962), 235 f.; Jacoby, loc. cit.

τοῖς περὶ τὸν Ἀντίπατρον: i.e. Antipater; see 41. 5 n. (cf. *Mor.* 341 c, γράφων πρὸς Ἀντίπατρον); there is no good reason to doubt the authenticity of this letter; see *PACA* 4 (1961), 13.

10. ὑπὲρ ἕνδεκα μυριάδας: 100,000 infantry and 10,000 cavalry (Diod. 17. 36. 6; Curt. 3. 11. 27). Arrian (2. 11. 8) gives a total of 100,000, including 10,000 cavalry; Justin (11. 9. 10) 61,000 infantry, 10,000 cavalry and 40,000 prisoners.

προλαβόντα τῇ φυγῇ: 'got a start in his flight'. τῇ φυγῇ is a dative of means. Cf. *Cic.* 47. 3, where τῇ φυγῇ should be read; Xen. *Cyn.* 7. 7, προλαβεῖν τῷ δρόμῳ. Diod. 16. 94. 4, προλαβὼν τῆς διώξεως, 'getting a start on his pursuers', is clearly different.

τὸ δ' ἅρμα καὶ τὸ τόξον: Arr. 2. 11. 5 f. mentions also Darius' shield and his mantle (κάνδυς), Curt. 3. 11. 11 (12. 5) only the mantle.

11. εὐζώνων: Generally used of hoplites without heavy shields, and of light troops. Here it means 'without surplus equipment or heavy baggage'.

ὑπερβάλλοντα πλήθει: 'in very great quantity'. According to Arr. (2. 11. 10) they found *only* 3,000 talents!

τῆς ἀποσκευῆς: 'baggage'. On the use of ἀποσκευή in the Hellenistic age (as here) to include *persons*, see Walbank on Polyb. 1. 66. 7. Cf. *Eum.* 9. 6, ἔπειτα ταῖς ἀποσκευαῖς τοῦ Ἀντιγόνου περιπεσὼν καὶ λαβεῖν ῥᾳδίως δυνάμενος πολλὰ μὲν ἐλεύθερα σώματα, πολλὴν δέ θεραπείαν (servants) καὶ πλοῦτον. For the fact cf. Arr. 2. 11. 9, τὰς γυναῖκας σφῶν ξὺν τῇ ἄλλῃ κατασκευῇ εἰς Δαμασκὸν ἔτυχον ἐσταλκότες.

ἐν Δαμασκῷ: Arr. loc. cit.; Diod. 17. 32. 3; Curt. 3. 8. 12. It was captured shortly after by Parmenio (see ch. 24. 1).

ἐκείνῳ = ἑαυτῷ (see Kühner–Gerth 1. 649).

ἐξηρηκότας: According to Curt. 3. 11. 23 it was customary (*tradito more*) to receive the victor in the tent of the conquered king. For the fact cf. also Arr. 2. 12. 3; Diod. 17. 36. 5.

θεραπείας: 'retinue, body of attendants', a common meaning in Plutarch. See esp. *Eum.* 9. 6 (cited above); *Mar.* 19. 1, τῆς δὲ θεραπείας τὸ πλῆθος . . . ἀθρόοι κατέβαινον; *Ti. Gracch.* 5. 6.

13. ὅλκια κτλ: 'basins, pitchers, bathing-tubs and vases for perfumes'.

⟨δι⟩ησκημένα: ⟨καὶ⟩ ἠσκημένα (Sintenis) seems preferable. The compound διασκεῖν is rare and does not occur elsewhere in Plutarch, whereas there are some half-dozen instances of the simple verb in Plutarch; see, e.g. *Sull.* 16. 4; *Caes.* 42. 3; *Alc.* 24. 7.

αὐτό: = '*dapes ipsas*'. nam adhuc de lectis triclinaribus mensisque dixerat (Reiske).

τοῦτ' ἦν: Some translators take this to mean that Alexander found pleasure in this luxury and thought that he was at last a king. Du Soul, however, long ago pointed out that Alexander was expressing pity for Darius, for thinking that royalty consisted in mere wealth. He translates 'hoccine ergo erat, quod homines regnare putant!' So essentially Langhorne, who remarks (in a note on this passage) that Alexander was not corrupted by Persian luxury until long after this.

53

XXI. *Alexander's treatment of the captured Persian women illustrates his generosity and self-control.*

1. ἐν τοῖς αἰχμαλώτοις: Arr. 2. 11. 9, Diod. 17. 36. 2 ff., Curt. 3. 11. 4 f., and Justin 11. 9. 12 all mention the capture of Darius' mother, wife, and two daughters. The first three add his young son.

τὸ ἅρμα καὶ τὰ τόξα: see ch. 20. 10.

2. πέμπει Λεοννάτον: According to Arr. 2. 12. 3 ff., Ptolemy and Aristobulus (and others?) related that Alexander sent Leonnatus. His visit is mentioned also by Diod. 17. 37. 3 ff., Curt. 3. 12. 7 ff. Arrian then gives as a λόγος the story that Alexander himself, accompanied by Hephaestion, visited the captives on the following morning (cf. Diod. 17. 37. 5 f., Curt. 3. 12. 13 ff.). Plutarch here certainly follows the version of Aristobulus. He omits the picturesque story of Alexander's visit given by Cleitarchus (Jacoby, *F. Gr. Hist.* 2D, 503, on Ptolemy fr. 7). Justin 11. 9. 12 ff. merely mentions a visit by Alexander.

Λεοννάτον: Berve no. 466. *RE* 12. 2035 ff. (Geyer). He was related to the royal house. He is said by Suidas to have been educated with Alexander and was one of those who killed Philip's murderer, Pausanias (Diod. 16. 94. 4). It is therefore probable that he was a close friend of Alexander. He was at this time one of Alexander's Companions. In 332/1 he was appointed a Bodyguard (Arr. 3. 5. 5; 6. 28. 4), but did not apparently enjoy independent command until India. The 'story' that he mocked a Persian performing *proskynesis* (Arr. 4. 12. 2) may be true; if so, it would account for the check in his career (see Badian *TAPA* 91 (1960), 337). His greatest feat was to help to save Alexander in the Malli town (see ch. 63); for this and his other services he received a golden crown (Arr. 7. 5. 5). Thereafter his rise was swift and he commanded part of the army during the march through Gedrosia, winning a victory over the Oreitae. At Alexander's death he was one of the leading generals and was probably appointed guardian (with Perdiccas) of Roxane's unborn child. To him fell the important satrapy of Hellespontine Phrygia, but Antipater requested his help in the Lamian War, and he fell at the Battle of Crannon in 322. His courage and military gifts are undoubted (see Suidas s.v.), but his character makes it improbable that he would have survived long in the struggles among the successors. 'He was showy and unstable, he wanted to be king and could not wait' (Tarn, *CAH* 6. 463). On his love of hunting and his extravagance see ch. 40.

3. ἀπήντα: 'evenerunt'. See LSJ II. 2; Holden on *Ti. Gracch.* 17. 4.

4. θάψαι γὰρ ... ἔδωκε: Diod. 17. 38. 1 ff.; Curt. 3. 12. 13 ff.

συντάξεις: 'pensions, allowances'. Cf. *Arat.* 41, δώδεκα τάλαντα σύνταξιν ἐναύσιον; *Cleom.* 19.

5. γενομέναις αἰχμαλώτοις: No change from Ziegler's text is required. The words are in place here in a comment by Plutarch, much less so in a speech. At p. 205, 21 the reading of *Λ* is derived from this passage. The misplacement of the words in this line is perhaps due to homoeoarchon, γενναίας . . . γενομέναις.

6. λέγεταί γε: Arr. 4. 19. 6; Curt. 4. 10. 24; *Mor.* 97 d, 338 e, 522 a; Gellius *NA* 7. 8. 2 f.; Frontinus *Strat.* 2. 11. 6; Amm. Marc. 24. 4. 27; Athenaeus 13. 603 c.

7. ὡς ἔοικεν: This is Plutarch's own view; see ch. 4. 6.
ἔθιγεν . . . ἔγνω: 'was not intimate with'. θιγγάνειν in this sense, although not used in the best prose, is common in Plutarch. For γιγνώσκειν LSJ cite no classical examples. It also is common in Plutarch, e.g. *Eum.* 1. 7, Βαρσίνην γὰρ τὴν Ἀρταβάζου πρώτην ἐν Ἀσίᾳ γνοὺς ὁ Ἀλέξανδρος, ἐξ ἧς ἔσχεν Ἡρακλέα; *Pomp.* 36. 3, 53. 2, etc.

πλὴν Βαρσίνης: Tarn 2. 330 ff. has shown conclusively that Memnon's widow, the daughter of Artabazus, who *was* captured at Damascus, was not called Barsine, although Memnon's brother Mentor did have a wife of that name (Arr. 7. 4. 6). The Barsine captured at Damascus was the elder daughter of Darius, whom Alexander married at Susa. Parmenio did advise Alexander to *marry* Barsine in order to produce an heir (he had given Alexander the same advice before the campaign began, Diod. 17. 16. 2), and, as Alexander arranged to have Barsine and her sister taught Greek (Diod. 17. 67. 1; cf. πεπαιδευμένη δὲ παιδείαν Ἑλληνικήν, § 9 below), he may have intended from the beginning to make her his wife. Tarn now believes (op. cit. 335), against his former view (adopted by Jacoby, *F. Gr. Hist.* 2D, 512), that the confusion of the two women is due to Plutarch and not to Aristobulus, who knew too much to make such an error. This is by no means certain. Schachermeyr 289 still regards Barsine as the mistress of Alexander before his marriage to Roxane and talks of a son, i.e. presumably Herakles, a pretender set up in 309 by Polyperchon; cf. Berve 2. 103 f. On the name Barsine see ch. 70. 3 n.

Sources: Plut. *Eumenes* 1. 7 (cited above); Arr. 7. 4. 6—on these passages see Tarn 2. 333, n. 1—; Justin 11. 10. 2.

9. ⟨καὶ τὸ κάλλος⟩**: Ziegler transferred the words from their position in the manuscripts after γενναίας (p. 207, l. 2) and suggested that an adjective, e.g. ἐκπρεπεστάτη, had been lost after them. This is an unnecessarily complicated solution, and it seems preferable to retain the words in their original position and to adopt Stephanus' simple correction κατὰ τὸ κάλλος, 'as noble as she was beautiful'. A somewhat better rhythm might be obtained by transferring ἅψασθαι γυναικός to follow Ἀριστόβουλος; the homoeoteleuton Ἀριστόβουλος . . . κάλλος might be held to account for the dislocation. τοκάδος (Bernardakis), however, is tempting. The change is negligible and the sense excellent, if we take τοκάδος to mean 'fruitful', as at Strabo 4. 1. 2.

10. ἀλγηδόνες ὀμμάτων: cf. Herod. 5. 18. Alexander's remark, if authentic, is probably a reminiscence of Herodotus. We may be sure that Alexander knew him well and, although the story was no doubt current in Macedonia, this part of the dialogue is pure Herodotus.

11. παρέπεμπεν: 'he passed them by without any sparke of affection towards them, more than if they had been images of stone without life' (North). For the verb cf. Diod. 17. 79. 4, *Cat. min.* 43. 10. At *Mor.* 338 d Plut. uses παρῆλθε.

XXII. *In this chapter Plutarch assembles a number of anecdotes designed to illustrate Alexander's moral and physical continence.*

1. Φιλόξενος: Berve 2. 389 ff. (nos. 793–6), *RE* 20 (1941), 189 f., distinguishes four Macedonians of this name. This Philoxenus (no. 793, *RE* (1)) was appointed together with Coeranus to take charge of the war-chest after Harpalus' flight in 333; on the return of Harpalus in 331 he became collector of taxes in Asia Minor west of the Taurus mountains (Arr. 3. 6. 4), perhaps responsible for collecting the *syntaxeis* of the Greek cities and forwarding them to Alexander (Badian, *Studies . . . Ehrenberg* (1966), 55). Of his subsequent career we know only that in 324 he sent men to Athens to demand the extradition of Harpalus, and to Rhodes to arrest Harpalus' confidential slave (*Mor.* 531 a; Hypereides *Adv. Dem.* col. 8; Paus. 2. 33. 4), and that (at an unknown date) he intervened in Ephesus to arrest the murderers of the tyrant (Polyaenus 6. 49).

His title and functions at this date are uncertain. He is variously called ὁ τῶν ἐπὶ θαλάττῃ (πραγμάτων) στρατηγός and ὕπαρχος παραλίας or 'Ιωνίας (refs. in Tarn 2. 172 f., Badian, op. cit. 57). Tarn prefers the former alternative and deduces that Philoxenus was appointed to control the sea communications between Greece and Asia Minor. But this fails to account for the story of his intervention in Ephesus, which Tarn, admittedly, considers an invention. Badian (op. cit. 59 f.) suggests that when *syntaxeis* ceased to be levied (after Alexander discharged the Greek allies) Philoxenus was appointed to a position over the Greeks in and near Asia Minor analogous to that of Antipater in Europe; cf. Bengtson, *Phil.* 92 (1937), 126–55 at p. 140, and id., *Die Strategie in hellenistischer Zeit* I (München, 1937), 34 ff., 215 f. Bengtson's suggestion that Philoxenus succeeded Alcimachus (Arr. 1. 18. 1) is rightly rejected by Badian (loc. cit.) and A. Heuss (*Hermes* 73 (1938), 141, n. 1), while his contention that Philoxenus is identical with the satrap of Caria (Berve no. 794, *RE* (2)) mentioned shortly before Alexander's death (Arr. 7. 23. 1, 24. 1) cannot be proved or disproved.

Θεόδωρον: Nothing else is known of him. The incident must post-date 331, when Philoxenus went to Ionia.

ἔγραψεν: The letter is mentioned again by Plut. at *Mor.* 333 a, 1099 d, and by Athenaeus 1. 22 d. On this and the following two letters see *PACA* 4 (1961), 13.

τὴν ὄψιν ὑπερφυεῖς: 'of extraordinary beauty'.

τοιαῦτ' ὀνείδη προξενῶν κάθηται: 'should spend (waste) his time procuring such *shameful creatures*'. 'τοιαῦτα ὀνείδη means the boys' (Tarn 2. 322, n. 4). He cites the use of ὀνείδη by Oedipus to describe his daughters (Soph. *OT* 1494). Add Ar. *Ach.* 855, Dem. 21. 132 for ὄνειδος used of persons. For προξενεῖν = procure see *Caes.* 60. 2, *Sol.* 2. 6.

3. Ἅγνωνι: Berve no. 17. A native of Teos, who later (before 327) joined Alexander and appears to have belonged to the ἑταῖροι. See ch. 40. 1 for his luxurious mode of life, and ch. 55. 2 for his hostility to Callisthenes.

νεανικῶς: In all manuscripts νεανίσκῳ follows Ἅγνωνι, but it is clearly inapplicable to him. Du Soul's proposal to delete νεανίσκῳ and insert νεανίσκον after Κρωβύλον (adopted by Ziegler in his first edition) makes excellent sense, but his alternative suggestion, that νεανίσκῳ should be emended to νεανικῶς, is simpler; it is supported by the use of the adverb with the similar verb, καθάπτομαι, at *Cic.* 9. 7.

4. γύναια: γύναιον may be used as a term of endearment ('little woman') or in a derogatory sense; but here it is probably equivalent to γυνή, 'the "wives" of certain mercenaries' (part of their ἀποσκευή). For this use, cf. Diod. 17. 24. 2, γύναιον, ὄνομα μὲν Ἄδα, γένει δὲ προσήκουσα τῇ Καρῶν ἀρχῇ; *Pel.* 9.

Δάμωνα καὶ Τιμόθεον: Probably serving in the forces under Parmenio's command in 333/2, since the wife of Darius was captured in the autumn of 333; see 21. 1 (Berve 2. 115 (no. 241)). There is no other evidence. On the incident see Tarn 2. 325.

5. κατὰ λέξιν: 'word for word'. Plutarch makes it clear when he is quoting; cf. ch. 77. 1.

τῆς εὐμορφίας αὐτῆς: See the references at 21. 6.

6. μάλιστα συνιέναι θνητὸς ὤν: cf. *Mor.* 65 f, Ἀλέξανδρος μὲν γὰρ ἀπιστεῖν ἔφη τοῖς θεὸν αὐτὸν ἀναγορεύουσιν ἐν τῷ καθεύδειν μάλιστα καὶ ἀφροδισιάζειν, ὡς ἀγεννέστερος περὶ ταῦτα καὶ παθητικώτερος αὐτοῦ γιγνόμενος, and *Mor.* 717 f.

7. ἦν δὲ καὶ γαστρὸς ἐγκρατέστατος: cf. 23. 9.

τοῖς πρὸς Ἄδαν λεχθεῖσιν: Plutarch tells the same story (without mentioning Leonidas) at *Mor.* 127 b, 180 a, 1099 c.

ἦν . . . ἀπέδειξεν: Arr. 1. 23. 7 f.; Diod. 17. 24. 2. For her previous history see ch. 10. 1. On the capture of Halicarnassus, in which she assisted (Strabo 14. 657), she was put in charge of the whole of Caria. For the custom of adoption see Gelzer, *Rh. Mus.* 35 (1880), 517.

8. ὄψα καὶ πέμματα: ὄψα are cooked foods, eaten with bread and wine, πέμματα pastries, cakes, sweetmeats.

10. ἀγγεῖα: any sort of receptacle; here more probably a chest (so North, Perrin) than a wardrobe (Dryden, Langhorne).

ἐπισκοπῶν μή: 'taking care lest'. LSJ cite only *Epistle to the Hebrews* 12. 15 for this use, but see Kühner–Gerth, 2. 394, who give several examples from Plutarch.

XXIII. *Alexander's day. His attitude to drink and its effects on him. His increased expenditure on banquets.*

1. ἧττον ἢ ἐδόκει καταφερής: 'less addicted to drink than he was thought to be'.

Plutarch's views on Alexander's drinking habits vary with his sources. In his early work, *De Alexandri Fortuna* (*Mor.* 337 f) he indignantly denies that Alexander was addicted to drink; here and at *Mor.* 623 e (a discussion of the king's drinking habits) he gives Aristobulus' version (see Arr. 7. 29. 4). But at *Mor.* 623 f he remarks that Philinus (a Pythagorean friend of his) showed, by citing the Diary, that those who held this view were talking nonsense; for the Diary contained entries stating that 'Alexander slept all this day and sometimes the next as well after drinking (ἐκ πότου)'—for the value of this evidence see below. Here, as in ch. 4, Plutarch thinks of Alexander as ποτικός, and gives a physical explanation of his hard drinking. Stories of Alexander's drinking habits were obviously current soon after his death, spread by men like Ephippus of Olynthus (*F. Gr. Hist.* no. 126). He wrote, probably during the Lamian War, a hostile pamphlet on the deaths of Alexander and Hephaestion, which he attributed to excessive drinking; for a discussion of his scanty fragments, Pearson, *LHA*, 61 ff., with Badian's comments in *Gnomon* 33 (1961), 662 f. That Macedonian banquets were more riotous than Greek is shown by

Ephippus fr. 1, and by Athenaeus 128 a–130 c (the banquet of Caranus). On Philip's banquets see Theopompus fr. 236 (cf. Diod. 16. 86. 6–87. 1) and *Alex*. 9. 6 ff. There is no reason to doubt Arrian's statement (4. 8. 2) that by the time of Cleitus' murder Alexander's drinking had become more 'barbaric' (cf. Curt. 5. 7. 1). But Alexander was no drunkard, and there is much force in Plutarch's contention, here and at *Mor*. 337 f, that he let nothing hinder him when there was work to be done. See further G. H. Macurdy, *JHS* 50 (1930), 294 ff.

εἷλκεν: 'dragged out, prolonged'. Cf. *Pomp*. 41. 3; *Ti. Gracch*. 16. 2. καὶ ταῦτα: 'and that too only when he had abundant leisure'.

2. οὐκ οἶνος κτλ.: For the sentiment cf. *Mor*. 337 e, τὸ δὲ λαβόντα μεγάλην ἐξουσίαν ἐνεγκεῖν καὶ μεταχειρίσασθαι καὶ μὴ συντριβῆναι μηδὲ διαστραφῆναι τῷ βάρει καὶ μεγέθει τῶν πραγμάτων, ἀνδρός ἐστιν ἀρετὴν καὶ νοῦν καὶ φρόνημ᾽ ἔχοντος. See also *Mor*. 337 f.

θέα: In Plutarch = 'spectacle, performance'. Cf. *Cam*. 5. 1, μεγάλαι θέαι = *Ludi Magni*; *Caes*. 55. 4; *Brut*. 21. 3.

3. καθήμενος: cf. *Mor*. 338 d. For the Macedonian practice of sitting at meals, Tarn 2. 107 and n. 2.

διδάσκων: So Sintenis for the MSS. δικάζων. He compares ch. 32. 12, συντάττων τι τῆς φάλαγγος ἢ παρακελευόμενος ἢ διδάσκων ἢ ἐφορῶν παρεξήλαυνεν. Ziegler's transposition of τι τῶν πολεμικῶν to follow συντάττων in the present passage is perhaps unnecessary.

4. ἐπείγουσαν: 'pressing, urgent'. Cf. *Marc*. 24. 10, τῶν ἀρχαιρεσίων ἐπειγόντων; *Mor*. 108 f, τῆς ὥρας ἐπειγούσης, 'since time was pressing'.

ἐκ τῶν ἐφημερίδων: It has generally been considered certain that a Diary was kept, probably by Eumenes the ἀρχιγραμματεύς, which will have contained Alexander's orders, the reports he received, details of troops detached, embassies, and so on (see Berve 1. 50 f., Pearson, *Historia* 3 (1954/5), 434, and for possible parallels Wilcken, *Phil*. 53 (1894), 80 ff., Kaerst, *RE* 5. 2749 ff., s.v. 'Ephemerides'). Pearson (loc. cit.) has put forward strong arguments to show that the extant fragments all come not from the original Diary (though this did exist) but from a literary production, which has no claim to be considered an authentic record. This view has been widely accepted. Recently, however, A. E. Samuel, *Historia* 14 (1965), 1 ff., observing that all the extant frags. appear to deal with the last period of Alexander's life (he tentatively assigns the events described in §§ 1–6 of this chapter to Alexander's stay at Babylon), has argued that Alexander never kept an official Diary and that the fragments derive from the works of later writers (Eumenes, Diodotus, Strattis) composed on the basis of Babylonian records. These (as the extant records show) contained 'the precise dates of events, major occurrences in the land, and notices of the health of the king' (p. 11). This would explain the fact that the Ephemerides are cited only for Alexander's last days, but it is difficult to believe that the Babylonian records contained notices of Alexander hunting birds and foxes; the instances cited by Samuel do not suggest it.

See also n. to 76. 1.

6. ἀδολεσχίας: In classical Greek 'chatter, idle talk', but in Hellenistic Greek (as here) 'conversation'. cf. *Mor.* 697 d.

7. τότε ταῖς μεγαλαυχίαις: 'under the influence of drink he became unpleasant, because of the airs he gave himself, and acted like a bragging soldier; for not only was he himself carried away into making boastful claims but he allowed himself to be ridden by his flatterers'.

στρατιωτικός: 'inelegans' (Wyttenbach). But probably the notion of boastfulness is present as at ch. 48. 5, πολλὰ φιλότιμα καὶ στρατιωτικὰ παρρησιαζόμενος (of Philotas). The soldier, of course, was commonly depicted as boastful, e.g. Plautus' *Miles Gloriosus*.

ὑποφερόμενος: LSJ cite *Alc.* 18. 8. Add *Eum.* 6. 3, Ἀλεξάνδρου . . . ὑποφερομένου πρὸς τὸν Περσικὸν ζῆλον.

ἱππάσιμον: Unique in this metaphorical sense.

Curt. 8. 1. 22 ff. gives a similar picture of Alexander at the banquet at which Cleitus was murdered: 'in quo (sc. convivio) cum multo incaluisset mero, *immodicus aestimator sui*, celebrare quae gesserat coepit, gravis etiam eorum auribus qui sentiebant vera memorari'. Cf. Arr. 4. 8. 3. At *Mor.* 65 d (a passage reminiscent of the present one) Plutarch attributes the deaths of Callisthenes, Parmenio, and Philotas to the activities of the flatterers: ἦν δὲ ὁ Μήδιος τοῦ περὶ τὸν Ἀλέξανδρον χόρου τῶν κολάκων οἷον ἔξαρχος καὶ σοφιστὴς κορυφαῖος ἐπὶ τοὺς ἀρίστους συντεταγμένος . . . Ἄγνωσι δὲ καὶ Βαγώαις καὶ Ἀγησίαις καὶ Δημητρίοις ἀφειδῶς ἐνέδωκεν ἑαυτὸν ὑποσκελίζεσθαι, προσκυνούμενον καὶ καταστολιζόμενον καὶ ἀναπλαττόμενον ὑπ' αὐτῶν ὥσπερ ἄγαλμα βαρβαρικόν. On Medius, see ch. 75. 4; Hagnon, ch. 55. 2; Bagoas, ch. 67. 8; Demetrius, 54. 6. Agesias is not otherwise known.

8. ἐκάθευδε: *Mor.* 623 e; Athenaeus 10. 434 b (quoting the Diary).

9. τὰ σπανιώτατα: See ch. 50. 2 f.

διαπεμπόμενος: 'distributing', cf. *Mor.* 155 e, ὁρῶν τούτους ὥσπερ τὴν Βαθυκλέους κύλικα διαπεμπομένους ἀλλήλοις, ἑτέρῳ δὲ μὴ μεταδιδόντας; *Mor.* 215 a.

10. εἰς μυρίας δραχμὰς προῆλθεν: So Ephippus (*F. Gr. Hist.* no. 126, fr. 2) for 60 or 70 guests. Athenaeus 146 c–d remarks that this figure of

160 drachmae per head corresponds to the expenditure of the Persian king. Jacoby (ad loc.) considers that the figure of 10,000 drachmae was chosen quite arbitrarily, but Alexander, as Great King, probably felt compelled to take over this limit from Darius.

τοῖς ὑποδεχομένοις: 'those who entertained A.'

xxiv. *The Persian booty captured at Damascus. Alexander wins Cyprus and all Phoenicia except Tyre. His visions during the siege. His life in danger.*

1. τὴν μάχην τὴν ἐν Ἰσσῷ: ἐπὶ ἄρχοντος Νικοκράτους μηνὸς Μαιμακτηριῶνος (Arr. 2. 11. 10), i.e. November 333.

πέμψας εἰς Δαμασκόν: sc. Parmenio; see ch. 20. 10. Darius had left the bulk of his baggage there (Arr. 2. 11. 9 f., 15. 1; Curt. 3. 8. 12, 12. 27 ff.; Diod. 17. 32. 3).

2. ὠφελήθησαν: 'gained a very great deal of booty'. ὠφελεῖσθαι and ὠφέλεια are very common in Plutarch and Polybius in this technical sense; see Walbank on Polyb. 2. 11. 14, Holden on *Tim.* 29. 2.

οἱ τῶν Θεσσαλῶν ἱππεῖς: Heavy-armed cavalry, 1,800 strong (Tarn 2. 156 ff.; Marsden 69; Schachermeyr 117 (doubtfully) against Berve 1. 140 f., 178), raised to 2,000 before Gaugamela. In all the great battles they fought under Parmenio on the left of the battle-line, and played a distinguished part in 'holding' the enemy while Alexander won the battle on the right. In the Battle of Issus they had a very hard struggle (ἱππομαχία καρτερά) before eventually repulsing their opponents. They may be regarded as particularly Parmenio's troops and were employed on several missions under his command, e.g. Arr. 1. 24. 3, 2. 5. 1. The Pharsalian horse corresponds to Alexander's Royal Squadron. Together with the other allied troops they were discharged at Ecbatana, but many signed on again (Arr. 3. 19. 5 f.); see 42. 5 n.

3. ἀνιχνεύειν: 'track'; properly of dogs, e.g. Homer *Il.* 22. 192. For a similar use see *Caes.* 69. 2, ἀνιχνεύων ἄχρι τοῦ μηδένα λιπεῖν τῶν ἀπεκτονότων (of Octavian); *Mor.* 694 e.

4. οὐ μὴν ἀλλά: Despite the attraction of the enormous wealth to be had in Persia.

τὰ πρὸς θαλάσσῃ: Plutarch makes no mention of the strategic importance of Tyre or of the effect which its capture would have. (Contrast Arr. 2. 17—Alexander's speech to the leaders of the army.)

Κύπρον: For a useful summary of previous Cypriot history, see A. H. M. Jones, *The Cities of the Eastern Roman Provinces* (Oxford, 1937), 365 ff. and (in more detail) Sir George Hill, *A History of Cyprus* 1

(Cambridge, 1940), especially 143 ff. As far back as the history of the island can be traced it was divided into a number of city-states, and at this time there were nine principal cities ruled by kings (a list in Beloch 4. 2, 331). They had joined in the general revolt against Artaxerxes in 351 (Diod. 16. 42), and after its failure their highly-trained navies (together with the Phoenician fleet) were again at Persia's disposal. After Alexander had disbanded his navy (Arr. 1. 20. 1), he found that the siege of Tyre was held up because of Tyrian supremacy at sea, and it was the arrival of 120 Cypriot ships, together with 80 Phoenician (Arr. 2. 20. 1 ff.), that gave him control of the sea and contributed largely to his final victory.

Φοινίκην: Diodorus (17. 40. 2) is equally brief. Aradus, Marathus, Byblos and Sidon all surrendered (Arr. 2. 13. 7 f., 15. 6 f.; Curt. 4. 1. 5 f., 4. 1. 15 ff.).

5. Τύρον: The siege is described at length in the extant sources: Arr. 2. 16–24; Diod. 17. 40–6; Curt. 4. 2–4. Justin 11. 10. 10 ff. contributes nothing. Diod. 17. 46. 5 and Curt. 4. 4. 19 both give seven months as the duration of the siege, while Arr. 2. 24. 6 dates its capture in the month Hecatombaeon = July/Aug., 332. The start of the siege may therefore be placed in January. For the chronology, Beloch 3. 2. 314 f.

τριήρεσι διακοσίαις: A round number; actually 223 triremes plus a Macedonian 50-oared ship. Details in Arr. 2. 20. 1 f.

ὄναρ εἶδε: cf. Arr. 2. 18. 1 (probably from Aristobulus), ἀλλὰ καί τι θεῖον ἀνέπειθεν αὐτὸν ὅτι ἐνύπνιον αὐτῆς ἐκείνης τῆς νυκτὸς ἐδόκει αὐτὸς μὲν τῷ τείχει προσάγειν τῶν Τυρίων· τὸν δὲ Ἡρακλέα δεξιοῦσθαί τε αὐτὸν καὶ ἀνάγειν εἰς τὴν πόλιν. According to Curt. 4. 2. 17, Alexander ('haudquaquam rudis pertractandi militares animos') announced the dream in a speech to his troops.

τὸν Ἡρακλέα: i.e. Melcarth. On the Tyrian Hercules see Arr. 2. 16 and the examples cited by A. S. Pease on Cic. *De nat. deor.* 3. 16. 42. For a modern account, B. C. Brundage, *JNES* 17 (1958), 225 ff.

Alexander suspected the good faith of the Tyrians, and requested that he be allowed to enter the city to sacrifice to Hercules (Arr. 2. 15. 7; Curt. 4. 2. 2 ff.). According to Arrian the Tyrians stated they would admit neither Persians nor Macedonians; Curtius more plausibly says that they first indicated a temple of Hercules in Old Tyre at which Alexander could sacrifice. The Tyrians may have felt that they would have recognized him as their rightful king if they allowed him to sacrifice in the city (Wilcken, *SB Berlin* 1928, 577, n. 6; Glotz–Cohen 85); more probably the Tyrian resistance is to be connected with the general strategic plan of the Persian High Command (Marsden 7, citing Diod. 17. 40. 3).

6. ἔδοξεν ὁ Ἀπόλλων: According to another version (Diod. 17. 41. 7 f.; Curt. 4. 3. 21 f.; ? from Cleitarchus) one of the citizens announces this dream in a public assembly. Curt. then relates that the Tyrians bound the statue of Apollo to its base with a golden chain (so Diod. loc. cit.) and attached it to the altar of Hercules, 'quasi illo deo Apollinem retenturo'.

J. G. Frazer (on Pausanias 3. 15. 7) cites many other examples (ancient and modern) of the fettering of images to prevent desertion. He also points to the practice of the Romans, when besieging a city, of inviting the guardian gods of the city to join their side.

7. εἰληφότες: Castiglioni (*Gnomon* 13 (1937), 140) suggests συνειλη-φότες; but the simple verb is well attested in this phrase, e.g. Dem. 19. 132, Eur. *Ion* 1214.

τῷ κολοσσῷ: Diod. 13. 108. 4 calls this statue χαλκοῦς σφόδρα μέγας, and κολοσσός probably implies great size here, though it does not always do so.

Diod. (loc. cit.) tells us on the authority of Timaeus (fr. 106) that the statue was captured by the Carthaginians at Gela in 405 and sent to Tyre. Curt. 4. 3. 22 wrongly says it was taken at Syracuse.

Ἀλεξανδριστὴν καλοῦντες: cf. Diod. 17. 46. 6, ὁ δὲ βασιλεὺς τοῦ μὲν Ἀπόλλωνος τὰς χρυσᾶς σειρὰς καὶ τὰ δεσμὰ περιελόμενος παρήγγειλεν ὀνομάζειν τὸν θεὸν τοῦτον Ἀπολλὼ φιλαλέξανδρον.

8. ἑτέραν δ᾽ ὄψιν: Attested elsewhere only by Eustathius (*ad Dion. Perieg.*, 911), ὅτι σὰ Τύρος, τουτέστι 'σῇ' Δωρικῶς. Chares may be Plutarch's source, see Jacoby on Chares, *F. Gr. Hist.* no. 125, fr. 7; Pearson, *LHA* 56, n. 28.

10. διὰ μέσου δὲ τῆς πολιορκίας: The expedition is historical: Arr. 2. 20. 4; Curt. 4. 3. 1; Polyaenus 4. 3. 4. There is no other evidence for this incident.

Following the success of the Tyrian fire-ships, Alexander had gone to Sidon to collect his triremes there; while the Phoenician and Cypriot ships were being equipped and engines prepared, he undertook this expedition with a mixed force (details in Arr. loc. cit.). His motive was to prevent the attacks of the natives on the Macedonians gathering timber for ship-building (Curt. loc. cit.); cf. Antigonus' troops in 315 B.C. before the attack on Tyre (Diod. 19. 58. 1). Alexander returned to Sidon in ten days, τὰ μὲν βίᾳ τῶν ταύτῃ ἐξελών, τὰ δὲ ὁμολογίᾳ παραστησάμενος.

τῷ Ἀντιλιβάνῳ: The more easterly of the two great parallel mountain ranges running roughly north-west to south-east and enclosing the valley of Coele-Syria proper. The highest peak reaches nearly 10,000 ft. and the range is perpetually snow-covered. More details in Smith, *Dict. of Gk. and Roman Geography*, s.v. Antilibanus.

Λυσίμαχον: See ch. 5. 8.

Φοίνικος: Phoenix (see ch. 5. 8) accompanied Achilles to Troy, where he was one of the ambassadors sent to bring Agamemnon's offer of reconciliation (Homer *Il.* 9. 168 ff.).

12. τῇ κουφότητι: 'agility, fitness'. So in Arrian's *Anabasis* κοῦφος means 'fit', not 'light-armed', as the Loeb editor constantly translates it (see Tarn 2. 153, n. 4).

Χάρης: *F. Gr. Hist.* no. 125, fr. 7.

x x v. *Aristander correctly foretells the fall of Tyre and Gaza. Alexander sends a great quantity of frankincense to Leonidas, who had formerly reproached his extravagance.*

1. τὰ σημεῖα κατιδών: Plutarch uses the same phrase at *Caes.* 47. 5, where C. Cornelius at Patavium sees in the omens the victory of Caesar at Pharsalus.

2. ἐκέλευε . . . ἀριθμεῖν: 'he ordered that that day should be called the 28th instead of the 30th', i.e. Alexander intercalated a second 28th, and was doubtless prepared to continue the process until the city was taken.

For details of the Athenian calendar including a list of the months, see esp. A. G. Woodhead, *The Study of Greek Inscriptions* (Cambridge, 1959), 115 ff.; W. K. Pritchett and O. Neugebauer, *The Calendars of Athens* (Harvard, 1947). τριακάς is the last day of a 'full' month or a 'hollow' one; but in either case τρίτη φθίνοντος will be the 28th, since the day omitted in a hollow month was δευτέρα φθίνοντος or δευτέρα μετ᾽ εἰκάδας, i.e. the 29th. So Pritchett and Neugebauer, op. cit. 25; B. D. Meritt, *The Athenian Year* (Berkeley, 1961) denies this. If he is right, the month was probably hollow, since it seems more likely that Plutarch, or his source, understood Alexander to be giving Aristander one day's grace than two. This incident illustrates Alexander's support for his friends and his piety.

3. γενομένης δὲ λαμπρᾶς ἐπιβολῆς: 'when a furious assault developed'. LSJ cite only Polyb. 6. 25. 7 for ἐπιβολή in this sense; but see *Caes.* 44. 6, ἐπιβολῆς ἅμα τοσούτων ἱππέων γενομένης, Diod. 17. 48. 5; cf. also *Alex.* 26. 14. For λαμπρός, cf. Polyb. 10. 12. 5.

μηδὲ . . . καρτερούντων: 'and not even the soldiers in the camp remained there'. For καρτερεῖν = wait, a late prose usage, see *Dion* 51. 1

(with Porter's note); cf. also Arr. 4. 8. 9, οὐ καρτερήσαντα δὲ ἀναστρέψαι αὖθις (of Cleitus).

4. πολιορκοῦντι Γάζαν: Arr. 2. 25. 4–27. 7; Diod. 17. 48. 7; Curt. 4. 6. 7–30; Josephus *AJ* 11. 320, 325; Polyb. 16. 22a; Dion. Hal. *de comp. verb.* 18 = Hegesias (*F. Gr. Hist.* no. 142) fr. 5.

Gaza was an old Phoenician foundation, lying about 2½ miles from the sea in a well-watered and fertile area; 'the last town on the edge of the desert as you go from Phoenicia to Egypt' (Arr. ad loc.). All the remainder of Syrian Palestine came over to Alexander, but Gaza under a eunuch Batis (or Baetis) held out for two months (Sept./Oct. 332). On Batis, Berve no. 209.

βῶλος: 'glebam' (Curt.); λίθον (Arr.).

ὑφ' ἕν τῶν μηχανημάτων: Arr. 2. 26. 4 mentions the presence of engines, but says nothing of the bird being caught. Curt. 4. 6. 11, less plausibly, says the bird stuck fast on the tower smeared with bitumen and sulphur.

τοῖς νευρίνοις κεκρυφάλοις: 'the net-work of sinews' (Perrin). κεκρύφαλος generally means 'a woman's hair-net', but Xen. *Cyn.* 6. 7 uses it of the belly of a hunting-net. Here the machine is almost certainly a torsion catapult, in which the tension was effected by twisted skeins of women's hair or the sinews of animals. νευρά and νεῦρον are both used of the strands of a torsion catapult. Alexander certainly possessed torsion catapults and the stone-throwing variety (πετρόβολος) is first attested shortly before this at the siege of Tyre (Tarn, *Hellenistic Military and Naval Developments* (Cambridge, 1930), 105); they were present at Gaza (Arr. 2. 27. 3). For a description of the catapult, Tarn, op. cit., 112 ff.; E. Schramm in Kromayer–Veith, *Heerwesen u. Kriegführung der Griechen u. Römer*, 220 ff.; for Alexander's catapults, cf. Marsden, *JHS* 80 (1960), 224.

5. ἐτρώθη . . . εἰς τὸν ὦμον: by a catapult, Arr. 2. 27. 2; by an arrow, Curt. 4. 6. 17, who also mentions a wound from a stone on the leg.

ἔλαβε δὲ τὴν πόλιν: The entire garrison (10,000, Curt.) fell fighting, and the women and children were enslaved. Alexander subsequently resettled the city with neighbouring tribesmen.

Plutarch says nothing of an attempt on Alexander's life by an Arab who pretended to surrender, or of Alexander dragging Batis round the walls in imitation of Achilles (Curt. 4. 6. 15 f., 29; Hegesias fr. 5.) On this last incident, Tarn 2. 266 ff.; Pearson, *LHA* 247 f.

6. Ὀλυμπιάδι: A. had sent presents to Olympias after the Granicus battle (Berve 2. 287). Dedications at Delphi by Olympias in 331 are probably recorded in an inscription (*SIG* 252 N, 5 ff., with n. 3).

Κλεοπάτρᾳ: The sister of Alexander; see ch. 10. 6.

Λεωνίδῃ: See ch. 5. 7. The incident is mentioned by Plutarch *Mor.* 179 e–f and Pliny *NH* 12. 62.

λιβανωτοῦ: The Attic–Euboeic talent weighed about 60 lb. Hence Alexander is said to have sent approximately 13½ tons of frankincense and 2½ tons of myrrh. Huge quantities of incense were burnt at sacrifices; Herodotus (1. 183), for example, tells us that the Chaldaeans offered up 1,000 talents on the great altar at Babylon when they kept the feast of 'Zeus'.

7. τῆς ἀρωματοφόρου: Theophrastus (*Hist. Plant.* 4. 4. 14; 9. 4. 4 ff.) mentions Syria and especially Arabia as the chief sources of incense.

XXVI. *The foundation of Alexandria. Alexander decides on a visit to Ammon at Siwah.*

1. κιβωτίου δέ τινος: 'a small chest or casket', the νάρθηξ of ch. 8. 2.

τοῖς . . . παραλαμβάνουσι: presumably the troops sent to Damascus, ch. 24. 1 (where the same phrase is used).

2. οὐκ ὀλίγοι τῶν ἀξιοπίστων: Of these we can identify only Onesicritus (ch. 8. 2).

3. Ἀλεξανδρεῖς: F. Pfister, *Alex. d. Gr. in den Offenbarungen der Griechen, Juden, Mohammedaner und Christen* (Berlin, 1956), 13, n. 2, suggests that Plutarch refers to a local Alexandrian history which included the work of Heracleides, whom he takes to be Heracleides Ponticus.

Ἡρακλείδῃ: 'H. nescioquis' (Ziegler, *Plutarchus, Vit. Par.* (Teubner ed.), 4. 2, Index 1). Perhaps Heracleides Lembus (*OCD* s.v. (3)), a civil servant who worked at Oxyrhynchus and was living at Alexandria in 170 B.C. He wrote ἱστορίαι and (probably) a book on Homer; frs. in Müller, *FHG* 3. 167 ff.

οὔκουν . . . Ὅμηρος: 'it seems that Homer was no idle companion, not one who contributed nothing'.

ἀσύμβολος properly means 'not paying one's share', of people contributing to a feast. The two words occur together again at *Coriolanus* 6 in the famous parable of Menenius Agrippa where the limbs complain that the belly sits in the body idle and contributing nothing (ἀργοῦ καὶ ἀσυμβόλου καθεζομένης).

4. τῆς Αἰγύπτου κρατήσας: Arr. 3. 1. 1 ff.; Diod. 17. 49. 1 f.; Curt. 4. 7. 1 ff. Mazaces, the Persian satrap of Egypt, since he had no troops and the Egyptians were hostile, surrendered the country to Alexander when he reached the border at Pelusium. Alexander proceeded up the

Nile to Memphis, where he was enthroned as Pharaoh, perhaps on 14 November 332 (Beloch 3. 2. 315). He then returned to the coast.

πόλιν ... συνοικίσας: Arr. (3. 1. 5–2. 2), like Plutarch, places the foundation of Alexandria *before* the visit to Ammon. This is undoubtedly Ptolemy's version—Aristobulus may have put it after the visit (C. B. Welles, *Historia* 11 (1962), 276, and n. 22)—and has been accepted by all modern writers. Welles (op. cit. 271 ff.), however, has advanced convincing arguments for dating the foundation *after* the visit (so Diod. (17. 52), Curt. (4. 8. 1 f.), Justin (11. 11. 13), Ps.-Call. (1. 31 ff.)—a version which goes back to Cleitarchus, and perhaps to Callisthenes (Welles, op. cit. 276, n. 21)). He makes three main points: (1) Alexander *must* have obtained a god's opinion before founding the city; this was provided by Ammon's oracle (Ps.-Call. 1. 30. 5); (2) Ptolemy probably did not visit Siwah and is wrong in taking Alexander back direct to Memphis, a journey whose feasibility has not been proved; (3) (most convincing) The date of Alexandria's birthday celebration is the date of its foundation; this was Wilcken's view also, but he wrongly dated it to 20 January, instead of 7 April (Welles, op. cit. 284 and n. 67).

5. ἀνὴρ πολιός: Welles (op. cit., 284) holds it possible that the dream of Homer actually took place in connection with an incubation in the Sarapeium of Rhacotis. This seems unlikely.

νῆσος ἔπειτά τις ...: Homer *Od.* 4. 354 f.

6. Φάρον: Strabo 17. 791 ff. (cf. Diod. 17. 52. 3 ff.) gives an excellent description of Pharos and Alexandria, as they existed in his day—a good map (No. xiii) at the end of vol. 8 of the Loeb edition. Pharos lies rather less than a mile off the coast, some twenty miles west (μικρὸν ἀνωτέρω) of the Canobic (most westerly) mouth of the Nile Delta, near the fishing village of Rhacotis.

διὰ χώματος: The Great Harbour on the Eastern side and the Harbour of Good Return (Eunostos) on the western were separated by a mole seven stades long. It formed a bridge to the western end of the island, and until the time of Julius Caesar served also to carry an aqueduct (Strabo 17. 1. 6).

7. ἀνείληπται: 'it has been joined to the mainland'. ἀνῆπται, proposed by Powell (*JHS* 59 (1939), 238) seems necessary. No instance of ἀναλαμβάνειν occurs in this sense, whereas ἀνάπτειν = 'make fast to' is common, e.g. Eur. *HF* 1011, ἀνήπτομεν πρὸς κίονα; cf. *Cam.* 8. 7.

εὐφυΐᾳ διαφέροντα: εὐφυΐα here = favourable situation; ἡ δὲ εὐκαιρία πολύτροπος, as Strabo remarks. Bounded by two stretches of water, the Mediterranean to the north and Lake Mareotis to the south, it was rendered cool by the north-west winds blowing all summer, and healthy by the water on either side. The rise of the Nile prevented the formation of marshes and the silting of the harbour. Diod. (17. 52. 3) also stresses its defensibility.

ταινία γάρ: lit. 'for it is a long strip of land, separating by an isthmus of moderate width a large lake (the Mareotis) and the sea, which terminated in a large harbour'.

ἦν ἄρα: 'was *after all*'. Alexander *now* saw that Homer, who had advised him to site his city here, was a great architect.

συναρμόττοντας: Emendation is unnecessary. The architects were to *make* the shape of the city *conform* to the topography. For this sense of συναρμόττειν, cf. *Mor.* 38 f., συναρμόττειν τῇ προσοχῇ τὴν ἀκρόασιν ... οὐ μανθάνουσιν.

8. τῶν δ' ἀλφίτων λαμβάνοντες: Arrian 3. 2. 1 f. (a λόγος, οὐκ ἄπιστος), Curtius 4. 8. 6 (a *fama*), and Strabo 17. 1. 6 (792) all mention the marking-out of the city by grain. In Arrian and Strabo this is a *pis aller*, as in Plutarch, and the good omen consists simply in its use; for barley-meal denoting an abundance of food, cf. Amm. Marc. 22. 16. 7. For Curtius, as for Plutarch, it is the arrival of flocks of birds that indicates the future prosperity of the city. The use of the meal may well be historical, for Curtius attributes to Macedonian custom the use of *polenta* to mark out the site of a city and he is 'good on Macedonian customs' (Tarn 2. 106–7). See, e.g., 9. 3. 4; 8. 4. 27 ff.; 10. 9. 12; 6. 11. 10 and 38; cf. 7. 2. 1, etc.

κυκλοτερῆ κόλπον ἦγον: 'They described a rounded area, to whose inner arc straight lines succeeded, starting from what might be called the skirts of the area and narrowing the breadth uniformly, so as to produce the figure of a chlamys.' (Tarbell, *CPhil.* 1 (1906), 285, n. 1.)

The chlamys, a military cloak of Thessalian or Macedonian origin, became part of the dress of the Athenian ephebe. It appears to have been a four-cornered garment, with a rounded skirt and a narrow collar, either cut square or circular. On its shape (for which this passage provides the chief evidence), see Tarbell, op. cit. 283 ff. The comparison of the site of Alexandria to a chlamys was a stock one; cf. Diod. 17. 52. 3; Strabo 17. 1. 8 (793); Pliny *NH* 5. 62. Strabo often compares the shape of the inhabited world to a chlamys.

ὑπελάμβανον: We should perhaps read ἀπελάμβανον, 'straight lines *cut off* the inner arc'.

10. τῶν μάντεων: Esp. Aristander, Arr. loc. cit.

11. ὥρμησεν εἰς Ἄμμωνος: Arr. 3. 3–4 (cf. 7. 8. 3); Diod. 17. 49–51;

Curt. 4. 7. 5–30; Justin 11. 11. 2–12; Strabo 17. 1. 43 (814) = Callisthenes fr. 14 (a); Ps.-Call. 1. 30; Iul. Val. 1. 23.

Amon (more correctly Amūn), originally a local god of (Egyptian) Thebes, became a national god with the rise of the eighteenth dynasty and was identified with the Sun-god Amon-Ra. Ammon was 'merely Amon transplanted to Siwah with his name modified to mean, or suggest, god of the sands' (Tarn 2. 348). He had a famous oracle at the oasis of Siwah some 400 miles west of Thebes (see esp. J. Leclant, 'Per Africae Sitientia', *BIAO* 49 (1950), 193 ff., with full refs. to ancient sources and modern literature). The oracle had been known to the Greeks (through Cyrene) since at least the time of Pindar, and had come to rival Dodona and Delphi; on the widespread knowledge of Ammon in Greece before 331, see esp. C. J. Classen, *Historia* 8 (1959), 349 ff.

Alexander's visit to Siwah has been endlessly discussed; for a select bibliography see Bengtson 334, n. 2. Various motives for his journey are given by the ancient sources: (1) His 'longing' (πόθος, Arrian; φιλοδοξία, Strabo; *ingens cupido*, Curtius): on this, see Ehrenberg, 52 ff.; (2) The desire to surpass the achievements of his ancestors, Perseus and Hercules (Strabo, Arrian); (3) To learn about his relationship to Ammon (Arrian, Curtius, Justin); (4) To consult Ammon about the site for a city, Alexandria (Ps.-Call. 1. 30. 5); see Welles, op. cit. 275. Callisthenes, writing no doubt as Alexander wished him to write, gave the official version. The crucial version is Arrian's (at 3. 3. 2) καί τι καὶ αὐτὸς τῆς γενέσεως τῆς ἑαυτοῦ ἐς Ἄμμωνα ἀνέφερε, and the conclusion that Alexander set out ὡς καὶ τὰ αὐτοῦ ἀτρεκέστερον εἰσόμενος ἢ φήσων γε ἐγνωκέναι; cf. Curt. 4. 7. 8, Iovem quem generis sui auctorem . . . aut credebat esse aut credi volebat. Wilcken, *SB Berlin* (1928), 576 ff. argued that Arrian's sources were Callisthenes (for the first two reasons) and Cleitarchus (for the passages quoted above); so essentially Tarn 2. 347 ff., although he holds, more reasonably, that Arrian's immediate source was Aristobulus. This combination of Callisthenes and Cleitarchus is unlikely in itself, and Strasburger, 29 ff., 60, has advanced powerful (many would say convincing) arguments in favour of regarding Ptolemy as the sole source of Arr. 3. 3. 1 f. (and of Curtius). Pearson *LHA* 161 (and n. 62) does not accept this, preferring Aristobulus, but he does not answer Strasburger's arguments. Wilcken and Tarn held that the conclusion was an invention by Cleitarchus and could be discounted. If, however, we accept Ptolemy as Arrian's source, as most scholars do, it is difficult to deny that Alexander went to Siwah to find out about his relationship with Ammon, though Ptolemy, who was out of sympathy with Alexander's ideas about Ammon (F. Taeger, *Charisma* 1 (Stuttgart, 1957), 192), is sceptical of what took place at Siwah. We may believe, too, that Alexander will have known, before he went, that the priest would greet him as 'Son of Ammon'; for it is difficult to believe that he would not have enquired about the procedure at Siwah. In view of the use which Callisthenes made of the greeting (or oracle, as he seems to have described it; see below), it is legitimate to say that Alexander went to have his divine sonship proclaimed. This does not mean that Callisthenes said Alexander was divine; for to be the son of a god was not the same thing as being a god (Tarn 2. 362; Berve 1. 94; cf. Badian, *Gnomon* 33 (1961), 661, 'the difference is crucial'). Certainly attempts (e.g. by Kaerst 1. 382) to connect his visit with a desire for world rule are misconceived (see R. Andreotti, *Saeculum* 8 (1957), 131, n. 30). It is likely, in fact, that *many* motives influenced Alexander (see esp. G. Radet, *REA* 28 (1926), 218 ff.), including the desire to secure the western frontier of Egypt (C. A. Robinson Jr., *AJP* 70 (1949), 199). Probably also the danger and difficulty will have attracted Alexander, as Plutarch suggests.

ὁδὸν μακράν: Alexander proceeded west to Paraetonium (Mersa Matruh), a distance of 200 miles, then turned south-west, following the modern caravan route to the oasis.

τὸν μὲν . . . τὸν δέ: The lack of water and the effect of the south wind are mentioned by all our sources.

12. πάλαι λέγεται: Herodotus 3. 26. 3, ἐπειδὴ ἐκ τῆς Ὀάσιος ταύτης ἰέναι διὰ τῆς ψάμμου ἐπὶ σφέας, γενέσθαι τε αὐτοὺς μεταξύ κου μάλιστα αὐτῶν τε καὶ τῆς Ὀάσιος, ἄριστον αἱρεομένοισι αὐτοῖσι ἐπιπνεῦσαι νότον μέγαν τε καὶ ἐξαίσιον, φορέοντα δὲ θῖνας τῆς ψάμμου κ α τ α χ ῶ σ α ί σφεας, καὶ τρόπῳ τοιούτῳ ἀφανισθῆναι.

μυριάδας . . . πέντε: Herod. 3. 25. 3.

14. τὸ θυμοειδές: On Alexander as θυμοειδής, see ch. 4. 5.

ἄχρι τῶν****πραγμάτων . . . ἀήττητον: A difficult passage. To the emendations cited by Ziegler add θαυμάτων, read by G. Radet in *REA* 28 (1926), 225, n. 7, and φαντασμάτων, 'bis in den Bereich der Wahnvorstellungen' (H. Erbse, *Rh. Mus.* 100 (1957), 282 f., who compares *Mor.* 900 f and 83 c). None is convincing (Ziegler himself postulates a lacuna), or necessary. Plutarch is not being critical of Alexander, who to him is a hero rising superior to τύχη and overcoming every kind of obstacle. Most translators appear to retain the manuscript text, punctuating (rightly) after ἀήττητον, and to understand ἄχρι τῶν πραγμάτων to mean 'which he carried into his undertakings' (Perrin; so, essentially, Ax and Ruegg). But it is, I think, preferable to take the phrase, whose position is emphatic, with ἀήττητον (proleptic). We may translate literally 'his spirited nature bore his ambition onward (to be) invincible as far as *things*', i.e. rendered his ambition invincible not only against men but even against *non-human* obstacles, the τόπους καὶ καιρούς of the next line. On Fortune in the *Life* see the Introduction, p. lxii.

XXVII. *Alexander's journey to Siwah. The proceedings at the oasis.*

2. ὕδωρ πολύ: The heavy rain is attested by all our sources; ὕδωρ πολύ (Arr. 3. 3. 4); πολὺς ὄμβρος (Diod. 17. 49. 4); largum imbrem (Curt. 4. 7. 14); cf. Callisthenes fr. 14 (*a*). It is attributed to divine help also by Arrian and Diodorus. Curtius mentions water carried by camels in leather bottles; it had given out by this time.

διαρκεῖς ὑετοί: 'persistent showers'.

νοτερᾶς . . . ξυμπεσούσης: 'becoming moist and compact'.

3. τῶν ὅρων . . . συγχυθέντων: Arr. 3. 3. 4 also mentions the obliteration of landmarks by the sand blown up by the south wind; cf. Diod. 17. 49. 5.

ὁδηγοῖς: LSJ cite only Polyb. 5. 5. 15; Add *Fab.* 6 (bis); *Luc.* 21; *Crass.* 29 (bis).

κόρακες: Aristobulus καὶ ὁ πλείων λόγος (including Callisthenes fr. 14 (*a*), Diod. 17. 49. 5 and Curt. 4. 7. 15) gave this version (Arr. 3. 3. 6). Aristobulus mentions two crows, Curtius *complures*. Guidance by birds was, of course, a well-known τόπος; see, e.g., Ar. *Av.* ad init., Verg. *Aen.* 6. 190. Ptolemy, however, wrote that the army was guided (to Siwah *and back*) by two talking snakes! (Arr. loc. cit.). Jacoby (on Ptolemy fr. 8) connects this with the role of the snake in the worship of Ammon, Tarn (1. 43, n. 2) with the worship of Sarapis, while Kaerst (1. 387, n. 1) thinks Ptolemy's version may have been influenced by the stories of Olympias and the snake (see ch. 3. 3).

4. ὡς Καλλισθένης φησί: *F. Gr. Hist.* no. 124, fr. 14 (*b*). Diod. (loc. cit.) mentions the cawing of the crows (κλάζοντες). Curt. (loc. cit.) gives Plutarch's other piece of information (ἑπομένων . . . ἀναμένοντες). This makes it certain that Cleitarchus gave both versions, from Callisthenes.

5. εἰς τὸν τόπον: Simply 'to the oasis' (Wilcken, *SB Berlin* (1930), 164, n. 1). No need for change. For descriptions of the oasis, see Arr. 3. 4. 1 ff.; Diod. 17. 50; Curt. 4. 7. 16 ff. For a modern account see Leclant, *BIAO* 49 (1950), 193 ff.

ὁ μὲν προφήτης . . . προσεῖπεν: In Plutarch, as in 'the vulgate', the priest greets Alexander as son of Ammon. Whether Callisthenes wrote that the priest *greeted* Alexander as son of Zeus or that the words were an *oracle* is disputed. Berve (*Gnomon* 5 (1929), 374 ff.) and Mederer

(53 ff.) argued vigorously in favour of the latter view, which appears to be supported by the text of Strabo; see Pearson's excellent analysis, *LHA* 33 ff. But most scholars are convinced by Wilcken's arguments; see his articles in *SB Berlin* (1928), 576 ff., especially 585, and 1930, 159 ff., and cf. F. Oertel, *Rh. Mus.* 89 (1940), 66 ff., and P. Jouguet, *BIE* 26 (1943/4), 91 ff. Wilcken pointed out that Strabo is selecting from Callisthenes' narrative the point which he considered best illustrated his flattery (κολακεία). It is, therefore, arguable that Strabo has placed the priest's words out of their proper place in Callisthenes' account. Moreover it is likely, on general grounds, that the priest would have greeted Alexander in his capacity as Pharaoh as son of Ammon; it is clear that in either case Callisthenes had equated Ammon with Zeus. On the question whether the greeting took place in the hearing of Alexander's companions (as seems almost certain) or in the temple, which Alexander entered alone, see H. Lamer, *Klio* 24 (1930/1), 63 ff., and C. F. Lehmann-Haupt, ibid., 185 f.

ὁ δ' ἐπήρετο: The 'vulgate' writers—Diod. 17. 51. 2 ff.; Curt. 4. 7. 26 ff.; Justin 11. 11. 9 f.—do not make it clear whether Alexander went into the temple alone, but Callisthenes (ap. Strabo) states unequivocally that he did; it is doubtful, therefore, whether the questions put by the king, and the priest's replies, have any claim to be regarded as genuine. Arrian (3. 4. 5) merely said that Alexander was pleased with what he had heard, ὅσα αὐτῷ πρὸς θυμοῦ ἦν. It is, of course, possible that the priests divulged details of what went on inside the temple (cf. Pearson, *LHA* 35, n. 71), or even that Alexander himself disclosed them (Schachermeyr, 209). C. B. Welles, *Historia* 11 (1962), 281, n. 48, inclines to accept the 'vulgate' version, but it is more commonly held to have been invented by Cleitarchus, on the basis of his knowledge that Alexander had received the answers he desired (so Tarn 1. 43; Wilcken 125; Mederer 64).

For the construction with ἐπέρεσθαι, see 41. 4 n.

8. ἐν ἐπιστολῇ: Almost all scholars accept as genuine, e.g. Tarn 2. 348, n. 2; Wilcken, *SB Berlin* (1928), 586 ff.; Schachermeyr 510, n. 139. Kaerst's objections (*Phil.* 51 (1892), 612) are trifling; see *PACA* 4 (1961), 13. See, however, the Introduction, p. lx, n. 1.

τινὰς ... μαντείας ἀπορρήτους: 'certain secret prophecies'. For this meaning of ἀπόρρητος ('to be kept secret') Berve, *Gnomon* 5 (1929), 375, n. 1, cites Herodotus 9. 45. Cf. also *Nic.* 5. 4, 23. 3, *Mor.* 332 f.

Wilcken (op. cit., 592 f.) suggested, improbably, that these oracles were concerned with world rule. Tarn (2. 354) is probably correct in thinking that the priest explained the spiritual nature of the relationship of Ammon to Alexander.

9. ἔνιοι δέ φασι: Pearson, *LHA* 35, n. 72, thinks that these 'later writers were worried by the possible inability of the priest of Ammon to speak Greek'. Jacoby (*F. Gr. Hist.* 2D, 421 f.) considers that they were writers hostile to Alexander, who attempted to discredit his relationship to Ammon by attributing the greeting to an error. It might be thought, more probably, a *favourable* invention (if it is an invention), in view of the enormous importance of such *lapsus linguae* as omens throughout antiquity.

It is quite likely that the priest could speak Greek. Tarn (2. 348) points to the regular intercourse between Siwah and Greece. Cf. Classen, *Historia* 8 (1959), 349 ff.

10. λέγεται: At *Mor.* 180 d, the incident takes place at Siwah and Alexander's remark immediately follows the priest's greeting of him as son of Ammon. Tarn 2. 435 ff. regards it as 'a plain statement that all men are brothers, and, if true, . . . the earliest known, at any rate in the ancient world'. Andreotti, *Historia* 5 (1956), 289 f., properly rejects the story as mere romance. For a convincing refutation of Tarn's arguments, see Badian, *Historia* 7 (1958), 426 f.; cf. Andreotti, loc. cit. Psammon (not known elsewhere) is simply a variation of Ammon, suggested by the deserts surrounding Siwah.

11. ὡς πάντων μὲν ὄντα κτλ.: An adaptation of the common Homeric phrase πατὴρ ἀνδρῶν τε θεῶν τε. κοινόν is inserted to contrast with the following ἰδίους.

xxviii. A digression on Alexander's attitude to divinity.

We find in Plutarch's writings only scorn for the ruler-cult. Deification he regarded as foolish and ephemeral, bringing no lasting glory (*Mor.* 360 c–d). He considers the proposal of the Athenian Stratocles to call the envoys sent to Demetrius θεωροί a 'most monstrous device' (ὑπερφυέστατον ἐνθύμημα), and holds that the 'absurd flattery' of the Athenians threw Demetrius' unstable intellect completely off balance. There can be little doubt that Plutarch, Arrian (see § 6), and Cassius Dio (e.g. 43. 41. 3) are all influenced by their attitude to the cult of the Roman Emperor and read back the conditions of their own times into this quite different situation. In the present chapter Plutarch sets out with obvious approval what he believes to have been Alexander's real attitude towards deification; elsewhere (*Mor.* 330 f–331 a) he talks of Alexander's supposed descent from Ammon as mere poetic flattery. Cf. also *Mor.* 65 d (quoted on ch. 23. 7).

For further details see esp. K. Scott, 'Plutarch and the Ruler Cult', *TAPA* 60 (1929), 117–35, and F. Taeger, *Charisma* 2. 527 ff.; esp. 528, n. 189, 531, n. 203.

1. περὶ τῆς ἐκ θεοῦ γενέσεως καὶ τεκνώσεως: 'of his divine birth and parentage' (Perrin). Tarn (2. 355, n. 7) wrongly takes τέκνωσις to mean 'adoption'. It is common in Plutarch in the sense of 'procreation'; see esp. *Lycurg.* 15. 11; *Sol.* 20. 6; *Mor.* 562 a; *Dion* 3. 6, σπουδάζοντι περὶ τὴν ἐκ ταύτης τέκνωσιν, 'he was eager to have a child by her'; cf. ch. 3. 3.

ὑποφειδομένως ἑαυτὸν ἐξεθείαζε: 'somewhat infrequently assumed his divinity'.

2. περὶ Σάμου γράφων Ἀθηναίοις: On the authenticity of this letter and the light which, if genuine, it throws on the character of Alexander towards the end of his life, see *CQ* N.s. 3 (1953), 151 ff., and cf. F. Hampl in *Studies . . . Robinson*, 823. It was written probably early in 323 B.C. in reply to an Athenian protest following the promulgation of the Exiles' Decree in the previous year (Diod. 17. 109. 1; 18. 8. 2 ff.). According to this, the Athenian cleruchs would require to evacuate Samos (Diod. 18. 8. 6); see also *SIG* 312.

ἐγὼ μὲν . . . ἔδωκα: '*I* would not have given'; not 'I *cannot* have given' (Perrin).

3. ὕστερον δέ: Plutarch errs in placing the wound after the letter. It was sustained by Alexander while besieging Massaga, the capital of the Assacenians, at the end of 327 B.C. (*Mor.* 341 b with Arr. 4. 26. 4; cf. Curt. 8. 10. 28).

περιαλγής: A very strong word used of oxen burnt by faggots (*Fab.* 6. 8) and of Antiochus hit in the mouth by a stone (*Cat. Mai.* 14. 1). In fact, the wound was trifling (Arr. loc. cit.).

ἰχώρ, . . . θεοῖσιν: Homer *Il.* 5. 340.

For the anecdote see also *Mor.* 180 e, 341 b. It goes back to Aristobulus (fr. 47 = Athenaeus 251 a); according to him the Homeric line was quoted by the Athenian pancratiast, Dioxippus (Berve no. 284), to flatter the king. In Diog. Laert. 9. 60 Anaxarchus deflates his divine pretensions, while in Seneca (*Suas.* 1. 5) Callisthenes quotes the line ironically. Tarn (2. 358, n. 5) is doubtless right in holding that Dioxippus quoted the Homeric line and was snubbed by Alexander, who remarked; 'It's not ichor, it's blood'. In Curt. 8. 10. 29 and Seneca *Ep.* 59. 12 Alexander remarks that the pain of his wound shows he is mortal.

4. Ἀνάξαρχος ὁ σοφιστής: Berve no. 70; W. D. Ross, *OCD* s.v. A native of Abdera and a follower of the atomist Democritus. He accompanied Alexander on his expedition, and in 323 persuaded him to enter Babylon. In our sources (e.g. Arr. 4. 9. 7 ff.; Athenaeus 6. 250 f) he is depicted as one of the king's flatterers, perhaps because of the desire of the Peripatetics to contrast him with Callisthenes; nevertheless he was the teacher of Pyrrho, the sceptic, and there is no reason to doubt that he was not an idealist, as Callisthenes may have been. See further, chapters 52–3.

Both anecdotes are related by Athenaeus 6. 250 f on the authority of Satyrus (fr. 18, *FHG* 3. 164). According to Diogenes Laertius (9. 58) the remark about the satraps' heads was directed at Nicocreon, king of Salamis (see ch. 29. 3), but more probably this is an invention designed to explain their subsequent hostility. Nicocreon was notorious for pounding Anaxarchus to death in a mortar; see Diog. Laert. 9. 59; *Mor.* 449 e; many other refs. in Berve 2. 35, n. 1.

καταφαυλίζων: 'depreciating' (ἅπ. λεγ.).

5. ἐξευτελίζοντα καὶ κατειρωνευόμενον: 'disparaging and mocking'.

6. τετυφωμένος: As the Stoics maintained; see the Introduction, pp. lxi f.

τῇ δόξῃ τῆς θειότητος: Arrian (7. 29. 3) also tends to regard Alexander's claim to be the son of Ammon as a mere device designed to impress his subjects, ὅτι δὲ ἐς θεὸν τὴν γένεσιν τὴν αὑτοῦ ἀνέφερεν, οὐδὲ τοῦτο ἐμοὶ δοκεῖ μέγα εἶναι αὐτῷ τὸ πλημμέλημα, εἰ μὴ καὶ σόφισμα ἦν τυχὸν ἐς τοὺς ὑπηκόους τοῦ σεμνοῦ ἕνεκα.

XXIX. *Alexander's disappointment at Thessalus' defeat in the tragic contest at Tyre does not prejudice him against the winner. He rejects Darius' peace offer.*

1. εἰς δὲ Φοινίκην: To Tyre, where he sacrificed a second time to Hercules and held athletic and literary contests (Arr. 3. 6. 1; Curt. 4. 8. 16).

χορῶν κυκλίων: Dithyrambic choruses, opposed to those arranged in a rectangle. See A. W. Pickard-Cambridge, *Dithyramb, Tragedy and Comedy* ed. 2 (Oxford, 1962), 32; id. *Dramatic Festivals*, 245.

2. ἐχορήγουν: 'acted as Choregi'. For their duties, see esp. Pickard-Cambridge, *Dramatic Festivals*, 87 ff.

οἱ κληρούμενοι κατὰ φυλάς: 'Those who were chosen by lot by tribes'. ταῖς φυλαῖς, suggested independently by Schaefer and by H. Richards (*CR* 17 (1903), 336) for the MSS. τὰς φυλάς, gives equally good sense. While the tribes selected the choregi for comedies, the Archon appointed the tragic choregi (Arist. *Ath. Pol.* 56. 3).

3. Νικοκρέων: Berve no. 568. As Pnytagoras is mentioned by Arrian (2. 20. 6; 22. 2) as king of Salamis during the siege of Tyre, Nicocreon

must have succeeded his father in 332/1. For his coins, B. V. Head, *Historia Numorum* (Oxford, 1911), 744.

Πασικράτης : Berve no. 610. His son Nicocles accompanied Alexander.

τοῖς ἐνδοξοτάτοις ὑποκριταῖς : The conclusion of this incident in the *Moralia* (334 d–e) well illustrates the difference between the *Life* and the speeches *De Alexandri Fortuna*. There Alexander is said to have felt that, while he must be superior to all men, yet he must submit to Justice.

Ἀθηνοδώρῳ : Victor at the Dionysia in 342 and 329, and perhaps also at the Lenaea in 342 (see J. B. O'Connor, *Chapters in the History of Actors and Acting in Ancient Greece* (Chicago, 1908), 73 f.). Since he must have been in Athens in 332 to make a contract to appear at the Dionysia, he probably joined Alexander in Egypt (cf. Arr. 3. 1. 4). He performed in 324 at the wedding feast at Susa (Chares fr. 4).

Θεσσαλῷ : See on ch. 10. 4.

5. τὸν ἀγῶνα τῶν Διονυσίων : The greatest festival of Dionysus, often called *Δ. τὰ ἀστικά* (or ἐν ἄστει) or *Δ. τὰ μεγάλα*. On the date, 8th–15th Elaphebolion (March/April), see Pickard-Cambridge, *Dramatic Festivals*, 63 f.

ἀπήντησε : 'did not appear at the Dionysiac festival'. ἀπαντᾶν is the usual legal term for appearing in court.

τὴν ζημίαν : 'The liability of artists to fines of this kind is laid down in the Euboean law (*IG* 12. 9. 207), c. 290 B.C., and elaborate provisions are made' (Pickard-Cambridge, *Dramatic Festivals* 287, n. 8).

6. Λύκωνος : The famous comic actor from Scarphe in E. Locris, who headed a troupe of actors at this time (*Mor.* 334 e). He also appeared at Susa in 324 (Chares fr. 4). See, further, *RE* 13, 2303 (no. 13).

7. Δαρείου δὲ πέμψαντος ἐπιστολήν : 1. Arrian mentions *two* embassies: (*a*) 2. 14, while Alexander was at Marathus (after Issus), offering friendship and alliance and requesting the release of the Persian captives; (*b*) 2. 25, during the siege of Tyre, offering Alexander the hand of one of Darius' daughters and the cession of all territory west of the Euphrates, together with payment of 10,000 talents. 2. Diodorus also gives two (Schwartz's attempt (*RE* 4, 1884) to show that Diodorus mentioned three embassies is rightly rejected by Kaerst 1. 376, n. 2 and Berve 2. 122, n. 1): (*a*) 17. 39, when Darius had reached Babylon after Issus, requesting the release of the captives for a large ransom (20,000 talents, 17. 54. 1) and offering to cede all territory west of the River Halys and to conclude a treaty of alliance with Alexander;

(b) 17. 54, shortly before Gaugamela—terms similar to Arrian (b), except that the ransom is 30,000 talents. 3. Curtius has *three* embassies: (a) 4. 1. 7 ff., while Alexander is at Marathus—terms similar to Arrian (a), but there is no mention of an alliance and a ransom is offered; (b) 4. 5. 1 ff., during the siege of Tyre—terms similar to Diodorus (a), except that no ransom is mentioned; (c) 4. 11, before Gaugamela—terms similar to Diodorus (b). 4. Justin (11. 12. 1 ff.) also lists three embassies, but without indication of time—terms similar to Curtius (though abbreviated).

It is generally (and rightly) held that there were only two embassies, to Marathus and Tyre. Berve (2. 121 ff.) regards the terms given in Diodorus (a) and Curtius (b), i.e. the ransom and the cession of territory west of the River Halys, as an invention patterned on the terms of the second embassy. Marsden 6 ff. may, however, be correct in thinking that the envoys were empowered to make these concessions in any bargaining that might arise. His suggestion that they originate with 'the mercenaries' source' (hence are unknown to Arrian's source) is acceptable only in the sense that Cleitarchus may have obtained them orally from Darius' mercenaries.

The letter cited by Plutarch is clearly that received by Alexander during the siege of Tyre (the terms agree exactly with those in Arr. 2. 25. 1 ff., including the figure of 10,000 talents), although he has wrongly dated it to Alexander's *second* visit to Tyre. Schwartz, *RE* 2, 913 (cf. Strasburger 29) and Pridik 55 think that Arrian uses Aristobulus; but the striking similarities between Arr. 2. 14. 4–9 and Curt. 4. 1. 10–14 suggest that, since there is no evidence that Curtius used Aristobulus, both drew on Ptolemy for the first letter; presumably then for the second as well. For further arguments in favour of Ptolemy as Arrian's source see Schachermeyr 508, nn. 125, 127. (The similarities which Pearson, *Historia* 3 (1953–4), 450, sees between Arr. 2. 14. 8 f. and Alexander's letter to Cleomenes (Arr. 7. 23. 8) are not striking and in any case may be due to Alexander's own wording.) The resemblances between Plutarch and Arrian are best explained by supposing direct use of Callisthenes by Plutarch, and indirect use (through Ptolemy) by Arrian.

8. Παρμενίωνος εἰπόντος: This anecdote occurs also in Diod., Curt., and Arr. (as a λόγος). It doubtless originates with Callisthenes, who shows Parmenio in an unfavourable light in the battle of Gaugamela (ch. 33. 10)—see Kaerst 1. 378, n. 1. Its authenticity is perhaps supported by ch. 21. 9, where Parmenio encourages Alexander to marry Barsine, i.e. Stateira, and produce a legitimate heir.

On the significance of the remarks for the outlook of Alexander and Parmenio, see Wilcken 111 f.

9. τῶν φιλανθρώπων: cf. Arr. 2. 25. 3, *ἐκέλευέ τε αὐτὸν ἥκειν, εἴ τι εὑρέσθαι ἐθέλοι φιλάνθρωπον παρ' αὐτοῦ.*

xxx. Death of Darius' wife. News of Alexander's kindness to her arouses his suspicions, but these are dispelled and he prays that, if the Persian Empire is fated to fall, Alexander may rule.

1. τῆς Δαρείου γυναικὸς ἀποθανούσης ἐν ὠδῖσι: The wife of Darius was captured at Issus in November 333 (ch. 21. 1). That she died in childbirth is doubtless true, and her death should be placed in the spring of 332, soon after the embassy to Alexander during the siege of Tyre. The misdating of this embassy caused Plutarch to put her death at this point. Diodorus (17. 54. 7) also puts her death after the second embassy. Curtius (4. 10. 18 ff.) and Justin (11. 12. 6 f.) place it *before* the embassy, which is indeed the result of Alexander's treatment of Darius' wife. Justin, like Plutarch, attributes her death to childbirth, Curtius to the hardships of travel.

ἔθαψεν οὖν . . .: Alexander's grief was such that his motives were questioned (*Mor.* 338 e). According to Curtius (4. 10. 23), he buried her with funeral rites in the native Persian manner.

2. τῶν δὲ θαλαμηπόλων: 'one of the eunuchs of the bed-chamber', cf. Arr. 4. 20. 1. For the episode, *Mor.* 338 e; Athenaeus 13. 603 c (Carystius); Curt. 4. 10. 25 ff.; Itin. Al. 57. Arr. loc. cit. gives it as a λόγος, and places it soon after Issus; the wife of Darius is still alive.

Τίρεως ὄνομα: Tyriotes (Curt. loc. cit.). Not otherwise known.

3. πληξάμενος τὴν κεφαλήν: Perhaps a reminiscence of Herod. 3. 14, *ἀνακλαύσας μέγα καὶ καλέσας ὀνομαστὶ τὸν ἑταῖρον ἐπλήξατο τὴν κεφαλήν.*

τοῦ Περσῶν δαίμονος: Plutarch (*Mor.* 369 d ff.; cf. 1026 b) gives a correct account of the main feature of Persian religion, the existence of a good and an evil principle in conflict with each other. The former, Zoroaster called a θεός, Oromazes, the latter a δαίμων, Areimanius.

On Zoroaster (Zarathustra) see esp. Olmstead 94 ff.; G. B. Gray in *CAH* 4. 205 ff.; J. Bidez and F. Cumont, *Les Mages hellénisés*, 2 vols. (Paris, 1938).

The idea that a whole people is led or misled by its Daimon is rare; cf., however, *Mor.* 324 b, where ὁ ʽΡωμαίων μέγας δαίμων remains constant in support of the Roman people.

γυναῖκα καὶ ἀδελφήν: So § 10 and Gellius *NA* 7. 8. 3. Their father, Arsanes (or Arsames), had himself married his sister, Sisygambis

(Berve no. 711). Earlier Darius II (Ochus), the grandfather of Sisygambis, had married his half-sister, Parysatis.

5. Στατείρᾳ: Berve no. 721. Her name occurs here alone.

ἀναλάμψειε: Powell, *JHS* 59 (1939), 238, proposed ἀνάψει. The manuscript reading ἀναλάμψει is supported only by a single example from the Greek Anthology of ἀναλάμπειν used transitively. All six examples in Plutarch are intransitive. On the other hand, there are ten examples of ἀνάπτειν used transitively. Castiglioni (*Stud.* I. 144) suggests the optative ἀναλάμψειε, 'may Oromasdes kindle again'. ἀνάψειε, therefore, is probably the correct reading.

ὁ κύριος Ὠρομάσδης: i.e. Ormazd, Ahura Mazda. 'At the head of the pantheon stood the sky, whose name of Dyaosh was cognate of the Greek Zeus (cf. Xenophon *Cyropaedeia, passim*); more often he was the "Lord", Ahura, or the "Wise", Mazdah. In time these manifestations of the supreme power were united as Ahura-Mazdah, the "Wise Lord".' (Olmstead 24.) To Zoroaster he was sole God, but by the time of Darius I he was "the greatest of the gods". (Olmstead 96, 471.) See also the works cited on § 3, and R. Ghirshman, *Iran* (Penguin, 1954), 155 ff.

8. Μίθρου τε φῶς: 'The sun god, god of justice and redemption . . . a very old Iranian deity' (Ghirshman op. cit., 156); 'the guardian of the plighted word' (Olmstead 132; cf. 24 f., 130). For an oath by Mithra, see Xen. *Cyr.* 7. 5. 53.

μᾶλλον ἂν κατ' ἀξίαν κτλ.: 'Would not my misfortune have been more compatible with my honour, if I had met with an angry and savage enemy' (Perrin). Darius means that his misfortune would not have involved his wife's dishonour, as the next sentence makes clear. Reiske's ἂν ἤ misses the point.

9. τί γὰρ εὐπρεπὲς . . . συμβόλαιον: 'what honest communication' (North). συμβόλαιον is any form of connection or association, not necessarily commercial; see *Arat.* 20. 4, and *Mor.* 980 d, ὁ κροκόδειλος θαυμαστὸν ἑαυτὸν ἐπιδείκνυται πρὸς κοινωνίαν καὶ χάριν ἐν τοῖς πρὸς τὸν τροχίλον συμβολαίοις (consuetudo, usus).

11. ⟨τὰς⟩ χεῖρας ἀνατείνας: For the addition of the article, see Ziegler *Rh. Mus.* 84 (1935), 374. To his examples add e.g. *Rom.* 18. 8; *Cam.* 12. 4; *Arist.* 7. 8 and esp. Athenaeus 13. 603 c (of the same incident).

12. τὴν Περσῶν ἀρχήν: In support of ἀρχήν, the reading of C, Ziegler cites Arr. 4. 20. 3, σὺ νῦν μάλιστα μὲν ἐμοὶ φύλαξον Περσῶν τε καὶ Μήδων τὴν ἀρχήν, and Curt. 4. 10. 34, primum mihi stabilite regnum.

εἰς ὀρθὸν ... σταθεῖσαν: Ziegler compares Soph. *OT* 50.

13. Κύρου: Cyrus, 'the Great', who overthrew the Median Empire and established the Achaemenid dynasty.

xxxi. *The events leading up to the battle of Gaugamela.* (See, apart from the general works, Marsden 11 ff.)

1. ἑκατὸν μυριάσι ... καταβαίνοντα: Plutarch agrees essentially with Arr. (3. 8. 6), 1,000,000 infantry and 40,000 cavalry, and Diod. (17. 53. 3), 800,000 infantry and 200,000 cavalry. These are mere propaganda figures (Tarn 1. 25). Justin (11. 12. 5), repeating his figures for Issus, gives 400,000 and 100,000. Curtius' figures (4. 12. 13) are much lower, 200,000 infantry and 45,000 horse. Schachermeyr 222 regards them as trustworthy, based on a captured Persian battle-order used originally by Callisthenes. But, although Aristobulus (Arr. 3. 11. 3) mentions the capture of this order of battle, there is no indication that it contained detailed figures for the Persian forces. Marsden 32 ff. reaches a total of *c.* 34,000 for the cavalry, which cannot be far out; he despairs, justifiably, of estimating the infantry.

5. Ἐρατοσθένης: *F. Gr. Hist.* no. 241, fr. 29.

6. τὴν δὲ μεγάλην μάχην: According to Arrian (6. 11. 4) ὁ πᾶς λόγος maintained that the battle was fought at Arbela, but Ptolemy and Aristobulus said it took place near the village of Gaugamela, though Arbela, being a city and sounding better, stole the credit of being the site of the great battle; so also Strabo 16. 1. 3, who says that 'the Macedonians' announced that the battle had taken place at Arbela and transmitted this to 'the historians'. Callisthenes evidently began the change, as Strabo (17. 1. 43), on his authority, refers to the prophecy of Ammon that Alexander would be victorious at *Arbela.* At 16. 1. 3 (? following Aristobulus), he rightly refers to Gaugamela.

The battle took place at Tell Gomel. Sir Aurel Stein (*Geog. Jour.* 100 (1942), 155 ff.) located this south of the Jebel Maglub, and held that the battle was fought on the plains of Keramlais south of the old route from Nineveh to Arbela. This view, accepted by Fuller 163 and Tarn 2. 189, must now be given up, since it seems established that Tell Gomel lay *north* of Jebel Maglub; see Schachermeyr 511, n. 153, Marsden 20. A full discussion in Streck, *RE* 7, 861 ff.

7. οἶκον καμήλου: So Strabo 16. 1. 3. Gaugamela really means 'the grazing place of the camel' (Olmstead 515, n. 4); cf. Streck loc. cit.

τῶν πάλαι τις βασιλέων: i.e. Darius I. Cf. Strabo loc. cit., ὠνόμασε δ' οὕτω Δαρεῖος ὁ Ὑστάσπεω. ...

ἀποτάξας: 'setting aside, earmarking'; cf. *Arist.* 27. 2.

8. ἡ ... σελήνη ... ἐξέλιπε: For the eclipse cf. Arr. 3. 7. 6; Curt. 4. 10. 2; Pliny *NH* 2. 180; Ptol. 1. 4. 2; Cic. *De Div.* 1. 121. It is dated by the reference to the Eleusinian mysteries, held at the time of the sowing in Boedromion (Sept./Oct.), to the night of 20/21 September 331. Plutarch, therefore, dates the battle to 1 October. So at *Cam.* 19. 5 he gives the date as Βοηδρομιῶνος πέμπτῃ φθίνοντος = 26 Boedromion = 1 October (see Beloch 3. 2. 315). The fact that he calls the battle Arbela, instead of the technically correct Gaugamela, does not mean that he is using a different source; he has read and digested his material, and writing in a non-specialist context he naturally uses the name by which the battle was commonly known (§ 6 above). In the same way he writes at *Alex.* 16 that the Granicus battle took place in the month of Daisios, but at *Cam.* 19 he writes Thargelion, the Attic equivalent.

What date Arrian had in mind is uncertain, probably 1 October; see Beloch's calculations (loc. cit.). His conclusions are challenged by Burn (*JHS* 72 (1952), 84 f.), who favours 27 September, and by Marsden (75, n. 4), who proposes 30 September; but Arrian's schedule of movements is vague enough to permit Beloch's interpretation, even if it does not require it. Marsden (loc. cit.) thought to find confirmation for his dating of Arrian in the present passage by emending the text to read ἐν δὲ δεκάτῃ ἀπὸ τῆς ἐκλείψεως νυκτί . . . (rather ἐν δεκάτῃ δέ, with the common postponement of δέ, to avoid the hiatus). But the emendation would not be justifiable, even if it were *certain* that Arrian intended 30 September, in view of the *Camillus* passage. Beloch with greater justification might claim support from Plutarch for his dating. Later (3. 15. 7), Arrian wrongly places the battle in the following month, Pyanepsion.

ἐν ὅπλοις συνεῖχε τὴν δύναμιν: Severely criticized by Arrian 3. 11. 1 f., καὶ εἴπερ τι ἄλλο, καὶ τοῦτο ἐκάκωσε τοῖς Πέρσαις ἐν τῷ τότε τὰ πράγματα; cf. Curt. 4. 13. 11 ff., Marsden 22.

ἐπιπορευόμενος τὰς τάξεις: lit. 'going through the ranks', cf. *Tim.* 12. 6, i.e. he held a general review of his troops.

9. ἱερουργίας . . . ἱερουργούμενος: 'carrying out some secret ritual'. At *Caes.* 9. 6, Plutarch uses ἱερουργία of the rites of the Bona Dea.

τῷ Φόβῳ σφαγιαζόμενος: Alexander is nowhere else recorded to have sacrificed to Phobos (cf. Berve 1. 86, n. 2), but there is no reason to follow most manuscripts in reading Φοίβῳ. The existence of Phobos as an independent deity (mentioned immediately after Zeus) is attested at Selinus in the fifth century (*SIG* 1122), and Plut. (*Cleom.* 8. 9) mentions a temple of Phobos in Sparta. More significantly, Aeschylus (*Sept.* 45) includes Phobos with Ares and Enyo in the ritual oath taken by the

Seven against Thebes, and both Scipio Africanus (Appian *Punica* 21) and Theseus (*Thes.* 27. 2) are said to have sacrificed to this god before battles. On Phobos, see *RE* 20, 309 ff. (Bernert) and Roscher's *Lexikon* s.vv. Personifikationen (griech.), col. 2140 (Deubner) and Phobos, cols. 2386 ff. (Weizsäcker). In Curt. (4. 13. 15) Alexander prays to Jupiter and Minerva Victoria.

10. τοῦ **Νιφάτου**: Classical writers, e.g. Strabo 11. 12. 4, generally place this mountain-range in southern Armenia; Pliny, *NH* 5. 98, connects it with the Taurus mountains. Plutarch evidently puts it much further south.

ἀτέκμαρτος . . . συμμεμειγμένη: 'a confused hubbub of voices.'

θόρυβος: As the majority of the manuscripts read θόρυβος καὶ φόβος, Schmieder suggested θ. καὶ ψόφος, perhaps rightly. ψόφος is found together with θόρυβος at *Alc.* 31. 3 and *Alex.* 60. 2. It is used of the noise of arms at *Cam.* 5. 6 and *Mar.* 28. 3.

11. ὤσασθαι **πόλεμον**: Ziegler compares *Cam.* 23. 4, ἀπώσασθαι πόλεμον ἀλλόφυλον καὶ βαρβαρικόν. For the simple verb, cf. *Mar.* 16. 1, νέφος τοσοῦτον πολέμου καὶ σκηπτὸν ὠσάμενοι. The expression is as old as Homer; cf. *Il.* 12. 276.

ἔπειθον: 'they tried to persuade'. Arr. (3. 10. 1 ff.) relates, as a λόγος, that Parmenio came to Alexander's tent and advised a night-attack. In Curt. (4. 13. 3 ff.) he gives this advice in a council called by the king. In both authors Alexander makes the same reply. Can this have been the occasion when, as Callisthenes said (ch. 33. 10), he was offended by Alexander's arrogance (ὄγκος)? Pearson, *LHA* 47 acutely notes that Callisthenes must have repudiated this charge, and points to the statement (Arr. 3. 10. 2) that Alexander's remark 'did not seem like excessive arrogance (οὐχ ὑπέρογκον) so much as proper confidence in the face of danger'. Parmenio may have been represented (? truthfully) as describing Alexander's remark as 'childish and foolish', while the others thought it showed confidence.

On the wisdom of Alexander's decision, see Arrian's sensible remarks (3. 10. 3 f.); cf. Burn 144 f.; Fuller 164.

12. μειρακιώδη καὶ κενὴν ἀπόκρισιν: 'a childish and foolish reply'. The words are similarly linked at *Crass.* 16. 1 and *Arist.* 8. 3. On μειρακιώδης, see Holden on *Them.* 3. 2.

13. τῶν προτέρων: i.e. at Issus.

14. ἀπὸ τηλικαύτης κτλ.: 'when he could draw from so great a host and so vast a territory' (Perrin). For the use of ἀπό, cf. *Luc.* 36. 1, ἀπὸ μείζονος δυνάμεως φοβερός; Cic. 23. 5, Κάτων . . . τοῖς ἐκείνων πολιτεύμασιν ἀπ᾽ ἴσης μὲν ἐξουσίας, μείζονος δὲ δόξης ἀντιτασσόμενος.

XXXII–XXXIII. *The Battle of Gaugamela and its preliminaries.*
The chief ancient accounts are Arr. 3. 11–15; Diod. 17. 57–61; Curt. 4. 13–16. The most detailed modern studies are those by G. T. Griffith, *JHS* 67 (1947), 77 ff.; Fuller 163 ff.; Marsden 40 ff.; cf. also Tarn 2. 182 ff., criticized at several points in the works cited, and by A. R. Burn, *JHS* 72 (1952), 85 ff. Plutarch's account is castigated by Tarn 2. 352 f., not without cause; but it is hardly 'the worst farrago of nonsense in the Greek language'. It contains one valuable piece of information—see 33. 4. It is little, if at all, worse than Curtius' version (cf. Burn op. cit., 87), which it resembles closely in several particulars—see 32. 5, the Bactriani; 32. 6, 33. 9, the two messages from Parmenio; 33. 2, Aristander and the eagle.

Tarn has not appreciated the structure of ch. 32. Plutarch begins (§ 1–3) by illustrating Alexander's confidence before the battle. Then in § 4 he states that the king displayed confidence in the battle as well (παρ᾽ αὐτὸν τὸν κίνδυνον). This he proceeds to prove by relating Alexander's remark when Parmenio's request for help reached him (§ 7). §§ 5–7 are, in fact, a digression to illustrate this, as the first words, ἔσχε γάρ, show. Plutarch then goes on to say that when he had sent this reply to Parmenio, Alexander put on his helmet (? to commence his attack). Plutarch's source evidently spoke of two requests for help (see 33. 9), and Plutarch had only a vague idea of when the first was supposed to have been made. §§ 8–12 are a digression on Alexander's armour and horses, as Tarn realized, introduced by the reference to the helmet. The imperfects προσήγετο and ἦρχε (§ 12) indicate that Plutarch is writing of Alexander's *normal* practice, and that he does not mean that Alexander *now* began the attack. τότε δέ is a vague expression; it resumes the narrative after 32. 3. Plutarch does not mean that Alexander put on his helmet and then addressed the Thessalians, as Tarn maintains. It is, indeed, by no means certain that Plutarch thought that they were under Alexander's personal command. He is selecting a particular incident, to show Alexander's interest in the Greeks, after which Alexander would ride along (παριππεύειν) to take up his position on the right; cf. the situation at Arr. 2. 10. 2.

1. λέγεται: Diod. 17. 56; Curt. 4. 13. 17 ff.; Justin 11. 13. 1 ff.

ἐπελθόντος ὄρθρου: For this reading see Ziegler (*Rh. Mus.* 84 (1935), 374). The manuscripts are divided between ἀπελθόντος and ἀπελθόντας, and most editors have adopted ἐπελθόντας, the reading of the Aldine ed.; this appears correct. Ziegler held that one would expect παρελθόντας or συνελθόντας rather than ἐπελθόντας and regarded the genitive as certain in view of τοῦ καιροῦ κατεπείγοντος below. But Plutarch nowhere combines ὄρθρου with a verb; at *Cam.* 41 and *Otho* 17 ὄρθρου is used absolutely; elsewhere he has περὶ (or πρὸς) τὸν ὄρθρον. At *Alex.* 76. 7 he writes ἐπελθόντων δὲ τῶν ἡγεμόνων.

παρ' αὐτῶν: 'on their own initiative'. Both Diodorus (ἀφ' ἑαυτοῦ) and Curtius attribute the order to Parmenio.

2. οὕτως: for the use of οὕτως before the main verb in a long sentence, see Ziegler *Rh. Mus.* 84 (1935), 370 f.

3. ἀπηλλαγμένοι τοῦ πλανᾶσθαι: cf. Curt. 4. 13. 23 f. Alexander had from the first aimed at bringing on a decisive battle, which would result in the death or capture of Darius. To have to undertake guerilla warfare against the Persians would be a lengthy and costly process. On Alexander's 'Grand Strategy' see Marsden 1 ff.

φυγομαχοῦντα: 'avoid action', often with the implication of cowardice. See esp. Diod. 17. 27. 2; *Caes.* 41. 2.

4. παρ' αὐτὸν τὸν κίνδυνον: 'during the battle itself'. For this use of παρά cf. § 10, παρὰ τὰς μάχας, and LSJ s.v. C. I. 10.

συνεστηκότα τῷ λογίζεσθαι: 'firm in his confident calculations' (Perrin).

5. ὑποτροπὴν καὶ σάλον: ὑποτροπή is properly a medical term = 'relapse, recurrence of an illness', but it is often used metaphorically; cf. *Luc.* 7. 6, τὴν Ἀσίαν ὅλην ὑποτροπὴ τῶν ἔμπροσθεν νοσημάτων εἶχεν. Here it means 'repulse, turning back'. σάλος means lit. 'the swell of the sea, the tossing of a ship'. It is used frequently by Plutarch, e.g. *Alex.* 11. 2, 68. 3; *Caes.* 33. 2, of disturbance in the state. At *Aem.* 18. 3 and here it is used of disturbance, movement in military formations.

κατὰ Παρμενίωνα: 'by, beside Parmenio'. For this use of κατά (not noticed by LSJ) see *JHS* 76 (1956), 28, n. 16, and esp. Arr. 2. 10. 3. Parmenio commanded the entire left wing (Arr. 3. 11. 10; Curt. 4. 13. 35, 16. 1) which was to perform its accustomed defensive role. For the units under his leadership, Arr. 3. 11. 10; 12. 4–5. They amounted to about 3,000 cavalry and 6,000 infantry excluding the phalanx (totals based on Marsden's figures, App. I, II). He was heavily outnumbered by the cavalry under Mazaeus (Curt. 4. 16. 1; not mentioned by Arrian); Marsden 55 puts their numbers at 14,000.

τῆς Βακτριανῆς ἵππου: This unit, 8,000 strong, was under the command of Bessus on the Persian *left* wing (Arr. 3. 11. 3). Curt. (4. 15.

20) also places them on the Persian right; according to him, they attack the Macedonian baggage.

Μαζαίου: Berve no. 484. Satrap of Syria and Mesopotamia. After the battle he withdrew to Babylon, which he surrendered to Alexander. The king received him with great honour and appointed him satrap of Babylon (Curt. 5. 1. 17; 44). His skill and courage in the battle—he came close to defeating Parmenio's forces—supply the reason. See Tarn 2. 185, 187.

περιπέμψαντος . . . προσβαλοῦντας: So Diodorus (17. 59. 5), who says he sent 2,000 Cadusians and 1,000 Scythians, Curtius (4. 15. 5), who mentions 1,000 cavalry, and Polyaenus (4. 3. 6), μοῖρα Περσῶν οὐκ ὀλίγη. Arrian says nothing of this manœuvre, although he mentions at a later stage in the battle (3. 14. 5) an attack on the baggage by 'some Indians and Persian cavalry'. These have generally been identified with 'the Parthians and some of the Indians, and the most and best of the Persians' (Arr. 3. 15. 1), whom Alexander met when attempting to reach Parmenio (see Griffith, JHS 67 (1947), 84, n. 26). As it appears impossible for the latter to have reached the Macedonian camp (at least 5 miles distant), plundered it and returned in the time available, Burn (JHS 72 (1952), 88 ff.) rejects Arrian's version of the attack and accepts the 'vulgate' version, given here by Plutarch. Marsden (59 f.), however, has since made it clear that the two groups mentioned above are quite distinct, and that 'the Parthians etc.' were never near the Macedonian camp. He points out that the first group was small. We may add that it was largely wiped out (Arr. 3. 14. 6). The objection to Arrian's account therefore vanishes. Fuller (175 ff.) has argued that the attack was made not on the Macedonian camp, but on the advanced baggage. Several of his arguments, e.g. that involving the time factor, are invalidated by his belief that the two groups are identical; on the other hand, an attack on the *camp* would mean that the second-line troops (infantry) had to march some five miles to overtake the Persians (Arr. 3. 14. 6). His case is not necessarily destroyed by Arrian's statement (3. 9. 1) that Alexander had decided to leave behind the baggage animals and the non-combatants in his fortified camp, since this decision was made when the battle was to take place next day.

It is perhaps just possible to accept as well the 'vulgate' account of an attack on the camp at an early stage, but, as it is closely linked to the two messages from Parmenio (see next note) and to the refusal of Darius' mother, Sisygambis, to leave, it is best rejected.

6. ἀπέστειλε . . . ἀγγέλους: Plutarch (33. 9) mentions a second message. Curtius also gives two messages (4. 15. 6; 16. 2); on this occasion

Polydamas (Berve no. 648) was sent. This first message is generally rejected, e.g. by Tarn 2. 352 f., Griffith, op. cit. 87 f., Marsden 61, n. 4. It is accepted, however, by Burn (157; *JHS* 72 (1952), 90). οἴχεσθαι τὸν χάρακα: 'the camp is lost'. Cf. *Crass.* 26. 2, οἴχεσθαι τὸν Πόπλιον, εἰ μὴ ταχεῖα καὶ πολλὴ βοήθεια παρ' ἐκείνου γένοιτο.

7. νικῶντες . . . τῶν πολεμίων: cf. Curt. 4. 15. 7.

8. ὑπένδυμα . . . ζωστόν: 'a Sicilian undergarment tied with a girdle'. θώρακα: Curtius (4. 13. 25) also says that Alexander wore a breast-plate on this occasion, though he rarely did so. Arr. 1. 15. 7 f., cited by Berve 1. 104 as evidence that Alexander wore a breast-plate at the Granicus, refers to the Persian. His use of one at Gaugamela or Issus, however, is confirmed by the Alexander mosaic from Pompeii, shown, e.g. by M. Rostovtzeff, *The Social and Economic History of the Hellenistic World* (Oxford, 1941), 1. 128; see further B. Andreae, *Das Alexander-mosaik* (Bremen, 1959) = *Opus Nobile* (Meisterwerke der antiken Kunst), Heft 14.

9. Θεοφίλου: Nothing further is known of him.

10. βαφῇ: The *temper* of the blade, produced by *dipping* red-hot iron in water.

τοῦ Κιτιέων βασιλέως: Pumathion (Berve no. 680).

11. ἐπιπόρπωμα: A cloak, not a belt, as many translators take it.

σοβαρώτερον: Here 'more elaborate'. Cf. 45. 2.

Ἑλικῶνος τοῦ παλαιοῦ: The son of Acesas and a native of Cyprus (Athenaeus 48 b). Both father and son were famed for their weaving in variegated colours, and a specimen of their work was dedicated at Delphi. The conjecture that Helicon lived in the time of Pheidias rests on no certain foundation. See further, *RE* 8, cols. 8 f. (Leonard).

τῆς Ῥοδίων πόλεως: The Rhodians surrendered to Alexander and sent 10 triremes to him during the siege of Tyre (Arr. 2. 20). The cloak was presumably sent at this time. They retained their oligarchic government, but had to accept a garrison. Curtius (4. 8. 12) implies that it was withdrawn early in 331, but Diod. (18. 8. 1; presumably based on Hieronymus of Cardia) states that the Rhodians expelled their garrison after Alexander's death. Berve (1. 247 f.), followed by Ehrenberg 18, accepts Diodorus' evidence: for the former view, see Tarn's persuasive, but not entirely convincing, arguments (2. 214 ff.; cf. 174); that a runaway slave took refuge in Rhodes does not prove beyond doubt the absence of a garrison.

12. ἄχρι μὲν . . . παρεξήλαυνεν: 'while he rode along the ranks, making some adjustment to the phalanx, giving encouragement or advice to his troops, or reviewing them'. For the practice cf. *Mor.* 793 e.

1. τότε δὲ τοῖς Θετταλοῖς κτλ.: By 'the other Greeks' Plutarch means the Greek allied cavalry (from the Pelop., Achaea, Phthia, Malea, Locris and Phocis) commanded by Erigyius (Arr. 3. 11. 10; Diod. 17. 57. 3 f.; Curt. 4. 13. 29). Both the Greek and Thessalian cavalry, led by Philip, were stationed on the extreme left. As Alexander commanded the Macedonian right, his address must have taken place some time before the commencement of the attack. See, e.g., Burn 151.

εἴπερ ὄντως Διόθεν . . .: *F. Gr. Hist.* no. 124, fr. 36. Tarn (2. 352 f.) contends that the prayer was invented by Callisthenes, since this is the only time Alexander is recorded by a reputable author to have called himself 'son of Zeus'; the Greek, as he notes, might simply mean 'Zeus-descended'. But as Callisthenes' purpose, to spread 'the noble lie' that the king was son of a god (Badian, *Gnomon* 33 (1961), 661), was certainly approved by Alexander, the force of his argument is greatly weakened. Moreover, as Hampl (*Studies . . . Robinson*, 822) has remarked, to have invented such a prayer would have made Callisthenes a liar in the eyes of the thousands who heard Alexander. It is notable that Alexander addresses this prayer to the *Greek* troops (see Jacoby on fr. 36); we should remember that when this portion of Callisthenes' history was published (after Parmenio's death) the Greek allies and many of the Thessalians would have returned home—for their discharge at Ecbatana see Arr. 3. 19. 5—and the possibility of refutation would have been very real.

2. Ἀρίστανδρος: cf. Curt. 4. 15. 26 ff., esp. 27, certe vates A., alba veste indutus et dextra praeferens lauream, militibus in pugnam intentis avem monstrabat haud dubium victoriae auspicium; he suggests, however, that it may have been an optical illusion.

Jacoby (ad loc.), although he ends fr. 36 at Ἕλληνας, thinks that Plutarch's account of Gaugamela goes back essentially to Callisthenes. Whether this is so or not, this incident probably derives directly from him.

συνεπαιωρούμενον: 'which continued hovering over' (ἅπ. λεγ.); cf. Curt., loc. cit., pendenti magis quam volanti similis apparuit.

κατευθύνοντα τὴν πτῆσιν: With τῇ πτήσει (all manuscripts) Ἀλέξανδρου may be understood from the preceding Ἀλεξάνδρου, 'directing A. with its flight'. But Benseler's emendation removes the awkward hiatus.

3. ἐπικυμαίνειν τὴν φάλαγγα: 'the infantry rolled on like a flood after the cavalry, which had charged at full speed against the enemy'.

4. πρὶν δὲ συμμεῖξαι κτλ.: Plutarch ignores the initial Persian attempt to outflank the Macedonian right, which led to heavy fighting there, and the subsequent reinforcement of the outflanking troops by cavalry from the left centre (Arr. 3. 13–14. 1). It was this last manœuvre which opened up the gap to the left of Darius, towards which Alexander charged. Marsden 57 ff. emphasizes rightly that ὡς ἐπὶ αὐτὸν Δαρεῖον (Arr. 3. 14. 2) means 'in the direction of Darius', not 'at Darius' (cf. Schachermeyr 224 and n. 156). Alexander then swung his great wedge (ἔμβολον) of cavalry to the left and made for Darius (εἰς τὰ μέσα συνελαύνοντος Ἀλεξάνδρου τὸ νικώμενον, ὅπου Δαρεῖος ἦν); cf. Marsden, loc. cit.

5. τῆς βασιλικῆς ἴλης: The Persian Horse-Guards, 1,000 strong, who surrounded Darius in the very centre of the Persian line, the normal position for the Persian King (Arr. 2. 8. 11; Xen. *An.* 1. 8. 21); Diod. (17. 59. 2) and Curt. (4. 14. 8) wrongly say that he commanded the Persian left.

συνεσπειραμένοις: 'formed in close order'; from συσπειράω, see LSJ s.v. σπεῖρα II. Cf. Xen. *An.* 1. 8. 21, and Wyttenbach on *Mor.* 157 b.

παρατεταγμένοις: 'drawn up to receive'. Reiske conjectured παρατεταμένοις (from παρατείνειν) = *intentis, exspectantibus*; but needlessly, since παρατάσσειν may govern the infinitive (see LSJ s.v.).

6. δεινὸς ὀφθεὶς ἐγγύθεν Ἀ.: For a short time it became a hand-to-hand fight (Arr. 3. 14. 3). For the situation, cf. also Diod. 17. 60. 2 ff., Curt. 4. 15. 23 ff. Both describe a Homeric combat, in which the kings hurl spears at each other, Alexander killing Darius' charioteer.

7. περισπαίροντες: 'struggling convulsively', 'in their last agonies', as in Nicander *Theriaka*, 773; cf. the use of ἀσπαίρω in Homer. Bryan suggested περισπειρῶντες, 'winding themselves around'; but this would seem to require the middle—see LSJ, s.v. περισπειράω.

8. ἐρειπομένων εἰς αὐτόν: 'were being hurled back upon him'; a strong expression. ἐρείπομαι literally means 'to be thrown down, fall in ruins': it is used of the Macedonians throwing down the wall of the Malli town (*Mor.* 327 b), and of the effect of the earthquake at Sparta (*Cim.* 16. 4). For a military context, see *Brut.* 42. 6. Diod. (17. 60. 3) and Curt. (4. 15. 30 ff.) both agree with Plutarch that Darius did not flee until things were desperate. In Arrian (3. 14. 3), he is the first to turn and flee.

πτώμασι πεφυρμένοι: 'entangled with corpses'.

ἀποκρυπτόμενοι: 'hidden by'. If this is not a 'Callisthenicum τεράτευμα' (so Schaefer), the most likely emendation is Held's πτυρόμενοι (or ἀποπτυρόμενοι). This verb is used several times in the *Lives*, e.g.

Fab. 3. 1; *Marc.* 6. 10 (with dat.). Diod. 17. 34. 6 (of Darius' horses at Issus) is a close parallel: διὰ τὸ πλῆθος τῶν περὶ αὐτοὺς σωρευομένων νεκρῶν πτυρόμενοι; cf. 17. 57. 6, διὰ τὸν ψόφον πτυρόμενα (also of horses). περιβάς: On the verb, see ch. 6. 6. No other extant author mentions the abandonment of the chariot, but Arr. (3. 15. 5) mentions the capture of the chariot and Darius' weapons.

9. ἕτεροι . . . ἱππεῖς: For the first message, see 32. 6. Both Arr. (3. 15. 1 ff.) and Curt. (4. 16. 2 ff.) agree with Plutarch that Parmenio's message reached Alexander when he was in hot pursuit of Darius, and that he turned back to help Parmenio, who had defeated his opponents before Alexander reached him. Diod. (17. 60. 7), however, says that Alexander had advanced too far for the messenger to reach him, and that Parmenio extricated himself from his difficulty. That the message did reach Alexander is virtually certain: Diodorus' version is perhaps due to the belief (on the part probably of Diodorus' source) that a messenger *could* not have reached Alexander (Griffith, *JHS* 67 (1947), 87). For a possible solution of the difficulty see Griffith, op. cit., 82 ff., who suggests that the king did not gallop off in pursuit of Darius, but wheeled *right* after his breakthrough, to help his hard-pressed right flank-guard. For a criticism of this theory (accepted by Fuller 176 ff.), see Marsden 58 ff., who agrees that Alexander did not pursue Darius immediately, but holds that Alexander was already moving left to encircle the Persian centre and the Persian right when the message reached him.

10. ὅλως γὰρ αἰτιῶνται Παρμενίωνα: It seems clear (though Pearson, *LHA* 47, dissents) that Callisthenes was primarily responsible for the unfavourable portrait of Parmenio. Since Callisthenes obviously wrote as Alexander wished him to write (*pace* Tarn 2. 358), Berve (2. 303) rightly calls this 'the official version'. It was doubtless put about after Parmenio's murder (see ch. 49. 13), to counteract the hostile reaction to the deed. It was clearly Callisthenes who related a series of instances of 'bad' advice by Parmenio; cf. 16. 3, 29. 8, 31. 10 ff. In any one case it is never implausible, but the series as a whole is obviously tendentious. It is possible, of course, that later writers embroidered the theme and that Callisthenes is not responsible for *all* the incidents in which Alexander rejects Parmenio's advice. It scarcely needs to be said that Parmenio's part in the victory was substantial. Arr. (3. 15. 3) and Diod. (17. 60. 8) both comment on the heroism of the Thessalians; Diod. indeed remarks on Parmenio's skilful leadership, possibly in reply to his denigrators.

νωθρὸν γενέσθαι καὶ δύσεργον: 'sluggish and lifeless'. δύσεργος is generally used only of things; but cf. *Mar.* 33. 2, περὶ νεῦρα γεγονὼς νοσώδης καὶ σώματι δύσεργος ὤν (of the aged Marius).

τοῦ γήρως: Parmenio was nearly seventy at this time.

τὸν ὄγκον: 'arrogance, insolence'. For this meaning Pearson, *LHA* 47, n. 121, compares Isocrates 1. 30.

11. δ' οὖν: 'at any rate', whatever the truth may be; Plutarch, characteristically, does not attempt to judge between the two versions.

xxxiv. *Alexander is proclaimed 'King of "Asia"'. He seeks to win the favour of the Greeks.*

1. ἡ μὲν ἀρχὴ κτλ.: cf. Justin 11. 14. 6. At the Granicus Alexander had met only a fraction of the Persian army, and at Issus the narrowness of the pass had prevented Darius from employing his whole force. At Gaugamela, on ground chosen by the Persians, Alexander had defeated the largest army which Darius had been able to collect in almost two years. It was this battle which 'uncovered the nerve-centres of the empire' (Tarn 1. 51). The hard fighting which awaited the Macedonians in Bactria and Sogdiana was hardly anticipated immediately after Gaugamela.

βασιλεὺς . . . ἀνηγορευμένος: 'proclaimed king of the Persian Empire'. For this meaning of Ἀσία, see the examples cited by Tarn *Bactria* 153, n. 1, especially Arr. 3. 25. 3, where the pretender Bessus calls himself Artaxerxes and claims to be βασιλεὺς τῆς Ἀσίας.

Plutarch's statement, though unsupported, need not be doubted. That the proclamation was formally made by the assembly of the Macedonian army (so Wilcken 137, Schachermeyr 227 ff.) is much less certain. It was undoubtedly not competent to proclaim Alexander 'King of the Persian Empire', i.e. successor of Darius (see Berve, *Klio* 31 (1938), 145, n. 2; Altheim 1. 177); but, as the importance of the proclamation was political, not constitutional, it may have done so with Alexander supplying 'the idea and the formula' (Wilcken, loc. cit.). Alexander had earlier claimed after Issus to be κύριος τῆς Ἀσίας ἁπάσης, and had instructed Darius to write to him as βασιλεὺς τῆς Ἀσίας—a reference to his victory, not to his constitutional position. Even if the assembly did make such a proclamation, we need not believe that Alexander was using the assembly as a counter-weight to the influence of the nobles, or that it thereby admitted the independence of Alexander's Asiatic Empire (so Schachermeyr, loc. cit.).

τοῖς φίλοις ἐδωρεῖτο: cf. 39. 10, where Parmenio is given the house of Bagoas. Olympias wrote to Alexander, complaining of his generosity (39. 7).

2. φιλοτιμούμενος δὲ πρὸς τοὺς "Ελληνας: 'seeking to win the favour of the Greeks'. cf. *Flam.* 9. 5 (the same expression); *Cim.* 4. 7 (πρὸς τὴν πόλιν). Alexander ostentatiously marked his position as *Hegemon* of the Corinthian League, and, by connecting his victory with the ancient victories of Salamis and Plataea, emphasized the Pan-Hellenic character of the war.

ἔγραψε . . . καταλυθῆναι: 'he wrote that the tyrannies (i.e. among the Greeks in Asia Minor) *had been* put down and that they now enjoyed freedom'.

At the same time as Alexander was proclaiming himself the liberator of the Greeks in Asia Minor (now that the Crusade was over) pro-Macedonian tyrannies existed in several cities in Greece. The author of 'On the Treaty with Alexander' ([Dem.] xvii), a speech delivered in 331 by a bitter anti-Macedonian (G. L. Cawkwell, *Phoenix* 15 (1961), 74 f.), complains of tyrannies supported by Antipater at Sicyon (§ 16), at Pellene (§ 10, the ex-wrestler Chaeron (Berve no. 818; cf. Cawkwell, op. cit. 78 f.)), and in Messenia (§§ 4; 7, the brothers Neon and Thrasylochus (Berve nos. 550, 379)). These tyrannies were doubtless maintained by Alexander's orders, although later Antipater was made officially responsible (Badian, *JHS* 81 (1961), 28). On this occasion Alexander presumably acts independently, as *Hegemon*, without reference to the *Synhedrion* of the League.

ἰδίᾳ δὲ Πλαταιεῦσι . . . παρέσχον: The reference is to the decisive battle of the Persian war in 479 B.C., fought in the territory of Plataea. For the 'provision of the land', cf. *Arist.* 11. 3–9, esp. 8, ἔδοξεν τοῖς Πλαταιεῦσιν . . . ἀνελεῖν τὰ πρὸς τὴν Ἀττικὴν ὅρια τῆς Πλαταιΐδος καὶ τὴν χώραν ἐπιδοῦναι τοῖς Ἀθηναίοις, ὑπὲρ τῆς Ἑλλάδος ἐν οἰκείᾳ κατὰ τὸν χρησμὸν ἐναγωνίσασθαι. Plut. (loc. cit.) says that a proclamation was made at the Olympic Games. But when could this be? The next Olympic Games were not held until 328.

Despite the oath taken by the Greek states after the battle, guaranteeing the independence of the Plataeans and the security of their territory, Plataea was destroyed in 427 B.C., when her citizens fled to Athens and were granted citizenship. Restored to Plataea in 386, following the peace of Antalcidas, they were expelled in 373 by the Thebans, who again destroyed the city (Diod. 15. 46. 6; Pausanias 9. 1. 8). Philip II promised to restore the Plataeans, and is said to have done so in 338 after the battle of Chaeroneia (Pausanias 4. 27. 10; 9. 1. 8). But in 335 Plataea had apparently not been rebuilt, since the allies, following the destruction of Thebes, agree to rebuild and fortify Orchomenus and Plataea (Arr. 1. 9. 10). Presumably Plataea had still not been rebuilt by 331, and in 330 there were still Plataeans in Athens (Aeschines 3. 162).

3. ἔπεμψε δὲ καὶ Κροτωνιάταις: For the part played by the Crotonians in the Persian War, see Herod. 8. 47, τῶν δὲ ἐκτὸς τούτων οἰκημένων Κροτωνιῆται μοῦνοι ἦσαν οἳ ἐβοήθησαν τῇ Ἑλλάδι κινδυνευούσῃ μιῇ νηί, τῆς ἦρχε ἀνὴρ τρὶς πυθιονίκης Φάϋλλος. Herodotus (7. 145; 153 ff.) mentions no embassy to South Italy, but only one to Gelon, the tyrant of Syracuse. P. Treves, *CPhil.* 36 (1941), 333 ff., who doubts even the embassy to Gelon, suggests, perhaps rightly, that Phayllus was in Greece when war broke out and enrolled in his crew such Crotonians as were in Greece. At any rate it seems certain that Phayllus was acting in a private capacity, because of his special connection with the mother country through his athletic victories, and not as a representative of Croton. Not only is there no mention of the city on the memorial erected on the Acropolis (see below), but, more important, the name of Croton does not appear on the 'Serpent Column' (*GHI* 1, No. 19) erected at Delphi, containing the names of all states which had fought against the Persians. Phayllus' victories at the Pythian Games were won in the pentathlon (twice) and the stadium (Pausanias 10. 9. 2). A statue of him was erected at Delphi, and a memorial on the Acropolis at Athens, which is still extant (*GHI* 1, no. 21).

> Πᾶσι Φάϋλλος ἀγητὸς ὁ νικῶν τρὶς τὸν ἀγῶνα
> τομ Πυθοῖ καὶ νῆας ʳἑλών, ʳἀς Ἀσὶς ἴηλεν.

A late epigram (*Anth. Pal. App.* 297) credits him with a jump of 55 feet, which is perhaps credible as a hop, step, and jump (E. N. Gardiner, *JHS* 24 (1904), 179 ff.; W. W. Hyde, *AJP* 59 (1938), 407 f.). Aristophanes (*Ach.* 215; *Vesp.* 1206) refers to him as a noted runner of olden time.

ἰδιόστολον: For the word LSJ cite *Alc.* 1. 1, *i.* τριήρης, equipped at one's own expense; *Thes.* 26. 1, *i.* πλεῦσαι, sail in one's own ship. Add *Dion* 32. 4, ἔγνω καθ᾽ αὑτὸν *i.* πλεῖν ἐπὶ τὸν τύραννον, with an expedition of his own.

συμμεθέξων: Coraes' emendation συμμεθέξων, a verb which occurs only three times in Plutarch with the genitive, seems unnecessary. τι μεθέξων makes good sense. Phayllus, despite having only a single ship, is 'determined to have *some* share in the fighting'.

4. τις εὐμενής: The indefinite τις, like the Latin *quidam*, modifies or strengthens (as here) the force of the word to which it is attached; see Holden on *Them.* 22. 3; *C. Gracch.* 6. 1.

Alexander's motives were, of course, less disinterested than the good-hearted Plutarch supposes.

xxxv. *The discovery of naphtha. An almost fatal experiment with it. A digression on its nature and origin.*

1. ἅπασαν εὐθὺς ἐπ' αὐτῷ γενομένην: After the battle Alexander did not pursue Darius, who fled to Media, but followed the main road to Babylon, which was surrendered to him by Mazaeus (Arr. 3. 16. 1 ff.; Diod. 17. 64. 3 ff.; Curt. 5. 1).

τό τε χάσμα τοῦ πυρός: Naphtha. Strabo (16. 1. 15) mentions the presence of naphtha in Babylonia and Susis; Pliny *NH* 2. 235 also mentions its existence near Babylon and among the Austaceni (or Astaceni) in Parthia.

ἐν † Ἐκβατάνοις: Ecbatana, the Persian summer capital, lying to the north-east on the Median plateau, cannot be meant. Hence Sintenis deleted the words, and Reiske proposed to insert ὅμοιον τῷ before them. More probably another proper name underlies Ἐκβατάνοις. Ziegler suggests Ἀρτακηνοῖς or Ἀρβήλοις on the strength of Strabo 16. 1. 4 (738), ἡ δὲ χώρα Ἀρτακηνὴ λέγεται. περὶ Ἄρβηλα δέ ἐστι καὶ Δημητριὰς πόλις· εἶθ' ἡ τοῦ νάφθα πηγὴ καὶ τὰ πυρά. In this passage, however, Kramer, comparing Pliny *NH* 6. 41, emends Ἀρτακηνή to Ἀδιαβηνή, and Ἀδιαβηνοῖς seems the more probable reading in Plutarch.

2. ἀσφάλτῳ: For the solid asphalt, see Herod. 1. 179; 6. 119; Strabo 16. 1. 15.

εὐπαθὴς πρός: 'sensitive to' (cf. Plut. *Mor.* 661 c; 949 e). The tendency of naphtha to ignite is noted by Strabo 16. 1. 15 and Pliny *NH* 35. 179.

ἐξαπτόμενος: sc. ὁ νάφθας (Reiske). 'It is kindled by the very radiance about the flame' (Perrin).

4. ἡ ⟨ἐπι⟩νομή: In view of τὴν ἐπινομήν (§ 9 below), Reiske proposed ἐπινομή here. But νομή is attested by Polybius (1. 48. 5; 11. 4. 4), and, as Herodotus (5. 101. 1–2) uses within three lines ἐπενέμετο and νεμομένου with reference to fire, we may retain νομή here.

5. ἦν δέ τις Ἀθηνοφάνης: Strabo, 16. 1. 15 (743), mentions the incident without names or location. Tarn (2. 300) rejects the story, as naphtha cannot be put out by water. But since Strabo (probably following the same source as Plutarch—cf. πρὸς τὴν πεῖραν (Plut.); πείρας δὲ χάριν (Strabo)) emphasizes that the bystanders used a great quantity of water (πολλῷ σφόδρα κατ αντλοῦντες τῷ ὕδατι), it may be true. Schachermeyr 230 accepts it without comment.

6. εὐτελοῦς σφόδρα καὶ γελοίου: 'who had a ridiculously plain face'.

10. ἀνασῴζοντες πρὸς τὴν ἀλήθειαν: If the text is sound, this must mean lit. 'rescuing the myth to reality', i.e. seeking to find a realistic explanation for the myth.

Pliny (*NH* 2. 235) also mentions this explanation of the poison used by Medea, without any indication of the source. The Budé editor, who is unaware of the present passage, comments (p. 262), 'l'explication . . . émane certainement de théoriciens désireux d'expliquer les mythes par des causes naturelles, *comme les Stoïciens*'. Plutarch doubtless came across the reference to Medea in one of the many Stoic works he had read. The association of naphtha with Medea was probably made easier by the fact that much of the naphtha imported into Italy came from Media; see R. J. Forbes, *Studies in Ancient Technology* I (Leiden, 1955), 42, 84, who mentions the use of 'Median Fire' by Septimius Severus for central heating and hot water supply in the thermae.

τὸν τραγῳδούμενον . . . πέπλον: See Eur. *Med.*, 949, 1156 ff., for the effect of these on Glauce, the daughter of Creon.

11. ἀλλὰ φλογὸς κτλ.: lit. 'when a fire was placed near them, a swift attraction and connection, invisible to the senses, took place'. For this meaning of ὁλκή cf. *Aem.* 14. 2 and *Mor.* 424 e, where it is combined with φορά, 'movement, impulse'. The former passage is a good example of Plutarch's interest in science.

12. τοῖς μὲν ἄλλοις κτλ.: 'in other bodies they produce only light and heat, but in those which are dry and porous or are sufficiently moist and oily they gather, break into a furious blaze, and quickly transform the material'.

Reiske takes the manuscript reading πυριμανοῦντα to mean '(ea corpora) quae gestiunt ardere, quae furiose velut atque incitatissime minima quacumque de causa ignem corripiunt'. Ziegler (*Rh. Mus.* 84 (1935), 374 f.), however, regards it as corrupt, and reads πυριγονοῦντα from πυριγόνον (below). Neither word is attested elsewhere.

13. παρεῖχε δ' ἀπορίαν: 'There has been much discussion about the origin (of naphtha).' It is evident that at least one theory about the origin of naphtha has fallen out of the text.

εἴτε μᾶλλον κτλ.: 'or whether rather the liquid which feeds the flame flows from a soil which has an oily and fiery nature'.

14. ἐστιν ἡ Βαβυλωνία σφόδρα πυρώδης: Strabo (15. 3. 10) remarks that in Susis 'barley spread out in the sun bounces (ἄλλεσθαι) like parched barley in ovens'. He does not mention this in connection with Babylonia, although he tells us (16. 1. 14) that it produced larger crops of barley than any other country, producing three-hundredfold, whereas Susis only rarely produces two-hundredfold.

οἷον . . . ἐχόντων: 'as if inflammation made the ground throb'

(Perrin). For σφυγμός, 'throbbing, beating', esp. of the heart or artery, Wyttenbach on *Mor.* 132 d.

τοὺς δ' ἀνθρώπους . . . καθεύδειν: cf. *Mor.* 649 f, where many merchants are said to do this.

15. Ἅρπαλος: The same anecdote is told by Theophrastus, *Hist. Plant.* 4. 4, and by Plut. *Mor.* 648 c, where he names Theophrastus as his source. In the *Moralia*, he tells us that Harpalus was acting on Alexander's orders. See also Hugo Bretzl, *Die botanischen Forschungen des Alexanderzuges* (Leipzig, 1903), 234 ff.

φιλοκαλῶν: 'being an enthusiast'. At *Mor.* 648 d, Plutarch writes φιλονικῶν, which Ziegler suggests here.

ἐκράτησε: 'he was successful with'.

τὴν κρᾶσιν: In the *Moralia*, Plutarch attributes the failure to the fact that both the ivy and the soil are πυρώδης and their union produces excess of heat. Theophrastus (loc. cit.) says that the country does not admit ivy διὰ τὴν τοῦ ἀέρος κρᾶσιν.

16. τῶν μὲν οὖν τοιούτων παραβάσεων: Plutarch several times introduces into the *Lives* digressions of a scientific, or semi-scientific, nature: see e.g. *Cor.* 11 (Greek and Roman names); *Aem.* 14 (the sources of springs); *Lys.* 12 (meteorstones); *Nic.* 23 (physical speculation disregarded until Plato); cf. *Arist.* 6 and *Per.* 39 (discussion of the names 'Just' and 'Olympian'). He usually apologizes for the digression, as here, but at *Dion* 21 (Dionysius' treatment of Dion's wife, after which Dion turns to war) and *Tim.* 14 f. (Dionysius II in exile at Corinth) he justifies their relevance.

XXXVI. *The treasures captured at Susa.*

1. Σούσων κυριεύσας: Arr. 3. 16. 6 ff.; Diod. 17. 65–6; Curt. 5. 2. 8 ff.; Justin 11. 14. 9; Strabo 15. 3. 9 (731).

Alexander spent a little over a month at Babylon (Diod. 17. 64. 4; Curt. 5. 1. 39), then marched east to Susa (400 miles away), which he reached in three weeks. Susa was 'the old capital of Elam which had been the chief seat of government under the Achaemenids' (Wilcken 141); cf. Strabo 15. 3. 2 (728). It had surrendered to a Philoxenus (Berve no. 795), sent by Alexander directly after the battle of Gaugamela (Arr. 3. 16. 6).

τετρακισμύρια τάλαντα νομίσματος: So Justin loc. cit. Arrian and Curtius give 50,000 talents of silver, Diod. (17. 66. 1 f.) 40,000 talents of uncoined silver and gold plus 9,000 talents of gold Darics (see Welles' note ad loc.). Strabo (15. 3. 9) gives 40,000 or 50,000 talents for the booty in Susis and Persis, excluding Babylon and the camp at Gaugamela. For a list of the booty acquired by Alexander at Babylon, Susa, Persepolis, and Ecbatana, see Berve 1. 312 f. Cf. Bellinger 68 ff., esp. 68, n. 148. See also ch. 37. 4 n.

2. πορφύρας Ἑρμιονικῆς: Pliny (*NH* 9. 125), in discussing the sources of the best purple dye, does not mention Hermione, a seaport in Argolis (described by Pausanias 2. 35); but Alciphron (3. 10. 4) refers to the loss of a valuable slipper of Egyptian linen dyed in sea-purple from Hermione. Vitruvius (7. 13. 3) mentions the mixing of *ostrum*, 'a purple ooze like a liquid tear-drop', with honey, but says nothing of the use of olive-oil. In the Middle Ages honey was used with indigo dyes, similar to the purple. On Ancient Dyeing, see R. J. Forbes, *Studies in Ancient Technology* IV (Leiden, 1956), 98–148.

4. Δίνων: Dinon, perhaps a native of Colophon, was the father of the historian Cleitarchus. He wrote under the title of *Persica* a history of the Eastern Empires, in three συντάξεις each comprising several books. Plutarch used him extensively, evidently at first hand, to correct and supplement Ctesias in his *Life* of Artaxerxes. For his testimonia and fragments, see *F. Gr. Hist.* 3C, 690. This is fr. 23 b. The commentary is not yet published. See Pearson, *LHA* 226 f., for a useful discussion; although Dinon's interest in Cunaxa scarcely proves that he wrote after Gaugamela. Nothing, in fact, can be deduced about his dates from the extant fragments.

τὸ κυριεύειν ἁπάντων: The Persian Empire had taken over from the Assyrian and Babylonian empires the claim to rule the world, recognizing no other great power. See Schachermeyr 227 f.; Kaerst 1. 300 f.

XXXVII. *Alexander captures Persepolis where he spends four months. He decides not to re-erect the statue of Xerxes. The remark of Demaratus.*

1. τῆς δὲ Περσίδος . . . δυσεμβόλου: 'hard to enter owing to the roughness of the country'. The difficulties of Alexander's route are evident in Sir Aurel Stein's account in *Geog. Jour.* 92 (1938), 314 ff. (with illustrations, and an excellent map following p. 384). For the ancient sources see Arr. 3. 18. 1 ff.; Diod. 17. 68; Curt. 5. 3. 16–4. 34. Alexander sent his heavy-armed troops and baggage under Parmenio by the main road, while with a picked force he entered the hills (Schachermeyr 235). The 'Persian Gates' (or 'Susian Gates'—so Diod., Curt.) were held by 40,000 infantry and 700 cavalry under the satrap Ariobarzanes (Arr. 3. 18. 2—evidently the 'official' figures;

Diod. and Curt. give 25,000 and 300). Failing with a frontal attack, Alexander retired some four miles to the west, and it was at this point that a prisoner undertook to lead him by a circuitous and difficult route to the north to a position in the rear of the Persians. For the entire campaign see Fuller 226 ff.

δίγλωσσος ἄνθρωπος: Arr. (3. 18. 4) merely says αἰχμάλωτοι. Both Diod. (17. 68. 5) and Curt. (5. 4. 10) call him a Lycian captured by the Persians and employed as a shepherd. Neither says anything of a Persian mother, although Diodorus describes him as ἀνὴρ δίγλωττος, εἰδὼς τὴν Περσικὴν διάλεκτον.

2. τὴν Πυθίαν προειπεῖν: Curt. (loc. cit.) and Polyaenus (4. 3. 27) mention this oracle. But whereas Curtius writes 'ducem in Persidem ferentis viae *Lycium* civem fore', Polyaenus has ἦν δὲ λόγιον Ἀπόλλωνος, ὡς ἄρα ξένος λύκος ἡγεμών . . . γένοιτο. πρόσεισι δὲ τῷ Ἀλεξάνδρῳ βουκόλος, θηρείαν ἔχων στολήν, ὁμολογῶν ὅτι Λύκιος ἦν. . . . Reiske emended λύκος to Λύκιος, probably rightly, since θηρείαν ἔχων στολήν could easily produce λύκος. Parke–Wormell 1. 241, on the other hand, hold that λύκος is the original reading, and that 'the feeble pun between Λύκιος and λύκος is eked out in one version by the further detail that the guide was dressed in a wolf-skin'. In any case, they rightly suppose that the oracle is an invention.

3. φόνον . . . γενέσθαι συνέπεσε: Zumetikos 40 f., referring to Arr. 3. 18. 6 and Diod. 17. 68. 7, argued that the slaughter took place at the Persian Gates. But there is no mention of the slaughter of prisoners in either author, and Herwerden rightly saw that the end of the story about the Lycian guide and the narrative of (or at least a reference to) the capture of Persepolis has fallen out of the text: the treasure mentioned in the next sentence is that seized at Persepolis. The letter evidently refers to the massacre of the inhabitants described by Diod. (17. 70. 2) and Curt. (5. 6. 6). Arrian, in a very summary account of events at Persepolis, says nothing of it, and it is ignored in the standard accounts (e.g. Tarn, Wilcken); Droysen 1. 231, n. 64 rejects it as an invention of Cleitarchus. It is accepted, however, by Schachermeyr 236, 512, n. 163, who thinks Cleitarchus drew on the recollections of Greek mercenaries, and Mederer 77, who stresses the hostility of the population to Alexander (Diod. 17. 69. 1; Curt. 5. 5. 2; perhaps implied by Arr. 3. 18. 10, ἐντεῦθεν δὲ αὖθις σπουδῇ ἤλαυνεν ἐς Πέρσας, ὥστε ἔφθη ἀφικέσθαι πρὶν τὰ χρήματα διαρπάσασθαι τοὺς φύλακας). It is impossible to say whether the letter is genuine or not: Zumetikos 40 f., holds that it is, for the odd reason that a forger would not have thought of excusing Alexander's cruelty by such a letter! Pridik 102 ff. thinks it probably a forgery, but his reasons are not cogent.

4. νομίσματος . . . πλῆθος: i.e. 40,000 talents (see ch. 36. 1). Strabo 15. 3. 9 (731) puts the total for Susis and Persis at 40,000 or 50,000 talents, and, according to other versions, a total of 180,000 for *all* the treasure assembled at Ecbatana; so also Diod. 17. 80. 3. Justin (12. 1. 3) gives 190,000. Diod. (17. 71. 1) and Curt. (5. 6. 9) both give 120,000 talents for the treasure at Persepolis.

ἐκκομισθῆναί . . . καμήλοις: Diod. (17. 71. 2) mentions πλῆθος ἡμιόνων and 3,000 camels, Curt. (5. 6. 9) 'iumenta et camelos'. Arr. 3. 19. 7 says that Parmenio was ordered to convey the Persian treasure to Ecbatana and hand it over to Harpalus. Strabo 15. 3. 9 (731) confirms this. Diodorus wrongly says that Alexander intended to take part with him and to store the remainder at Susa, while Curtius apparently thinks that Alexander intended to take it all with him. 'Clearly this (i.e. the treasure assembled at Ecbatana) was Alexander's capital for the financing of the campaign in Afghanistan and India' (Bellinger 71). Bellinger points out (72 f.) that there is no evidence that the treasure was converted into coins at Ecbatana (as Berve 2. 76 f. suggests), unless these were Darics. His admirably circumspect discussion of the fate of the treasure highlights our ignorance of Alexander's finances in the East.

6. ἀναλαβεῖν: 'to refresh'.

τέσσαρας μῆνας αὐτόθι διήγαγε: Since Alexander reached Persepolis early in February 330 (Beloch 3. 2. 318), he cannot, if Plutarch is correct, have left before the end of May. Yet Strabo (15. 2. 10 (724), ? based on Aristobulus) mentions his arrival in the territory of the Paropamisadae ὑπὸ Πλειάδος δύσιν, which is generally taken to refer to the *morning* setting of the Pleiades, i.e. 6 November. But if this assumption is correct, we must reject the evidence either of Plutarch or of Strabo; for in a little over five months Alexander cannot have covered nearly 2,500 miles, including a stop at Ecbatana: see C. A. Robinson, *AJP* 51 (1930), 22 ff. Robinson rejects Plutarch's statement and suggests that Alexander stayed at Persepolis for only seven weeks or so: this view conflicts with Curtius' evidence (see below) and cannot be correct. Schachermeyr 514, n. 175, follows Tarn and Wilcken in rejecting Strabo's date, but regards the problem as insoluble. But in *Classical Weekly* vol. 28, no. 16 (1935), 124 f., Tom B. Jones makes the likely suggestion that Strabo (I should prefer to say his source) refers to the *evening* setting of the Pleiades, i.e. April 329, and that his statement does not conflict with Plutarch. Although ancient writers generally refer to the morning setting (see, however, Pliny *NH* 18. 246), Curtius (5. 6. 12) tells of an expedition carried out by Alexander while at Persepolis 'sub ipsum Vergiliarum occasum'. This can refer only to the *evening* setting of the Pleiades in April.

Alexander will then have reached the region south of the Hindu Kush early in April 329 (or perhaps in March, since ὑπό may mean 'just before' as well as 'just after'; see Arr. 5. 12. 4). This allows ample time for Alexander's journey, and enables us to accept Arrian's evidence (3. 28. 1), that Alexander travelled in heavy snow—unlikely from September to November (Schachermeyr loc. cit.). Strabo (loc. cit.) also says that Alexander wintered south of the Hindu Kush (διαχειμάσας δ' αὐτόθι). This must be rejected; evidently Strabo has misunderstood his source and, like most modern writers, has taken ὑπὸ Πλειάδος δύσιν to refer to November.

7. λέγεται δέ, . . .: On Demaratus see 9. 12 n. For this anecdote, cf. ch. 56. 2. It is told again at *Ages.* 15. 4, where Plutarch remarks that the Greeks would have been more likely to weep, when they reflected that the overthrow of the Persian Empire was left to Alexander because of the internal struggles of the Greeks, and at *Mor.* 329 d. There the incident takes place in *Susa*; this is borne out by Curt. (5. 2. 13 ff.) and Diod. (17. 66. 3 ff.), according to whom Alexander sat on the royal throne there.

XXXVIII. *Thais encourages Alexander to burn the palace at Persepolis.*

1. μέλλων ἐξελαύνειν ἐπὶ Δαρεῖον: Plutarch appears to place the burning of the palace immediately before the end of Alexander's stay at Persepolis. No conclusions can be drawn from Arrian's summary account of events at Persepolis, but Plutarch's dating is supported by Curtius' narrative. According to this the burning took place after an expedition (not mentioned by Arrian) against the Mardi and neighbouring tribes; this began about 20 April and lasted for thirty days (5. 6. 12 ff.). It was followed, he implies (5. 7. 2), by several days of feasting, of which the burning was the climax, and by Alexander's departure for Media. Diod. (17. 73. 1) places the same expedition *after* the fire, and Strabo (15. 3. 7) mentions an expedition to Pasargadae after it, but these statements cannot stand against Curtius' precise chronology. The fire, then, must be dated to the end of May.

ἐπὶ κῶμον ἥκοντα: Diodorus (17. 72) presents 'a picture with all the features of a Dionysiac Komos' (Mederer 73). This is evidently the version of Cleitarchus, who made Thais responsible for the burning of the palace (*F. Gr. Hist.* no. 137, fr. 11 = Athenaeus 13. 576 d–e). Curtius (5. 7. 2 ff.) attempts to rationalize it; e.g. in his account the presence of women is a sign of Alexander's decadence. Plutarch stands considerably closer to Diodorus than to Curtius, *pace* Tarn 2. 48. It is not correct to say that in his version Alexander is going downhill, as in Curtius; women were clearly present in Diodorus as well. The essential point is that in Plutarch and Diodorus Thais occupies the centre of the stage. For a good examination of these accounts, see Pearson, *LHA* 218 f.; cf. Mederer 71 ff.

γύναια: simply 'women'; cf. ch. 22. 4.

2. Θαΐς: Berve no. 359. The famous Athenian courtesan, after whom Menander named one of his comedies. Athenaeus (loc. cit.) remarks that she became after Alexander's death the mistress of Ptolemy, by whom she had three children, Leontiscus, Lagus, and Eirene (not *two*, as Berve, 2. 175, n. 4, who omits Lagus). In fact, as Tarn (2. 324, n. 7) points out, Thais was probably already his mistress; at any rate an inscription (*SIG* 314) lists Lagus, son of Ptolemy, a Macedonian, as the winner in the two-horse chariot race (a man's event) at the Arcadian festival, the Lycaea, in 308/7. Lagus presumably came to Greece in 308 with his father (*CAH* 6. 494–5). ὕστερον is, of course, to be construed with βασιλεύσαντος; Stewart and Ax wrongly connect it with ἑταίρα.

4. τὸν Ξέρξου . . . οἶκον: For Xerxes' destruction of Athens in 480 B.C., see Herod. 8. 53.

Although Darius had laid down the general plan of the Persepolis buildings, Persepolis in its final form was the work of Xerxes (see Olmstead (Chicago, 1948), 272). The site has been excavated by Prof. Herzfeld and Dr. Schmidt of the University of Chicago with spectacular results. These are published in E. F. Schmidt *Persepolis*, 2 vols. (Chicago, 1953–7); the large-scale illustrations of the magnificent reliefs in vol. 1 should be consulted if possible. See also Olmstead, who gives (272 ff.) a detailed description of the palace.

5. ἐπισπασθείς: 'attracted, enticed'. On ἐπισπάω, a favourite word with Plutarch, see Wyttenbach on *Mor.* 39 a, and cf. ch. 49. 8.

7. ἤλπιζον γάρ . . .: 'For they hoped that the burning and destruction of the palace was the action of a man who was concerned with affairs in Greece and did not intend to remain among the barbarians'. Ziegler's suggestion (*Plutarchi Vitae* 4. 2, p. xx) to substitute εἴκαζον or ᾔκαζον for ἤλπιζον is unnecessary.

The reaction of the Macedonians must have come as an unwelcome surprise to Alexander.

8. οἱ δ' ἀπὸ γνώμης: Arr. 3. 18. 11 f., Strabo 15. 3. 6. Whether Callisthenes dealt with the incident, as Kaerst 1. 403 and Berve 2. 175 (no. 359) believe, is uncertain. The last event certainly dealt with by him is the battle of Gaugamela, and he is not cited by Plutarch in the extensive list of writers who wrote about the Amazon queen (ch. 46). For various explanations of the mention of the R. Araxes (fr. 38), which might suggest that Callisthenes' narrative reached 329, see Jacoby, *F. Gr. Hist.* 2D, 420 l. 41, 430 (on fr. 38), *RE* 10. 1699 f., In any case, Arrian reproduces Ptolemy and Strabo Aristobulus (see esp. Strasburger 35). Both give the 'official' view, that Alexander's intention was to punish the Persians for their destruction and burning of Greek temples. This is connected with the ostensible pan-Hellenic character of the expedition (Diod. 17. 4. 9, Arr. 2. 14. 4), and symbolizes the completion of this enterprise. It has found wide acceptance, e.g. by Tarn 2. 47 f. (who also suggests (1. 54) that the burning of the palace was 'a sign to Asia'), by Wilcken 144 f., and by Andreotti *Historia* 1 (1950), 590 ('certamente deliberato'), who thinks (*Saeculum* 8 (1957), 127 f.) that it was intended to exercise a moral effect on Darius, who had shown no sign of coming to terms.

However, Berve 2. 175, Mederer 69 ff., and Burn 163 f., have advanced strong arguments for preferring the 'vulgate' version. In particular Burn makes the point that 'this harking back to the "war of revenge" comes as an aberration at this time, when he (Alexander) was already developing his new policy, conciliating the Persians'; cf. Mederer 76, who also remarks (78 ff.) that the destruction of the palace as a considered act of policy might perhaps be considered reasonable at the beginning of Alexander's stay, when (according to the 'vulgate') there was massacre and looting (see 37. 3 n.); but, in fact, the burning did not take place until the end of May (see 38. 1 n.). Moreover G. T. Griffith (*Proc. Camb. Philol. Soc.* N.s. 10 (1964), 37, n. 3) has drawn attention to Plutarch's statement that there is general agreement (ὁμολογεῖται) that Alexander quickly changed his mind and gave orders for the fire to be extinguished. He makes the important (? decisive) point that, if this is correct and if Alexander had ordered the burning of the palace as an act of policy, we should have a unique instance of vacillation on Alexander's part.

δ' οὖν: This reading should be retained. Plutarch means 'whatever the truth may be, at any rate it is agreed. . .'.

μετενόησε: cf. Curt. 5. 7. 11, ipsum, ut primum gravatam ebrietate mentem quies reddidit, *paenituisse constat.* Arr. 6. 30. 1 mentions Alexander's regret for his action when he returned to Persepolis in 324.

In chs. 39–42. 4 Plutarch assembles a number of anecdotes designed to illuminate various aspects of Alexander's character. He resumes the narrative at 42. 5.

XXXIX. *Alexander's Generosity.*

1. φιλοφροσύνη: Plutarch has already commented on Alexander's graciousness as a boy (5. 1). At 59. 4 Alexander responds to Taxiles' φιλοφροσύνη with great generosity.

2. Ἀρίστων: Berve no. 138. The commander of the Paeonians, a hard-working light cavalry regiment from the borders of Macedonia, who led them probably from the start of the expedition and saw hard fighting in the three great battles (Arr. 1. 14. 1; 2. 9. 2; 3. 12. 3). Neither Ariston nor the Paeonians are heard of after Gaugamela. Tarn (2. 158) thinks they were sent home (? from Bactria); Berve suggests that they were merged with the Prodromoi. Both units are sometimes called 'Lancers' (See ch. 16. 3).

πολέμιον ἄνδρα: Satropates (Berve no. 699), a cavalry commander sent ahead before Gaugamela to make contact with Alexander's forces (Curt. 4. 9. 7). The incident is related by Curtius (4. 9. 25), according to whom Satropates was killed in a cavalry battle immediately after Alexander crossed the R. Tigris and shortly before the eclipse of 20 September 331. Arrian (3. 7. 5), however, says that the Macedonians met no opposition at this point (οὐδενὸς δὲ εἴργοντος), and mentions a cavalry battle four days after the eclipse (3. 7. 7–8. 2) in which the Paeonians were engaged and the enemy suffered casualties. It is likely, then, that the incident is to be located here. It provides, incidentally, a good illustration of the type of men that Alexander commanded.

προπίομαι: lit. 'drink to another, pledge him'; cf. ch. 67. 4. It then comes to mean 'make a present of the cup to the person pledged', and finally 'make a present' generally; see, e.g., ch. 59. 5, *Arat.* 14. 1; *Galb.* 17. 8; Dem. *De Cor.* 296, π. τὴν ἐλευθερίαν Φιλίππῳ.

3. τῶν πολλῶν τις Μακεδόνων: 'one of the Macedonian rank and file'.

ἑαυτῷ: = σεαυτῷ (see Kühner–Gerth 1. 572).

4. Φωκίωνι: The famous Athenian general and statesman (402–318 B.C.). He rendered considerable service to Athens in the field, especially in the decade 350–340, and was general forty-five times in all; in politics, however, he was convinced of the futility of resistance to Macedon, consistently favouring accommodation with Philip and Alexander and the avoidance of provocation. Before Chaeroneia he advocated a settlement, and after the battle he was sent with Demades and Aeschines to treat with Philip. Again, after the destruction of Thebes in 335, he and Demades secured the withdrawal of Alexander's demand for the surrender of the leading Athenian statesmen (see on ch. 13. 1). At his meeting with Alexander he is said (*Phoc.* 17. 6 ff.) to have made a great impression on the king, whose friendship he retained until his death (see the anecdote in *Phoc.* 18. 8). After his defeat of Darius, Alexander is said, on the authority of Chares, to have included χαίρειν only in his letters to Antipater and Phocion (*Phoc.*

17. 10). He rejected Harpalus' advances (*Phoc.* 21. 3 ff.), and after Alexander's death attempted to dissuade the Athenians from embarking on the Lamian War. Once again, after the Greek defeat at Crannon in 322, he was employed in (successful) negotiation with Macedon. In 318 he failed to save Peiraeus from the Macedonian, Nicanor, and was convicted of treason and executed.
The main source is Plutarch's *Phocion* (other references in Ziegler's ed.); the *Life* by Cornelius Nepos adds nothing of value. For his career during Alexander's reign, see Berve no. 816 (with full refs.). For the subsequent period, Tarn in *CAH* 6. 454 f., 459 f., 475 f. For a more sympathetic verdict on Phocion, see Hammond 650.
This anecdote is related at length by Plut. *Phoc.* 18. 1 ff. (cf. *Mor.* 188 c; Aelian *VH* 1. 25, 11. 9), where Alexander is said to have sent 100 talents.

ἔγραψεν ἐπιστολήν: Zumetikos 34 and Pridik 92 (no. 51) both hold, probably correctly, that Plutarch's source is Chares. They regard the letter as genuine. But about this letter, and the other letters in chapters 39 to 42, no decision is possible.

5. Σεραπίωνι: Berve 2. 352 f. (no. 701) regards the name as an anachronism (so Tarn (2. 360), who rejects the story altogether); he holds that the original Greek name has been replaced by the later common oriental name. But C. B. Welles (*Historia* 11 (1962), 288) justifiably uses the occurrence of the name as support for the existence of a cult of Sarapis in Alexander's day (see on ch. 76. 9). For the name Serapion at Athens, see S. Dow in *Harv. Theol. Rev.* 30 (1937), 221 ff.
Alexander evidently had at his headquarters a group of professional ball-players; cf. ch. 73. 7 οἱ νεανίσκοι οἱ ⟨συ⟩σφαιρίζοντες. Athenaeus 1. 19 a mentions a σφαιριστής of Alexander, Aristonicus of Carystus (Berve no. 129), who was made a citizen of Athens διὰ τὴν τέχνην and whose statue was erected at Athens. His statement is confirmed by a fragmentary inscription (*IG* 2. 358B—between 318 and 300 B.C.), which mentions also that Aristonicus was granted the high honour of σίτησις ἐν Πρυτανείῳ; see S. Dow *Harv. Stud.* 67 (1963), 77 ff. For the little that is known of Greek ball-games, see esp. E. N. Gardiner, *Athletics of the Ancient World* (Oxford, 1930), 230 ff.

6. Πρωτέᾳ: Berve no. 665. One of the sons of Lanike, Alexander's nurse (Athenaeus 4. 129 a; Aelian *VH* 12. 26), and nephew of 'Black' Cleitus. Elsewhere he is noted for his prowess in drinking (Ath. loc. cit.; Ael. loc. cit.), and Ephippus (*F. Gr. Hist.* no. 126, fr. 3 = Ath. 10. 434 a) mentions a drinking competition between him and the king during the last months of Alexander's life. Curtius (8. 2. 8) wrongly says (in a speech attributed to Alexander) that Lanike's (only) two sons were killed at Miletus.

7. τοῖς φίλοις καὶ τοῖς σωματοφύλαξι: Plutarch here probably uses φίλοι for the more correct ἑταῖροι; see on ch. 15. 5. On the two meanings of σωματοφύλακες, see Tarn 2. 139 ff. The word may denote (1) the Royal footguard, the *agēma* of the Hypaspists or may be used more commonly (as here) to designate (2) 'a few great officers, the so-called Bodyguards, who formed Alexander's personal Staff' (Tarn 2. 141); cf. Berve 1. 25 ff., with a list of known Bodyguards on p. 27.

ἡλίκον εἶχον ὄγκον: Most translators take the words to refer to πλούτων, e.g. North, 'The goods and riches . . . were very great.' But Perrin is evidently correct in translating 'What *lofty airs* his friends and bodyguards were wont to display over the wealth bestowed by him.' This is proved by ch. 41. 1, οἱ δὲ φίλοι διὰ πλοῦτον καὶ ὄγκον ἤδη τρυφᾶν βουλόμενοι. For this meaning of ὄγκος, cf. ch. 48. 3.

δι' ἐπιστολῆς: Tarn (2. 302) regards the letter as genuine on the ground that 'it is exactly what any mother of strong character, let alone an Olympias, must have written to a son in Alexander's position'. Pridik 133 f. and Zumetikos 136 also think it genuine; Kaerst (*Phil.* 51 (1892), 616 f.), however, has grave doubts about the authenticity of all the letters in ch. 39–42. None of them adduces any worthwhile argument for his view.

ἐνδόξους ἄγε: The manuscript reading, ἐνδόξως ἄγε is sound. ἄλλως is to be taken with both εὖ ποίει and ἐνδόξως ἄγε, 'in other ways (sc. than by giving them money) benefit your friends and hold them in honour'. ἄγειν + adverb is a rarer version of ἔχειν + adverb, as in Plato *Rep.* 528 c where ἐντίμως ἄγουσα αὐτά immediately follows ἐντίμως αὐτὰ ἔχει without any observable difference in meaning. νῦν δέ, which seems to have troubled Reiske, merely means 'as it is, by doing as you are now doing'.

πολυφιλίας: 'abundance of friends'. Plutarch wrote on this topic in the *Moralia*, 93 a–97 b.

ἑαυτόν: = σεαυτόν. See 39. 3 n.

8. πολλάκις δέ κτλ.: The same incident, *Mor.* 180 d, 332 f–333 a, 340 a. Diod. (17. 114. 3) mentions frequent letters from Olympias to Alexander complaining of Hephaestion and quotes the end of an outspoken reply by Hephaestion to Olympias.

9. Μαζαίου δέ κτλ.: On Mazaeus see ch. 32. 5. He had at least three sons. Artiboles (Berve no. 154) and Hydarnes (Berve no. 759) surrendered with him at Babylon, and were admitted to the *agēma* of the Companion Cavalry in 324. Antibelus (Berve no. 82) did not surrender to Alexander until Darius was taken prisoner by Bessus. Curtius (5. 13. 11) reports that Brochubelus, a son of Mazaeus, surrendered to

Alexander during the pursuit of Bessus. He is described as 'Syriae quondam praetor (satrap)'. Berve (s.v. Antibelos), who identifies him with Antibelus, suggests that he may have governed a part of Syria under Mazaeus, who was evidently satrap of Syria (Arr. 3. 8. 6). But the passage in Curtius should certainly be emended to read Brochubelus, Mazaei filius, Syriae quondam praetor*is*; is quoque transfuga. . . . The -*is* of *praetoris* may easily have been omitted before the following *is*. Although Berve (2. 84, n. 5) is almost certainly correct in regarding the incident as unhistorical, his reason, that no son of Mazaeus is recorded to have held a satrapy under Alexander (as ἔχοντι implies), is not conclusive; for our sources (even Arrian) are very vague in the use of terms like 'satrap'. Mazaeus' sons no doubt held high positions of some sort. For a table of satrapies and their governors (with few gaps), see Berve at 1. 276.

προσετίθει: A conative imperfect, 'attempted to add'.

10. Βαγώου: Presumably the chiliarch who poisoned Artaxerxes III (Ochus) in 338 and his son Arses in 336, but was promptly poisoned by Darius III whom he had set up as king. See Diod. 17. 5. 3 ff.; Arr. 2. 14. 5; Aelian *VH* 6. 8; *Mor.* 337 e, 340 b.

τῶν περισσῶν: For the text see Ziegler *Rh. Mus.* 84 (1935), 376.

11. ὡς ἐπιβουλευόμενον: i.e. by Olympias. The hostility of Antipater and Olympias is well attested: see e.g. Arr. 7. 12. 5 ff.; *Mor.* 180 d; Justin 12. 14. 3; Diod. 17. 118. 1. Arrian says that they never ceased writing letters to Alexander complaining of each other's behaviour. Olympias described Antipater as 'excessively arrogant' (ὑπέρογκος), while he described her as 'headstrong, sharp-tempered, and interfering'. Arrian indignantly rejects the rumour that Antipater's replacement in 324 by Craterus (see ch. 74) was due to the influence of Olympias: even if Alexander's remark (§ 13) is not 'sicher unhistorisch' (as Berve 2. 50, n. 1, maintains), he certainly did not allow his mother to interfere in affairs of state. Olympias, so far from getting the better of Antipater (so Diod., loc. cit.), felt obliged to retire to Epirus in 331: see also ch. 68. 4.

X L. *Alexander rebukes the luxury of his followers and sets them an example in the field and the chase.*

1. ἐκτετρυφηκότας: The ἐκ- is intensive, 'over-luxurious'. Athenaeus (12. 519 f) uses the compound of the Sybarites, who live ὑπὲρ τὸ μέτρον ἐκλελυμένως.

φορτικούς: The word combines the ideas of arrogance and vulgar display. At *Mor.* 708 c it is combined with νεόπλουτος, at *Cic.* 24. 3

with ἐπαχθής; cf. *Sull.* 5. 10, οἱ δὲ ὡς φορτικὸν ᾐτιάσαντο καὶ ἀκαίρως φιλότιμον. At *Cleom.* 13. 1, it is contrasted with εὐτελής and ἀφελής.

Ἄγνωνα: See chs. 22. 3 and 55. 2.

κρηπῖσιν: Man's half-boots, worn by soldiers (hence κρηπῖδες may stand for the soldiers themselves; see Gow on Theocritus 15. 6), and especially by Macedonians. See *Mor.* 760 b, ὁ Φάϋλλος ὑποδήσας τὴν γυναῖκα κρηπῖσι, καὶ χλαμύδα περιθεὶς καὶ καυσίαν Μακεδονικὴν ὡς ἕνα τῶν βασιλικῶν νεανίσκων παρεισέπεμψε λαθοῦσαν; *Aem.* 34. 1, κρηπῖδας ἔχων ἐπιχωρίους; Ant. 54. 8.

Λεοννάτῳ: For his career, see ch. 21. 2. Suidas comments on his liking for Oriental pleasure and royal magnificence.
    Athenaeus (12. 539 f.) and Aelian (*VH* 9. 3), both from Phylarchus (who perhaps derived his information from Chares via Duris—see Jacoby, *F. Gr. Hist.* no. 81, fr. 41), describe the extravagance of Alexander's followers and the luxury of the king's audience-chamber; cf. also Polyaenus 4. 3. 24, who explains the display as an attempt by Alexander to impress the 'barbarians'. The tone of both Athenaeus and Aelian is hostile to Alexander: no one dared to approach the king, because of his ἀξίωμα (Athenaeus) or because of the fear inspired by Alexander ἀρθέντος ὑπὸ φρονήματος καὶ τύχης ἐς τυραννίδα (Aelian). Both authors differ from Plutarch in assigning the dust (sand) to Perdiccas and Craterus, the nets to Leonnatus and Menelaus. Moreover the tone in Plutarch is altogether different. Jacoby plausibly suggests that he here follows Onesicritus. Certainly Alexander is shown as the philosopher in action: ἐπετίμησε πράως καὶ φιλοσόφως.

Φιλώτᾳ: See ch. 48. 1.

αὐλαίας: Generally 'curtain', e.g. ch. 49. 11, *Eum.* 14. 10 (of a litter). Here 'hunting-net'; αἷς περιστάντες τὰς θήρας ἐκυνήγουν (Athenaeus, loc. cit.).

τρίπτας δὲ καὶ κατευναστάς: 'masseurs and attendants'.

2. ὅτι τῶν καταπονηθέντων κτλ.: Perrin translates 'that those who conquer by toil sleep more sweetly than those who are conquered by their toil'; cf. 'eos iucundius, alios qui fatigant, quam fatiscentes quiescere' (Reiske). This seems doubtful reasoning. More probably Dryden is right in translating 'that those who labour sleep more sweetly and soundly than those who are laboured for'; so essentially North.

3. ἀπειθικὼς . . . τὰς χεῖρας: lit. 'having made his hands unaccustomed to touch his own body'; from ἀπεθίζω = 'disaccustom'.

πέρας: Not 'the end and object' (Perrin), but 'the end and *perfection*' (Dryden), 'des Siegers höchstes ist' (Ax). Ziegler cites Coraes, 'ἐπὶ τοῦ *κεφάλαιον ἢ κορωνίς, ἐνθάδε τὸ πέρας, ὡς ἄριστα ἡρμήνευσεν ὁ* Ἁ(myot), le comble de nostre victoire'.

4. περὶ τᾶς βασιλείας: τὰς L¹P, τῆς C. But the Spartan ambassador spoke Doric.

5. Κρατερὸς . . . ἀνέθηκεν: In fact, Craterus was killed in the autumn of 321 before he could carry out his intention. The dedication of this celebrated work was discovered at Delphi towards the end of the last century, and published by Homolle in *BCH* 21 (1897), 598 ff.: see also Perdrizet, *BCH* 22 (1898), 566 ff. and *JHS* 19 (1899), 273 ff. It showed that the dedication was carried out by Craterus' son, also named Craterus, who was known from Athenaeus (15. 696 e) to have founded a festival (the Κρατερεῖα) at Delphi in honour of his father. The dedication was probably not made until the early third century (Perdrizet, *BCH*). In it Craterus locates the hunt *οἰονόμων ἐν περάτεσσι Σύρων*, from which Willrich (*Hermes* 34 (1899), 231 ff.) concluded that it took place in the famous Persian 'reserve' at Sidon. This is generally accepted, e.g. Berve 1. 12; 2. 226 (no. 446), 243 (no. 482),—his statement (2. 155, n. 1) that Plutarch refers to the lion-hunt in Sogdiana is a mere slip—and is probably correct. It is possible (since the Greeks used the terms Σύρος and Ἀσσύριος, Συρία and Ἀσσυρία quite indiscriminately) that the scene should be located in Sogdiana, where Curtius (8. 1. 14 ff.) mentions a great lion-hunt. There is, however, no mention of Craterus, and Curtius refers to a wound sustained by Lysimachus in a lion-hunt *in Syria*. No conclusions about the time of the hunt can be drawn from Plutarch's mention of it at this time, since the events related in the digression may have occurred at any time.

If the hunt took place at Sidon, the Spartan ambassador may be Euthycles (Berve no. 312), who was under 'open arrest' in Alexander's camp at this time (Arr. 2. 15. 2 ff.). If the later hunt is meant, the ambassador could be one of those sent after the defeat of Agis (Curt. 6. 1. 20; Diod. 17. 73. 6), or of those who surrendered in Hyrcania (Arr. 3. 24. 4; Curt. 6. 5. 7). It is possible, too, as Perdrizet suggests (*BCH* 22 (1898), 567), that Plutarch has combined two separate incidents in the story. For Craterus, see on ch. 47. 9.

Λύσιππος: See ch. 4. 1. Pliny *NH* 34. 64 mentions among the works of Lysippus 'Alexandri venationem, quae Delphis sacrata est'; see the Budé ed. by H. Gallet de Santerre (with commentary on pp. 233 f.).

Λεωχάρης: The famous Athenian (?) sculptor who made *inter alia* statues in gold and ivory of Amyntas, Philip, Olympias, and Alexander for the Philippeion at Olympia (Pausanias 5. 20. 10). On his work see Pliny *NH* 34. 50, 79 (with commentary in Budé ed. pp. 206, 256 ff.), and G. M. A. Richter, *The Sculpture and Sculptors of the Greeks*, rev. ed. (New Haven, 1950) 284 ff.; cf. Lippold *RE* 12, 1992 ff., no. 2.

XLI. *Alexander at first tolerates the abuse of the M 1:ed onians. Examples of his goodwill towards them.*

1. ὄγκον: See on ch. 39. 7.

2. πάνυ πράως ... διέκειτο: So in ch. 40. 2 Alexander rebukes the luxury of his followers πράως καὶ φιλοσόφως. For his later reaction to their abuse, see ch. 42. 4.

3. τὰ μὲν μικρότατα: The μέν is answered by δέ at the beginning of ch. 42. 1, θαυμάσαι δ' αὐτὸν ἔστιν. ...

παραθήσομαι: 'I shall quote, adduce'. Cf. esp. *Per.* 17. 4, and the examples cited by LSJ B. 5.

4. Πευκέστᾳ: Berve no. 634. Peucestas first came into prominence when he helped to save Alexander at the Malli town (see ch. 63). For this he was awarded a golden crown, and despite being satrap-designate of Persia was honoured by being made a σωματοφύλαξ (Arr. 6. 28. 3 f.). As satrap of Persia he adopted Persian dress and learnt Persian, thereby earning Alexander's approval and the ill-will of the Macedonian leaders. He was present in Babylon in 323 during Alexander's last days (see ch. 76. 9). After Alexander's death he retained the Persian satrapy. Berve (2. 319) is no doubt correct in placing this incident (and that in ch. 42. 1) in 324 or 323, after Peucestas had taken up his post.

γράψον ... μή: 'whether'. μή = *num* is common in later Greek; see Kühner–Gerth 2. 394, n. 3. Cf. 22. 10 n.

5. τοῖς περὶ Ἡφαιστίωνα: i.e. Hephaestion, according to the very common later Greek practice of using a periphrasis with περί + accus. for the individual. Polybius (e.g. at 10. 14. 7) uses κατά in the same way.

περιπεσών: 'meeting with, encountering'. περιπίπτειν is very frequently used of sustaining a wound; see LSJ s.v. II. 3, and the passages cited by Holden at *Tim.* 4. 1.

6. ἔκ τινος ἀσθενείας: Berve (2. 21 f.) assumes that this refers to the bite of the bear (see § 4). But in that case, Plutarch would probably have expressed himself more definitely.

Ἀλέξιππον: Berve no. 43. Nothing further is known of him, or of Pausanias (Berve no. 616).

7. ἐλλεβορίσαι: 'dose with hellebore'. Alexander's interest in medicine stems from the teaching of Aristotle, whose father had been a doctor at the Macedonian court. See on ch. 7. 2.

8. τὴν Ἁρπάλου φυγήν: As nothing further is known of Ephialtes (Berve no. 330) or Kissos (Berve no. 420), this incident might refer either to Harpalus' first flight in 333 or to the second in 324 (see on ch. 8. 3). Castiglioni, who proposed (*Gnomon* 13 (1937), 141) κλοπήν for φυγήν on the ground that we would expect a mention of Harpalus' theft, evidently preferred the later date (so Stähelin, *RE* 7, 2399). But Berve (2. 161) is probably correct in holding that Alexander's surprise indicates the first flight; cf. Badian, *Historia* 9 (1960), 245, n. 1.

9. τοὺς ἀσθενοῦντας . . . ἀποστέλλοντος: For the dispatch of the veterans and invalids from Opis in 324, see Arr. 7. 8. 1 ff., and ch. 71. 2 ff.

Εὐρύλοχος Αἰγαῖος: Berve no. 324. Plutarch tells the story of Telesippa (Berve no. 743) twice in the *Moralia* (180 f–181 a, 339 c–d), and in both passages (not merely at 339 c, as Berve) he speaks of Antigenes of Pellene (ὁ Πελληναῖος). For a similar confusion between Antigenes and Atarrhias see ch. 70. 4.

ἐνέγραψεν: Ziegler, comparing ἀπογεγραμμένος (*Mor.* 181 a) and ἀπογραψάμενος (*Mor.* 339 d), both of the same incident, proposed (but did not read) ἀπέγραψεν. In general, ἐγγράφειν seems to be used in a technical sense of enrolment among the citizens, or in the senate or the ephebi, but Plutarch's terminology is not always strict and he does not always reproduce what he has written in the *Moralia*.

τίνων ἀνθρώπων: Powell (*JHS* 59 (1939), 238) suggests τίνος ἀνδραποδόν. But cf. *Mor.* 339 d, τίνος τὸ γύναιόν ἐστιν.

10. ὅπως πείθωμεν: Powell's addition of μένειν after πείθωμεν (loc. cit.) is attractive. He compares *Mor.* 181 a, "οὐκοῦν," ἔφη, "ὦ Ἀντιγένη, πείθωμεν τὴν Τελεσίππαν, ἵνα μείνῃ μεθ᾽ ἡμῶν. βιάζεσθαι γὰρ ἐλευθέραν οὖσαν οὐχ ἡμέτερον", and *Mor.* 339 c–d, "οὐκοῦν," εἶπε, "πείθωμεν αὐτὴν καταμένειν, ἐπαγγελλόμενοι καὶ διδόντες". (Cf. ἢ λόγοις ἢ δώροις). μένειν might easily have dropped out after πείθωμεν.

XLII. *Plutarch expresses surprise that Alexander had time to write on minor matters to his friends. Alexander later became exasperated at being abused. His self-denial during the pursuit of Darius.*

1. ἐπιστολῶν: Since ἐπιστολῶν cannot stand in the same sentence with the following οἷα, Reiske suggested ἐπιστέλλων. Richards (*CQ* 4 (1910), 18) emended οἷα to οἵας. But οἷα may stand with a colon after ἐσχόλαζεν; so Ziegler.

Σελεύκου: Berve no. 700. The future king and founder of the Seleucid dynasty. He is not mentioned until 326, when he commands the hypaspists against Porus, and is called a ἑταῖρος (Arr. 5. 13. 1, 4). Later at Susa (Arr. 7. 4. 6) he married the daughter of Spitamenes, Alexander's most difficult opponent in Bactria, and unlike the other leaders did not repudiate his marriage after Alexander's death. For his presence at Babylon in 323 see 76. 9. Berve (2. 352, n. 2) places this letter with probability in 324/3. Sintenis suggests Σέλευκον (as the object of κελεύων) for Σελεύκου, to avoid the hiatus. But Plutarch allows hiatus after proper names; see Kronenberg, *Mnemos.* 5 (1937), 311, and cf. ch. 39. 10, Βαγώου ἔδωκε, where the text should not be altered.

Νίκωνα: Mentioned only here.

Μεγαβύζῳ: Berve no. 491, s.v. Μεγάβυξος, the form of the name in the Priene inscription (*SIG* 282, 1) and Pliny *NH* 35. 93. Other writers, e.g. Strabo 14. 641, Xen. *An.* 5. 3. 6, and Herodotus, prefer Μεγάβυζος. Originally a Persian name (see Herod. 3. 70), it was transferred to the eunuch priests of Artemis (Diana) of Ephesus (*SIG* 282, Strabo, loc. cit.). The Megabyzus mentioned here is the native of Ephesus honoured by the citizens of Priene in 334/3 for his part in completing the temple of Athena Polias (*SIG* 282). This temple Alexander dedicated in 334 (*SIG* 277). Berve's dating of this letter to 324/3 (loc. cit.) seems quite arbitrary.

τῷ ἱερῷ: i.e. of Artemis of Ephesus.

2. τῷ κινδυνεύοντι: 'the accused'. A technical word (not noticed by LSJ): cf. *Arist.* 4. 2, οὐ βουλομένων ἀκούειν τοῦ κινδυνεύοντος τῶν δικαστῶν; *Cat. Mai.* 15. 4, κρινόμενος καὶ κινδυνεύων διετέλει; *Phoc.* 10. 8; *Cic.* 9. 5, 35. 1.

φυλάττηται: Read φυλάττῃ. The object of φυλάττῃ is his ear, τὸ ἕτερον τῶν ὤτων, with which καθαρόν and ἀδιάβλητον agree. The manuscript reading φυλάττηται has arisen from dittography, because of the influence of the following καί. φυλάττειν with a predicative adjective is (perhaps) unclassical, but not uncommon in Plutarch, e.g. *Per.* 16. 3, ἐφύλαξεν ἑαυτὸν ἀνάλωτον ὑπὸ χρημάτων; *Nic.* 27. 1, ἀήττητον ἐφύλαττε τὴν δύναμιν; *Ti. Gracch.* 19. 4. LSJ cite for this predicative use Antiphon 5. 47; Dion. Hal. *Thuc.* 34; Lucian, *D. Mar.* 5. 1; add Diod. 16. 45. 3, φυλάττων τὴν ὀργὴν ἀπαραίτητον. Jebb regards Soph. *OC* 625 f., τὸ σὸν μόνον πιστὸν φυλάσσων, as an example of this predicative use; not apparently LSJ.

In no case does the middle voice appear to be used.

ἀδιάβλητον: Either (1) 'unexceptionable', as *Mor.* 4 b, διδασκάλους γὰρ ζητητέον τοῖς τέκνοις, οἳ καὶ τοῖς βίοις εἰσὶν ἀδιάβλητοι, καὶ τοῖς τρόποις ἀνεπίληπτοι, or (2) 'not listening to slander, unprejudiced', as here and at *Brut.* 8. 1, οὐ μὴν οὐδὲ Καῖσαρ ἀνύποπτος ἦν πάμπαν οὐδ' ἀδιάβλητος πρὸς αὐτόν.

3. ἀλλ' ὕστερόν γ' . . .: 'But later the many accusations (which he had to listen to about others) made him harsh, and those that were false were believed because of those that were true.' ἐκτραχύνειν = 'exasperate' is frequent in this unclassical metaphorical sense in the *Lives*, e.g. *Alc.* 14. 4, *Marc.* 6. 2, *Sert.* 10. 7. Reiske and Sintenis rightly corrected παρόδων to πάροδον comparing especially *Agis* 2. 1, πλὴν ὅση πάροδον ἐπὶ τὰς πράξεις καὶ διὰ τοῦ πιστεύεσθαι δίδωσι, and *Mor.* 821 c, ἡ πάροδον ἐπὶ τὰς πράξεις διδοῦσα πίστις. But their deletion of πίστιν is unlikely in view of Polyb. 1. 35. 4, (τὸ εἰρηθὲν) δι' αὐτῶν τῶν ἔργων ἔλαβε τὴν πίστιν; cf. id. 7. 13. 2. The most probable solution (now adopted by Ziegler) is to read πάροδον ⟨καὶ⟩ πίστιν with Coraes.

4. ἐξίστατο τοῦ φρονεῖν: 'his reason forsook him' (Langhorne): A very strong expression. 'He lost discretion' (Perrin) is much too mild.

χαλεπὸς ἦν καὶ ἀπαραίτητος: This is particularly true of Alexander's later years. See ch. 57. 3, ἤδη δὲ καὶ φοβερὸς ἦν καὶ ἀπαραίτητος κολαστὴς τῶν πλημμελούντων (see the examples cited by Plutarch), and esp. Arr. 7. 4. 3, οὐ μὴν ἀλλὰ καὶ αὐτὸς Ἀλέξανδρος ὀξύτερος λέγεται γενέσθαι ἐν τῷ τότε (after his return from India) ἔς τὸ πιστεῦσαί τε τοῖς ἐπικαλουμένοις, ὡς πιθανοῖς δὴ ἐν παντὶ οὖσι, καὶ ἐπὶ τὸ τιμωρήσασθαι μεγάλως τοὺς καὶ ἐπὶ μικροῖς ἐξελεγχθέντας. Both adjectives are used of the elder Cato: *Cat. Mai.* 16. 4, ἐφοβοῦντο τὴν αὐστηρίαν τοῦ ἀνδρός, ἀπαραίτητον καὶ χαλεπὴν ἐσομένην.

ἄτε δὴ τὴν δόξαν κτλ.: For Alexander's concern with δόξα, see ch. 5. 5 n. Plutarch here attempts to find an excuse for Alexander's undoubted change towards greater severity.

5. τότε δ' ἐξήλαυνεν: Plutarch resumes his narrative, after the lengthy digression, from the end of ch. 38. The date is the end of May or the beginning of June 330 (see on ch. 37. 6). For what follows see Arr. 3. 19. 1–21. 8; Diod. 17. 73. 1 f.; Curt. 5. 8–13 (esp. for the events in the Persian camp). After Gaugamela Darius had fled to Media, and had assembled at Ecbatana a force of 6,000 infantry and 3,000 cavalry (Arr.). Diod. puts the figure at 30,000 infantry, Curt. adds 4,000 slingers and archers, and 3,300 cavalry. After some (ill-advised) thought of resistance, Darius decided to flee to Bactria via Rhagae (near Teheran) and the Caspian Gates. For his route see esp. G. Radet in *Mélanges Gustave Glotz* (Paris, 1932) 2. 767 ff., and (less correctly) A. F. von Stahl, *Geog. Jour.* 64 (1924), 312 ff.

ἀκούσας δὲ τὴν . . . σύλληψιν: At Tabae (Pali, see Radet op. cit. 772), just east of the Caspian Gates, Alexander learnt from the Babylonian Bagistanes that Darius had been arrested by Bessus, satrap of Bactria, Nabarzanes, and Barsaentes, satrap of Arachosia and Drangiana (Arr. 3. 21. 1; Curt. 5. 13. 2, who omits Barsaentes).

ἀπέλυσε τοὺς Θεσσαλούς: Alexander sent home the Thessalians, together with the other Greek allies, from Ecbatana (Arr. 3. 19. 5). Diod. (17. 74. 3) places the discharge of the allies after the death of Darius, Curt. (6. 2. 17) at Hecatompylos. Many Thessalians reenlisted and were eventually sent home after crossing the Hindu Kush (Arr. 3. 29. 5). C. A. Robinson, *AHR* 62 (1957), 333 ff., relying on Arr. 5. 27. 5, argued that they had mutinied in Bactria; but ἀπὸ Βάκτρων should there be emended to ἀπ' Ἐκβατάνων (Krüger).

Alexander, who had by now heard of Antipater's victory at Megalopolis, no longer needed the Greek allies even as hostages, and regarded his position as στρατηγὸς αὐτοκράτωρ (though not as ἡγεμών) at an end. See, e.g., Wilcken 147, Schachermeyr 238.

δισχίλια τάλαντα κτλ.: So Arr. (loc. cit.), δισχίλια παρ' αὐτοῦ τάλαντα ἐπιδούς, i.e. Alexander gave the 2,000 cavalrymen 1 talent each as a gift in addition to their pay. Diod. and Curt. (locc. citt.) confirm this, and add that the infantry received 1,000 minae each.

6. ἀργαλέαν καὶ μακρὰν γινομένην: Pompey's march against the Albani is described in very similar terms (*Pomp.* 35. 2, μακρᾶς αὐτὸν ἐκδεχομένης ἀνύδρου καὶ ἀργαλέας ὁδοῦ).

ἔνδεκα γὰρ ἡμέραις . . . σταδίους: This statement, accepted by Tarn (1. 56) 'Apparently the tradition made him cover the 400 miles to Shadrud in eleven days', is contradicted by Arrian's narrative; see now R. D. Milns, *Historia* 15 (1966), 256. It is probably due to the fact that Alexander reached *Rhagae* (Rei, about five miles south-east of Teheran) from Ecbatana in eleven days (Arr. 3. 20. 2). There he rested five days, ὡς ἀπέγνω κατὰ πόδας αἱρήσειν Δαρεῖον. It was the news of Darius' arrest which renewed Alexander's hopes of overtaking the king and sent him off in headlong pursuit. Darius was murdered near Damghan (von Stahl) or Shadrud (Radet), and Alexander covered either 210 miles (to Damghan) or 250 miles (to Shadrud) in (probably) less than seven days—Radet calculates 5 days, but this is certainly too short. The exact time taken depends on the time spent at Tabae, when Coenus was sent to forage: Arrian (3. 20. 4–21. 2) is not explicit. In any case it was 'a tremendous feat of endurance when it is remembered that it was mid-summer and much of the country waterless desert' (Fuller 113 f.).

ἀπηγόρευσαν: 'were worn out'.

κατὰ τὴν ἄνυδρον: ἀνυδρίαν, the reading of all manuscripts, except C, and of Zonaras, should be retained. For the noun in Plutarch, see ch. 26. 11 and *Ant.* 47. 1; for κατά = διά, which troubled Reiske, see LSJ s.v. B vi. 1 and Kühner–Gerth, 1. 479, where examples from Thucydides and Herodotus are cited. Cf. also ch. 49. 6, καθ' ὑποψίαν ἤδη τοῦ Φιλώτου, and Diod. 17. 34. 2, 'Οξάθρης . . . κατὰ τὴν ἀνδρείαν ἐπαινούμενος. There are about a dozen examples in the *Lives.*

7. ἔνθα δὴ Μακεδόνες ἀπήντησαν: This incident, 'one of Alexander's noblest deeds' (Arrian), is located in a number of different places. Arrian (6. 26. 1–3) recounts it during the crossing of the Gedrosian desert (probably from Aristobulus—so Schwartz *RE* 2, 1241 f., followed by Jacoby, *F. Gr. Hist.* no. 139, fr. 49, Strasburger 45, Pearson *LHA* 179; Kornemann 87 suggests Ptolemy as his source), but remarks that others put it among the Parapamisadae. Curtius (7. 5. 10 ff.) says it occurred in Sogdiana near the R. Oxus, while Frontinus (*Strat.* 1. 7. 7) places it in Africa, i.e. on the journey to Siwah. Polyaenus (4. 3. 25) mentions no location.

The details of the incident also differ: the chief difference is that in the versions of Plutarch and Curtius the Macedonians bring water for their sons, and Alexander returns the water to them; in the other version (Arrian, Polyaenus, Frontinus) there is no mention of the sons and Alexander pours out the water on the ground. Fränkel holds that Plutarch follows Cleitarchus because of the similarity to Curtius; but apart from other differences the locations vary, and in Curtius the water is poured into a *vas.* Both versions are, of course, designed to illustrate Alexander's ἐγκράτεια and μεγαλοψυχία. For the latter, cf. Curt. 7. 5. 9, 'amici ut meminisset orabant *animi sui magnitudinem unicum remedium deficientis exercitus esse'.*

XLIII. *The Death of Darius. Punishment of Bessus.*

§§ 1–4. Sources: Arr. 3. 21. 9 f.; Diod. 17. 73. 3 f.; Curt. 5. 13; Justin 11. 15; Aelian *NA* 6. 25; Ps.-Call. 2. 20. 5 ff.; Iul. Val. 2. 32 f.

1. ἑξήκοντα: This figure may not be far out. The final pursuit was made with 500 mounted infantry (Arr. 3. 21. 7) and, as Alexander covered some fifty miles during his furious night ride (ibid. 3. 21. 9), many must have dropped out. Curtius (5. 13. 21) gives the ridiculous figure of nearly 3,000.

2. πολὺν ἄργυρον καὶ χρυσόν: Darius had left Ecbatana with 7,000 talents from his Median treasure (Arr. 3. 19. 5).

διαφερομένας: 'wandering aimlessly'. Cf. *Cleom.* 37. 11, διαφέρεσθαι καὶ πλανᾶσθαι.

3. κατάπλεως: Does Plutarch mean 'full of javelins' or 'full of (javelin-) wounds'? It would be rash to deny that an author like Cleitarchus might have drawn a picture of Darius' body bristling with javelins, but it is more natural to take the phrase to mean 'full of wounds', and this interpretation is supported by Justin 11. 15. 5, multis quidem *vulneribus* confossum. This sense of ἀκόντισμα is not listed by LSJ, but seems to occur at *Tim.* 4. 3, πολλὰ μὲν ἀκοντίσματα, πολλὰς δὲ πληγὰς ἐκ χειρὸς ἀναδεξάμενος εἰς τὸ σῶμα. For the other view, however, cf. *Marc.* 10. 4, αὐτὸν ἐν τοῖς νεκροῖς εὑρεθέντα πολλῶν βέλων κατάπλεων τὸ σῶμα.

Darius was wounded by Nabarzanes and Barsaentes before they fled. Diod. (17. 73. 2) says, less exactly, that he was seized and murdered by Bessus.

μικρὸν ἀπολείπων τοῦ τελευτᾶν: Arr. (loc. cit.) merely says that Darius died of his wounds soon after, before Alexander had seen him. Diod. (loc. cit.) gives the same version, but adds that according to some writers Alexander found Darius still alive (ἔμπνουν ἔτι). Justin (11. 15. 5) says that he was discovered alive by 'one of the soldiers', whom Curtius (5. 13. 24) agrees with Plutarch in calling Polystratus, but the rest of Curtius' account is lost.

4. πέρας . . . δυστυχίας: 'the height of misfortune'. For this sense of πέρας see ch. 40. 3 n.

ᾧ ταύτην δίδωμι . . .: So Justin 11. 15. 13.

ἐξέλιπεν: 'he died'. For the absolute use of ἐκλείπειν, cf. ch. 57. 4; *Phoc.* 31. 1.

5. τὴν ἑαυτοῦ χλαμύδα: Plutarch is the only author to mention this incident. At *Mor.* 332 f he uses it to illustrate Alexander's philosophical conduct—οὐκ ἔθυσεν οὐδ' ἐπαιάνισεν ὡς τοῦ μακροῦ πολέμου τέλος ἔχοντος, ἀλλὰ τὴν χλαμύδα. . . . Schachermeyr 246 ff. regards this action as 'symbolising nothing less than an attempt to end the perpetual conflict between East and West'. A simpler view seems preferable. However, he makes the good point (513, n. 168) that Cleitarchus seems not to have dealt with the incident; otherwise Justin, in his detailed account of Darius' death, would have dealt with it.

6. Βῆσσον μὲν ὕστερον εὑρών: Berve no. 212. After the murder of Darius, Bessus fled to Bactria where he assumed the upright tiara, the symbol of royalty, and took the name of Artaxerxes (Arr. 3. 25. 3). When he failed to delay Alexander's advance by devastating the countryside north of the Hindu Kush, he fled across the R. Oxus into Sogdiana and his supporters dispersed (Arr. 3. 28. 3). In the summer of 329 he was arrested by the Sogdian barons, Spitamenes and

Dataphernes, who offered to hand him over to Alexander. According to Ptolemy he himself captured Bessus when the Sogdians fled (Arr. 3. 29. 7–30. 3); Aristobulus, however, appears to say (Arr. 3. 30. 5) that they brought Bessus to Alexander; for the text (where Πτολεμαίῳ should be excised or emended) see Jacoby on *F. Gr. Hist.* no. 138, fr. 14; Kornemann 10. Both Diod. (17. 83. 8) and Curt. (7. 5. 26, 36) agree that the conspirators brought Bessus to Alexander, but make no mention of Ptolemy. Ptolemy's version is generally preferred, e.g. by Pearson *LHA* 166, but Welles, *Miscellanea Rostagni*, 109 f., thinks 'it is likely that Ptolemy's memory or imagination has run away with him'.

After being scourged, Bessus was sent to Bactra where in the following year (328) he was tried for the murder of Darius (see Badian, *CQ* 8 (1958), 146, against Tarn's view that he was tried for assuming the royal tiara—add to Badian's evidence Curt. 7. 10. 10, from Ptolemy as Arr. 4. 7. 3 shows). He was sentenced to have his nose and ears cut off—a Persian punishment inflicted by Darius I on his rivals—then sent to Ecbatana to be put to death in an assembly of Medes and Persians (Arr. 4. 7. 3). Curtius, the only other author to mention the place of execution, at 7. 5. 43 says that this was to be where Darius was killed, but at 7. 10. 10 (from Ptolemy) Bessus is sent to Ecbatana. The 'vulgate' (Diod. loc. cit., Curt. 7. 5. 40 ff., Justin 12. 5. 10 f.) mentions that Bessus was handed over to Darius' brother, Oxyathres, for mutilation and punishment. According to Curt. and Justin he was to be crucified, but Diod. (agreeing in part with Plutarch) says that his body was cut up and the pieces then scattered (διεσφενδόνησαν).

διεσφενδόνησεν: 'dismembered, scattered as if from a sling'. Cf. *Marc.* 15. 3. Pearson *LHA* 10 points out that this was the form of punishment inflicted by Theseus on the robber Sinis, the *Pityocamptes*. He regards the story, probably correctly, as an invention designed to show Alexander following heroic precedents. Impaling, a Persian punishment, is more likely.

νείμασθαι: 'carried with it' (North).

7. τότε δὲ . . . ἀπέστειλε: To Persepolis to be buried in the royal tomb: Arr. 3. 22. 1; cf. Justin 11. 15. 15; Diod. 17. 73. 3; Pliny *NH* 36. 132.

Ἐξάθρην: Berve no. 586 s.v. *Ὀξυάθρης*: for the form of the name see Roos on Arr. 7. 4. 5. Renowned for his courage (Diod. 17. 34. 2), he had fought well at Issus and had remained faithful to his brother. His admission to the Companions (the only example of an Oriental admitted to this body) is confirmed by Curt. 6. 2. 11, 'fratrem Darei recepit in cohortem amicorum'. His daughter, Amastris or Amastrine (Berve no. 50), later married Craterus in the great wedding-feast at Susa.

For the 'Companions', see on ch. 15. 5.

XLIV. *Alexander reaches the Caspian Sea. The Theft of Bucephalas.*

1. Alexander enters Hyrcania: Arr. 3. 23. 1 ff.; Diod. 17. 75; Curt. 6. 4. 1 ff.; Justin 12. 3. 4.

μετὰ τῆς ἀκμαιοτάτης δυνάμεως: Presumably the 20,000 infantry and 3,000 cavalry mentioned at ch. 47. 1.

αὐτός: Alexander divided his forces into three, sending Erigyius by the main road with the baggage and dispatching Craterus against the Tapurians (Arr. loc. cit.) or leaving him to protect Parthiene (Curt. loc. cit.). They rejoined him at Zadracarta (Arr. 3. 23. 6; Curt. 6. 4. 23 calls it Arvae).

εἰς Ὑρκανίαν κατέβαλε: κατέβαλε is Ziegler's simple correction of κατέλαβε, the reading of all the manuscripts. There appears to be no parallel to καταβάλλειν in the sense of 'go down', although admittedly ὑπερβάλλειν (see 57. 1) and εἰσβάλλειν are used intransitively. If this emendation is not correct, it seems unlikely that εἰς Ὑ. κατέλαβεν bears the later Greek meaning 'he arrived in H.', as Reiske holds. This meaning, however, might possibly have led a copyist to insert εἰς; alternatively εἰς might be due to the preceding -εως. If this is so, Ὑ. κατέλαβεν would mean simply 'he occupied H.'.

πελάγους ἰδὼν κόλπον: The view that the Caspian Sea was a gulf of the Ocean is as old as Hecataeus (see below, § 2). Herodotus (1. 202 f.) implicitly rejected this by emphasizing that the Caspian was a lake (ἡ δὲ Κασπίη θάλασσά ἐστι ἐπ' ἑωυτῆς, οὐ συμμίσγουσα τῇ ἑτέρῃ θαλάσσῃ . . . ἡ δὲ Κασπίη ἐστι ἑτέρη ἐπ' ἑωυτῆς), and the correct view still occurs in Aristotle (*Meteor.* 354 a) and in the 'Gazetteer of Alexander's Empire' (Diod. 18. 5. 2–6. 3) dating probably from 324/3 B.C. (see Tarn 2. 309 ff.). Whether the *Meteorology* was published by 334 or not (for a judicious discussion of the date, H. D. P. Lee in the Loeb. ed., pp. xxiii–xxv), Alexander will have started with Aristotle's geography in his head—the statement in Alexander's speech at the Hyphasis (Arr. 5. 26. 1) that the Caspian is a gulf does not represent his own opinion; rather the geography is that of Eratosthenes (Tarn 2. 288). But after he had discovered that the Persian Gulf was a gulf he came to have doubts about Aristotle's geography, and planned an expedition to find out whether the Caspian was a lake or was connected with the Ocean (Arr. 7. 16. 1 ff.). This expedition probably never took place and Patrocles, the admiral of Seleucus and Antiochus I, who explored the Caspian about 284/3 B.C., unfortunately decided that it was a gulf. Eratosthenes accepted this view and it became standard; see esp. Strabo 2. 74; 11. 509. Although the great geographer Claudius Ptolemy restated the truth in the second century A.D., the 'Gulf Theory' prevailed (with few exceptions—see Thomson 390) until the fourteenth century. Plutarch here reproduces the view current in his day; see, e.g., Curt. 6. 4. 19; Pliny *NH* 2. 168, 6. 36. Other references in *RE* s.v. Kaspisches Meer (Herrmann).

οὐκ ἐλάττονα . . . φανέντα: 'non minus hoc esse quam Pontum Euxinum Cleitarchus putat' (Cleitarchus fr. 12, ap. Pliny *NH* 6. 36); πάρισον ἡγεῖται τὸ πέλαγος τοῦτο τῷ Ποντικῷ (Patrocles ap. Strabo 11. 7. 1). Tarn's contention (2. 17 f.) that Cleitarchus is dependent on Patrocles and therefore wrote after 280 B.C. has been generally and rightly rejected. Cleitarchus may merely have guessed the size of the Caspian (so Pearson *LHA* 227; cf. Schachermeyr 503, n. 72) or both may be dependent on Polycleitus (Jacoby on Polycleitus, *F. Gr. Hist.* no. 128, fr. 7). Brown, *AJP* 71 (1950), 139, suggests, less probably, that Onesicritus may be their source. Plutarch here probably follows Polycleitus.

γλυκύτερον δὲ τῆς ἄλλης θαλάττης: 'Alii sunt qui Maeotiam paludem in id (i.e. Caspium mare) cadere putent et argumentum afferant aquam, quod dulcior sit quam cetera maria' (Curt. 6. 4. 18). This is derived from Polycleitus (*F. Gr. Hist.* no. 128, fr. 7 = Strabo 11. 7. 4), ὑπόγλυκυ εἶναι τὸ ὕδωρ, either directly (so Tarn 2. 104, n. 1) or, more probably, by way of Cleitarchus (Jacoby ad loc.). Tarn (2. 7 ff.) argues that the reference to 'nearly sweet' water (Ath. 14. 625 a, τὸ μὴ γλυκὺ μὲν ἐγγὺς δὲ τούτου λέγομεν ὑπόγλυκυ) proves that Polycleitus means by ἡ Κασπία θάλαττα the Aral Sea, into which flowed the Oxus and the Jaxartes (believed to be the Tanais—see next note). The knowledge of the Aral, in Tarn's view, derived from the Chorasmian king, Pharasmanes, who visited Alexander's headquarters at Bactra (Arr. 4. 15. 4) and told him of the Jaxartes flowing into a great sea (the Aral, on which his own kingdom lay), containing snakes and 'sweet' water. Later writers, e.g. Curt. loc. cit., Diod. 17. 75. 3, not knowing of the existence of the Aral, transferred the 'sweet' water to the Caspian. Tarn's argument seems to be well based. The average salinity of the Caspian is 13 per thousand, i.e. 13 lb. of salt to 1,000 lb. of Caspian water, and although the water is drinkable in the north owing to the inflow of the Volga, Alexander knew nothing of the north. The considerably greater saline content in the south renders the water undrinkable. The average salinity of the Aral is considerably lower (10·7 per thousand), and the water is certainly drinkable at the points where the Oxus and the Jaxartes enter it. (Figures from the *Enc. Brit.*, 1963 ed.) For criticism (not all valid) of Tarn's interpretation of the Strabo passage see Pearson, *CQ* N.S. 1 (1951), 80 ff.; cf. *LHA* 75 ff.

τῆς Μαιώτιδος λίμνης ἀνακοπήν: 'an overflow from Lake Maeotis'. For ἀνακοπή see Wyttenbach on *Mor.* 76 f.

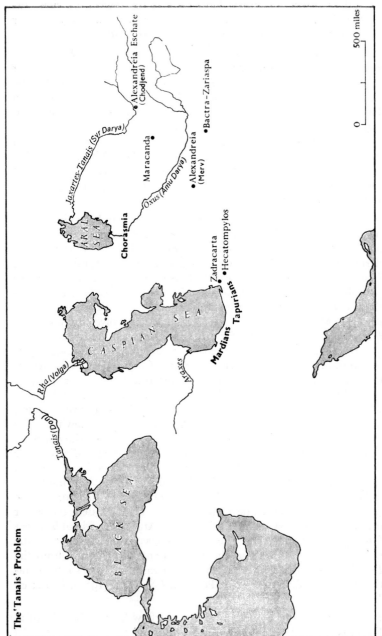

The 'Tanais' Problem

FIG. I.

The view that the Maeotis and the Caspian Sea were connected occurs also in Curt. 6. 4. 18 f. (cited in the previous note) and Strabo 11. 7. 4, where he sharply criticizes 'certain flatterers of Alexander' for uniting the Maeotis and the Caspian, λίμνην καὶ ταύτην καλοῦντες καὶ συντετρῆσθαι φάσκοντες πρὸς ἀλλήλας ἀμφοτέρας, ἑκατέραν δὲ εἶναι μέρος τῆς ἑτέρας.

If the *Meteorology* antedates his expedition, Alexander may have been influenced by Aristotle's belief (*Meteor.* 1. 13. 29 f. (351ᵃ)) that there was an underground connection between the Caspian and the Black Sea. Doubtless the confusion between the Jaxartes and the Tanais/Don played a part. Aristotle (*Meteor.* 1. 13. 15 (350ᵃ)) held that the Tanais branched off from the Araxes to enter the Maeotis, and Herrmann (*RE* 10, 2278) suggested that owing to the similarity of the names the Araxes was confused with the Jaxartes, which was consequently linked with the Tanais. This may be correct, but Aristobulus (ap. Arr. 3. 30. 7, ? following Polycleitus) tells us that 'the local tribesmen called the lower Jaxartes the Tanais, and said that it flowed into the 'Caspian'. On the other hand, if the name given by the tribesmen to the Jaxartes was not Tanais, but a name of similar sound, Aristotle's view may have disposed Alexander and his followers to identify it with the Tanais/Don. Polycleitus (Strabo, loc. cit.) reasoned that if the Jaxartes/Tanais entered the 'Caspian' this could be no other than Lake Maeotis, into which (as everyone knew) the Tanais/ Don flowed. Strabo regards the identification of the Jaxartes with the Tanais as part of a 'stratagem' by Alexander's followers to increase his reputation; as the Tanais was the recognized boundary between Europe and Asia, Alexander could be held to have conquered all Asia. But the 'stratagem' is probably a figment of Strabo's imagination: he is overfond of criticizing his predecessors and anyone who held, as he did, that the Caspian was a gulf of Ocean, could not but believe Polycleitus to be dishonest.

2. τούς γε φυσικοὺς ἄνδρας: The Ionian geographers, especially perhaps Hecataeus. See Tarn 2. 5, and H. Schrader in *Hermes* 43 (1908), 61.

τεσσάρων κόλπων εἰσεχόντων: 'four gulfs running in from the outer Sea'. εἰσέχειν is frequent in this sense in Herodotus; see, e.g., 1. 193; 2. 11, 138; 3. 78.

This is Eratosthenes' geography, reproduced by Strabo 2. 5. 18 (121), ἡ καθ' ἡμᾶς οἰκουμένη γῆ περίρρυτος οὖσα δέχεται κόλπους εἰς ἑαυτὴν ἀπὸ τῆς ἔξω θαλάττης κατὰ τὸν ὠκεανὸν πολλούς, μεγίστους δὲ τέτταρας. ὧν ὁ μὲν βόρειος Κασπία καλεῖται θάλαττα, οἱ δ' Ὑρκανίαν προσαγορεύουσιν. . . . Strabo then enumerates the Persian and Arabian Gulfs and lastly the Mediterranean ('mare nostrum'). Plutarch (*Mor.* 944 b–c) mentions the same four gulfs.

3. ἐνταῦθα: Arrian, in his panegyric on Bucephalas (5. 19. 6), places the incident in the territory of the Uxii, between Susa and Persepolis, but Diodorus (17. 76. 5 ff.) and Curtius (6. 5. 18 f.), drawing on a common source, perhaps Cleitarchus, locate it among the Mardi, west of Hyrcania. In both, Alexander proceeds from threats to action before Bucephalas is restored; in Arrian, as in Plutarch, the threat is sufficient. Plutarch uses the incident to illustrate Alexander's φιλανθρωπία.

4. ἀναπέμψειαν: 'send back'. LSJ cite only Pindar for this meaning of ἀναπέμπειν: but cf. *C. Gracch.* 6. 1, ἐκεῖνος δ' ἔπεισε τὴν βουλὴν ἀπο-δομένην τὸν σῖτον ἀναπέμψαι ταῖς πόλεσι τὸ ἀργύριον; Lysander 6, 1. The more obvious meaning '*bring* back' (cf. πέμπω, 'conduct, escort') is not attested.

XLV. *Alexander's adoption of 'barbarian' dress is disliked by the Macedonians, who nevertheless agree because of his valour.*

1. ἐντεῦθεν: From Zadracarta, the capital of Hyrcania, where Alexander had spent fifteen days after the expedition against the Mardi (Arr. 3. 25. 1). In Curtius also Alexander proceeds from Zadracarta (= Arvae) into Parthia (combining 6. 5. 22 and 6. 5. 32), although here (and in Diodorus and Justin) his departure follows the visit of the Amazon Queen (see ch. 46. 1).

ἐνεδύσατο τὴν βαρβαρικὴν στολήν: The adoption of a mixed dress by Alexander is obviously a political measure, like the introduction of *proskynesis* (see ch. 54. 3), designed to win over the conquered peoples and especially to secure the co-operation of the leading Persians. It is extravagantly praised by Plutarch at *Mor.* 329 f. (esp. 330 b–c). The same point of view is evident at ch. 47. 5.

Although Arrian (4. 7. 4, 8. 4, 9. 9), Curtius (6. 6. 4), and Justin (12. 3. 8 f.) speak only of a Persian or Median dress, this does not mean that they conflict with Plutarch's statement. They follow a hostile source which concentrates on the fact that Alexander wore (some) Persian or Median garments (see Andreotti *Saeculum* 8 (1957), 131 f. and n. 32). So Plutarch can talk of Alexander putting on τὴν βαρβαρικὴν στολήν. Diodorus (17. 77. 5) confirms the adoption of the diadem, the white chiton, and the girdle, and the rejection of the ἀναξυρίδες and the κάνδυς. On the development of Alexander's dress, see also Berve 1. 15 ff., and E. Neuffer, *Das Kostüm Alexanders des Grossen* (Giessen, 1928), especially 35 ff. These writers accept the statement of Ephippus (*F. Gr. Hist.* no. 126, fr. 5 = Ath. 12. 537 e–538 b) that at banquets Alexander (? towards the end of his life) wore the costume of various gods—Ammon, Hermes, Heracles. His account is regarded by Pearson *LHA* 65 as untrustworthy, but see Badian, *Gnomon* 33 (1961), 663. See also 23. 1 n.

Plutarch's source here is probably Eratosthenes, cited at *Mor.* 330 a (see on § 2), who had a variety of primary sources to draw on.

βουλόμενος . . . νόμοις: ' wishing to associate himself with the customs of the country'. For συνοικειοῦν see Wyttenbach on *Mor.* 355 b.

ἀπόπειρά τις ὑφεῖτο: ὑφίημι is commonly used with ἐνέδρα, 'to set an ambush', and the tone of the passage is well rendered by H. Richards (*CR* 17 (1903), 334), 'he was *furtively* making experiment'. He plausibly suggests that Plutarch wrote ὑφίετο.

2. ἀλλόκοτον: 'monstrous, unprecedented'. It is used e.g. of the senatorial decree expelling Italians from Rome in 122 B.C. See also Wyttenbach on *Mor.* 149 b.

ἀναξυρίδας: The baggy Eastern trousers, sometimes of leather (Herod. 1. 71), frequently mentioned with the tiara and the kandys as typical Persian dress; see Plut. *Mor.* 330 a (cited below) and Xen. *Cyr.* 8. 3. 13, ὁ Κῦρος . . . ὀρθὴν ἔχων τὴν τιάραν καὶ χιτῶνα πορφυροῦν μεσόλευκον, ἄλλῳ δὲ οὐκ ἔξεστι μεσόλευκον ἔχειν, καὶ περὶ τοῖς σκέλεσιν ἀναξυρίδας ὑσγινοβαφεῖς, καὶ κάνδυν ὁλοπόρφυρον; cf. also Herod. 5. 49, 7. 61; Xen. *Cyr.* 1. 3. 2; *An.* 1. 5. 8. Strabo 11. 13. 9 (526) remarks that the ἀναξυρίδες and the tiara were introduced from Media into Persia.

κάνδυν: An upper garment of wool, often purple, with long wide sleeves.

τιάραν: The conical Persian head-dress, a sort of turban, worn especially on solemn occasions. The royal head-dress was high and erect and encircled with a diadem (Xen. *An.* 2. 5. 23), while that of the common Persian was soft and fell over on one side. At Arr. 3. 25. 3 Bessus, the Bactrian satrap, is reported τὴν τιάραν ὀρθὴν ἔχειν and to be claiming that he was king of Asia.

τῆς Μηδικῆς: At *Mor.* 330 a Plutarch writes Ἀλέξανδρος οὐ τὴν ἐσθῆτα προσήκατο τὴν Μηδικήν, ἀλλὰ τὴν Περσικὴν πολλῷ τῆς Μηδικῆς εὐτελεσ-τέραν οὖσαν. τὰ γὰρ ἔξαλλα καὶ τραγικὰ τοῦ βαρβαρικοῦ κόσμου παραιτησά-μενος, οἷον τιάραν καὶ κάνδυν καὶ ἀναξυρίδας, ἐκ τοῦ Περσικοῦ καὶ Μακεδονικοῦ τρόπου μεμειγμένην τινὰ στολὴν ἐφόρει, καθάπερ Ἐρα-τοσθένης ἱστόρηκεν. Hence Coraes and Schmieder proposed Μακε-δονικῆς here. But Zonaras (p. 296, ll. 1–2), τῆς μὲν Μηδικῆς ἀτυφοτέραν, τῆς δὲ Περσικῆς σοβαρωτέραν, evidently found Μηδικῆς in his text of Plutarch. Moreover, Plutarch does not always reproduce in the *Life* what he has written in the *De Alexandri Fortuna* (see Badian, *Historia* 7 (1958), 437, n. 48), and his intention in the two passages is different. In the *Moralia* he is particularly concerned with the idea of fusion, the linking of Europe and Asia. Here his main point is the effect that the adoption of non-Macedonian dress has upon the Macedonians: see Andreotti, *Saeculum* 8 (1957), 131 f. and n. 32. It is possible that he cites Eratosthenes wrongly in the *Moralia*, where he writes from memory (Badian, loc. cit.); less probably, in view of the reminiscences of the earlier passage, his source may not be Eratosthenes here.

ἀτυφοτέραν ... οὖσαν: 'more modest than the one, and more stately than the other'. ἐκείνης redit ad Medicam vestem, ταύτης ad Persicam (Reiske); for a similar inversion of the normal usage, see ch. 8. 4.

3. χρηματίζων: 'giving audience': see Holden on *Sull*. 5. 4, who cites *inter alia* Polyb. 3. 66. 6; Diod. 17. 2. 2. Plutarch uses the verb in this sense at *Caes*. 60. 4.

4. ἐπιχωρεῖν: 'pardon', LSJ s.v. (3), who cite also *Mor*. 482 a.

5. ὅς γε κτλ.: All the translators misunderstand this passage. They take Plutarch to mean that Alexander, *at the time he adopted a mixed dress*, had recently sustained these wounds, and thereby convict him of a serious error. But the sentence in §§ 5–6 is a unit, and ἔναγχος can be understood only as relative to the crossing of the Jaxartes. This is borne out, at least as regards the first wound, by two passages in the *Moralia*; 341 b, ἐν Μαρακάνδοις τοξεύματι (sc. πληγεὶς) τὴν κνήμην ὥστε τῆς κερκίδος τὸ ὀστέον ἀποκλασθὲν ὑπὸ τῆς πληγῆς ἐξαλέσθαι, and 327 a, where the wound occurs *near Maracanda*. Curtius (7. 6. 3) also places it in this region, while Arrian (3. 30. 11) more accurately locates it on the R. Jaxartes, to which Alexander had advanced from Maracanda in the summer of 329. He is probably also correct in talking of damage to Alexander's *fibula* (περόνη) rather than to his *tibia* (κέρκις).

The second wound is also mentioned in the *Moralia*, where Plutarch wrongly locates it in Hyrcania, περὶ τὴν Ὑρκανίαν λίθῳ τὸν τράχηλον, ἐξ οὗ καὶ τὰς ὄψεις ἀμαυρωθεὶς ἐφ' ἡμέρας πολλὰς ἐν φόβῳ πηρώσεως ἐγένετο (341 b). This wound occurred in Sogdiana shortly before the crossing of the Jaxartes. Curtius (7. 6. 22 f.) relates that Alexander was struck on the neck by a stone 'ita ut oculis caligine offusa collaberetur, ne mentis quidem compos' during the siege of a town of the Memaceni (otherwise unknown).

This town Arrian calls Gaza (4. 2. 1); he does not mention a wound there, but at 4. 3. 3 he writes that during the siege of nearby Cyropolis βάλλεται λίθῳ αὐτὸς Ἀλέξανδρος βιαίως τήν τε κεφαλὴν καὶ τὸν αὐχένα. This is no doubt correct.

For a complete list of Alexander's wounds see W. Nachstädt's dissertation *De Plut. Declamationibus quae sunt De Alex. Fortuna* (Berlin, 1895), 38–44.

ἀχλὺν ὑποδραμεῖν: 'a mist stole over', an Epic expression; cf. Homer *Il.* 5. 696.

τὸν Ὀρεξάρτην: This is Aristobulus' (correct) form for the R. Jaxartes (Tanais) = Syr Darya; see Tarn 2. 9 and n. 2, where he cites Arr. 3. 30. 7 (= fr. 25) and 7. 16. 3 (= fr. 54). There the manuscripts have Ὀρξάντης and Ὀξυάρτης respectively. Pearson *LHA* 163, n. 74, thinks that Ὀξυάρτης may be the correct form, but as this is a well-known man's name this is extremely improbable. Later writers, e.g., Strabo 510 ff., Ptol. 6. 12–14, Pliny *NH* 6. 49, all call the river Jaxartes (Ἰαξάρτης).

ὃν αὐτὸς ᾤετο Τάναϊν: For possible explanations of this, see ch. 44. 1.

τοὺς Σκύθας τρεψάμενος: For the incident see Arr. 4. 4, esp. §§ 8–9 (from Aristobulus); he attributes Alexander's illness to drinking foul water. Curt. 7. 9. 11 ff. does not mention dysentery; it is the effect of the wound in the neck which causes Alexander's withdrawal. Sintenis proposed to read ἵππῳ for ἐπί on the strength of *Mor.* 341c, ἐδίωξεν ἵππῳ πεντήκοντα καὶ ἑκατὸν σταδίους, ὑπὸ διαρροίας ἐνοχλούμενος. But Plutarch does not always reproduce the *Moralia* verbatim in the *Life*, as indeed ἑκατόν for πεντήκοντα καὶ ἑκατόν shows. Plutarch relates this episode out of chronological order to illustrate his ἀρετή (§ 4), the courage and perseverance he displays, undeterred by wounds and illness.

XLVI. *The Visit of the Amazon Queen.*

1. ἐνταῦθα: Gisinger (*RE* 21, 1705) and Welles (on Diod. 17. 77. 1) hold that ἐνταῦθα refers back to εἰς Ὑρκανίαν at the beginning of ch. 44—'The reference to Alexander's flying expedition across the Jaxartes at the end of sect. (i.e. chapter) 45, which has misled scholars, is a parenthesis' (Welles ad loc.). In this case Plutarch, like Cleitarchus (below), will have located the meeting in Hyrcania. But Jacoby (*F. Gr. Hist.* 2D. 491 foot), Tarn 2. 326 ff., and Pearson *LHA* 77, are certainly correct in holding that ἐνταῦθα refers to the Orexartes of the preceding chapter. The question is settled by Alexander's letter to Antipater (§ 3 below), in which Plutarch says that Alexander wrote that the Scythian king offered him marriage with his daughter, but that he (Alexander) made no mention of the Amazon Queen. Now as we know from Arrian (4. 15. 1 ff.) and Curtius (8. 1. 9 f.) that envoys from the Scythian king reached Alexander in Bactria with such an offer, it is clear (whether the letter is genuine or not) that Plutarch thinks of the (supposed) meeting between Alexander and the Amazon as taking place beyond the Jaxartes and not in Hyrcania. This chapter is attached to the digression at the end of ch. 45 (see previous note). Plutarch returns to Hyrcania and the main narrative in ch. 47.

οἱ πολλοί . . .: There is much to be said for Tarn's view (2. 308) that a monograph on the Amazons is the source of the list of writers given here. This, of course, does not rule out the possibility that Plutarch has added to the original list from his own wide reading; but it seems unlikely that he had read *all* the authors cited.

For the suggestion that Plutarch's source was Ister see below.

Κλείταρχος: On Cleitarchus see the Introduction pp. lvii ff. His version may be deduced from the versions of Diod. 17. 77. 1–3; Curt. 6. 5. 24–32, and Justin 12. 3. 5–7. Curtius locates the meeting precisely at Zadracarta (see on 45. 1), and the queen remains there for thirteen days (so Diod. and Justin) until Alexander satisfies her desires. According to Cleitarchus the Amazons came from the R. Thermodon, which he evidently thought of as not far west of the Caspian Gates (Strabo 11. 5. 4 = fr. 16). For his geography see especially Pearson *LHA* 214, n. 14, 220 f.; Tarn 2. 328 f.

Πολύκλειτος: A member of a well-known family in Larisa. He is often said, e.g. by Berve, to have been the grandfather of Antigonos Doson, but in view of the frequency of the name in Thessaly Pearson *LHA* (71) rightly hesitates to accept this or any other identification proposed. He accompanied Alexander and wrote in at least eight books a work entitled *A History of Alexander* or perhaps more probably *Stories of Alexander*, which was used by Cleitarchus and Eratosthenes. If we may judge by the ten extant fragments (five preserved by Strabo), he was particularly interested in geography and natural history. But fr. 3 reveals his insight into the character of the Persian imperial economy; see Pearson *LHA* 73. Strabo 11. 7. 4 (= fr. 7) considered him one of the 'flatterers' of Alexander; but probably wrongly—see the notes to ch. 44. 1.

For his fragments see *F. Gr. Hist.* no. 128. A good discussion in Pearson *LHA* 70–7; cf. also *RE* 21, 1700–7 (Gisinger); Berve no. 651.

Ὀνησίκριτος: See Introduction, pages lvi f.

Ἀντιγένης: *F. Gr. Hist.* no. 141, fr. 1. Apart from this, Antigenes is cited only for the name of a Macedonian river. It is improbable that he should be identified with the famous Macedonian infantry leader, or the soldier mentioned in ch. 70. 4 (Berve nos. 83, 84).

Ἴστρος: Ister, probably a native of Paphos, belonged to the circle of Callimachus and was perhaps once his slave. There is no other evidence of his date. He was an antiquary rather than a historian, and his numerous works appear to have been collections of material from 'classical' literature, grouped together on special topics. The chief of these dealt with Athenian antiquities in at least fourteen books, and was probably confined to the mythical period; at any rate it is never cited for historical matters.

The extant fragments are collected in *F. Gr. Hist.* 3B, no. 334, with commentary in 3B Supplement, 618 ff.; see also *RE* 9, 2270 ff. (Jacoby), and L. Pearson, *The Local Historians of Attica* (Philadelphia, 1942), 136–44. Plutarch cites Ister also at *Mor.* 403 e and at *Thes.* 34. 3, where he criticizes him for a strange story about Aithra in terms which suggest that he had Ister's book before him. A. von Gutschmid (*Kleine Schriften* 5 (1894), 155 f.) has suggested, not implausibly, that Ister is Plutarch's source for this list of writers. For the context 'one might think of Theseus' expedition to the Amazons or their attack on Athens' (Jacoby, 3B Supplement, 643, on fr. 26).

2. Ἀριστόβουλος δὲ καὶ Χάρης: See Introduction, pages liv lv. f.

Πτολεμαῖος: See on 10. 4. Ptolemy 'never (so far as is known) explicitly contradicted anyone' (Tarn 2. 27, 331, citing Strasburger 50, 55). Arr. 5. 14. 5 is Arrian's own criticism, not Ptolemy's—see *PACA* 4 (1961), 19, n. 24 *contra* Pearson *LHA* 172–3. Perhaps, therefore, he merely omitted any reference to the incident.

Ἀντικλείδης: The first Athenian known to have written a book on Alexander. His date is uncertain, perhaps early third century. His chief work was a περὶ Νόστων dealing with 'Returns' from the Heroic Age onwards, but he wrote also a History of Delos. He appears to have been more of an antiquary than a historian, but as with Ister no decision is possible. As he rationalized the story of the judgement of Paris, it is not surprising that he rejected the Amazon story.

See further *F. Gr. Hist.* no. 140; *RE* 1, 2425 f. (Schwartz); and especially Pearson *LHA* 251–3, who prints an additional papyrus fragment referring to the Mardi.

Φίλων ὁ Θηβαῖος: Nothing is known of Philon or Hecataeus (*RE* 7, 2666 f. (no. 2)) or Philip the Chalcidian (*RE* 19, 2349 (no. 38)). Philip of Theangela in Caria (*RE* 19, 2349 (no. 40); *F. Gr. Hist.* no. 471) wrote a Carian chronicle in the third century, of which only three substantial fragments survive.

I should prefer to retain the order of all manuscripts except C, in which πρὸς δὲ τούτοις Ἑκαταῖος ὁ Ἐρετριεὺς follows Φίλιππος ὁ Θεαγγελεύς. Ziegler adopts the order given by C, on the ground that it would be natural for Plutarch to put two authors of the same name together (*Rh. Mus.* 84 (1935), 376 f.). This is scarcely cogent, and it seems more natural to mention five authors and to *add* another three than to name two and add six.

Jacoby (*RE* 7, 2666) suggested that Plutarch mentions first the Alexander-historians and adds (πρὸς δὲ τούτοις) those writers who dealt with the Amazons in other works. But we know so little of the last four authors that it is quite uncertain what scheme, if any, Plutarch followed.

Δοῦρις ὁ Σάμιος: *F. Gr. Hist.* no. 76 fr. 46. Duris succeeded his father Scaeus as tyrant of Samos and studied under Theophrastus at Athens. Apart from works on literature and art, he wrote a Samian chronicle and a History of Agathocles, used by Diodorus in Bks. 19–21. His most quoted work was his Μακεδονικά, commencing in 370/69 and going down to at least 281, in which the history of Philip and Alexander occupied Bks. 2–9. He was a prominent example of the 'tragic' style, whose exponents strove to involve the emotions of their readers (see esp. F. W. Walbank in *Historia* 9 (1960), 216 ff.).

πλάσμα: 'a pure invention'. π. is often combined with μῦθος, as at *Thes.* 28. 1, *Mor.* 17 a, etc.

3. ἔοικεν: This is a *deduction* by Plutarch from the fact that Alexander writes to Antipater describing in detail (ἀκριβῶς) the visit of the Scythian envoys (see on § 1 (ἐνταῦθα) above) and makes no mention of the Amazon Queen. Cf. 7. 5, where Plutarch deduces the content of Aristotle's teaching from the letters.

Welles (on Diod. 17. 77. 3) points out that 'disbelief in Amazons as such is a modern phenomenon', and that Plutarch doubts the story not because Amazons did not exist, but because it is poorly attested. Plutarch writes at length about them at *Thes.* 27. Even Arrian (7. 13. 2–6) does not doubt their existence at any earlier period, although he does not believe they survived to Alexander's day. Strabo's attitude (11. 5. 3 f.) is essentially the same.

4. λέγεται: After his victory over Ptolemy in 306 at Salamis in Cyprus Antigonus assumed the royal title, and was followed in 305 by the other rulers including Lysimachus (*CAH* 6. 498 f.; Glotz–Cohen 4. 1. 333). Brown (6 f.) therefore holds that this incident proves that the fourth book of Onesicritus' work had not been published by 305 (so also Berve 2. 289 and Andreotti, *Historia* 1 (1950), 584). Most scholars, including Brown and Berve, have therefore rejected the anecdote in Lucian (*Hist. Conscr.* 40), in which Onesicritus reads extracts from his work to Alexander, since it is unlikely that Onesicritus spent nearly twenty years in the composition of three books. But, as Fisch (*AJP* 58 (1937), 132) and Griffith (*CR* n.s. 1 (1951), 169) have pointed out, there is no reason to think that Onesicritus was reading what he had only recently written. Schachermeyr (502, n. 67) suggests, less probably, that Onesicritus read his book to Lysimachus when he was still satrap. We may therefore accept the evidence of Lucian.

Since Cleitarchus used Onesicritus (Jacoby *RE* 11. 652 f., *F. Gr. Hist.*

2D. 469; Strasburger *RE* 18, 466), an early date for Onesicritus is established if Jacoby (*RE* 11, 626) is correct in his contention that Cletiarchus' book appeared *c.* 310; see also Introduction, p. liv and n. 1. In § 97 of the *Testamentum Alexandri*, contained in §§ 87–123 of the Metz Epitome, Onesicritus (*F. Gr. Hist.* no. 134, fr. 37) is cited for failing to give a list of the persons who attended the party given by Medios (see ch. 76) at the very end of Alexander's life. R. Merkelbach (*Die Quellen des griechischen Alexanderromans* (München, 1954), 54 f., 124 ff.) has put forward strong reasons for supposing that this *Testamentum* was a pamphlet written in 321 by a partisan of Perdiccas in the struggle against Antipater (for this, see e.g. *CAH* 6. 474). If this view is correct, Onesicritus in all probability began his book during the King's lifetime and completed it within two years of his death; see Merkelbach, op. cit., 145, n. 1.

XLVII. *Alexander persuades the Macedonians to continue the campaign. He pursues his 'policy of fusion'. The conflict between Hephaestion and Craterus.*

Plutarch now returns to Hyrcania and the main narrative (see ch. 45, last note). For the incident, see also Diod. 17. 74. 3, Curt. 6. 2. 15–4. 1, Justin 12. 3. 2–4; in all three it takes place in Parthia, before Alexander enters Hyrcania, but Curtius locates it at Hecatompylos, Diodorus two days before Alexander entered the city. The occasion for the speech is the feeling of the Macedonians that the death of Darius marked the end of the campaign, but in Diodorus the discharge of the allied Greek troops follows the speech, in Curtius they are already discharged. In Curtius, also, Alexander wins over the generals before addressing the whole army.

Arrian does not mention the incident.

1. κατὰ χώραν: Presumably in Parthia, although nothing is said of an advance into Hyrcania. τοὺς δ᾽ ἀρίστους may refer to the ἀκμαιοτάτη δύναμις of 44. 1.

⟨πεῖραν⟩ προσέβαλε: 'he applied a test'. The supplement is due to Ziegler (*Rh. Mus.* 84 (1935), 377 f.), who compares *Brut.* 12. 3, where, however, the phrase occurs only by emendation. The anonymous προσέλαβε (without πεῖραν) = 'he won over' is probably correct; see on the (vexed) text of this paragraph my note in *CPhil.* 51 (1956), 170 ff.

†ἐνύπνιον: ἐνώπιον, 'face to face' was suggested by Ziegler in the first edition of his Teubner text; he compared Curtius 6. 3. 8, 'vestris armis continentur, non suis moribus, et qui *praesentes* metuunt, in absentia hostes erunt'. Later (*Rh. Mus.* 84 (1935), 377 f.) he withdrew

his suggestion, since ἐνώπιον is not used elsewhere by Plutarch, in favour of ἐν ὅπλοις ⟨παρόντας⟩. H. Erbse (*Rh. Mus.* 100 (1957), 279 n. 15), has since proposed ἐνόπλους ὄντας. But if the passage in Curtius is regarded as parallel (as it is by Ziegler and Erbse), ἐνώπιον (with perhaps the emendation of ὁρώντων to ὀρρωδούντων) is more probable. Ziegler did not observe that Plutarch is here quoting verbatim (σχεδὸν αὐτοῖς ὀνόμασιν) from a letter, and the wording may be that of the author, whether Alexander or another.

2. οὐ μὴν ἀλλ' ἀφιέναι γε . . .: The text of this section is certainly corrupt. Ziegler retains the manuscript reading ἔφη, καί, adopts Bekker's emendation ἀφιέναι for ἀπιέναι (so all manuscripts), and conjectures a lacuna after ἐγκαταλέλειπται. A simpler solution, to emend ἔφη καί to ἐφῆκε, 'he allowed', was proposed by Coraes and adopted by Sintenis and Perrin. This, however, would seem to require the alteration of τοὺς βουλομένους to τοῖς βουλομένοις, as indeed Coraes suggested. The need for change may be avoided by reading ἀφῆκε with the same meaning. For this use of ἀφιέναι cf. Eur. *Med.* 373, τήνδ' ἀφῆκεν ἡμέραν | μεῖναί μ', Herod. 3. 25, τοὺς Ἕλληνας ἀπῆκε ἀποπλέειν, 6. 62, and elsewhere (see Powell's Lexicon). For its use in Plutarch see *Cim.* 8. 8 (where Ziegler wrongly emends to ἐφῆκεν) and *Alex.* 60. 15. Alternatively, we may translate ἀφῆκε as 'he sent away', and construe ἀπιέναι with τοὺς βουλομένους.

ἐθελόντων: with στρατεύειν is read by most editors and translators. Bryan suggested ἐθελοντῶν, 'volunteers', which is perhaps more vigorous.

κτώμενος: 'while seeking to win', a conative present participle.

3. ἐν τῇ . . . ἐπιστολῇ: On the authenticity of this letter, see *PACA* 4 (1961), 15. This *need* not be the same letter as that mentioned in the previous chapter, which must have been written after Alexander reached the Jaxartes (see 46. 1 n.); although, of course, it may be.

ἐξέκραγον: So Curt. 6. 4. 1, 'summa militum alacritate, iubentium quocumque vellet ducere, oratio excepta est'.

5. ἐκείνους τε προσῆγε: Although all manuscripts have ἐκεῖνα, Ziegler's ἐκείνους (*Rh. Mus.* 84 (1935), 378) is surely correct. ὁμοίου ἑαυτόν must be followed by a personal object and τοῖς ἐπιχωρίοις is therefore masculine. Yet ἐκεῖνα immediately following would cause a reader to understand it as a neuter noun.

6. τρισμυρίους παῖδας: For the arrival of those youths at Susa in 324 see 71. 1. Diod. (17. 108. 1–3) says that they were formed into a unit as a counter-balance (ἀντίταγμα) to the Macedonian phalanx after the mutiny at the Hyphasis (wrongly called Ganges), and the subsequent unruliness and ridicule of Ammon. This date (325) seems too late, although Wilcken (187) accepts it. More probable is Curtius' statement (8. 5. 1) that Alexander issued orders for its formation in Bactria in 327, immediately after his marriage to Roxane (accepted by Schachermeyr 294, Robinson 160, Tarn 1. 77). Arr. 7. 6. 1 describes the youths on their arrival at Susa in 324 as ἡβάσκοντας ἤδη, implying that they had had a long training. Plutarch does not date the order to 330 in Hyrcania, as is sometimes said, e.g. by Radet 240; §§ 5–12 of this chapter are 'eidology' (see Introduction, p. xl), and the narrative is resumed with ch. 48. It is likely that he thinks of the same date as Curtius, who however assigns a very different motive to Alexander; in Curtius Alexander, intending to invade India, issues the order 'obsides simul habiturus et milites'.

7. τὰ περὶ 'Ρωξάνην: 'his marriage to Roxane.'
Roxane (Berve no. 688), whose name means 'Little Star' (Rawlinson, *Bactria* (1912), 46, n. 2), was the daughter of the Bactrian baron, Oxyartes, and was captured on the Sogdian rock (Arr. 4. 18. 4, 19. 5; Polyaenus 4. 3. 29), sometimes called the Rock of Ariamazes (Curt. 7. 11. 1 ff.). It is usually said (e.g. by Berve loc. cit.) that the marriage took place later on the rock of Chorienes (for the siege see Arr. 4. 21. 1–10; Curtius calls him Sisimithres). This rests only on the testimony of Strabo 11. 11. 4 (517) who, however, confuses the two rocks. He supposes that Oxyartes' wife and children were captured on the rock of Sisimithres, i.e. he thinks of Roxane's capture and the marriage as taking place on the same rock; this is, of course, the first (Sogdian) rock. Their marriage was painted by Aëtion in a picture later seen in Italy by Lucian and described by him (*Imag.* 7; *Herod.* 4–6).
Plutarch gives a different view of Alexander's motives in the *Moralia*. At *Mor.* 338 d his marriage to Stateira (see ch. 70) is said to have been a matter of policy, whereas he was in love with Roxane (ἐρασθείς; cf. *Mor.* 332 e, where the same word is used and he is praised for acting φιλοσόφως in not offering her violence). All our sources affirm that Alexander was overcome by her beauty, and most scholars accept this. An exception is Tarn, who thinks Alexander never loved any woman except his mother; he seems concerned, however, to eliminate any weakness of this sort in Alexander (see 2. 319 ff., Appendix 18, 'Alexander's Attitude to Sex'). He points out (*CAH* 6. 397, though omitted at 1. 76) as proof of Alexander's lack of passion that Roxane did not bear him a child until after his death; but the Metz Epitome (ch. 70) may well be correct in the mention of a son who died on the Hydaspes in the autumn of 326 (accepted by Berve loc. cit., Wilcken 176). But Plutarch (again followed by modern scholars, e.g. Bury 796) is doubtless correct in seeing policy *as well as*

passion in the marriage. Tarn (2. 326, n. 3) credits Plutarch with being the only author to suggest a political motive; see, however, Curt. 8. 4. 25, 'in amorem . . . ita effusus est ut diceret ad stabiliendum regnum pertinere Persas et Macedones conubio iungi'. Alexander hoped, as in fact happened, that by this marriage he would conciliate the Bactrian barons and bring the long struggle to an end (see Hammond 623). Whether it was 'symbolic of the union of Europe and Asia' (Bury 796) seems questionable.

8. τοῖς ὑποκειμένοις πράγμασιν: His policy of fusion.

ὑπερηγάπησαν: cf. 9. 4.

9. Ἡφαιστίωνα: Berve no. 357. Hephaestion was about the same age as Alexander, and was brought up with him and is clearly the dearest of Alexander's friends (Curt. 3. 12. 16). At Troy he appears as 'Patroclus' to Alexander's 'Achilles' (Arr. 1. 12. 1); although Arr. gives the story as a λόγος, it is very probably true. If so, it confirms (what might be suspected) that in their youth at any rate Alexander and Hephaestion were 'lovers'. This aspect of their relationship helps to explain Alexander's extravagant reaction to Hephaestion's death; see the notes to 72. 3 ff. His intimacy with Alexander and his privileged position (obviously resented by the leading Macedonians) is illustrated by several incidents, e.g. Olympias' letter at 39. 8, and especially when Darius' mother mistakes Hephaestion for Alexander (Diod. 17. 37. 5; Curt. 3. 12. 17; Arr. 2. 12. 6, a λόγος). Tarn (2. 57, 78) considers Hephaestion's intimacy with Alexander antedated on the ground that he is not mentioned among his companions at 10. 4. This is not conclusive, and the view that the anecdotes about him are derived from 'a source that wrote up Hephaestion' takes no account of the evidence of Curtius.

It is significant that it was through Hephaestion that Demosthenes attempted to conciliate Alexander in 331, as Marsyas of Pella (no. 489) attests (*F. Gr. Hist.* nos. 135–6, fr. 2); cf. Aeschines 3. 162. Marsyas was well qualified to know the truth, as he was the half-brother of Antigonus (see 70. 4 n.) and wrote a detailed history of Alexander, with whom he had been brought up (T. 1).

Of his military career we hear nothing until Gaugamela, where he was wounded (though not leading the Hypaspists; so Diod. 17. 61. 3 accepted by Berve 2. 170; these were under the command of Nicanor (Arr. 3. 11. 9). Doubtless he was a cavalry officer). After the death of Philotas he was appointed joint commander (with Cleitus) of the Companion Cavalry, and rapidly proved his ability in Bactria, Sogdiana, and India, where he frequently held independent commands. Alexander's regard for him (partly due to Hephaestion's understanding of and support for his policy of fusion) is shown by the creation in 324 of the post of Chiliarch or Grand Vizier; this was perhaps due also to his ability to deal with Asiatics. It marked him out as second only to Alexander; cf. Tarn 1. 117. A less attractive side of his character is shown by his relations with Craterus and Eumenes (see *Eum.* 2; cf. Arr. 7. 13. 1, 14. 9), and by his part in the deaths of Philotas and Callisthenes (ch. 49. 12; 55. 1). At Susa he married Drypetis, the sister of Stateira (ch. 70).

συμμετακοσμούμενον: 'changing his habits together with him', i.e. co-operating in his policy of fusion. συμμετακοσμεῖσθαι is ἅπ. λεγ. in this sense. For the simple verb, see *Num.* 5. 4, *Phil.* 9. 6, and for the noun, *Mor.* 75 e; *Sull.* 7. 3 (with μεταβολή); Arr. 4. 9. 9.

Κρατερόν: Berve no. 446; *RE* Supplementband 4, 1038–42 and especially 1046–8 (Geyer). Craterus was perhaps the outstanding soldier in Alexander's army and one of his Companions. He began the expedition as a battalion commander, and at Issus and Gaugamela commanded all the infantry on the left of the phalanx, under Parmenio. After Parmenio's death he became Alexander's second-in-command and often operated independently with conspicuous success in Bactria (see esp. Arr. 4. 17. 1–2, 22. 1). In 325 he brought back the troops who returned from India through the interior of Persia, while Alexander marched through Gedrosia. His marriage to Amastris, a niece of Darius, lasted only until 322 and was without issue. In 324 he was entrusted with the task of leading the veterans back to Macedonia, and was ordered to replace Antipater in Macedonia (71. 8 n.). For his position after Alexander's death, see esp. Badian, *Gnomon* 34 (1962), 383. He was killed in 321 in a battle against Eumenes.

His loyalty to Alexander was unquestioned and he deserved (and got) Alexander's respect; cf. Arr. 7. 12. 3, τὸν πιστότατόν τε αὐτῷ καὶ ὅντινα ἴσον τῇ ἑαυτοῦ κεφαλῇ ἄγει, and Curt. 6. 8. 2, 'regi carus in paucis'. The affection of his soldiers for him is shown by *Demetr.* 14. 2 and especially *Eum.* 6. 3, where his opposition to Alexander's adoption of Persian habits is mentioned. As there is no other evidence for the πολλὰς ἀπεχθείας which Craterus is thereby said to have incurred, it may be doubted whether he was an outspoken opponent of Alexander's policy.

Geyer (1046) rightly rejects the suggestion that all the passages which attest Craterus' exceptional standing among the Macedonians were invented by Duris; the two passages cited may derive from Chares.

10. φιλαλέξανδρον . . . φιλοβασιλέα: cf. Diod. 17, 114. 2; *Mor.* 181 d.

11. ὑπούλως ἔχοντες: A favourite phrase of Plutarch; cf. *Luc.* 22. 5,

Dion 54. 4, *Arat.* 40. 1. Wyttenbach (on *Mor.* 44 a) defines ὕπουλος as 'tamquam ulcus latens, occultum et insidiosum odium': so at Alexander's accession πᾶσα δ' ὕπουλος ἦν Μακεδονία πρὸς Ἀμύνταν ἀποβλέπουσα καὶ τοὺς Ἀερόπου παῖδας (*Mor.* 327 c).

συνέκρουον: 'came into collision'. Generally transitive, as at *Pel.* 14. 1, but here used like προσκρούειν, e.g. at *Eum.* 2. 1, οὐ μὴν ἀλλὰ καὶ προσέκρουσε πολλάκις Ἀ.

ἅπαξ δέ κτλ.: See *Mor.* 337 a (in less detail).

ἔμπληκτον: 'senseless', a very strong word. LSJ cite *Rom.* 28. 5, ἔμ. καὶ μανικός. Cf. also *Eum.* 3. 10, ἔμπληκτον ὄντα καὶ φορᾶς μεστὸν ἀβεβαίου καὶ ὀξείας ἀπογνούς (of Leonnatus); *Mor.* 149 b, ἔμπληκτος καὶ ἀλλόκοτος (where see Wyttenbach).

12. ἐπώμοσε τὸν Ἄμμωνα: So, according to Arrian (*Ind.* 35. 8), Alexander swears (ἐπόμνυσιν) by Zeus of the Greeks and Libyan Ammon that he was more pleased at the safety of his fleet (which he had believed lost) than because he had conquered all Asia. See also Tarn 2. 351 and n. 5.

XLVIII–XLIX. 12. *The 'Conspiracy' of Philotas.*

1. Φιλώτας: Berve no. 802. The eldest son of Parmenio, brother of Nicanor and Hector; related by marriage to several distinguished Macedonian families. He is said by Plutarch (ch. 10. 3) to have been one of Alexander's boyhood friends; nevertheless, he must have been considerably older than Alexander. He commanded the Companion Cavalry since the beginning of the expedition, and it seems unlikely that even Parmenio's son would have been given this post in his early twenties (Welles, *Miscellanea Rostagni*, 108). Once or twice he held independent commands (Arr. 1. 19. 8, 24. 3). His courage and military ability were undoubted, but his passion for sport and luxury was notorious even among the Macedonian nobility (see on ch. 40. 1). In addition he was inordinately proud of his family position, and given to boasting (below).

καρτερικός: 'capable of endurance'.

3. ὄγκῳ δέ: 'self-importance, arrogance'; cf. 41. 1 (39. 7). ὄγκῳ δέ is correlative with ἀξίωμα μέν in l. 1. Plutarch (*Mor.* 339 b) contrasts his invincibility in battle with his enslavement to pleasures, women, and money. For his boasting see Curt. 6. 8. 3, 'neque (Craterus) ignorabat, saepe (Philotan) Alexandri auribus *nimia iactatione virtutis atque operae gravem fuisse et ob ea non quidem sceleris, sed contumaciae tamen esse suspectum*'.

βάρει πλούτου: 'abundance of wealth'; on βάρος in this sense, see Denniston on Eur. *El.* 1287 (where the manuscript reading is sound). In Curt. 6. 11. 3 he has wagons laden with gold and silver! For Philotas' high-handed actions see Curt. 6. 11. 1–4, where Bolon, a Macedonian officer, after Philotas' arrest reminds the soldiers how often he had driven the soldiers out of their quarters to make way for his servants (purgamenta servorum). This passage obviously needs to be received with caution.

τῷ σολοίκῳ καὶ παρασήμῳ: 'in bad taste and in a manner that did not ring true'. σόλοικος, lit. 'speaking incorrectly, using bad Greek', hence 'awkard, in bad taste' (see Porter on *Dion* 17. 6); παράσημος, 'marked falsely, counterfeit', especially of money, e.g. Ar. *Ach.* 518.

χείρων . . . γίνου: 'be less of a hero' (Burn 179).

4. ὅτε γάρ κτλ.: by Parmenio in 333 b.c., following the Battle of Issus (Oct. 333); see on 24. 1.

Ἀντιγόνη: Berve no. 86. In the *Moralia* (339 d–f) Plutarch calls her Antigone of Pella, and remarks that she was captured by Autophradates in Samothrace. This was presumably earlier in 333 when, after the death of Memnon, Autophradates (Berve no. 188) and Pharnabazus won over several islands including Tenedos (Arr. 2. 2. 1–2). Although our sources do not mention it, there may have been a raid on Samothrace; at any rate Plutarch's account does not suggest that Antigone was captured while sailing to the island (so Berve 2. 96, n. 3). I know no evidence for Burn's suggestion (180) that Antigone was sold to a slave-dealer after the capture of Pydna by Philip in 356.

5. στρατιωτικά: 'boastful', cf. 23. 7, where the word is used of Alexander. For an (? imaginary) instance of his boastfulness see *Mor.* 339 e.

ἀπεκάλει: See 11. 6.

τὸ τῆς ἀρχῆς ὄνομα: Castiglioni (*Gnomon* 13 (1937), 141) would add καὶ δόξαν after ὄνομα, comparing *Caes.* 69. 1, ταύτης (sc. ἀρχῆς) οὐδὲν ὅτι μὴ τοὔνομα μόνον καὶ τὴν ἐπίφθονον καρπωσάμενος δόξαν παρὰ τῶν πολιτῶν.

6. ἐκείνου . . . ἕτερον: ἐκείνης . . . ἑτέραν, Helmbold (*CPhil.* 32 (1937), 285), citing *Mor.* 339 f, τούτους τοὺς λόγους ἡ Ἀντιγόνα ἐξήνεγκε πρός τινα τῶν συνήθων γυναικῶν, ἐκείνη δὲ πρὸς Κρατερόν.

7. φοιτᾶν εἰς ταὐτὸ τῷ Φ.: 'to continue her meetings with Philotas'. For this construction see the examples cited by Holden on *Per.* 32. 1; add *Pomp.* 35. 6.

XLIX.

2. κατέσχεν: 'he restrained himself'.

εἴτε . . . εἴτε: Probably Plutarch's own suggestions. In the *Moralia* (339 f) he oddly remarks that Alexander did not disclose his suspicion of Philotas for more than *seven* years! Presumably he dated this to the beginning of Alexander's reign, assuming that Alexander had always disliked Philotas, if it is not a rhetorical exaggeration. Both Ptolemy and Aristobulus (Arr. 3. 26. 1) say that a report of Philotas' treason was made to the king in Egypt, but that Alexander did not believe it because of his long friendship with Philotas and the favour he had shown to him and his father.

3. ἐν δὲ τῷ τότε χρόνῳ: In 330 B.C. at Phrada, the capital of Drangiane (Diod. 17. 78. 4). Its name was later changed to Prophthasia (Steph. Byz. s.v. *Φράδα*), presumably because of the detection of the conspiracy. It is usually held to be identical with the modern Farah (so Schachermeyr 513, n. 173; Berve 1. 293), but see Tarn *Bactria* 14, n. 4.

On the 'conspiracy' of Philotas see also Arr. 3. 26. 1–3; Diod. 17. 79. 1–80. 2; Curt. 6. 7–11; Justin 12. 5. 3; Strabo 15. 2. 10 (724).

The official version given by Ptolemy (Arr. loc. cit.) was that Philotas was convicted ἄλλοις τε ἐλέγχοις οὐκ ἀφανέσι καὶ μάλιστα δή (that he had failed to inform Alexander of the existence of a plot against him). This version is accepted by Tarn (1. 62 ff.) and, with reservations, by Wilcken (163 ff.); but its inadequacy is well demonstrated by Badian (*TAPA* 91 (1960), 324–38 esp. 331 ff.); see also Berve (2. no. 802) and Schachermeyr (266–75, esp. 269 f.). In particular he points out that Arrian's words mean quite simply that there was *no* evidence that Philotas had conspired against Alexander (so already Otto ap. Berve 2. 395, n. 3).

Badian, however, argues that Alexander had for years determined to remove Philotas and his father Parmenio, and by this time had succeeded in undermining Parmenio's reputation and had left him behind on communications. In the death of Nicanor, Parmenio's second son and commander of the Hypaspists, he saw his opportunity: Philotas was left behind to attend to the funeral and in the period before he rejoined the army, probably at Phrada, Alexander hatched the plot against him. But unless we allow a very large measure of coincidence this interpretation requires that we reject most of the evidence of the sources. We must suppose that there was *no* plot against Alexander, and that the king had arranged with Dimnus and the others that the (false) information be communicated to Philotas. Even if we accept this, how could Alexander *know* that Philotas would

fail to pass on the information? ἐπιβουλευόμενος (49. 1) refers to the
fact that he is being watched without his knowledge.

He was certainly
kept under surveillance and his utterances, faithfully reported to
Alexander, would naturally prejudice the king against him; but that
is not to say that he had determined to 'liquidate' Philotas.

Berve and Schachermeyr also hold that Alexander planned the
destruction of Philotas and Parmenio, but they suggest more plausibly
that the king seized the opportunity afforded by Philotas' failure to
inform him of the plot (which really existed), and with characteristic
speed and ruthlessness accomplished his object.

It is equally probable, and certainly more in accord with the sources,
that there was an actual plot against Alexander, in which Philotas
was not involved and to which he gave little credence, and that his
many enemies seized the opportunity of his silence to persuade the
king that Dimnus was too insignificant to be the leader of the conspiracy. They could urge that Philotas had had ample time to inform
him and had not done so; he must therefore be involved in the plot,
indeed be the instigator of it or the agent of Parmenio. After all Philotas
had for some time been guilty of making indiscreet remarks, depreciating Alexander. The king, moreover, knowing the hostility his adoption
of Persian dress and ceremonial had aroused, would be ready to
believe the worst of one who so obviously disapproved.

F. Cauer, 'Philotas Kleitos Kallisthenes', *Neue Jahrb. f. Kl. Philol.*,
Supplementband 20 (1894), 8 ff., is still worth reading.

Λίμνος: Berve no. 269. He is mentioned only in this incident. Ziegler
(*Rh. Mus.* 84 (1935), 378 f.) retracts his earlier suggestion that Λίμνος
(so all manuscripts) should be altered to Δίμνος to conform to the
spelling in Diodorus and Curtius. He points to the lack of parallels to
the form Dimnos by contrast with Limnaios and Limnos, a name
borne by three prominent Macedonians in the third and second centuries B.C. But we should have to assume either a parallel corruption
in Curtius or that he already had before him a Greek text with a corrupt form. The change of Δίμνος into the commoner Λίμνος, Δ to Λ,
would be easy, and Δίμνος is doubtless correct.

Χαλαίστρας: A town in Macedonia at the mouth of the R. Axius; cf.
Herod. 7. 123.

[χαλεπῶς]: 'Facile noscitatu est, χαλεπῶς esse vitiosam iterationem
verae lectionis Χαλαίστρας' (Reiske).

Νικόμαχον: In Diodorus (17. 79. 2) he is persuaded to take part in the
plot, but 'being very young' discloses it to his brother. Curtius, though
more rhetorical, agrees with Plutarch that Nicomachus was not
a conspirator.

4. ἐντυχεῖν: 'communicate to, converse with'; so in § 6 below. See Holden on *C. Gracch.* 6. 3.

6. πρὸς ἕτερον: Pearson *LHA* 60, suggests that Chares the Chamberlain is meant and that he is Plutarch's source here. But it is the page Metron, in charge of the armoury (Curt. 6. 7. 22). The proposal to restore *Μέτρωνα* to the text is needless; Diod. (17. 79. 4) merely says 'one of the royal pages'.

παρεδήλωσαν: 'they gradually revealed that Philotas'. LSJ are wrong in separating this passage from the closely parallel *Crass.* 18. 5, ἡσυχῇ δὲ παρεδήλουν καὶ οἱ μάντεις, ὡς ἀεὶ πονηρὰ σημεῖα καὶ δυσέκθυτα προφαίνοιτο τῷ Κράσσῳ διὰ τῶν ἱερῶν, and translating 'inform against'. Both passages indicate the gradual (and ? reluctant) revelation of unpopular information.

7. ὡς ἠμύνετο συλλαμβανόμενος κτλ.: The other authorities differ. Curt. (6. 7. 29 f.) relates that, when summoned, Dimnus stabbed himself and died in the presence of Alexander without revealing anything. In Diod. (17. 79. 5), D. also stabs himself, but only after he had revealed everything to Alexander.

8. τοὺς πάλαι μισοῦντας αὐτόν: Curtius (6. 8. 1) tells of a council of Alexander's friends (no names given), summoned by the king to hear Nicomachus' evidence, in which Craterus spoke against Philotas and persuaded the other members. The elaborate arrangements for the arrest are made by Craterus, Leonnatus, Hephaestion, Coenus, Erigyius, and Perdiccas (6. 8. 17).

9. ὄργανον: 'a mere tool'. LSJ cite for this meaning only Soph. *Ajax* 380 (see Jebb; Kamerbeek goes astray). Add Xen. *Cyr.* 5. 3. 47, the general should know the names of his commanders whom he must use as *tools* (ὀργάνοις), just as the doctor should know the names of his instruments, and esp. *Ant.* 72. 3, Ἀλεξᾶς . . . τῶν Κλεοπάτρας ἐπ' Ἀντώνιον ὀργάνων τὸ βιαιότατον. Cf. also *Mar.* 35. 1; *Crass.* 2. 7, where slaves are said to be ὄργανα ἔμψυχα (so Arist. *Eth. Nic.* 1161ᵇ4); Cic. *Ad fam.* 11. 14, ὄργανον enim erat meum senatus.

ἀπὸ μείζονος ἀρχῆς: Philotas, and perhaps also Parmenio.

10. ἀναπετάσαντος τὰ ὦτα: cf. 42, 2–4, where Plutarch obviously has this incident, among others, in mind.

11. συλληφθεὶς ἀνεκρίνετο . . . ταῖς βασάνοις: Diod. (17. 80. 2) and Curt. (6. 11. 8 ff.) also say that torture was used. Tarn and Wilcken ignore its use, presumably since Arrian does not mention it. But his account is very summary. Berve (2. 396) doubts whether it was used, but Schachermeyr (271 and 514, n. 180) and Badian (*TAPA* 91

(1960), 332) point to its use in the case of the conspiracy of the pages and of Callisthenes (see Arr. 4. 14. 3, on Ptolemy's authority). In these instances Berve (1. 210) conjectures that the army assembly gave permission for the use of torture.

κατακούοντος: The compound is elsewhere used of eavesdroppers; see Strabo 14. 1. 32; cf. Plato *Protag.* 314 c.

12. τοῖς περὶ τὸν ʽΗ.: Hephaestion. See 41. 5 n.

XLIX. 13. *The murder of Parmenio.*

Sources: Arr. 3. 26. 3 f.; Diod. 17. 80. 1 ff.; Strabo 15. 2. 10; Curt. 7. 2. 11–34; Justin 12. 5. 3.

Παρμενίωνα: Parmenio had been left behind in charge of Media (Diod. 17. 80. 3; Curt. 6. 8. 18). Robinson (*AHR* 62 (1957), 333 f.) has suggested that he had already been deposed from his command and arrested, perhaps for disobedience. He points out that Parmenio had not marched to Hyrcania as he had been instructed to do (Arr. 3. 19. 7) and that the troops he was to have commanded later reached Alexander in Parthia (3. 25. 4); he refers also to Arrian's statement that the generals in Media had been placed over the army commanded by Parmenio (ἐπὶ τῆς στρατιᾶς ἧς ἦρχε Π. τεταγμένοι ἦσαν). But Alexander may have countermanded his orders, and Arrian's narrative is by no means complete.

Philotas does not seem to have incriminated his father even under torture (Curt. 6. 11. 33), and it is clear from the silence of Ptolemy that no charge was brought against him. His condemnation by the army assembly (Diod. 17. 80. 1, Curt. 6. 11. 39) is a mere fiction. Robinson, however, has argued (*AJA* 49 (1945), 422 ff.) that the execution of Parmenio was judicial and that he was put to death by a Macedonian law which enacted that relatives of conspirators *must* die. But, as Tarn (2. 270 ff.) points out, the *lex* (or rather *mos*) had been temporarily suspended, and Parmenio was condemned, according to Curtius, on the evidence of a (supposed) treasonable letter (6. 9. 13 ff.). It was 'plain murder' (Tarn 1. 64).

Parmenio's murder has been regarded by Badian (*TAPA* 91 (1960), 333) as the culmination of the same scheme as the execution of Philotas. He rejects Tarn's view (1. 64), that Alexander *had* to kill Parmenio, since a great general could not simply be 'retired' but must rebel or die, on the ground that the Macedonian monarchy was not governed by the law of the jungle (he cites the case of Alexander the Lyncestian who had not yet been put to death, although suspected of high treason), and that of the many Macedonian officers who disappear from view some certainly survived Alexander. But Parmenio was not just another officer; he was Alexander's second-in-command, he held a vital position astride Alexander's communications—which Alexander would never have given him had he suspected his loyalty— and he was in control of a vast amount of money. He could not simply disappear. Badian's strongest argument is that Parmenio was not of royal blood and consequently could never aspire to the throne. Even so A. could not afford the risk that Parmenio might rebel; this is borne out by the need to assassinate him before he heard of Philotas' death.

ἐξορμήσαντα διαβῆναι: This is not mentioned elsewhere. Both he and Antipater suggested that Alexander should first provide an heir (Diod. 17. 16. 2).

δύο . . . πρότερον ἀποθανόντας: Parmenio's second son, Nicanor (Berve no. 554), had commanded the Hypaspists from the start of the expedition; he had fought in the three great battles and taken part in the pursuit of Bessus. He died of sickness soon after leaving Hyrcania for Bactria (Arr. 3. 25. 4; Curt. 6. 6. 18 f., 6. 9. 27).

The youngest son, Hector (Berve no. 295), died of exhaustion after his ship had capsized in the Nile and he had swum ashore (Curt. 4. 8. 7 ff.). Julian *Ep.* 82, p. 108 (Bidez–Cumont), wrongly places his death on the Euphrates.

XLIX. 14–15. *Antipater's negotiations with the Aetolians.*

ταῦτα πραχθέντα: In addition, Parmenio's son-in-law, Alexander of Lyncestis (Berve no. 37), the sole survivor of the Lyncestian royal house, was brought to trial at this time, condemned, and put to death, obviously because he might be used as a pretender to the throne. He had been suspected of complicity in the murder of Philip, but had acknowledged Alexander and was retained in the Companions. Subsequently he commanded the Thracian cavalry, but shortly before Issus (autumn 333) was arrested on suspicion of conspiring with the Persians to kill Alexander, and kept in custody. On his execution see Badian *TAPA* 91 (1960), 325, 335 f.

μάλιστα δ᾽ Ἀντιπάτρῳ: For Antipater's fears see Diod. 17. 118. 1, Justin 12. 14. 1 ff.

As Badian acutely observes (*JHS* 81 (1961), 37, n. 159), Plutarch presents, as he often does, a logical as a chronological connection. The negotiations should be placed in 324 after the proclamation at Susa of the 'Exiles' Decree' (*SIG* 312, 11 ff.). The Decree, which *inter alia* ordered the Aetolians to give up Oeniadae, was later proclaimed to the exiles at the Olympic Games (end of August) by Nicanor (Berve no. 557); see Diod. 17. 109. 1, Curt. 10. 2. 4, Justin 13. 5. 2. The text, which will have differed from the instructions sent to the Greek cities by Alexander, is given by Diod. 18. 8. 2 ff.; see especially A. Heuss

Hermes 73 (1938), 134 f. According to Diodorus (18. 8. 6) most states welcomed the decree except the Athenians and Aetolians. Diodorus and Plutarch are clearly describing the same incident and following the same source, perhaps Hieronymus (Badian loc. cit.). Berve (2. 50) rightly stresses that Antipater would have little sympathy for Alexander's divine aspirations (see especially Suidas s.v. *Ἀντίπατρος*), and for his altered view of the monarchy, while the policy of fusion would mean little to him (cf. Schachermeyr 426). But he rejects Plutarch's statement that Antipater entered into treasonable relations with the Aetolians, because of his 'unswerving loyalty' to the king and the fact that he was subsequently employed on various important tasks. So, too, G. T. Griffith *PACA* 8 (1965), 15, n. 16, who suggests that Antipater's negotiations with the Aetolians about Oeniadae, in his capacity as regent, might easily be misrepresented by an enemy. See, however, Badian op. cit. 36 ff., and further on 74. 2, 77. 2.

L–LII. 2. *Alexander murders Cleitus. His grief at the deed.*

Sources: Arr. 4. 8. 1–9. 4; Curt. 8. 1. 20–2. 12; Justin 12. 6. 1–16. Cf. *Mor.* 71 c; Seneca *Ep.* 83. 19; *De ira* 3. 17. 1.

For a good analysis of the three main versions, see T. S. Brown, *AJP* 70 (1949), 236 ff.; cf. Berve 2. 207 f., Kornemann 249 ff., and A. Aymard *Mélanges Henri Grégoire* I (Brussels, 1949), 43 ff. Cauer, op. cit. (on 49. 3), 38–58, is still useful, but R. Schubert, *Rh. Mus.* 53 (1898) contains little of value. Plutarch's version is preferred by most scholars (e.g. Brown, Berve, Schachermeyr 297 ff., Wilcken 166), particularly because of its lack of bias and its many details; Ed. Meyer (*Kleine Schriften* 1. 319 ff.), however, prefers Arrian. Even Kornemann adopts Plutarch's version, despite his belief that Arrian reproduces Ptolemy; this is not the general view (see Strasburger 40), but may be correct (see Brown 237, Pearson *LHA* 170); at any rate, the use of λέγουσι (Arr. 4. 8. 2) does not rule out the possibility (see Kornemann 21 ff.). Plutarch's source is generally held to be Chares, probably correctly, although only Kornemann 249 ff. offers any worthwhile arguments.

1. οὐ πολλῷ δ' ὕστερον: In fact, not till two years later, in the autumn (Wilcken 166) rather than the summer (Tarn 1. 73) of 328. The murder took place at Maracanda (the modern Samarkand) in Sogdiana (Curt. 8. 1. 19; from Ptolemy, Tarn 1. 73, n. 1).

τὰ περὶ Κλεῖτον: 'The murder of Cleitus'. On Cleitus see 16. 11 n.

A short time before this Artabazus, the satrap of Bactriana, had resigned because of old age (Arr. 4. 17. 3), and Cleitus had been appointed to succeed him but had not yet done so (Curt. 8. 1. 19, provinciam eius (sc. Artabazi) *destinat* Clito; Arr. (loc. cit.) mentions Amyntas (Berve no. 60) as Artabazus' successor). Schachermeyr (296 f.) argues that the appointment meant that Cleitus was shelved and separated from the king's circle and the fighting men, in consequence of his lack of enthusiasm for and perhaps even opposition to Alexander's plans. This view ignores the importance of the satrapy.

οὕτω μὲν ἁπλῶς πυθομένοις: 'those who simply learn the immediate circumstances' (Perrin), not 'however simply related' (Langhorne). λόγῳ μέντοι, by contrast, makes this clear.

2. τὴν αἰτίαν κτλ.: The provocation which Alexander received, and the fact that it took place at a drinking party.

τῷ Κλείτου δαίμονι: 'Cleitus' evil genius'. This has nothing to do with the Platonic *daimon*, for which see Introduction, p. xx. In popular belief each man received at birth a *daimon* which accompanied him throughout life; it might be either good or bad. Cf., e.g., Plato *Phaedo* 107 d and *Caes.* 69, μέγας δαίμων (of Caesar) and κακὸς δαίμων (of Brutus). See further Nilsson in *OCD* s.v. and *RE* Supp. 3, 267–322, especially 287 ff.

τὴν ἀκμήν: 'its freshness'.

4. κατεσπεισμένων: 'consecrated, marked out for sacrifice'. From κατασπένδω = 'libare'; cf. 69. 7, κατασπείσας ἑαυτόν.

5. Κλεομένει: Wyttenbach's certain correction of Κλεομάντει (all manuscripts). Cleomantis is otherwise unknown, while we hear (Arr. 7. 26. 2) of a Cleomenes who was present in the temple of Sarapis just before Alexander's death (see 76. 9).

Although he conjectures that this Cleomenes (No. 432) was a Greek priest or seer, Berve oddly lists 'Cleomantis' (no. 430) without query or discussion. The corruption was doubtless caused by the presence of τοῖς μάντεσιν (Ziegler, *Rh. Mus.* 84 (1935), 379).

ἐκθύσασθαι: 'that sacrifices of expiation be made on behalf of Cleitus'. 'proprium et elegans *expiandi per sacrificia* notione verbum' (Wyttenbach on *Mor.* 149 d): see the examples cited by LSJ. At 41. 6 Alexander also sacrifices in consequence of a dream. For Alexander's consultations of seers, fewer after 330 (at least in our sources), see Berve 1. 90 ff.

7. οὐ μὴν ἔφθασε . . . ἐκθυσάμενος: 'before the sacrifices on behalf of Cleitus had been performed' (Stewart), rather than 'Cleitus did not finish his sacrifice' (Perrin).

Διοσκούροις: So Arrian 4. 8. 2; Alexander neglected to make his

annual sacrifice to Dionysus and sacrificed instead to the Dioscuri.
The reason is unknown. This leads on (in Arr.) to a comparison
between the Dioscuri, who were raised to the Gods for benefiting
mankind (Tarn 2. 57, n. 1), and Alexander, and to remarks about the
divinity of Alexander. In Curtius (8. 5. 10) the comparison of Alexander and the Dioscuri occurs during the *proskynesis* episode.

8. πότου . . . συρραγέντος: All accounts make it clear that both
Alexander and Cleitus had drunk excessively. Arrian himself (4. 8. 2)
comments on the barbaric nature of Alexander's drinking, and
Schachermeyr (298) is clearly right in emphasizing that drink sparked
off the latent antagonism between the two men.

Πρανίχου τινός κτλ.: Evidently one of the minor poets who accompanied Alexander; on these see Tarn 2. 55 ff. Nothing is known of
Pranichos or Pierion. For *Πρανίχου* Bekker suggested *Πανίχου* and
Latte *Παιανίχου*, comparing *IG* 7. 27, 21. But there is no certainty—
Ziegler *RE* 22, 1689.

εἰς τοὺς στρατηγοὺς . . . ἡττημένους: The defeat is historical. Late in
the previous year (329) Alexander had sent an inadequate force to
meet Spitamenes who was besieging Maracanda (Arr. 4. 3. 7; Curt.
7. 6. 24 less probably says he was established in the city) and, partly
owing to divided command, the Macedonian force was almost wiped
out (Arr. 4. 5. 2–6. 2; Curt. 7. 7. 30 ff.). For an analysis of the accounts of Curt. and Arr., see Pearson *LHA* 167 f. For Alexander's
responsibility, Schachermeyr 283, 299.

9. τῶν δὲ πρεσβυτέρων: Philip's men. Berve (2. 207, n. 6; 208, n. 1)
stresses the personal nature of the quarrel, but personal and political
motives cannot be separated. Cleitus' death was not a political killing,
but it would be idle to deny that Cleitus' actions were conditioned by
his attitude to Alexander's policy or that his views were shared by
many of the older Macedonians (see 53. 1).

βελτίονας: Ziegler suggests βελτίονας ⟨γεγονότας⟩, but if a participle is
required ὄντας (Richards, *CR* 17 (1903), 337) seems more likely to
have been omitted after βελτίονας.

10. ἀποφαίνοντα: 'representing (falsely)'; cf. Plato, *Protag.* 349 a, ἁ.
σεαυτὸν ἀρετῆς διδάσκαλον. The imputation of cowardice struck the
enraged Cleitus 'like a whiplash' (Berve 2. 207).

11. τὸν ἐκ θεῶν: Alexander as son of Ammon. See ch. 27. 5.

τῷ Σπιθριδάτου ξίφει: When Cleitus saved Alexander's life at the
Granicus (see on 16. 9 ff.). In Arrian's account (4. 8. 6) Cleitus
apparently made much of this incident, τά τε ἄλλα καὶ πολὺν εἶναι

ἐξονειδίζοντα Ἀλεξάνδρῳ ὅτι πρὸς αὑτοῦ ἄρα ἐσώθη, ὁπότε ἡ ἱππομαχία ἡ ἐπὶ Γρανικῷ ξυνειστήκει πρὸς Πέρσας. According to Curtius (8. 1. 39) Cleitus did not taunt Alexander with having saved his life on this occasion, although he had done so frequently in the past.

τὸν νῶτον ἐπιτρέποντα: Ziegler adopts Reiske's emendation, but no change is required. The MSS. ἐκτρέποντα implies 'taking to one's heels' as well as 'turning one's back on' (Schachermeyr 299 f.). We may compare Eur. *Bacch.* 798 f., καὶ τόδ' αἰσχρόν, ἀσπίδας | θύρσοισι βακχῶν ἐκτρέπειν χαλκηλάτους; see Dodds' note ad loc.

τηλικοῦτος κτλ.: 'so high and mighty as to renounce Philip and call yourself son of Ammon'. εἰσποιεῖν implies 'forcing oneself upon' (Schachermeyr, loc. cit.); cf. *Ant.* 80. 4, εἰσποιῶν δὲ μὴ προσηκόντως ἑαυτὸν τῇ Ἀκαδημείᾳ, where Philostratus is said to be 'destitute of any right to call himself a member of the Academy'.
In Curtius also (8. 1. 42) Cleitus refers mockingly to Ammon.

LI.

1. ἑκάστοτε: As ταῦτα presumably refers to both Cleitus' taunts, this was evidently not the first time that he had made derogatory remarks about Alexander's divine sonship.

2. ἐπιδεῖν: 'to live to see'.

ξαινομένους: ξ. is used properly of carding wool, hence to 'lacerate, flog'. See especially *Mor.* 239 c, οἱ παῖδες παρ' αὐτοῖς ξαινόμενοι μάστιγι δι' ὅλης τῆς ἡμέρας ἐπὶ τοῦ βωμοῦ τῆς 'Ορθίας Ἀρτέμιδος; cf. *Publ.* 6. 4.

Περσῶν δεομένους: There is no need to follow Pearson (*LHA* 60) in believing that Chares is Plutarch's source here because an introduction is involved.

4. Ξενόδοχον . . . Ἀρτέμιον: Nothing is known of these men. Berve (2. 84, n. 4) rightly rejects Schubert's suggestion (op. cit. 103) that they brought the fruit (50. 3).

5. ⟨ἐὰν⟩ ἃ βούλεται λέγειν: 'bidding Alexander allow him to speak out freely what he wished to say'. Richards (*CR* 17 (1903), 337) had already suggested λέγειν ⟨ἐὰν⟩. But no supplement is needed; the sense is that A. should speak out and not whisper to his neighbours— referring to his previous remark. The fact that A. *couldn't* repeat the remark for the Macedonians to hear and the insolence of being told what to do was very powerful provocation.

τὴν Περσικὴν ζώνην . . .: Cf. Xen. *Cyr.* 8. 3. 13 (cited at 45. 2).

προσκυνήσουσιν: See ch. 54. 3.

ἔπαισεν αὐτόν: Berve (2. 208, n. 3), comparing *Mor.* 737 a, where the king pelts Anaxarchus with apples, thinks that Alexander throws the apple in scorn rather than in anger; but this seems quite inappropriate here. Schubert (loc. cit.) refers to the μηλομαχία in Chares (fr. 9), and thinks that this shows that Chares is Plutarch's source here!

6. Ἀριστοφάνους: No σωματοφύλαξ named Aristophanes is known. Tarn (2. 141, n. 2) thinks he is probably imaginary, or (just possibly) that we should read στρωματοφυλάκων, 'Gentlemen of the Bed-Chamber' (cf. 57. 5). But an Aristonous is known later (325) as one of the Bodyguards (Arr. 6. 28. 4), and Palmerius emended the manuscript reading to Ἀριστόνου. Berve (2. 69, n. 2) described the emendation as 'arbitrary and false in fact', since we are concerned with a member of the Hypaspists, but Ziegler (*Rh. Mus.* 84 (1935), 379 f.) rightly pointed out that the Hypaspists (on whom Alexander calls) are there contrasted with the Bodyguards. For the two meanings of σωματοφύλαξ, see ch. 39. 7.

περιεχόντων: The English translators seem correct in understanding the verb to mean 'surround' (the usual meaning) rather than 'hold fast', as Ax and Ruegg; cf. especially *Nic.* 27. 2, ταχὺ τῶν πολεμίων περισχόντων καὶ συλλαβόντων αὐτόν; *Brut.* 17. 3. I should prefer to read the aorist περισχόντων here, since there is no example in Plutarch of the present tense in this sense, unless we read περιεχούσης at *Phoc.* 34. 1, where, however, Ziegler reads περισχούσης with C.

Μακεδονιστί: The problem of the Macedonian language has been much discussed. For a good brief discussion see Beloch 4. 1. 1–9. See further the works cited by Bengtson 295, nn. 1, 3, and add A. B. Daskalakis, *The Hellenism of the Ancient Macedonians* (Thessaloniki, 1965), Section B, who concluded that the Macedonians spoke a dialect of Doric Greek. N. G. L. Hammond, however, reviewing the original (Greek) edition (*CR* N.S. 12 (1962), 270), suspects that they spoke 'a patois which was not recognizable at once as normal Doric Greek but may have been a north-west-Greek dialect of a primitive kind'. It may be significant that Thucydides (3. 94) describes the Aetolians as ἀγνωστότατοι γλῶσσαν.

τοῦτο δ᾽ ἦν κτλ.: The only evidence. It might, however, be an interpolation, someone's fairly obvious guess.

τοὺς ὑπασπιστάς: i.e. the agēma of the Hypaspists, which 'still had the duty of safeguarding his (Alexander's) person in peace time, which they fulfilled at Opis when most of the army mutinied' (Tarn 2. 138). See also Berve 1. 122 f.

When he found his dagger gone, Alexander suspected treachery and may even have shouted that he was being treated as Darius had been (so Arr. 4. 8. 8, Curt. 8. 1. 47).

τὸν σαλπιγκτήν . . .: 'ut ad regiam armati coirent' (Curt. loc. cit.). At a Macedonian banquet a trumpeter gave the signal for the libation after the meal (Tarn 2. 442 and n. 2).

8. οἱ φίλοι: Aristobulus (Arr. 4. 8. 9) mentions Ptolemy; in his version also Cleitus returns and is then killed by Alexander. Curtius' version (8. 1. 48 ff.) is typically hostile to Alexander, who lies in wait for Cleitus and runs him through as he leaves last.

Εὐριπίδου . . .: *Andr.* 693. Ziegler marks a lacuna after νομίζεται. He points to (a) the plural, τὰ ἰαμβεῖα ταῦτα, (b) the evidence of Curtius (8. 1. 28 f.), (c) the hiatus νομίζεται | οὕτω, and (d) Zonaras p. 296, l. 29. Aymard (*Mélanges Grégoire*) I, 44 f.) adduces as an additional reason the use of περαίνω (= bring to an end), which (he holds) implies that Plutarch's quotation extended to several verses.

Of Ziegler's reasons (c) is invalid: There are about twenty examples in the *Lives* of hiatus before and after a quotation; cf. esp. *Pelop.* 1, ἐκτελέσαι | οὕτω, and *Pomp.* 53 ὑποκονίεται | οὕτως. The other three are indecisive. The use of the plural ἰαμβεῖα probably means that Plutarch's source quoted several verses, and Curtius' paraphrase of vv. 694 ff. may indicate that *his* source did likewise; but neither reason proves anything about *Plutarch's* text, since he may have quoted only the single line, adding καὶ τὰ λοιπά, as Zonaras does. Aymard's reason is similarly indecisive; see H. U. Instinsky, *Historia* 10 (1961), 252. The question is insoluble.

There is no reason to doubt that Cleitus could have uttered these verses of Euripides (see Berve 2. 208, n. 5; Brown, *AJP* 70 (1949), 238, n. 68). His poetry was doubtless well known in Macedonia since his stay at the court of Archelaus (see Schmid, *Gesch. d. griech. Lit.* 1. 3 (1940), 627 ff.). Alexander certainly knew the poet well: he quotes *Med.* 288 (10. 7), an unidentified fragment (53. 2), and *Bacch.* 266 (53. 4). Harpalus sent him the tragedies of Euripides (8. 3), and according to Nicobule (*F. Gr. Hist.* no. 127, fr. 2) he recited a passage from the *Andromeda* at the party before his death (see 75. 4).

For the view that Plutarch (? or Chares) has moved the verses, which *were* uttered earlier in the dispute (cf. Curtius 8. 1. 28 f.), to enhance the pathetic and tragic effect, see Aymard op. cit., 46 f.

10. βρυχήματος: The verb βρυχάομαι is used generally of the sounds of wild animals, but it occurs as early as Homer (*Il.* 13. 393) of the death-cry of a man. The noun occurs only here and at *Mar.* 20. 2, τῶν Ἀμβρώνων ὀδυρμὸς ἦν διὰ νυκτός, οὐ κλαυθμοῖς οὐδὲ στεναγμοῖς ἀνθρώπων ἐοικώς, ἀλλὰ θηρομιγής τις ὠρυγὴ καὶ βρύχημα μεμιγμένον ἀπειλαῖς καὶ θρήνοις. This well illustrates its animal character.

11. γενόμενος παρ' ἑαυτῷ : ' when he came to himself'. Cf. *Mor.* 564 a, αἱ δ' οὔτ' ἤκουον, οὔτ' ἦσαν παρ' ἑαυταῖς, ἀλλ' ἔκφρονες καὶ διεπτοημέναι.

ἑλκύσασθαι κτλ.: So Curt. 8. 2. 4; Justin 12. 6. 8. Arrian (4. 9. 3) notes that most historians did not mention this incident.

LII.

1. τήν τε νύκτα κτλ.: Arr. (4. 9. 4), Curt. (8. 2. 11) and Justin (12. 6. 15) concur in saying three days. Possibly Plutarch found three days in his source and changed it for dramatic effect.

ἀποσιώπησιν: 'becoming silent', i.e. the silence which followed his lamentation.

2. Ἀριστάνδρου: Aristander is not mentioned by the other authors, although Arrian (4. 9. 5), perhaps from Ptolemy (Brown, *AJP* 70 (1949), 239), relates that some of the seers attributed the misfortune to the anger of Dionysus at being neglected by Alexander. This appears to be an attempt to exculpate Alexander. Curt. (8. 2. 12) writes of a decree by the Macedonians that Cleitus had been justly killed.

τήν τ' ὄψιν ... καὶ τὸ σημεῖον: See, respectively, 50. 6, 50. 5.

LII. 3–7. *Callisthenes and Anaxarchus console Alexander.*

Brown (op. cit., 240) draws attention to the similarity of the accounts of Plutarch and Arrian (4. 9. 7 f.), which 'makes it almost certain that they were following the same source, though not directly'. He suggests this may have been Callisthenes: but it is far from certain that his work reached so far (see 38. 8 n.).

3. οἰκεῖον: 'a relative', not 'a friend' (as Ax) ; in fact, his nephew (see 55. 8).

Ἀνάξαρχον: See ch. 28. 4.

4. ἠθικῶς: Perrin, punctuating after πράως and ἀλύπως, translates correctly: 'Callisthenes tried by considerate and gentle means to alleviate the king's suffering, employing insinuation and circumlocution so as to avoid giving pain.' All other translators are content to paraphrase, and often omit part of the sentence. περιϊέναι appears to be used metaphorically elsewhere only at *Mor.* 1125 e, κύκλῳ π. For ἠθικῶς = 'gently, tactfully', cf. *Mor.* 72 b.

6. τὴν Δίκην ἔχει κτλ.: Arrian (4. 9. 7 f.), who mentions only Δίκη, ascribes this view to οἱ πάλαι σοφοὶ ἄνδρες; cf. Sophocles *OC* 1381 f. ἡ παλαίφατος | Δίκη ξύνεδρος Ζηνὸς ἀρχαίοις νόμοις. It is clear from [Dem.] *Adv. Aristogeiton* 11 that this was an Orphic doctrine—see O. Kern, *Orphicorum fragmenta* (1922), 158; but the connection of Dike with Zeus is as old as Hesiod (*Op.* 256 ff.). The view that Themis was the partner of Zeus goes back at least to Pindar (*Ol.* 8. 21 ff.), ἔνθα Σώτειρα Διὸς ξενίου | πάρεδρος ἀσκεῖται Θέμις | ἔξοχ᾽ ἀνθρώπων; for the connection, cf. id. *Nem.* 11. 8 (with Farnell's note).

Anaxarchus puts his own construction on the old myth, and is severely criticized by Arrian (loc. cit.) and by Plutarch, both here and at *Mor.* 781 a where he expresses himself in very similar terms. For the sentiment cf. Thrasymachus in Plato, *Rep.* 339 c, and Herodotus (3. 31), who mentions a law that whatever the king of Persia did was right.

7. τὸ δ᾽ ἦθος: See Introduction, pp. xxxviii f.

χαυνότερον: 'more vain, conceited'. Cf. Plato, *Laws* 728 e, χαύνους τὰς ψυχὰς καὶ θρασείας ποιεῖ; *Sull.* 30. 5; *Lyc.* 6. 5.

αὐτὸν δὲ δαιμονίως ἐνήρμοσε: 'made himself marvellously popular'.

αὐστηρόν: cf. 53. 2 n.; Curt. 8. 8. 21, haudquaquam aulae et assentantium accomodatus ingenio.

LII. 8–9. *Callisthenes and Anaxarchus.*

8. λέγεται: There is no other evidence for this incident.

ὑπὲρ ὡρῶν κτλ.: 'during a discussion about the climate and the temperature of the air'. For τὸ περιέχον = 'atmosphere', see the instances collected by Holden at *Sull.* 7. 3.

τοῖς λέγουσι: 'those who maintained', not, as Perrin, 'maintain'. λέγουσι represents an imperfect.

9. ἐν τρίβωνι: The τρίβων was often worn by Spartans, see, e.g., *Nic.* 19. 4, εἰ διὰ παρουσίαν ἑνὸς τρίβωνος καὶ βακτηρίας Λακωνικῆς οὕτως ἰσχυρὰ τὰ Συρακουσίων ἐξαίφνης γέγονεν (referring to Gylippus), and by philosophers, especially Stoics and Cynics. At *Mor.* 782 b (cf. 332 a) Alexander envies τὸν τρίβωνα καὶ τὴν πήραν, ὅτι τούτοις ἦν ἀνίκητος καὶ ἀνάλωτος Διογένης.

κατάκεισαι: 'you recline' at meals.

καὶ τοῦτο προσπαρώξυνε: 'this *also added* to the irritation of Anaxarchus'. They had other reasons for quarrelling.

LIII–LIV. 2. *Callisthenes and Alexander*.

1. κόλακας: Jacoby (*F. Gr. Hist.* 2D. 412) well compares *Mor.* 65 d (cited on 23. 7) for Alexander's flatterers.

τοῖς πρεσβυτέροις: The older men in particular objected to Alexander's 'orientalism'; cf. Curt. 8. 5. 20, 'seniorum praecipue, quibus gravis erat inveterati moris externa mutatio'.

τὴν λεγομένην . . . πρόφασιν: So *Mor.* 1043 d, Καλλισθένει τινὲς ἐγκαλοῦσιν, ὅτι πρὸς Ἀλέξανδρον ἔπλευσεν ἐλπίζων ἀναστήσειν Ὄλυνθον, ὡς Στάγειρα Ἀριστοτέλης. Jacoby (*RE* 10, 1676, *F. Gr. Hist.* 2D. 412) and Berve (2. 193) regard this as a mere doublet of the story of Aristotle and Stagira (see ch. 7. 3). Brown, however, remarks (*AJP* 70 (1949), 233, n. 42) that it would have been surprising had Callisthenes *not* been concerned about Olynthus. He points out that Eumenes had previously tried to influence Alexander in favour of his native Cardia.

ἀνέβη: Though ἀνέβη by itself might mean simply 'to go to Alexander's court', it appears from *Mor.* 1043 d (cited in previous note) that Plutarch thought that Callisthenes joined Alexander after the start of the expedition; Val. Max. 7. 2. ext. 11 and Amm. Marc. 18. 3. 7 point to a similar tradition. Jacoby (*RE* 10, 1675) offers no proof that πρὸς Ἀλέξανδρον ἔπλευσεν is 'an almost technical expression' meaning 'zu Hofe gehen'; but he is correct in accepting the evidence of Diog. Laert. (5. 4) that Aristotle left Callisthenes in Pella in 335/4 when he went to Athens to found his school. The named fragments of Callisthenes' history support the view that he was with Alexander from the start.

2. βαρύτητι: 'gravity, seriousness', as the translators render it, scarcely brings out the force of the word. It is clearly derogatory; 'unpleasantness' or even 'resentment' is perhaps nearer the mark. Plutarch frequently combines it with ὄγκος and ὑπεροψία. Not surprisingly he uses it twice of Marius (*Mar.* 43. 2, *Sert.* 5. 1). Callisthenes appears to have been an unpleasant character. Arrian (4. 10. 1) comments that he had 'something of the boor (ὑπαγροικότερον)' in his character; he does not approve (4. 12. 6–7) of Callisthenes' arrogance and rudeness (ὕβρις καὶ σκαιότης), and thinks Alexander was justifiably angry at his untimely freedom of speech and foolish arrogance (ἄκαιρος παρρησία καὶ ὑπέρογκος ἀβελτερία).

μισῶ σοφιστήν κτλ.: Euripides fr. 905 (Nauck, *TGF*).

3. λέγεται δέ ποτε κτλ.: Philostratus (*Vit. Apoll.* 7. 2) also mentions this incident. Good discussions of this period may be found in Brown,

AJP 70 (1949), 245 ff.; Jacoby *RE* 10, 1680 f.; Berve 2. 195 ff.; Schachermeyr 318 ff. (Jacoby 1681 (followed by Brown 246) strangely writes as if there were *two* incidents involving quotations from Euripides and Homer.) The chronology is uncertain, but it is probable that this episode took place *after* Callisthenes' refusal to perform '*proskynesis*' (so Brown, Jacoby, Schachermeyr; Berve is doubtful); cf. 54. 5 n. If this is so, Plutarch (as at 49. 14 and elsewhere) will have arranged his material logically, not chronologically; certainly this incident follows naturally from Alexander's remark. Callisthenes' presence after the murder of Cleitus (see 52. 3) guarantees his good relations with the King at that time. The '*proskynesis*' affair appears decisive in the relationship of the two men (Jacoby, Berve). We should probably place near the end of Callisthenes' life another incident, when Callisthenes refused to drink Alexander's health in unmixed wine (Athenaeus 434 d, based on Chares (fr. 13); he cites also Aristobulus (fr. 32), and Lynceus of Samos; cf. *Mor.* 454 e, 623f): it is well discussed by G. H. Macurdy, *JHS* 50 (1930), 294 ff.

Plutarch relates the incident to illustrate Callisthenes' lack of σοφία; it is susceptible of a more sinister interpretation. Alexander, having decided to 'liquidate' Callisthenes for thwarting the attempt to introduce '*proskynesis*', deliberately encouraged the 'guileless antiquarian' (Brown) to discredit himself in the eyes of the Macedonians. For (independent) interpretations on these lines, see Brown and Schachermeyr. (Cf. Balsdon, *Historia* 1 (1950), 372, n. 46, 'a deliberate attempt by Alexander to create a rift between Callisthenes and the Macedonians'.)

εὐροῆσαι πρὸς τὴν ὑπόθεσιν: 'spoke so eloquently on the topic'. The verb occurs only here in this sense (normally = 'be successful, prosperous'); for a similar sense of the noun, see Plato, *Phaedr.* 238 c, εὔροιά τίς σ' εἴληφεν; *Cic.* 4. 1; and, further, Holden on *Per.* 20. 3.

4. κατ' Εὐριπίδην: *Bacch.* 266 f., ὅταν λάβῃ τις τῶν λόγων ἀνὴρ σοφὸς | καλὰς ἀφορμάς . . . (Speech of Teiresias to Pentheus). For the meaning of ἀφορμάς, 'an honest case to argue', see Dodds ad loc. (Alexander does not quote the words ἀνὴρ σοφός; ? because Callisthenes was obviously not σοφός—as he had remarked!)

5. ἐν δὲ διχοστασίῃ κτλ.: A favourite quotation of Plutarch, source unknown; cf. *Nic.* 11. 3; *Sull.* 39. 3; *Mor.* 479 a (where the manuscripts give ἔμμορε for ἔλλαχε).

6. τοῖς Μακεδόσιν: βαρὺ ἐγγενέσθαι μῖσος τοῖς *M.*; so all manuscripts. Transposed by Ziegler to avoid the hiatus. For his reasons for preferring this solution, see *Rh. Mus.* 84 (1935), 381.

LIV.

1. ὁ Ἕρμιππος: Hermippus of Smyrna, a biographer of the late third century. A pupil of the eminent Callimachus, but much influenced by the Peripatetic school. He wrote a vast work entitled βίοι τῶν ἐν παιδείᾳ διαλαμψάντων on philosophers, writers, and lawgivers. Plutarch uses him as his main source in the *Lives* of Solon and Lycurgus and cites him four times in the *Demosthenes*. For a brief sketch of his work see D. R. Stuart, 163–5; details in *RE* s.v. (6). His fragments are collected by Mueller in *FHG*, 3. 35–54.

Hermippus is our only authority for this story, as Badian (*Gnomon* 33 (1961), 661) rightly emphasizes, and in view of his reputation as a romancer (see *CAH* 7. 261, Walbank in *OCD*) the details at least must be received with caution. Schachermeyr (518, n. 210) suggests that Hermippus derives his information from Theophrastus; but there is no evidence.

τὸν ἀναγνώστην: A slave trained to act as reader; cf. Cicero, *Ad Att.* 1. 12. 4. Nothing more is known of Stroebus.

πρὸς αὐτόν: It is inconceivable that Callisthenes could have cited the following verse two or three times to Alexander without being punished. Berve (2. 197) indeed regards this as evidence that the account has been 'touched up' in the Peripatetic tradition. Hence Ziegler adopted K. Latte's suggestion αὐτόν for the manuscript αὑτόν; Droysen (ed. 2, 2. 90 = 1. 312) had already translated 'sagte dreimal zu sich selbst'. But the picture is an unlikely one. Schachermeyr (loc. cit.) suggests that αὑτόν refers not to Alexander, but to Stroebus. This is possible, but ἀπιόντα makes it improbable that the remark was made to Stroebus and his presence is difficult to justify. The most likely solution is that Berve's view is correct.

κάτθανε καί κτλ.: *Il.* 21. 107, where Achilles addresses Lycaon, son of Priam.

2. ἔοικεν: Plutarch's own view (cf. 7. 5 n.).

νοῦν δ' οὐκ εἶχεν: Lydus, *De Mens.* 4. 77 (p. 131, 8 Wünsch) remarks ὅτι ὁ Ἀριστοτέλης τὸν Κ. ἀπέσκωψεν εἰπὼν τὸν μὲν περιττὸν νοῦν ἔχειν, τὸν δὲ ἀνθρώπινον ἀποβεβληκέναι; cf. Diog. Laert. 5. 5, where Aristotle rebukes Callisthenes for his freedom of speech against Alexander, quoting Homer *Il.* 18. 95, Ὠκύμορος δή μοι, τέκος, ἔσσεαι, οἷ᾽ ἀγορεύεις. Jacoby (*RE* 10. 1678) holds that Lydus and Plutarch express two separate judgements, not two versions of the same judgement, and that the verdict in Plutarch (made after Callisthenes' death) *proves* that the good relations between Aristotle and Alexander were not affected. But there is nothing to indicate that Aristotle's remark was made after

Callisthenes' death; indeed the reverse would seem more probable. Aristotle may be referring as much to Callisthenes' earlier glorification of Alexander as to his subsequent opposition.

LIV. 3–6. *The Affair of the* Proskynesis.

Sources: Arr. 4. 10. 5–12. 5; Curt. 8. 5. 5–21; Justin 12. 7. 1–3; Val. Max. 7, 2 ext. 11; Amm. Marc. 18. 3. 7; Tatianus *adv. Gr.* 2, p. 2, 25 (Schw.).

Arr. (4. 12. 3–5) gives Chares' version as a λόγος. He also relates as a λόγος a quite different version, in which Alexander makes an agreement with the Greeks and the leading Medes and Persians to discuss the subject of divine honours. Anaxarchus speaks in favour of the proposal to grant Alexander divine honours, but is strongly opposed by Callisthenes, and the Macedonians are told not to perform *proskynesis* in future. For an analysis of the versions of Plutarch, Arrian, and Curtius see esp. Balsdon, *Historia* 1 (1950), 371 ff. and Brown, *AJP* 70 (1949), 242 ff. Most scholars agree that Chares' account is to be preferred.

3. τὴν γε προσκύνησιν: In Persia an inferior performed *proskynesis* before his superiors, and all Persians performed it before the King. It originally denoted the act of bringing the right hand to the mouth and blowing a kiss through the rounded first finger and thumb; later it acquired the meaning of abasement, going down on one's knees (more properly called προσπίπτωσις); see Balsdon op. cit. 372 ff. and the works cited in n. 56—add B. M. Marti; *Language* 12 (1936), 272 ff. and G. C. Richards, *CR* 48 (1934), 168 ff., who suggests that it was akin to the 'salaam'. E. J. Bickerman (*Parola del Passato* 91 (1963), 241 ff.) has argued that the gesture of blowing a kiss was the normal practice and that abasement was exceptional. In particular, he holds that the term προσκυνεῖν used by Chares (§ 4, below) does *not* imply abasement. But it is clear from the examples he cites that *this* practice was widespread; it is remarkable that he does not refer to Herod. 7. 136, the earliest (and best) evidence. There is no doubt that Alexander proposed to introduce 'prostration'.

Although it has been maintained that the Persians worshipped their king as a god, it seems certain that they did not and that *proskynesis* was not a cult act, but a social practice (see esp. Balsdon op. cit., 375, n. 66 for refs. to modern views on either side; add Brown op. cit., 240 and F. Taeger, *Charisma* 1 (Stuttgart, 1957), 94, on the negative side. But as the Greeks (and Macedonians) accorded *proskynesis* only to the gods, they naturally concluded that the Persian King was regarded as a god by his subjects; see esp. Isocrates, *Paneg.* 151, Xen. *An.* 3. 2. 13, and (later) Curt. 8. 5. 11, Persas quidem . . . reges suos inter deos colere. This is evidently Plutarch's view.

It is possible, therefore, to maintain either that Alexander aimed at introducing a uniform *court* practice for Macedonians, Greeks, and Persians or that (for various reasons) he intended to institute worship of himself. Both views have many supporters. The latter is maintained by Glotz–Cohen, 4. i. 136 f. (A. desired worship for its own sake); Tarn 1. 79, 2. 362 (in the interest of his policy of fusion—'but deification it must have meant'); Robinson, *AHR* 62 (1957), 338 ff. ('to put an end to wavering support and possible plots by becoming an autocrat'); Badian, *Gnomon* 33 (1961), 661 (Callisthenes is attested to have opposed *deification*); Schachermeyr 302 ff. (to establish his autocracy); cf. F. Hampl, *La Nouvelle Clio* 6 (1954), 116; Bengtson 353 and n. 4.

To Robinson (and Schachermeyr) we may reply that there would be an end of plots only if the Macedonians *believed* Alexander to be a god; this was obviously not the case. Tarn's contention can be met if we make the reasonable assumption that the (social) significance of the Persian practice and Alexander's purpose in introducing it were made clear to the leading Greeks and Macedonians; this was presumably Hephaestion's task. It is true that Callisthenes makes a lengthy speech opposing divine honours for Alexander (Arr. 4. 11), but this occurs in a λόγος of unknown authorship. I see no reason to suppose that this speech is based on good tradition. Callisthenes' opposition is intelligible enough on the supposition that he, like the Macedonian leaders, was opposed to the equalization of Greeks (and Macedonians) and Persians. We have no reason to suppose that his views on 'barbarians' differed from those of Aristotle. 'He saw in it (*proskynesis*) a barbaric and ridiculous mode of reverence, by which the free Greek was depressed to the level of the barbarians he despised' (Wilcken 170); cf. Balsdon, *Historia* 1 (1950), 378.

The arguments in favour of the view that Alexander intended the introduction of a uniform court procedure are convincingly set out by Balsdon, op. cit., 376 ff. He stresses the desirability of uniformity and points out in particular that to forbid *proskynesis* would have led to the belief that 'Alexander was not a real king'. He well emphasizes that Alexander must have intended to limit the ceremony to formal occasions, and that it is improbable that, with the invasion of India in prospect, he was troubled about establishing a theocratic basis for his rule.

L. R. Taylor (*The Divinity of the Roman Emperor* (Connecticut, 1931), 256, n. 1) is mistaken in thinking that Plutarch in this paragraph refers to the first story in Arrian (4. 10. 5–12. 2), and that 'the incident from Chares that follows is another story'. She consequently rejects the view that Alexander abandoned his attempt to introduce *pros-kynesis* (op. cit., 265, n. 31).

4. Χάρης δ' ὁ Μ.: See Introduction, pp. lv f.

φιάλην: A broad, flat bowl used for libations. It was sometimes made of silver or of gold, as here; cf. Arr. 4. 12. 3.

πρὸς ἑστίαν: The importance of this altar in the ceremony has been much discussed, and is still disputed. Since the words do not occur in Arrian's version, Berve (*Klio* 20 (1926), 179 ff.) regarded them as an addition to Chares' account made by a writer influenced by the practice at a Roman drinking party. But there is every reason to suppose that Plutarch used Chares' book and that the words should be retained.

P. Schnabel (*Klio* 19 (1924), 113 ff.; ibid. 20 (1926), 398 ff.), who maintained that Alexander was attempting to introduce worship of himself, interpreted Plutarch to mean that the guests received the cup from Alexander, who was reclining on the couch (ἐν τῷ συμ-ποσίῳ), crossed to the altar on which stood an image of the king, drank and performed *proskynesis* to the image, then returned to Alexander and kissed him at the couch (ἐν τῷ συμποσίῳ). L. R. Taylor (*JHS* 47 (1927), 53 ff.), agreed with this interpretation of the passage and suggested that the object of the *proskynesis* was the *daimon* or *fravashi* of the king. But these views are to be rejected; in Plutarch's text, on which they rely, προσκυνῆσαι clearly governs Ἀλέξανδρον, not ἑστίαν and Demetrius' words, οὗτος γάρ σε μόνος οὐ προσεκύνησε, are decisive; see Tarn, *JHS* 48 (1928), 206 ff., and Balsdon, *Historia* 1 (1950), 379 ff.

Two other interpretations have gained considerable support. In 1927 W. Otto suggested (in Ἐπιτύμβιον H. Swoboda dargebracht, 194 ff.) that the ἑστία was a brazier, on which burned the eternal fire of Persia (for this see, e.g., Xen. *Cyr.* 8. 3. 12); he thought that the *proskynesis* ceremony had no connection with divinity, but showed Alexander's conversion to oriental practices. This view has been accepted by Jacoby (*F. Gr. Hist.* 2D. 435 ff.) and by Bengtson (340, n. 2), but is open to Balsdon's objection (loc. cit.) that it is doubtful whether ἑστία can mean a brazier. He also refutes Schachermeyr's fanciful reconstruction (302 ff.) in which, developing Otto's suggestion, he maintained that Alexander, by having *proskynesis* made to the eternal fire (his own idea), sought to secure recognition of his divinity. The other (more probable) interpretation was advanced by L. R. Farnell in *JHS* 49 (1929), 79 ff. He remarked that a ἑστία was part of the furniture of a Greek drinking party and that to it the first libation was offered; he reminds us of the phrase ἀφ' Ἑστίας ἄρχεσθαι. He also considers it possible that Chares 'has carelessly thrown in a Greek touch, which the careful Arrian discards'; but it is difficult to credit that Arrian knew that it wasn't a Persian practice and deliberately avoided an anachronism which Chares (the Royal Chamberlain!) had been guilty of.

[ἐν τῷ συμποσίῳ]: The phrase occurs in the previous sentence, where it is clearly required; hence Sintenis deleted the words as a doublet, probably rightly. They come in awkwardly after the first instance and are not necessary for the sense of the passage, *pace* Schnabel (loc. cit.), who argued vigorously that they mark the return of the guest to Alexander's couch after his performance of *proskynesis* at the altar.

5. οὐ προσέχοντος: If this detail is true, it suggests that at this stage Callisthenes was in no sense 'a marked man', and confirms the order of events advocated at 53. 3. Was Callisthenes perhaps placed accidentally in the position of 'leader of the opposition'?

6. Δημητρίου: The son of Pythonax (Berve no. 258). He is listed among the flatterers of Alexander at *Mor.* 65 d.

διακλῖναι τὸ φίλημα: 'Alexander refused to kiss him.' So Arrian 4. 12. 5, τὸν Ἀλέξανδρον οὐ παρασχεῖν φιλῆσαι ἑαυτόν. For the verb, cf. *Ant.* 12. 3, ἐκείνου (sc. Καίσαρος) δὲ θρυπτομένου καὶ διακλίνοντος (the diadem).

μέγα φθεγξάμενον: Typical of Callisthenes' arrogance and lack of tact.

L V. *The Conspiracy of the Pages. The Arrest of Callisthenes. Various versions of his fate.*

Sources: Arr. 4. 13–14; Curt. 8. 6–8.

1. ὑπογινομένης: The present participle represents the imperfect indicative, 'while such estrangement (between Alexander and Callisthenes) *was* growing up'. Jacoby (*F. Gr. Hist.* 2B. 633) wrongly accepts Coraes' ὑπογενομένης. The form γίνομαι is regular in Plutarch; see (in this *Life*) 10. 1, 22. 6, 36. 3, 42. 6, 63. 11.

Ἡφαιστίων ἐπιστεύετο: In view of his sympathy with Alexander's aims, Hephaestion would be the obvious person to choose to make arrangements for the experiment. Whether he lied to save his face must remain uncertain; see Schachermeyr 313.

Plutarch's obvious disbelief of Hephaestion's statement is shared by several modern scholars, e.g. Berve 2. 171, Brown, *AJP* 70 (1949), 244; Jacoby *RE* 10, 1679 f.

2. Λυσίμαχοι: Only one person is meant. This is often taken to be Lysimachus the Bodyguard (Berve no. 480), most recently by Pearson

LHA 57, n. 30 (probably). Berve, however, argues convincingly that Plutarch means Alexander's teacher (Berve no. 481), mentioned in chs. 5 and 24. Justin (15. 3. 6) writes that Lysimachus the Bodyguard was a pupil of Callisthenes; Jacoby (*RE* 10, 1676), however, doubts his statement.

Ἄγνωνες: On Hagnon see ch. 22. 3.

ὡς ἐπὶ καταλύσει τυραννίδος: Arrian (4. 10. 3 f.) relates as a λόγος that when Philotas asked Callisthenes whom the Athenians honoured most he answered the tyrannicides, Harmodius and Aristogeiton, and pointed to Athens as a city where a tyrannicide could find refuge. These stories deserve no credence; they are part and parcel of the portrait of Philotas the conspirator. Curtius (8. 6. 24 f.) reports with reserve stories that Callisthenes listened sympathetically to the pages.

τὰ μειράκια: For the interest of the young, cf. also 53. 1. Hermolaus was reputed to be a keen student of philosophy and for this reason a follower of Callisthenes (Arr. 4. 13. 2). Callisthenes would act as the tutor of the Royal pages.

On the Royal pages see Berve 1. 37 ff. The institution dates from Philip's time; among their duties they attended the king while hunting and guarded him at night (Arr. 4. 13. 1).

3. τῶν περὶ Ἑρμόλαον: Presumably a genuine plural, not merely Hermolaus himself, since several pages were involved; their names in Arr. 4. 13. 3 f.; Curt. 8. 6. 8 f.

Both Curtius and Arrian (a λόγος) attribute to Hermolaus only a personal motive for the conspiracy. He had been whipped on Alexander's orders for forestalling the king in killing a wild boar. Nevertheless in the speech which Hermolaus is represented as making at his trial (Arr. 4. 14. 2, Curt. 8. 7. 1 ff.) he claims that his action was due to hatred of Alexander's conduct—executions of Philotas and Parmenio, murder of Cleitus, adoption of Persian dress, *proskynesis*, etc.

Tarn (1. 81) and Wilcken (170) regard the conspiracy as an act of revenge without political significance, as does Berve (2. 153), who detects in the speeches the same (false) tendency as in the Cleitus affair to connect events with the change in Alexander's monarchy and the opposition to it. But Cleitus' outburst was caused partly by his attitude to Alexander's policy, and we have no reason to suppose that the pages were less sensitive to the events of the last two years than Cleitus. The punishment inflicted on Hermolaus, we may be confident, was not unparalleled or inconsistent with the discipline of the corps; it need not be denied that the punishment may have rankled, but by itself it would seem a quite inadequate motive for the murder of the king. For the view that 'the conspirators thought of themselves as tyrannicides' see Schachermeyr 315 ff. He points to the extent of the conspiracy and to the punishment of Callisthenes which, he holds, could only have taken place if the conspiracy was political.

προβαλόντι: 'propounding the question how'. Cf. *Pomp.* 48. 8, ἐρωτήματα τοιαῦτα προύβαλλε τίς ἐστιν. . . .

4. τὴν χρυσῆν κλίνην: Alexander as Great King, ? who thought of himself as a god.

5. οὐδεὶς .. κατεῖπε: According to Arr. (4. 14. 1), both Ptolemy and Aristobulus (fr. 33) stated that the pages incriminated Callisthenes, but most writers denied this. Arrian himself seems to disbelieve them when he writes (4. 12. 7), that because of Callisthenes' unreasonable frankness and his arrogance his accusers were readily believed when they asserted that he participated in the conspiracy or even when they maintained that he was the instigator of it. Curt. (8. 8. 21) also considers him innocent. Alexander's letter to his generals (§ 6 below) proves that Ptolemy and Aristobulus were not telling the truth. Of modern scholars only Tarn (2. 301) and Robinson (*AHR* 62 (1957), 341) think Callisthenes guilty.

διὰ τῆς ἐσχάτης ἀνάγκης: i.e. under torture, βασανιζομένους (§ 6); στρεβλούμενοι (Arrian); 'excruciatos' (Curtius). Torture was also used against Philotas, and (according to Ptolemy) against Callisthenes.

6. Ἀλέξανδρος . . . γράφων: The authenticity of this letter is proved by the names of the recipients. Early in 327 Alexander had sent Craterus, Polyperchon, Attalus, and Alcetas to Pareitacene to deal with the rebellion of Catanes and Austanes in Bactria (Arr. 4. 22. 1). At this time (and only at this time) Polyperchon was operating independently in Bubacene (Curt. 8. 5. 2), and the other three generals were detached. It is hardly to be supposed that a forger would be aware of this. See further *CQ* N.S. 5 (1955), 219 ff.; *PACA* 4 (1961), 15 f. (no. 27).

7. ὕστερον δὲ γράφων . . .: Kaerst (*Phil.* 51 (1892), 608) claimed that this letter was a forgery, since Chares did not mention this danger to Aristotle and we hear of no danger to him except these threats. But Alexander's anger may have been short-lived (cf., however, 74. 5), and if Chares *did* mention his threats to Aristotle, Plutarch would not have repeated them after citing the letter. The trial of Callisthenes in Aristotle's presence (55. 9) might be regarded as the punishment envisaged in the letter. The real objection to acceptance of the letter is the threat to Athens at this time; see further *PACA* 4 (1961), 16 (no. 28).

κατελεύσθησαν This punishment is confirmed by Arr. 4. 14. 3

(a λόγος), τοῦτον (Hermolaus) μὲν δὴ αὐτόν τε καὶ τοὺς ξὺν αὐτῷ ξυλληφθέντας καταλευσθῆναι πρὸς τῶν παρόντων. Stoning to death was a Macedonian custom; see Curt. 6. 11. 10, 38; 7. 2. 1. At Curt. 7. 1. 9 Alexander the Lyncestian is run through with lances; but this is not a judicial punishment.

τοὺς ὑποδεχομένους: The Athenians.

ἄντικρυς ... ἀποκαλυπτόμενος: 'revealing his intentions outright'. For ἀποκαλύπτεσθαι see Diod. 17. 62. 5, and especially 18. 23. 3.

8. ἀνεψιᾶς Ἀριστοτέλους: This is confirmed by Suidas (s.v. *Καλλισθένης Δημοτίμου*), who calls him a pupil of Aristotle and the son of his first cousin (ἀνεψιαδοῦς). Cf. 52. 3.

9. ἀποθανεῖν δ' αὐτόν ...: So Arr. 4. 14. 3, citing Ptolemy for the former view, and for the latter Aristobulus, whose source is evidently Chares (so Jacoby, *F. Gr. Hist.* 2D. 517, 35, Pearson *LHA* 171, Rabe 58 f.). Since Ptolemy sought to exculpate Alexander by asserting (falsely) that Callisthenes was guilty and that he was justly executed we may accept his hanging as historical; the versions of Arrian (loc. cit.) and Curtius (8. 8. 21) do not imply that he was hanged *immediately*, as Pearson (*LHA* 56, 171, 191) states. We can, therefore, accept the statement of Chares that Callisthenes was carried around with the army for seven months, a circumstantial account unlikely to have been invented. On the other hand, both he and Aristobulus tended to depict Alexander favourably and their version of Callisthenes' natural death which would absolve him from blame is accordingly suspect. For this view of the matter see Wilcken 171, Schachermeyr 321, Glotz–Cohen 1. 138, Berve 2. 197.

ἐν τῷ συνεδρίῳ: The assembly of the Corinthian League. Callisthenes would presumably have been charged with plotting against the *Hegemon* in the person of Alexander.

[ἐν Μαλλοῖς Ὀξυδράκαις]: The conspiracy took place early in 327 at Bactra; see Strabo 11. 517, as emended by Schachermeyr 518, n. 211, and cf. Arr. 4. 22. 2. As Alexander was not wounded in the Malli town until early 325, Schaefer deleted the reference to the Malli. It is probably an unintelligent gloss; certainly it is not likely that Plutarch, who had made a special study of A.'s wounds (see the dissertation cited at 45. 5), thought that a wound 'in India' necessarily meant the one in the Malli town. Alexander is recorded to have sustained two wounds late in 327, neither serious; see Arr. 4. 23. 3, Curt. 8. 10. 6 and Arr. 4. 26. 4, Curt. 8. 10. 28 respectively.

ὑπέρπαχυν ... φθειριάσαντα: 'having become excessively fat and lousy'. There is no need to suppose that Chares meant that Callisthenes suffered from the imaginary disease, phthiriasis, from which

Sulla was supposed to have died; for this see *Sull.* 36. 3–4 (with Holden's note). Chares' version was subsequently much elaborated, and in some accounts Callisthenes was kept captive in an iron cage; see especially Justin 15. 3. 3 ff., Diog. Laert. 5. 5. Other references in Berve 2. 198, n. 1.

LVI. *The Death of Demaratus the Corinthian.*

Plutarch artistically places this chapter after the death of Callisthenes. His punishment of an enemy is contrasted with the generous treatment of a friend, and the manner of their deaths is also contrasted.

1. ὕστερον: The death of Callisthenes must have taken place towards the end of 327 (see 55. 9 nn.).

Δημάρατος: See ch. 9. 12.

ἀναβῆναι: As Demaratus fought at the Granicus (Arr. 1. 15. 6), Plutarch must mean that he joined Alexander at the start of the expedition.

καὶ θεασάμενος . . .: Sintenis proposed to delete this sentence as an intrusion from ch. 37. 7. It is extremely difficult to account for its presence in so careful a writer as Plutarch, but no solution seems possible. Mere excision will not serve, since the third sentence does not follow on naturally from the first.

2. ἀρρωστίας: Used especially of a lingering ailment (e.g. of Nicias' illness at Syracuse).

ἐκηδεύθη: 'attend to a corpse, bury'. A poetic word used in later prose.

LVII. *Alexander prepares to invade India. His punishment of wrongdoers. His despondency at bad omens dispelled by the discovery of petroleum at the River Oxus.*

1. μέλλων δ' ὑπερβάλλειν: Alexander left Bactra at the end of spring 327—ἐξήκοντος ἤδη τοῦ ἦρος (Arr. 4. 22. 3).

This incident is related by Polyaenus (4. 3. 10) among the stratagems of Alexander; he also places it immediately before the invasion of India. Curtius (6. 6. 14 ff.) locates it, with less probability, in Parthiene, after Bessus has assumed the royal diadem and before the Macedonians enter Bactria.

⟨εἶτα⟩ καὶ ⟨τάς⟩ . . .: Inserted by Ziegler from Zonaras (p. 297, ll. 12 f.), συνεσκευασμένων τῶν ἁμαξῶν, πρώταις μὲν ταῖς οἰκείαις ἐνῆκε πῦρ, εἶτα καὶ ταῖς τῶν φίλων, καὶ μετὰ ταῦτα καὶ τὰς τῶν Μ. καταπρῆσαι ἐκέλευσε.

The supplements are perhaps supported by Polyaenus loc. cit., πρώτας ὑπέπρησε τὰς βασιλικὰς ἁμάξας, εἶτα τὰς τῶν ἄλλων.

3. ἀπαραίτητος κολαστής: At the end of the long digression after the burning of Persepolis (42. 4) Plutarch remarks that Alexander became χαλεπὸς καὶ ἀπαραίτητος when he was maligned.

καὶ γὰρ Μένανδρόν κτλ.: Nothing further is known of these events or of Menander or Orsodates.

4. διδύμους: i.e. testicles.

αὐτῆς: i.e. κεφαλῆς. Sintenis retains the manuscript αὐτοῦ, but αὐτῆς (Coraes) seems a necessary emendation.

βδελυχθείς: 'disgusted at the portent'. Although LSJ cite only this example and Ar. *Ach.* 586, βδελύττομαι is a favourite word in Plutarch. See *Nic.* 11. 2; *Luc.* 5. 4; *Cleom.* 13. 2; *Ant.* 80. 3; etc.

τῶν Βαβυλωνίων: The priests of the Babylonians, 'wrongly called Chaldaeans by the Greeks and Romans' (Wilcken 140), in accordance with whose instructions Alexander had sacrificed at Babylon. The 'Chaldaeans' later warned Alexander not to enter Babylon (cf. ch. 73. 1). For the position of priests in Semitic lands, see Berve 1. 98.

περιστήσῃ τὸ δαιμόνιον: 'Heaven might devolve his power upon an ignoble and impotent man' (Perrin). περιίστημι is used particularly of bringing round to a worse state, often with chance or fate as the subject. See Isocrates 6. 47 (cited by LSJ), and esp. *Luc.* 19. 5, where Lucullus laments the fact that when he had wished to emulate Sulla (who had saved Athens) ἐμὲ . . . εἰς τὴν Μομμίου (who destroyed Corinth in 146) δόξαν ὁ δαίμων περιέστησεν.

5. ὁ ἐπὶ τῶν στρωματοφυλάκων: The Macedonian who was set over those in charge of the royal equipage. We may compare ch. 23. 5, τοὺς ἐπὶ τῶν σιτοποιῶν καὶ μαγείρων.

παρὰ τὸν Ὦξον ποταμόν: Arrian (4. 15. 7 f.)—based on Ptolemy (so Strasburger 41, Kornemann 144, Jacoby, *F. Gr. Hist.* 2D. 516, 38)—and Curtius (7. 10. 13 f.) both agree in placing the incident on the R. Oxus, the boundary between Bactria and Sogdiana. This was in the spring of 328. Strabo (11. 11. 5) mentions the discovery of petroleum near the R. Ochus, but he probably refers to the same incident since the two rivers were not clearly distinguished by the Alexander-historians (Strabo, loc. cit.).

ἀνεκάλυψε: Photius reads ἀπεκάλυψε, but no change is required. See especially *Mor.* 776 e, ποταμοῦ τινος ἀενάους πηγὰς ἀνακαλύπτων.

ὑγροῦ λιπαροῦ καὶ πιμελώδους: 'oily and fatty liquid'.

6. ἀπαντλουμένου κτλ.: 'When they drew off the top (surface), it at once gushed forth pure and translucent, apparently no different from oil in smell or taste, and altogether indistinguishable in brightness and oiliness, and that too although the soil does not even bear olives.'

7. λέγεται: There is no other evidence for this.

8. ἐξ ὧν γράφει πρὸς Ἀ.: Athenaeus (2. 42 f) mentions that Alexander wrote about the discovery of 'oil' in Asia: presumably he had this letter before him. Kaerst oddly thinks that the fact that both writers mention it proves it to be a forgery; see *PACA* 4 (1961), 16.

9. οἱ δὲ μάντεις: Arrian (loc. cit.) mentions only Aristander: Ἀρίστανδρος δὲ πόνων εἶναι σημεῖον τοῦ ἐλαίου τὴν πηγὴν ἔφασκεν· ἀλλὰ καὶ νίκην ἐπὶ τοῖς πόνοις σημαίνειν.

πόνων γὰρ ἀρωγήν: ? A reminiscence of Plato, *Menex.* 238 a, μετὰ δὲ τοῦτο ἐλαίου γένεσιν, πόνων ἀρωγήν, ἀνῆκεν (sc. ἡ ἡμετέρα γῆ) τοῖς ἐκγόνοις.

LVIII. *Alexander displays his confidence, courage, and resolution.*

Plutarch makes no attempt at a connected narrative. The capture of Sisimithres' rock took place during the winter of 328/7—for the chronology see Tarn 1. 72, n. 1—and Aornos was taken in the following winter. Plutarch selects these incidents merely in order to illustrate various aspects of Alexander's character.

The term 'rock' refers to 'the abrupt and isolated rocky hills which are not uncommon in Asia and which made excellent fortresses' (Welles on Diod. 17. 28. 1).

1. τραύμασι νεανικοῖς: In the *Moralia* (327 a–b, 341 a–c; cf. 344 c–d) Plutarch gives lists of Alexander's numerous wounds: see the tables in Nachstädt's dissertation cited at 45. 5. The most famous (and the most serious) of his wounds was that sustained among the Malli (see ch. 63. 2 ff.).

ἀπορίαι τῶν ἀναγκαίων κτλ.: If Plutarch has any particular period in mind, he is presumably thinking of the situation described by Arrian (4. 21. 10) in the winter of 328/7.

2. αὐτὸς δέ κτλ.: cf. ch. 26. 14. Arrian also comments on Alexander's confidence and boldness at the siege of Chorienes' rock. Oxyartes (see below) comments to Chorienes (4. 21. 7), βίᾳ μὲν γὰρ οὐδὲν ὅ τι οὐχ ἁλωτὸν εἶναι Ἀλεξάνδρῳ.

3. τὴν Σισιμίθρου ... πέτραν: Also called the rock of Chorienes (Arr. 4. 21. 1–9). Sisimithres was one of the petty chiefs in the east of

Sogdiana (Paraitacene) and the rock was situated on the R. Vakhsh south of Faisabad. For Strabo's confusion about the rocks see 47. 7 n. and on the erroneous geography in Curtius and Strabo see *RE* 3, 2424 (Kaerst).

ἀπότομον: So Arrian 4. 21. 2, αὐτὴ δὲ ἀπότομος πάντοθεν. . . . Φάραγξ δὲ κύκλῳ περιείργει τὴν πέτραν βαθεῖα.

Ὀξυάρτην: Berve no. 587. The father of Roxane, and one of the Bactrian nobility (see ch. 47). He is to be distinguished from Oxyathres, the brother of Darius. Curtius (8. 2. 19 ff.) seems to think of two men, Oxartes (here) and Oxyartes, who is introduced at 8. 4. 21 apparently for the first time. In Arrian Chorienes (Sisimithres) requests Alexander to send Oxyartes to him; in Curtius Alexander sends him to persuade Sisimithres to surrender.

He fled with Bessus and Spitamenes over the R. Oxus to Nautaca. After Bessus' death he continued to resist and only surrendered to Alexander after the capture of his wife and daughters (see ch. 47). Later, at the end of 326, he was appointed satrap of the Parapamisadae and continued to administer this satrapy after Alexander's death (Diod. 18. 3. 3).

5. ἑτέρᾳ δ' ὁμοίως ἀποτόμῳ: The rock Aornos, identified by Sir Aurel Stein in 1926 as Pīr-Sar, north-east of Peshawar on the Indus: see his article in *Geog. Jour.* 70 (1927), 515 ff., and his book, *On Alexander's Track to the Indus* (London, 1929). The siege is described by Arrian (4. 28. 8–30. 4), Diodorus (17. 85), and Curtius (8. 11. 1–25); cf. Justin 12. 7. 12 f. A good modern account in Fuller 248–254 (with excellent photographs).

⟨ἔχων⟩: Some supplement is clearly necessary. Ziegler (*Rh. Mus.* 84 (1935), 383) suggested ἔχων or ἄγων, and printed ἔχων. ἄγων is perhaps more likely to have dropped out after προσβαλών.

καὶ διὰ τὴν ἐπωνυμίαν: Cf. Curtius 8. 11. 10, Alexander, quem rex nominis, quod sibi cum eo commune esset, admonuit. The youth might have been expected to be brave in any case, but being called Alexander he was the more bound to display courage.

6. τῇ καλουμένῃ Νύσῃ: Nysa was situated in Swat, between the rivers Cophen and Indus, and was traditionally founded by Dionysus (Arr. 5. 1. 1; 2. 1); Strabo (688) is properly sceptical. Tarn 1. 90 considers the Nysaeans Iranian immigrants, while George Woodcock, *The Greeks in India* (London, 1966), 21 ff., argues that they were descendants of Darius' Greek soldiers.

This incident is not mentioned elsewhere, although Curtius (8. 10. 7 ff.) describes a siege and an attempt by the defenders to break out. Arrian (loc. cit.) says nothing of fighting.

νεῖν οὐκ ἔμαθον: However, Diodorus (17. 97. 2) implies that Alexander was able to swim.

7. ἐπεὶ δὲ καταπαύσαντος: There is no need to suppose a lacuna before ἐπεί. Plutarch is describing very briefly a number of incidents merely in order to illustrate the king's character.

πρέσβεις: Their chief, Acuphis, and thirty of their leading men (Arr. 5. 1. 3). Curtius (8. 10. 11) also mentions their surrender.

ἀθεράπευτος: 'unkempt' (R. M. Jones *CPhil*. 15 (1920), 400) or 'covered with blood and dust' (Stewart, McCrindle) rather than 'without an attendant' (Perrin) or 'without any pomp or ceremony' (North, Langhorne). See the λόγος at Arr. 5. 1. 4, παρελθεῖν τε δὴ ἐς τὴν σκηνὴν τὴν Ἀλεξάνδρου τοὺς πρέσβεις καὶ καταλαβεῖν καθήμενον κεκονιμένον ἔτι ἐκ τῆς ὁδοῦ ξὺν τοῖς ὅπλοις τοῖς τε ἄλλοις καὶ τὸ κράνος [αὐτῷ] περικείμενον καὶ τὸ δόρυ ἔχοντα. θαμβῆσαί τε ἰδόντας τὴν ὄψιν . . ., and cf. Arr. 7. 11. 1, οὔτ᾽ ἐθεράπευσε τὸ σῶμα (of Alexander after the mutiny at Opis).

8. πρᾳότητα: A certain emendation by Ziegler. λαμπρότητα could mean only 'brilliance' or 'magnificence', which is impossible in the context. Moreover Isocrates (5. 116) combines πρᾳότης and φιλανθρωπία, and at *Nic.* 12. 4 the manuscripts confuse πρᾳότης and λαμπρότης.

9. σὲ μὲν ἄρχοντα κτλ.: Alexander appointed Acuphis ὕπαρχος in place of the ruling aristocracy of 300 (Arr. 5. 2. 2); for the use of ὕπαρχος in Arrian see Tarn 2. 173, n. 1. Arrian relates this incident as a λόγος; he tells us that Alexander also requested 300 cavalry, and in view of Acuphis' reply remained content with them. They were later sent home from the R. Hydaspes (Arr. 6. 2. 3).

LIX. *Alexander's treatment of Taxiles. He massacres the Indian mercenaries and punishes the 'philosophers'.*

1. ὁ δὲ Ταξίλης: The ruler of the great city of Taxila (Takshasila) and the surrounding territory between the Indus and the Hydaspes (Arr. 5. 3. 6, 8. 2). Taxila has been extensively excavated by Sir John Marshall; his results are contained in three magnificent volumes, *Taxila* (Cambridge, 1951). It lay some twenty miles north-west of the modern Rawalpindi, at the meeting-place of the three great trade routes from Bactria, Kashmir, and the Ganges valley, and was 'the principal seat of Hindu learning in Northern India, to which scholars of all classes flocked for instruction, especially in the medical sciences' (Smith *EHI* 61; cf. Marshall op. cit., 1. 43 f.).

Taxiles was the ruler's official title; his own name is given by Curtius (8. 12. 14) as Omphis (i.e. Āmbhi), less correctly by Diodorus

(17. 86. 4) as Mophis. As Curtius rightly puts it, 'Taxilen appellavere populares, sequente nomine imperium, in quemcumque transiret'; see also Radet 291, who compares Porus = the Paurava monarch, Abisares, Sophytas, and Phegelas, the rulers of Abhisara (Kashmir), Saubhûta, and Bhagala respectively.

When Alexander was in Sogdiana (328–7), Taxiles had sent envoys making submission (Diod. 17. 86. 4; Curt., 8. 12. 5), in order to gain the king's support against his enemies, Porus (see ch. 60) and Abisares, the ruler of Kashmir, and had assisted Hephaestion to bridge the Indus. For his lavish gifts to Alexander see Arr. 5. 3. 5 f.; Curt. 8. 12. 10.

τῆς Ἰνδικῆς . . . τὸ μέγεθος: So Strabo 15. 1. 28 (698), φασὶ δ' εἶναί τινες τὴν χώραν ταύτην Αἰγύπτου μείζονα. The source of Plutarch and Strabo, and ultimately of the accounts in Diodorus and Curtius, is probably Onesicritus; see H. Strasburger, *Bibl. Or.* 9 (1952), 207.

εὔβοτον δὲ καὶ καλλίκαρπον: (Strabo, loc. cit.). Taxila lay in an extensive fertile valley, 11 miles long by 5 miles wide, nearly 1,800 feet above sea level. For its fertility see Marshall op. cit., 1. 2 f.

2–4. The conversation is reported more briefly at *Mor.* 181 c. Berve (2. 370, n. 3) comments on its Cynic tendency and assigns it tentatively to Onesicritus. He rightly doubts its claim to be considered historical.

5. λαβὼν δὲ δῶρα πολλά: Curtius (8. 12. 15) mentions golden crowns to Alexander and his followers and 80 talents of coined silver.

δοὺς πλείονα: Curtius adds gold and silver table vessels, Persian robes, and thirty caparisoned horses.

προέπιεν: ἐδωρήσατο (Zonaras). For this meaning of the verb see ch. 39. 2.

τοὺς μὲν φίλους κτλ.: So Curt. 8. 12. 17 f. 'This lavish generosity . . . probably was prompted more by policy than by sentiment' (Smith, op. cit., 62). Taxiles led a contingent of 5,000 men to serve with Alexander (Arr. 5. 8. 5). This fact and his gifts show that he became a vassal-king.

6–7. ἐπεὶ δέ κτλ.: This incident occurred during the siege of Massaga in the country of the Assaceni (*mod.* Swat), east of the River Guraeus (Arr. 4. 25. 7–26. 1). Arrian agrees with Diodorus (17. 84) and Plutarch that Alexander made a settlement with the mercenaries, but relates (27. 3 f.) that he massacred them because, after agreeing to serve with him, they were about to desert. Tarn (1. 89) thinks, perhaps correctly, that 'the thing may have been some horrible mistake perhaps due to defective interpreting and to Alexander's growing impatience'.

8. οἱ φιλόσοφοι: The Brāhmans of Sind are meant. They inspired the revolts of Musicanus (Arr. 6. 16. 5, 17. 2) and Sambus (Diod. 17. 102. 7, 103. 1 ff.). 'The power behind the throne was the Brāhman community, and here for the first time we come upon an opposition inspired by the conception of a national religion' (E. Bevan in *CHI*. 378). For Plutarch's confusion of the Gymnosophists (Ascetics) and Brāhmans, see ch. 64.

This incident is placed out of chronological order because of the logical connection of thought; see on ch. 49. 14.

LX. *The Battle of the R. Hydaspes. Alexander's treatment of Porus.*

Sources (for §§ 1–10): Arr. 5. 8. 4–18. 5; Diod. 17. 87–8; Curtius 8. 13. 5–14. 33; Justin 12. 8. 1–4; Polyaenus 4. 3. 9, 22; Frontinus 1. 4. 9.

1. ἐν ταῖς ἐπιστολαῖς: For arguments in favour of the authenticity of this letter see *PACA* 4 (1961), 16–18. It is at variance with Arrian's account in only two important details (see below, §§ 7–8) and contains additional information, e.g. on the duration of the battle (§ 11).

ἐν μέσῳ τῶν στρατοπέδων: See Arr. 5. 9. 1. Alexander probably encamped either at Jhelum, where the modern Grand Trunk road from Taxila via Rawalpindi crosses the Hydaspes, or at Haranpur some forty miles south of Jhelum. Haranpur suits better Strabo's statement (15. 1. 32) that Alexander travelled *south* from Taxila, and the distance from Taxila to Haranpur over the Salt Range tallies almost exactly with the 120 (Roman) miles given by Pliny (*NH* 6. 62) for Alexander's march; the distance from Taxila to Jhelum by the Grand Trunk road is about twenty miles less.

According to Arrian (5. 11. 1) Alexander crossed the river about 150 stades (*c*. 17½ miles) from his camp at a point where the river made a notable bend (ἐπέκαμπτεν λόγου ἀξίως) and where a large, wooded island lay opposite a headland. Curtius (8. 13. 17) adds that near the bank was a deep gully (*fossa praealta*), capable of concealing cavalry. Sir Aurel Stein (*Geog. Jour.* 80 (1932), 31 ff. ; *Archaeological Reconnaissances in NW India and SE Iran* (London, 1937)) claimed to have found this point at Jalalpur, exactly 17½ miles upstream from Haranpur, where there is a suitable headland and where the Kandar Kas provides such a *fossa*. Unfortunately the bend in the river is slight and its course cannot be supposed to have altered significantly. This led Tarn (2. 198) to prefer the theory of B. Breloer (*Alexanders Kampf gegen Poros* (Stuttgart, 1933); *Alexanders Bund mit Poros* (Leipzig, 1941), 79 ff.). According to him Alexander crossed about 13 miles above Jhelum, at a place which satisfies all the conditions except that the islands are small; he then marched south for 15 miles and engaged Porus opposite

Jhelum, between the river and the Pabbi Range. However, Stein (*Arch. Rec.* 21), has stressed the extremely broken nature of the terrain at this point—'it is cut up by torrents into a continuous succession of ravines'—which makes it very difficult, if not impossible, to believe that the operations described by Arrian took place here. The area opposite Jalalpur, on the other hand, offers ample room for the Indian battle line and for the cavalry manœuvres on the Indian left. If it is perhaps too much to say that Stein 'demolishes' Breloer's theory (so Fuller 185, n. 2), it seems probable that Alexander crossed at Jalalpur. But only the discovery of Nicaea or Bucephala (see ch. 61. 2) will settle the matter (Tarn 2. 198).

For a good discussion of the question, with criticism of earlier views, see Fuller 181 ff.

ἀντιπρῴρους: Sintenis rightly preferred ἀντιπόρους, 'on the opposite side of the river', the reading of P. ἀντίπρῳρος, lit. 'with the prow towards, ready for action', is almost always used of ships. Xenophon (*HG* 7. 5. 23) applies it to an army, τὸ στράτευμα ἀντίπρῳρον ὥσπερ τριήρη προσῆγε, and Arrian (5. 17. 7) compares the elephants retreating to ships backing water, ὥσπερ αἱ πρύμναν κρουόμεναι νῆες; both instances show that the word was permissible as a simile, but not as a matter-of-fact metaphor. The error is doubtless due to the mention of the Hydaspes.

2. ψόφον ποιεῖν κτλ.: For the situation see Arrian 5. 10. 2–4, esp. 4, Ἀλέξανδρος δὲ ὡς ἐξείργαστο αὐτῷ ἄφοβον τὸ τοῦ Πώρου εἰς τὰς νυκτερινὰς ἐπιχειρήσεις. Alexander, realizing that it was impossible to cross in the face of the elephants, which untrained horses will not face, feinted to cross at various points. Porus eventually ceased to send out his elephants to meet the threats and contented himself with placing scouts along the bank.

3. τῶν πεζῶν μέρος: The hypaspists, the regiments of Cleitus and Coenus, the archers and the Agrianians. Meleager, Attalus, and Gorgias were posted with the mercenary infantry between the main camp and the crossing point: they were to cross as Alexander's force passed them on its march down the opposite bank (see Tarn 2. 190). Craterus was left in the main camp with two regiments and the 5,000 Indian troops—his orders, Arr. 5. 11. 4.

ἱππεῖς δὲ τοὺς κρατίστους: The *agema* of the Companions, four cavalry regiments (inc. the Bactrian, Sogdian, and Scythian cavalry), and the horse-archers, a total of 5,300 in all. The mercenary cavalry in the intermediate camps presumably crossed with the infantry and took part in the battle. Craterus retained his own cavalry regiment and some native cavalry.

νῆσον οὐ μεγάλην: Arrian's authorities differed: Aristobulus (5. 14. 3) described it as small (μικρά), Ptolemy (5. 13. 2) as μεγάλη. Curtius 8. 3. 17 and Arrian 5. 11. 1 refer to a different island.

5. τραχὺν δέ κτλ.: 'After the storm the Hydaspes, roaring down in high flood, had scoured a deep channel.' This tallies with Arrian's account (5. 13. 3).

αὐτοὺς δέ δέξασθαι: 'The ground between the two currents gave his men no sure footing, since it was broken and slippery.' (Perrin).

6. Ὀνησίκριτος εἴρηκεν: *F. Gr. Hist.* no. 134, fr. 19. Pearson (*LHA* 105) is rightly cautious about the interpretation of the remark. M. H. Fisch (*AJP* 58 (1937), 132) thinks that it represents part of Alexander's attempt to win over Athenian and Greek public opinion. If it was ever uttered, it must have been much earlier; for it is very doubtful whether Alexander was worried about this *at this stage*. But Brown 53 is probably right to attribute the remark to Onesicritus' rhetoric.

Only the quotation is to be credited to Onesicritus; Strasburger (*RE* 18, 466) rightly rejects the view that he gave a detailed description of the battle.

7. ἄχρι μαστῶν βρεχομένους: So Arrian 5. 13. 3.

τῶν πεζῶν ... προϊππεῦσαι: 'led his cavalry in advance of his infantry'.

λογιζόμενος κτλ.: Arrian (5. 14. 2) gives a fuller account of Alexander's reasons for riding ahead with his cavalry. He envisages three possibilities: if the Indians attack in full force he will (*a*) defeat them with his cavalry or (*b*) hold them until his infantry comes up; (*c*) if the Indians flee he will be able to inflict the greatest loss on them. But Alexander must surely have reckoned on a sortie by the Indian cavalry, as Plutarch relates. On the other hand he will not have expected to defeat the entire Indian force, including elephants, with his cavalry unsupported by infantry—see *PACA* 4 (1961), 17. On the limitations of ancient cavalry see F. E. Adcock, *The Greek and Macedonian Art of War* (Berkeley 1957), 48 ff.

8. τῶν γὰρ ἱππέων κτλ.: This is the force commanded by Porus' son, which was sent out to oppose Alexander's landing. For the conflicting versions of these events see Arrian 5. 14. 3–6. On the size of the Indian force the sources differ: Ptolemy gave 2,000 cavalry and 120 chariots, Aristobulus only 60 chariots, and Curtius 4,000 cavalry and 100 chariots (led by Porus' brother). For a discussion of these figures see *PACA*, loc. cit.

Arrian (5. 15. 2) confirms Plutarch's figures for the Indian losses. The chariots were rendered useless in the action by the thick mud.

9. συμφρονήσαντα: 'realizing'; see 9. 14 n. Previously Porus had to reckon with the possibility of a feint (Fuller 190).

μετὰ πάσης τῆς δυνάμεως: In ch. 62. 1 Plutarch, perhaps from the letter, gives Porus' forces *in the battle* as 20,000 foot and 2,000 cavalry. Other figures are higher: Arrian (5. 15. 4) 30,000 infantry, 4,000 cavalry, 300 chariots and 200 elephants; Curtius (8. 13. 6) the same figures except for 85 elephants; Diodorus 50,000 infantry, 3,000 cavalry, 1,000+ chariots and 130 elephants.

πλὴν ὅσον . . . ἀπέλιπε: A few elephants and a small infantry force. Porus had decided that Alexander constituted the main threat.

10. αὐτὸς μὲν ἐνσεῖσαι κτλ.: On the tactics of the battle see Fuller 193–7 and *JHS* 76 (1956), 26–31. The only essential point of difference is whether Coenus rode round behind or in front of the Indian line. Fuller prefers the latter, more reasonable, alternative, but Arrian's version of the orders given to Coenus clearly means that he was to stick closely to the rear of the cavalry on the Indian right when they crossed (presumably behind their own line) to support their left flank threatened by Alexander. θάτερον κέρας means the *Indian left* and τῷ δεξῷι the *Indian right*.

11. γενομένης δὲ τροπῆς ἑκατέρωθεν: 'both wings having been routed'. For this stage in the battle see Arrian 5. 17. 3–7.

ὅθεν . . . εἶναι: For the infinitive in a relative clause see W. W. Goodwin *A Greek Grammar* § 1524. ἔωθεν (Solanus) is an improbable conjecture.

ὀγδόης ὥρας: Plutarch is the only authority for this statement. He does not trouble to relate that Craterus crossed the river at Haranpur and continued the pursuit of the fleeing Indians.

12. οἱ δὲ πλεῖστοι κτλ.: Arr. 5. 19. 1; Diod. 17. 88. 4; Curt. 8. 14. 13; It. Alex. 111; Epit. Mett. 54. 60–63; Suidas, s.v. Πῶρος; Ps.-Call. 3. 4. 3; Iul. Val. 3. 7.

ὑπεραίροντα κτλ.: lit. 'exceeding the height of four cubits by a span'. Plutarch is giving the Greek (Attic) cubit of 18¼ in., and Porus' height is therefore 6 ft. 8½ in., an evident exaggeration. Arrian (5. 19. 1) says he was 'over 5 cubits' and Diodorus (17. 88. 4) gives his height as 5 cubits. If the Greek cubit is meant Porus would be 7½ ft. tall, but Tarn (2. 170) has argued convincingly that there was a short Macedonian cubit of about 13–14 in., which their source was using. Porus will then have been about 6 ft. tall, very tall compared with the average Greek.

ἱππότου . . . ὁ ἐλέφας: 'looked as large on his elephant as an ordinary man did on a horse because of his great height and bulk'.

13. σύνεσιν δὲ θαυμαστὴν ἐπεδείξατο: At *Mor.* 970 d Plutarch cites this incident as an instance of animal wisdom. Aelian (*NA* 7. 37) uses Plutarch's essay (see A. F. Scholfield in the introduction to the Loeb ed. of Aelian). Diod. (17. 88. 6) and Curt. (8. 14. 37–40) say nothing of this, although the animal attempts to defend the king. Cf. Strabo, 15. 1. 42 (705).

ἀνακόπτων: 'beating back'. LSJ cite only Thuc. 4. 12 in this sense: but the word is common in Plutarch, e.g. *Caes.* 44. 12, *Sull.* 21. 6, *Dion* 30. 9, *Mor.* 324 a, etc.

περιρρυῇ: 'slip off'; from περιρρέω, LSJ II. 3. So *Mor.* 970 d (of the same incident).

14. ἐπεὶ δὲ ληφθέντα κτλ.: This famous incident is mentioned thrice in the *Moralia* (181 e, 332 e, 458 b), by Arrian (5. 19. 1–3, a λόγος) and by Themistius *Or.* 7. 88 d. Cf. Curt. 8. 14. 41 ff.

15. ἀφῆκεν αὐτὸν ἄρχειν: 'allowed him to rule'. For this meaning of ἀφίημι see ch. 47. 2 n.

[καὶ] τῆς αὐτονόμου: Ziegler adopts Reiske's emendation of the manuscript reading, καὶ τοὺς αὐτονόμους, but, with the necessary deletion of καί, the manuscript reading (with a comma after χώραν) makes perfectly good sense. Hephaestion was sent against the autonomous tribes along the R. Hydraotes (Ravi), while Alexander marched against the Cathaeans. The capture and destruction of their capital, Sangala, near Amritsar is described by Arrian 5. 22. 5–24. 8. He mentions also the Oxydracae and the Malli (see ch. 63. 2 ff.) further to the south (5. 22. 2; 6. 4. 3).

προσέθηκε χώραν: Porus' existing territory lay between the Hydaspes (Jhelum) and the Acesines (Chenab)—see Strabo 15. 698. To this was added that of the Glausae (or Glauganicae) including 37 towns and many villages (Arr. 5. 20. 4), that of the 'bad' Porus and other independent tribes along the Hydraotes (Arr. 5. 21. 5 f.), and of the Cathaeans east of the river (Arr. 5. 24. 8). After the mutiny on the Hyphasis (Beas) he was given all the territory up to that river (5. 29. 2), and before Alexander sailed down the Indus he appointed Porus *king* of all Indian territory captured till then—7 tribes and over 2,000 cities (6. 2. 1). Cf. Diod. 17. 89. 6; Curt. 8. 14. 45; Justin 12. 8. 7; Epit. Mett. 61. For full details of Porus' kingdom, see Berve 1. 288–90. Cf. Smith *EHI* 89.

Alexander had already enlarged Taxiles' kingdom, which now extended to the Jhelum; 'he meant the two rajahs to balance each other' (Tarn 1. 97; cf. Glotz–Cohen 1. 151).

πεντεκαίδεκα μὲν ἔθνη κτλ.: Strabo (15. 1. 4 (686) and 15. 1. 33

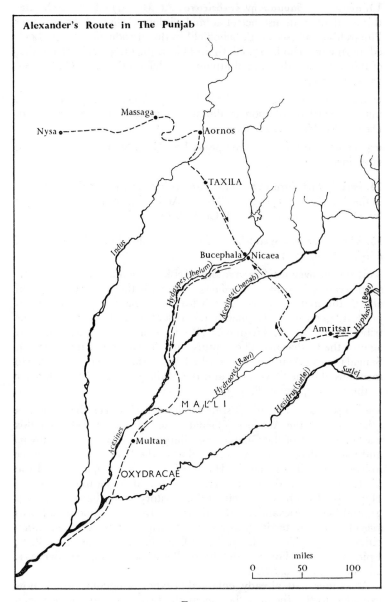

FIG. 2.

(701)), gives 9 tribes and 5,000 cities; so also Pliny *NH* 6. 59. Their information is derived from Onesicritus—see Pearson *LHA* 106 and n. 88. Arrian's figures (5. 20. 4; 6. 2. 1) are more moderate.

16. ἄλλης δὲ τρὶς τοσαύτης: Reiske suggests, perhaps rightly, that with the manuscript text, ἄλλην . . . τοσαύτην, ἧς Φ. . . ., φασιν εἶναι may be understood from the previous sentence.

The satrapy of Philip (Berve no. 780) originally embraced the territory between the Indus and the Hydaspes (Arr. 5. 8. 3; *Ind.* 19. 4) but in the autumn of 326 he is called 'satrap' of the land west of the Indus towards Bactria (Arr. 6. 2. 3). He must then have taken over Nicanor's satrapy (cf. Arr. 4. 28. 6). Later his satrapy included the territory of the Malli and the Oxydracae as far as the confluence of the Acesines and the Indus (Arr. 6. 14. 3; 15. 2). In 325 Philip was murdered by his mercenaries, and Taxiles and Eudamus were ordered to administer his satrapy as a temporary measure (Arr. 6. 27. 2). See also *CHI* 383 f.

LXI. *The death of Bucephalas and the foundation of Bucephalia.*

1. ὁ Βουκεφάλας: See ch. 6. 1.

ὡς οἱ πλεῖστοι λέγουσι: Strabo 15. 1. 29 (698); Diod. 17. 95. 5; Curt. 8. 14. 34; Gellius *NA* 5. 2. 4; cf. Justin 12. 8. 4 (B. wounded). As Gellius cites Chares in § 2 of his account of Bucephalas, this version may go back via Cleitarchus to Chares; see Jacoby, *F. Gr. Hist.* 2D. 437, 20.

ὡς δ' Ὀνησίκριτος: *Fr. Gr. Hist.* no. 134, fr. 20. So Arrian (5. 19. 4–5) from Aristobulus, who probably took it from Onesicritus, as Jacoby (*F. Gr. Hist.* 2D. 477) suggests. Aristobulus also gives Bucephalas' age as 30, probably correctly, *pace* A. R. Anderson, *AJP* 51 (1930), 11 ff. Dr. Green informs me that the most common life-span for a stallion is 28–32 and that the optimum selling age would be seven, just about the earliest age at which Alexander could have broken Bucephalas.

2. συνήθη καὶ φίλον: See Arrian's tribute (loc. cit.).

Βουκεφαλίαν: So spelled in *Mor.* 328 f, Strabo loc. cit. Arrian calls the city τὰ Βουκέφαλα, Diodorus ἡ Βουκέφαλα, others simply Βουκέφαλα. For a complete list see G. Radet in *REA* 43 (1941), 34 n.

Alexander founded two cities after his victory, the other being called Nicaea (Arr. loc. cit.; Diod. loc. cit.; Curt. 9. 1. 6, 3. 23; Strabo loc. cit.; Justin 12. 8. 8; Epit. Mett. 62). Against all modern writers who mention the matter, Tarn (2. 236 f.) has argued that Bucephala was built on the *east* bank of the river and Nicaea at the crossing-point on the west bank. He bases his case on a list of cities given by Claudius Ptolemy (7. 1. 45 f.) in which Bucephala appears to be placed on the east, and regards the evidence of the Alexander-historians as indecisive. But Arrian (5. 19. 4) seems to put it on the west side of the river; certainly we might expect Nicaea to be founded on the battlefield.

3. λέγεται δέ: sc. Ἀλέξανδρος.
On the name Περίτας see F. Mentz, *Phil.* 88 (1933), 199, who connects it with the Macedonian month Περίτιος = February, when (presumably) the dog was born or acquired by Alexander. We hear (Pollux *Onom.* 5. 46) that Alexander had another dog called Τριακάς, born on the 30th of some month (?). See Mentz op. cit., 421, who points to the practice of naming slaves in this way.

Pollux (*Onom.* 5. 42) relates on the authority of Theopompus (*F. Gr. Hist.* no. 115 fr. 340) that Peritas was an Indian dog bought for 100 *minae*. On the valour of these dogs see Strabo 15. 1. 31, Diod. 17. 92. 2 f., Curt. 9. 1. 31 ff. (from Onesicritus?).

Σωτίων: A Peripatetic writer, whose date depends on the connection with Potamon. A list of his works in *OCD* s.v. (2), *RE* 3A, 1237 f.

Ποτάμωνος: An eminent rhetorician from Mytilene (born *c.* 75 B.C.) who served on embassies to Caesar (in 47 and 45) and to Augustus (in 25). Numerous inscriptions testify to the gratitude of his fellow-citizens. He practised in Rome and also wrote historical works, including *On Alexander the Great* and encomia of Brutus and Caesar, of which only this fragment remains. He died at the beginning of Tiberius' reign, at the age of about 90.
Details in *F. Gr. Hist.* no. 147, *RE* 22, 1023-7 (Stegemann).

LXII. *The mutiny at the Hyphasis.*

Sources: Arr. 5. 25. 1-29. 1; Diod. 17. 93. 2-95. 2; Curt. 9. 2. 1-3. 19; Strabo 15. 1. 27, 32; Justin 12. 8. 10-17; Pliny *NH* 6. 62; Orosius 3. 19. 5; Epit. Mett. 68-9; Philostr. *vit. Apoll.* 2. 43; Suidas s.v. Βραχμάν.

1. τοῦ πρόσω τῆς Ἰνδικῆς . . .: Immediately after the victory over Porus Alexander ordered the construction of a fleet on the Hydaspes (Diod. 17. 89. 4, Curt. 9. 1. 3—based on Onesicritus; see Schachermeyr, *Jax Festschrift* 126 f.). Droysen (1. 357) argued that this showed unmistakably that Alexander's march eastwards was a mere raid, and Breloer (*Alexanders Bund mit Poros* (Leipzig, 1941), especially 115 ff.) and Andreotti (*Saeculum* 8 (1957), 140 ff.) hold that Alexander wished merely to create an extended safety zone, in the interests of trade (Breloer) or to facilitate the embarkation of his troops and to strengthen the position of Porus (Andreotti); cf. Hampl, *La Nouvelle Clio* 6 (1954), 102 ff.

Many scholars, however, consider that Alexander intended to proceed along the Ganges to reach the Eastern Ocean; see, e.g., Wilcken 173 f., Radet 299 ff., and (most fully) Schachermeyr, op. cit. 123 ff. Alexander, he suggests, had time while the timber for the ships was seasoning to reach the Ocean and return (we might add that there was no need to *use* the fleet as soon as it was ready), and stresses the large build-up of troops. Both these points seem valid, but do not prove that Alexander intended to reach the Ocean. Nor do considerations of the extent of Alexander's geographical knowledge *prove* anything. It is likely that he knew of the existence of the Ganges (below, § 2), and he was (surely) well informed about the region between the Hyphasis and the Upper Ganges (only 250 miles away); see esp. Andreotti 143, who stresses his contacts with the Indian princes, and note the position of Taxila at the end of the Royal road from the East (59. 1 n.). But it is perhaps less certain than Andreotti believes that Alexander would have been deterred by the knowledge of the difficulties involved in his march.

Advocates of the view that Alexander intended to march to the Eastern Ocean rely heavily on Alexander's statement (in his speech at the Hyphasis—Arr. 5. 26. 2) that it was not far to the Ganges and the Eastern Ocean. This speech is taken by most scholars to be essentially genuine; see especially Kornemann 78 ff., 148, who concludes that it is based on Ptolemy: But for dissentients see the scholars cited by Andreotti op. cit., 144, n. 66, especially Tarn 2. 287 ff., who is certainly correct in maintaining that the geography is not Alexander's; he did not think of the Caspian (Hyrcanian) sea as a Gulf of Ocean.

Alexander's objective may have been less well-defined than is commonly thought. He may have intended to advance until effective resistance ceased; see Arr. 5. 24. 8, although this may be Arrian's own comment rather than Ptolemy's.

2. δισμυρίοις πεζοῖς . . .: Perhaps from Alexander's letter cited in ch. 60.

τὸν Γάγγην . . .: The Ganges is mentioned in Alexander's speech at the Hyphasis (above), and is certainly to be restored in Diod. 18. 6. 2 (so E. Meyer, *Klio* 21 (1927), 185; D Kienast, *Historia* 14 (1965), 184). This list of satrapies was compiled in the last year of Alexander's life (see Tarn 2. 309 ff.), but Diodorus derives it from Hieronymus and the mention of the Ganges may be due to Hieronymus (so Kienast) or to Diodorus himself (so Meyer). Finally, Diod. 17. 93. 2 and Curt. 9. 2. 1–3, obviously drawing on a common source, tell how the Indian ruler Phegeus informed the king that the Ganges (32 stades wide) was to be reached by a twelve days' journey *across the desert*, and that beyond the river lived the Prasii (Tabraisii, Diod.) and the

Gandaridae. Their common source cannot be other than Cleitarchus. Tarn (2. 281) holds that his information is derived from Megasthenes, but as Megasthenes gave 100 stades as the width of the Ganges (Strabo 15. 702; Arr. *Ind.* 4. 7) Cleitarchus (who probably wrote before M.; see Intro. p. liv) cannot have obtained a figure of 32 stades from him. Nor is his source Onesicritus (see Schachermeyr op. cit., 134). More important, Kienast has observed that Cleitarchus describes the Thar desert, far to the south of Alexander's route; whether the story is a legend (as Tarn 2. 281 maintains) or not, it has no connection with Alexander. Unless his statement at the Hyphasis is genuine, we can judge only from probabilities. When we consider the opportunities available to Alexander and the close cultural unity of Northern India, it is more likely than not that he had heard of the Ganges. The extent of his knowledge can only be conjectured.

Tarn (2. 281) holds that Plutarch thinks of Alexander as having *reached* the Ganges. It seems more likely that like Diodorus and Curtius he regards the Ganges as a distant objective. Schachermeyr (loc cit.) points to his use of ἐλέγοντο and πυνθανόμενοι.

δύο καὶ τριάκοντα σταδίων: So Diod. 17. 93. 2 (from Cleitarchus); elsewhere (2. 37. 2, 18. 6. 2) he gives 30 stades. Schachermeyr (op. cit. 133) regards 32 stades as roughly right for the Upper Ganges, but the width of the Ganges where it debouches on to the plains south of Haradwar is only about one mile in the rainy season.

3. ἐλέγοντο γάρ . . .: Diod. (loc. cit.) and Curt. (9. 2. 3 f.) give somewhat lower figures—20,000 cavalry, 200,000 infantry, 4,000 elephants and 2,000 chariots.

The Gandaridae are linked with the Praisii or Prasii (= Easterners) only in this episode. The Prasii are the inhabitants of the great kingdom of Magadha, with its capital at Pataliputra near Patna on the Ganges. Detailed knowledge of them reached the Greeks only through Megasthenes (below). For the view that the Gandaridae were a branch of the people of Gandhara and lived just east of the Beas see Tarn 2. 279 ff.; cf. Kiessling *RE* s.v. Their connection with the Prasii (evidently facilitated by the existence of a tribe called Gangaridae at the mouth of the Ganges) may have led to the confusion of the Hyphasis (Beas) with the Ganges. At any rate Justin (12. 8. 9) relates that Alexander actually defeated the Prasii and the Gandaridae.

4. Ἀνδρόκοττος: The evidence for the form of the name is assembled by Ziegler at *Rh. Mus.* 84 (1935), 383. Briefly, apart from the present chapter, there are only four passages, Arr. *Ind.* 9. 9, Strabo 2. 70, App. *Syr.* 55, and *Mor.* 542 d, in which the name begins with *A*.; otherwise always with Σ. In the first two passages (as in § 9 below) it follows a word ending in -s. On the basis of this evidence, I should prefer to avoid the hiatus by reading Σανδρόκοττος, as Ziegler does in his first edition.

Chandragupta was the founder of the Mauryan dynasty and the grandfather of Asoka. Justin (15. 4. 15) and the Jain and Brahman traditions say that he was of humble birth (accepted by Smith *EHI* 42, 117), but the Buddhist tradition that his father was chief of the Maurya clan is probably to be preferred—see *CHI* 470. He annihilated the Macedonian garrisons and overthrew the last of the Nanda dynasty at Pataliputra. His accession is generally placed *c.* 322 (the Buddhist tradition), but the Jain tradition would put it in 312. Justin (15. 4. 20) appears to support the earlier date—*pace* Tarn *Bactria* 47, n. 1.

Σελεύκῳ . . . ἐδωρήσατο: Probably in the summer of 304—on the date see Beloch 4. 1. 142, n. 2. Tarn (*JHS* 60 (1940), 84 ff.) shows conclusively that 500 is used in Indian writings to denote 'a large and important number'. As the greatest number of elephants recorded in the possession of any king is 150, he suggests that Megasthenes' informant used the equivalent of 500, which the interpreter translated as πεντακοσίους. The number will have been smaller, perhaps in the region of 150; the elephants played an important part in the defeat of Antigonus and Demetrius at Ipsus in 301 (*CAH* 6. 504).

Megasthenes several times visited the court of Chandragupta (Arr. 5. 6. 2) as the envoy of Seleucus, and to him the Greeks owed almost all their detailed knowledge about India east of the Hyphasis. He is a major source of Strabo's *Geography*, and Diodorus (2. 35–42) and Arrian in his *Indica* reproduce his book. Fragments in *F. Gr. Hist.* 3C no. 715; the commentary is not yet published. On his life and work see *RE* 15, 230–326 (O. Stein).

Strabo (15. 724) and Appian (*Syr.* 55), who reproduces Megasthenes, relate that as part of an agreement, which secured peace between the two dynasties for about 120 years, Seleucus ceded several frontier provinces west of the Indus—on the details, Tarn *Bactria*, 100, refuting extravagant views. Both authors mention a compact which Appian calls a κῆδος, Strabo an ἐπιγαμία. This must mean that a daughter (or niece) of Seleucus married Chandragupta or his son Bindusara (Tarn, op. cit. 174, n. 3), not that there was *ius conubii* between the two peoples or the two families (so *CHI* 431). It is sometimes said that there is no evidence that the two armies met (e.g. *CHI* 431, 472), but Appian (*Syr.* 55) explicitly says that Seleucus crossed the Indus and fought (ἐπολέμησε) Androcottus (i.e. Chandragupta). In any case Seleucus had to make the best terms he could in view of the urgent call for help from his allies, Lysimachus, Cassander, and Ptolemy.

Pliny *NH* 6. 68, gives 600,000 infantry, 30,000 cavalry and 9,000 elephants, and Smith (*EHI* 125 f.) points to the enormous forces used by Indian kings in later times. Chandragupta's empire eventually extended to the Bay of Bengal in the East and to Mysore in the south, so that 'all India' is not much exaggerated.

5. εἰς τὴν σκηνὴν καθείρξας ἔκειτο: Plutarch omits the speeches of Alexander and Coenus given by Arrian (5. 25. 3–27. 9) and Curtius (9. 2. 12–3. 15). Following the refusal of the Macedonians to obey, Alexander shut himself up in his tent and waited for two days in the hope that they would change their minds. When they did not (and clearly did not intend to) he came out and offered sacrifice with a view to crossing the river. This was unfavourable! Arrian (Ptolemy) says nothing of the consolation of Alexander's companions or of the entreaties of the soldiers.

6. ἐπικλασθείς: 'moved to pity, with his resolution shaken'. For the verb see Holden on *Them.* 10. 5.

7. ὅπλα μείζονα κτλ.: The fullest account in Diodorus (17. 95. 1–2); cf. Curt. 9. 3. 19, Justin 12. 8. 16. Alexander encloses a space three times as large as his existing camp with an enormous ditch and rampart; he constructs two beds (7½ ft. long) for each soldier and two mangers twice the normal size for each horse. All this in order to suggest to the natives that the Macedonians were giants. No modern scholar accepts these fancies, which Tarn (2. 62) suggests originated in the minds of the poets with Alexander and were passed on by Cleitarchus (2. 84). Smith (*EHI* 78) inclines to the view that they were travellers' tales.

8. ἱδρύσατο δὲ βωμοὺς θεῶν: Arrian (5. 29. 1–2—from Ptolemy) mentions the erection of twelve altars (one for each Olympian) as high as the highest towers and even broader, as a thank-offering to the gods for his victorious progress and a memorial of his labours. Diodorus (17. 95. 1) gives their height as 50 cubits. Strabo (3. 5. 5 (171)) says that Alexander was imitating Hercules and Dionysus; certainly Hercules was reputed to have erected 12 altars in the far west (Wilcken 187; Schachermeyr 363). We may attribute to Philostratus' imagination, or to legends current in his day, his reference (*Vit. Apoll.* 2. 43) to altars 30 stades west of the Hyphasis inscribed 'To Father Ammon and Herakles his brother, to Athena Providence, to Zeus of Olympus, to the Cabiri of Samothrace, to the Indian Sun, and the Delphian Apollo', as well as a bronze column (στήλη) inscribed 'Here Alexander stopped'.

οἱ Πραισίων βασιλεῖς: Chandragupta and his successors. Plutarch's statement is unconfirmed and his source unknown. At *Mor.* 542 d he refers to Chandragupta honouring Alexander.

διαβαίνοντες: Pliny *NH* 6. 62, says that Alexander crossed the Hyphasis and set up altars on the eastern bank—probably wrongly, although Alexander *might* have crossed to show that the *river* had not stopped him. Philostratus (above) implies the western bank.

9. Ἀλέξανδρον εἶδε: Many scholars assume without warrant that Chandragupta met and spoke to Alexander. Glotz–Cohen 1. 152, actually assert that he promised Alexander 'd'utiles concours'. But Chandragupta was in no position to do so, having fled from Magadha to escape death following an unsuccessful coup (Justin 15. 4. 16, reading *Nandrum* for the manuscript *Alexandrum*).

παρ' οὐδὲν ἦλθε: Ziegler's tentative οὐδὲν ⟨ἂν⟩ is unnecessary. Chandragupta said that Alexander came within an ace of overthrowing Nanda and conquering Magadha. He is thinking of what happened in his own case and means that Alexander had only to continue his march and there would have been a popular uprising. I see no reason to suppose (so Tarn 2. 283; *Bactria*, 155) that this remark springs from Demetrius' victorious advance to Pataliputra *c.* 182 B.C.

τοῦ βασιλέως: Dhana Nanda, the ninth (and last) of the Nanda dynasty. Diod. 17. 93. 3 and Curt. 9. 2. 6–7 both relate that his father, a poor barber, had usurped the throne with the aid of the queen, whom he had seduced.

δυσγένειαν: LSJ are clearly wrong in translating 'meanness', although the king *was* mean. North correctly translates 'base parentage', and most translators agree.

LXIII. *Alexander sails down the Indus. He is seriously wounded among the Malli.*

1. ἐντεῦθεν: Plutarch is misleading because he is summarizing. Alexander had returned to the Hydaspes, where he repaired Nicaea and Bucephala which had been damaged by the rains (Arr. 5. 29. 5; *Ind.* 18. 1). Diod. (17. 95. 3), Curt. (9. 3. 21), and Justin (12. 9. 1) all say that he returned to the Acesines, a mere error if their (common) source is not writing loosely: the Hydaspes flows into the Acesines. Aristobulus, ap. Strabo (15. 1. 17 (691), 1. 32 (700)), confirms the Hydaspes.

Alexander set out from Bucephala early in November 326, 'a few days before the setting of the Pleiades' (Strabo 15. 1. 17).

τὴν ἔξω θάλασσαν: What Arrian (6. 1. 1, 20. 2) calls ἡ μεγάλη θάλασσα; cf. ch. 73. 1. ἡ ἔξω θάλασσα in contrast to ἡ ἐντὸς θάλασσα = the Mediterranean (Arr. 6. 1. 3).

πολλὰ πορθμεῖα . . . πηξάμενος: Nearchus ap. Arr. *Ind.* 19. 7 gives 800 (not to be emended to 1,800 (as Schmieder ad loc.); see Jacoby *F. Gr. Hist.* 2D. 451 on Nearchus fr. 1 at 19. 7) as the total of warships, transports for troops and horses, and provision ships. Diod. and Curt. (locc. citt.) give a total of 1,000, which is generally accepted. Berve (1. 164, n. 6), however, prefers Ptolemy's figure of 2,000 at Arr. 6. 2. 4 and accepts Schmieder's emendation. But Ptolemy, who is fond of increasing numbers (Jacoby ad loc.), will have included everything that floated (see Smith *EHI* 89, n. 1).

On the river system of the Punjab, 'the land of the Five Rivers', see especially Arr. 5. 4. 2, 6. 14. 5; *Ind.* 3. 10, 4. 8. The Hydaspes, the Hydraotes, and the Hyphasis all flow into the Acesines, which then flows into the Indus.

2. προσβάλλων: 'putting in at' (not 'attacking'), as at *Mar.* 41, 3, προσβαλὼν Τελαμῶνι τῆς Τυρρηνίας καὶ ἀποβάς; cf. Thuc. 6. 4, 8. 12.

ἐχειροῦτο πάντα: Diodorus mentions the surrender of the Siboi (17. 96. 1–2) and operations against the Agalasseis, north of the confluence of the Hydaspes and the Acesines (17. 96. 3–5). Cf. Curt. 9. 4. 2 ff.; Strabo 15. 1. 33 (701); Justin 12. 9. 2.

τοῖς καλουμένοις Μαλλοῖς: The Malli (Malavas) and the Oxydracae or Sudracae (Kshudrakas—see Welles on Diod. 17. 98. 1) were independent tribes living north of the confluence of the Acesines and the Hydraotes, east of the river (see Tarn 2. 280, n. 2). They are described by Arrian (6. 4. 3) as 'the most numerous and war-like of the Indians in these parts', and Diodorus (17. 98. 1) gives their combined forces as 80,000 infantry, 10,000 cavalry, and 700 chariots; so essentially Curt. 9. 4. 15. Fuller (259), however, regards these totals as 'probably much exaggerated'. For the strategy of the Mallian campaign see Fuller 259–63. The town meant here is described by Strabo as πολίχνη τις and by Plutarch (*Mor.* 327 b, 344 c) as ἀνώνυμος κώμη, ἄδοξος πολίχνη; it is therefore not Multan, but a village probably some 80 or 90 miles to the north-east (Smith *EHI* 96, n. 1).

Arrian (6. 11. 3) remarks that 'tradition is unanimous' (ὁ πᾶς λόγος κατέχει) that the event occurred among the Oxydracae. In fact it took place among the Malli; the Oxydracae took no part in the operations and subsequently surrendered to Alexander. Arrian probably means all authors (known to him) except Ptolemy and Aristobulus. It is likely that Plutarch's source is Aristobulus.

3. πρῶτος . . . ἀναβάς: Thinking that the Macedonians were

malingering, Alexander seized a ladder and mounted the wall (Arr.
6. 9. 3). This was the second time that Alexander had had to mount
the wall first in order to shame the Macedonians into attacking—for
the first occasion see Arr. 6. 7. 5 f.

ὀλιγοστὸς ὤν: 'with a few companions'. Cf. *Caes.* 49. 5; *Fab.* 16. 6.
According to the 'vulgate' authors (Diod. 17. 99. 4; Curt. 9. 5. 1 f.;
Justin 12. 9. 5, *sine ullo satellite desiliit*) Alexander leapt down *alone*
within the wall and was seriously wounded *before* Peucestas and the
others joined him. But Arrian (6. 10. 1—from Ptolemy) confirms that
Peucestas, Abreas, and Leonnatus all leapt down with Alexander.

4. τιναξαμένου . . . φέρεσθαι: Arrian (6. 9. 5) comments on the
splendour of his armour. In the *Moralia* (343 e), in a highly rhetorical
passage, Plutarch remarks of Alexander's leap τίνι ἄν τις εἰκάσειεν
ἢ πυρὶ κεραυνίῳ. . . οἷον ἐπὶ γῆν κατέσκηψε φάσμα Φοίβου φλογοειδέσιν
ὅπλοις περιλαμπόμενον; cf. Homer *Il.* 4. 75–80.

5. μετὰ δυεῖν ὑπασπιστῶν: Arrian (6. 11. 7) remarks that all writers
agree that Peucestas was one of those who saved Alexander, but that
there is no agreement about the others. This is borne out by the extant
sources. Arrian himself (6. 9. 3, 11. 7) mentions Leonnatus the bodyguard and Abreas, who was killed. Diod. (17. 99. 4) gives 'Peucestas
and several others', and Curtius (9. 5. 14 f.) names Timaeus, Leonnatus, and Aristonus as well as Peucestas. At *Mor.* 327 b Plutarch names
Ptolemy and Limnaeus, and at *Mor.* 344 d adds Leonnatus. It seems
certain at least that Peucestas and Leonnatus saved Alexander, since
they received golden crowns at Susa explicitly for this feat (Arr. 7. 5.
4 ff.).

Arrian (6. 11. 8) regards the inclusion of Ptolemy as the greatest
blunder of the Alexander-historians; among these he certainly includes Cleitarchus, who (with Timagenes) is cited by Curtius (9. 5.
21) for the statement that Ptolemy was present in the battle.

6. βέλος: The arrow is said by Plut. (*Mor.* 341 c) and Curt. (9. 5. 9)
to have been two cubits (3 ft.) long. Earlier Curtius (8. 9. 28) had
written that the Indians 'sagittas emittunt maiore nisu quam effectu'!

8. Ἀλέξανδρος ἀπέκτεινεν: So Diod. 17. 99. 3, Curt. 9. 5. 11, Justin
12. 9. 12, and Plutarch at *Mor.* 344 d; but Arrian (6. 10. 2) merely
says he kept defending himself.

9. πληγεὶς ὑπέρῳ κατὰ τοῦ τραχήλου: Doubtless from Aristobulus;
see *Mor.* 341 c, ὑπελάσας ⟨δὲ πρὸς τὸ τεῖχος πληγὴν ὑπέρου⟩ ἔλαβε κατὰ
τοῦ αὐχένος, ὡς Ἀριστόβουλος ἱστόρηκε. The supplement is due to
Jacoby, who lists other suggestions on fr. 46. Here and in the *Moralia*,
327 b, 341 c, and 344 d, Plutarch relates that this blow followed the

wound by the arrow; Diod. (loc. cit.) and Curt. (9. 5. 7), with more probability, mention previous blows. However, Arrian (6. 11. 7) states that Ptolemy asserted that there was only the wound in the breast, although some said that Alexander was struck on the helmet by a club *before* this.

11. παραυτίκα ... ἦν λόγος: Cf. Arr. 6. 12. 1.

τῆς ἀκίδος: 'the barb'. 'hamos inesse telo' (Curt. 9. 5. 23).

12. τριῶν δακτύλων ... τεσσάρων: i.e. about 2″×3″. A δάκτυλος was about 7/10th of an inch. At *Mor.* 344 c Plutarch gives the dimensions as four fingers broad and five fingers long. As F. C. Babbitt remarks (in the Loeb ed.), 'Plutarch the rhetorician increases by one finger's-breadth the dimensions of the arrow-point which are given by Plutarch the biographer in his *Life of Alexander*'.

ἔγγιστα θανάτου συνελαυνόμενος: 'brought near to death's door' (Perrin).

13. πολὺν χρόνον κτλ.: According to Arrian Alexander sailed down the Hydraotes to the main camp at the junction with the Acesines as soon as he was able, in order to convince the Macedonians that he was still alive and to dispel their fears. Curtius has a different version: it was in order to put an end to the hopes of the Indians which had been raised by the report of his death. Alexander sets out seven days after his wound.

14. χώραν ... καταστρεφόμενος: Especially the kingdoms of Musicanus and Oxycanus (Porticanus); see Arr. 6. 15. 1–16. 2; Diod. 17. 102, 1–5; Curt. 9. 8. 4–16; Strabo 15. 1. 33 f., cf. 15. 1. 22; Justin 12. 10. 1. For modern accounts see Smith *EHI* 98 ff., *CHI* 376 f. Both writers stress the difficulty of identifying the tribes mentioned, owing to their names being preserved in Greek and the considerable changes in the course of the river since Alexander's day. Cf. Glotz–Cohen 1. 157, n. 187.

LXIV. *Alexander and the Gymnosophists.*

τῶν δὲ Γυμνοσοφιστῶν κτλ.: The revolt of Sambus is historical—see Arr. 6. 16. 3–5; Diod. 17. 102. 6 f.; Curt. 9. 8. 13–15. He had been appointed satrap of the Indian hillmen, but on hearing that his enemy Musicanus had been confirmed in his kingdom he had fled across the Indus. His relatives made submission at Sindimana (perhaps Sihwan—but see Smith *EHI* 101, n. 4). Diodorus and Curtius (following Cleitarchus) report that 80,000 Indians were put to death, and the Brahmans who were responsible for the revolt were executed, as were those who incited Musicanus to revolt (Arr. 6. 16. 5; 17. 2). In general Greek writers failed to distinguish clearly between the Brahmans and the ascetics described in ch. 65, but Nearchus (Strabo 15. 1. 66) states that the Indian 'sophists' were divided into Brahmans, who followed the king as councillors, and the 'men who followed Nature'. Megasthenes (Strabo 15. 1. 59) also distinguished between the Brahmans and Garmanes (i.e. Sramans, Buddhist ascetics). The interrogation of the Indian Gymnosophists by Alexander is found in two main versions. The first group, in which there are ten questions, comprises Plutarch, the so-called Metz Epitome §§ 79–84 contained in a tenth-century Latin MS. (see *Epitoma rerum gestarum Alexandri*, ed. P. H. Thomas (Leipzig, 1960)), and Berlin papyrus 13044 of *c.* 100 B.C. (ed. U. Wilcken, *SB Berlin* 1923, 161 ff., *A. der Gr. u. die indischen Gymnosophisten*). The second group consists of the various versions of the Alexander-Romance (see Tarn *Bactria* 429, n. 7). Boissonade *Anecdota Graeca* I. 145 preserves a text similar to the writers of the first group, but containing only nine questions. The relationship of the various versions is disputed; see Wilcken, op. cit. 174 and Tarn *Bactria*, 429.

Wilcken (loc. cit.) has shown the essential difference between the account of Onesicritus (see ch. 65) and the common original of the two groups. This was clearly written also by a Cynic, but he, unlike Onesicritus, represents Alexander in an unfavourable light; see also Brown 47. The setting represents a powerful and unscrupulous ruler face to face with a wise man—a favourite type of anecdote with the Cynics (see K. von Fritz, *Philologus* Supplbd. 1926, 1 ff., who calls it 'The Sage and Tyrant' type).

The episode is certainly unhistorical. The meeting between Alexander and the Gymnosophists is to be placed in Taxila (see Arr. 7. 1. 5–6, perhaps from Nearchus—Tarn *Bactria* 428, n. 2). It is not clear whether Plutarch differs from the Metz Epitome, where Sambus appears among the Malli, although his historical kingdom lay on the lower Indus, but the similarities between the two accounts are so striking that he probably did not.

LXV. *Onesicritus visits the Indian wise men and converses with Dandamis and Calanus.*

1. δωρησάμενος: With a gift of clothing(!), according to the Metz Epitome and the papyrus.

Strabo 15. 1. 63–5 (715–16) gives a much fuller version of Onesicritus' account of his meeting with the Gymnosophists. It is clear that he claimed to have met them near Taxila—see Megasthenes, cited by

Strabo 15. 1. 68 (718); Arr. 7. 2. 2-4, who almost certainly used Onesicritus. Wilcken (*SB Berlin* 1923, 175), however, considers that Onesicritus invented the whole episode, vivid and consistent though it is, since Aristobulus (ap. Strabo 15. 5. 61 (714)) relates that two of the 'sophists' frequently took dinner standing at Alexander's table. He regards this account as irreconcilable with Onesicritus' statement (in Strabo) that he was sent because Alexander did not think it proper to go himself. Tarn (*Bactria* 428, n. 2) also considers Onesicritus' story fiction, since Arrian (7. 1. 5-6) relates a λόγος that Alexander himself met certain Indian wise men; so Ps.-Call. 3. 11 ff.; Hippolytus philosophus, ap. Diels, *Doxographi Graeci*[3] (Berlin, 1958), 574. But the motivation in Plutarch is to be preferred to that in Strabo. According to him—and his source is Onesicritus no less than Strabo's—Onesicritus was sent to *request* (δεόμενος) the sages to come to Alexander. His statement is supported by Megasthenes (Strabo 15. 1. 68; Arr. 7. 2. 2), where it is expressly stated that Alexander's messengers summoned Mandanis to visit Alexander. The versions of Strabo and Plutarch can be reconciled if we suppose that Onesicritus was sent to *ask* the sages to visit Alexander, but was instructed not to use force to compel them. His mission may well have taken place before Aristobulus saw the Indian 'sophists' in Taxila; indeed their presence there may have been the result of Onesicritus' request; for this view see Brown 46.

But even if Onesicritus did meet the Gymnosophists, it is clear that the doctrine of the wise men is 'good Cynic doctrine' (Brown 45), and does not reflect Indian philosophy. Either Onesicritus used the occasion to expound Cynic doctrines (so Brown 39 ff.), or he regarded these ascetics as true Cynics (Wilcken op. cit., 181); see further Pearson *LHA* 99.

2. τῶν Διογένει . . . συνεσχολακότων: 'one of the pupils of Diogenes the Cynic'. For the verb cf. *Dem.* 5. 7, ὑπομνήμασιν . . . ἐν οἷς ἐγέγραπτο τὸν Δημοσθένη συνεσχολακέναι Πλάτωνι; *Cic.* 4. 5 (in a list of his teachers).

τὸν μὲν Καλανόν: See on ch. 69. 6.

ὑβριστικῶς πάνυ καὶ τραχέως: Mandanis rebuked Calanus ὡς ὑβριστήν, especially after he had censured arrogance (ὕβρις) himself.

ἀποδύντα τὸν χιτῶνα: Onesicritus was wearing the Macedonian chlamys, the kausia, and the high boots (κρηπῖδες).

παρὰ τοῦ Διός: J. E. Powell (*JHS* 59 (1939), 238) makes the attractive suggestion that Plutarch wrote παρ' αὐτοῦ τοῦ Διός. With this reading Calanus means even if Onesicritus had come from Zeus himself, not merely from *the son of Zeus*. It is evident that Onesicritus had described Alexander as the son of Zeus to the Indians; see Arr. 7. 2. 3; Strabo 15. 1. 68 (718).

3. Δάνδαμιν: Kaerst *RE* 4, 2099 and Berve 2. 116 s.v. *Δάνδαμις* (no. 243) hold that Plutarch and Arrian (7. 2. 3) preserve the correct form. Pearson *LHA* 98, n. 58, and J. W. McCrindle *Ancient India* (Calcutta, 1877), 387, prefer Mandanis, Strabo's form (15. 1. 64, 68). **περὶ Σωκράτους κτλ.**: Plutarch summarizes; for the fuller version see Strabo 15. 1. 65. Dandamis means that the Greek philosophers are slaves to convention in not going naked and living the simple life like Gymnosophists. On this passage see Brown 42 ff.

4. ἄλλοι δέ φασι: Certainly not Megasthenes; possibly Nearchus, whose account has largely disappeared. For what remains see Arr. *Ind.* 11. 7, Strabo 15. 1. 66. Nearchus seems to have been on bad terms with Onesicritus; see on 66. 3.

5. ἐκαλεῖτο δὲ Σφίνης: 'The Greeks, catching among the Indian words of greeting which he exchanged with his fellow-countrymen the word kalyāṇa, "lucky", came to call him Kalanos' (E. R. Bevan in *CHI* 359). However, Kroll (*RE* 10, 1544) and Berve (s.v. *Καλανός*, no .396) hold that Kalanos may be the Greek version of the Indian name.

6. τὸ παράδειγμα τῆς ἀρχῆς: In his Roman Oration (§ 18) Aelius Aristides uses a similar *παράδειγμα*. The seer Oebaras tells Cyrus, the founder of the Persian Empire, that if he wanted to be king, 'he ought to go marching around to every part of his empire will he nill he for he saw what happened to the leather bag (*τὴν βύρσαν*): the parts on which he set foot became depressed and touched the ground, while the parts off which he stepped rose up again, and were depressed once more only with another trampling' (trans. J. H. Oliver in his edition of the speech, 'The Ruling Power', in *Trans. Am. Philos. Soc.* N.S. 43 (1953), 871–1003). In his commentary on this section (p. 912) Oliver comments that 'It is clear that Aristides had the story directly or indirectly from Ctesias'. As Onesicritus also uses Ctesias (see Jacoby *F. Gr. Hist.* 2D. 473, 34 ff.), it is possible that he has adapted this illustration to suit Alexander.

βύρσαν ... κατεσκληκυῖαν: 'a dry and shrivelled hide': from *κατασκέλλομαι*, 'become a skeleton, wither away'.

LXVI. *Alexander reaches the Indian Ocean. He dispatches his fleet along the coast and marches through Gedrosia.*

1. ἡ δέ ... ἀνάλωσεν: Plutarch continues his narrative from ch. 63. 14. It is not clear what distance Plutarch envisages as occupying 7 months. Aristobulus (fr. 35, ap. Strabo 15. 1. 17 (692)) says that Alexander left the Hydaspes (i.e. Bucephala) 'a few days before the setting of the Pleiades', i.e. beginning of November 326, and arrived at Pattala 'about the rising of the dog-star', i.e. about the middle of July 325. This period he calls 10 months. Pliny *NH* 6. 60, reckons only 5 months, although this may refer only to the voyage from the confluence of the Acesines and the Indus. The site of Pattala, where the Indus bifurcates, is probably either Bahmanabad (Smith *EHI* 103, n. 1) or Hyderabad (Berve 1. 272; Radet 314). Alexander remained there until about the end of August (see Beloch 3. 2. 305) engaged in the construction of a harbour and dockyards, and in the preparations for Nearchus' voyage.

ἐμβαλὼν δὲ ταῖς ναυσίν . . .: During this period he investigated the two branches of the Indus to discover which was the safer for the fleet. The following events occurred when he reached the Arabian Sea after sailing down the western branch—see Arr. 6. 19. 3–5, *Ind.* 20. 10; Diod. 17. 104. 1; Curt. 9. 9. 27; Justin 12. 10. 4–6.

Σκιλλοῦστιν: Κιλλουτὰ δὲ τῇ νήσῳ τὸ ὄνομα ἔλεγον (? the natives)— Arrian 6. 19. 3 (following Nearchus—Jacoby *F. Gr. Hist.* 2D, 467 on fr. 32–3). There were two islands; Cillouta lay within the delta, the other (unnamed) some 200 stades south in the ocean, at the mouth of the delta; cf. Diod. loc. cit.

2. ἔθυε τοῖς θεοῖς . . .: According to Arrian (loc. cit.) Alexander sacrificed at both islands on consecutive days to the gods to whom Ammon in an oracle had ordered him to sacrifice; he then proceeded out to sea, sacrificed to Poseidon and the other sea gods, poured a libation, and uttered a prayer that Poseidon would bring his fleet safe to the Persian Gulf.

Altheim (1. 204) has connected the sacrifices at the islands with the alleged response given by the oracle at Siwah promising Alexander world rule (see ch. 27. 6), but Hampl (*La Nouvelle Clio* 6 (1954), 110, n. 1) firmly and rightly rejects this view. The sacrifices are to be connected with those made by Alexander when he set off down the Hydaspes (Arr. *Ind.* 18. 11; 6. 3. 1); they are his thank-offering for a successful journey down the rivers.

With regard to the sacrifice in the Ocean, Wilcken 196 writes that 'in the proud and happy consciousness that he (Alexander) had reached a limit of the world, he offered to Poseidon . . . a great sacrifice of gratitude for the past and prayer for the future'; cf. V. E. Ehrenberg (*Festschrift M. Winternitz* (Leipzig, 1933), 287 ff.). But Arrian's narrative offers no hint of this and Hampl, op. cit. 107 ff., points out that Alexander sailed only a short distance from the delta in his search for land.

τὴν φύσιν ἐπεῖδε: 'examined the nature of the ocean and the shore'. For ἐπεῖδον cf. ch. 63. 1 and *Mar.* 13. 2, Σκιπίωνος γὰρ . . . βουληθέντος ἐπιδεῖν μὴ μόνον τὰ ὅπλα μηδὲ τοὺς ἵππους ἀλλὰ καὶ τοὺς ὀρεῖς καὶ τὰς ἁμάξας. Alexander personally went with his cavalry three days' march along the coast observing the nature of the country and ordering wells to be dug; subsequently he sent troops to continue this work.

3. τὰς μὲν ναῦς . . . Ὀνησίκριτον: On the strained relations between the two men see especially Jacoby *F. Gr. Hist.* 2D. 469 (on T. 4–6), Brown 8–10, 105 f., Pearson *LHA* 83 f. Onesicritus was steersman (κυβερνήτης) of the king's ship on the voyage down the Indus (Arr. 6. 2. 3; *Ind.* 18. 9) and may have been Chief Steersman (ἀρχικυβερνήτης), as Strabo 15. 1. 28, 2. 4, and Plut. *Mor.* 331 e call him, on the voyage from the Indus to the Persian Gulf (so Pearson loc. cit.; *contra* Jacoby loc. cit.). But he lied when he claimed to be admiral (Nearchus ap. Arr. 6. 2. 3), for this post belonged to Nearchus alone; Jacoby *F. Gr. Hist.* 2D. 470, justly criticizes Berve's attempt to place the two men on an equality. Curt. 9. 10. 3, 'Nearcho atque Onesicrito nauticae rei peritis imperavit', is probably based on Onesicritus.

The fleet was to sail along the coast into the Persian Gulf to rejoin Alexander at the mouth of the Euphrates (Arr. 6. 19. 5, *Ind.* 20 ff.; Diod. 17. 104. 3; Strabo 15. 2. 4 (721); Pliny *NH* 6. 96–100 = Onesicritus fr. 28). Nearchus was to leave the eastern branch of the Indus about the end of October, when the north-east monsoon was due, but the threatening attitude of the natives forced him to start about 21 September 325. Consequently he had to remain near the site of Karachi for 24 days until the monsoon began (Strabo 15. 2. 5; Arr. *Ind.* 21).

4. αὐτὸς δὲ πεζῇ . . .: The hardships of the desert march are vividly described by Arrian 6. 21. 3–26 and Strabo 15. 720–3. Cf. Diod. 17. 104–5; Curt. 9. 10. 4–16; Justin 12. 10. 7. On Alexander's motives for the march, see Arr. 6. 24. 2–3, Strabo 15. 1. 5 = Nearchus fr. 3 a, b; cf. Strabo 15. 2. 4 f.

According to Nearchus, Alexander chose this route in order not only to support the fleet with provisions and water but also to surpass Cyrus and Semiramis, who were said to have met with disaster in attempting to cross the desert with their armies. The latter motive (given by other writers also; see Arr. loc. cit.) need not be doubted: Alexander wished to cross the desert with a large force to restore his reputation (damaged at the Hyphasis) for superhuman achievement. We may compare his rivalry with Perseus and Heracles as a motive for the journey to Siwah (Arr. 3. 3. 1–2). Nearchus was the only writer to maintain that Alexander was ignorant of the difficulty of the route (Arr. 6. 24. 2)—an obvious attempt to exculpate the king.

δι' Ὠρειτῶν: Plutarch writes loosely or, perhaps more probably, has only a vague idea of the geography of the region; for the disaster which overtook Alexander occurred not among the Oreitae but in the Gedrosian desert. Strabo (15. 2. 1–2), in describing the satrapy of Ariana, proceeds from east to west along the coast and lists the Oreitae, the Ichthyophagi and the Carmanians. Gedrosia lies inland (ὑπερκεῖται) from the Ichthyophagi; cf. Arr. *Ind.* 26. 1.

The extent of the disaster is disputed. Tarn (1. 107) holds that Alexander had only 8,000–10,000 fighting men with him and that he 'extricated the army without much loss'; cf. Glotz–Cohen 1. 162, who give 10,000–12,000 men, and Robinson 206, who gives 15,000. On the other hand Strasburger, *Hermes* 80 (1952), 486 ff., puts the army with Alexander at not less than 60,000–70,000 fighting men of whom at most 15,000 will have survived; for similar figures cf. Beloch 3. 2. 344 f., Berve 1. 180 ff. The only evidence for Alexander's forces apart from Plutarch is given by Curtius 8. 5. 4 (120,000 fighting men at the start of the Indian campaign) and Nearchus ap. Arr. *Ind.* 19. 5 (120,000 fighting men at the start of the voyage down the Hydaspes). It seems clear that a high figure is more probable than a low one, as Nearchus is a reliable source, and that Strasburger is nearer the mark than Tarn; but all figures are estimates. The losses were enormous, and the responsibility was Alexander's; see Schachermeyr 382 f. On his route see Sir Aurel Stein, *Geog. Jour.* 102 (1943), 193 ff. with Strasburger's criticisms in *Hermes* 82 (1954), 251 ff.

6. ἀνθρώπων κακοβίων: The Ichthyophagi are meant; for the sheep see the description in Arr. *Ind.* 26. 7 and cf. Strabo 15. 2. 2; Diod. 17. 105. 5; Curt. 9. 10. 10.

προσφέρεσθαι: 'to take food or drink'. Cf. *Cic.* 3. 7, ἀρρωστίᾳ στομάχου μικρὰ καὶ γλίσχρα μόγις ὀψὲ τῆς ὥρας προσφερόμενος. The verb is very frequent in Plutarch in this sense; see Holden on *Dem.* 30. 5.

7. ἐν ἡμέραις ἑξήκοντα: At Pura, the capital of Gedrosia, which he reached sixty days after leaving the territory of the Oreitae, i.e. during November 325; see Strabo 15. 2. 7; Arr. 6. 27. 1; Diod. 17. 106. 1; Curt. 9. 10. 18. On the chronology of this period, Beloch 3. 2. 320 ff. Plutarch apparently thinks that Alexander *now* entered Gedrosia; so Curt. loc. cit., 'exercitus tandem in Cedrosiae fines perducitur'.

τῶν ἔγγιστα σατράπων ...: Phratraphernes, the satrap of Parthia, and Stasanor, satrap of Areia and Drangiane, are meant. According to Diod. 17. 105. 7 and Curt. 9. 10. 17 f. they received instructions from Alexander to send to the borders of Carmania camels and transport animals with provisions. In Arrian's version they did so on their own initiative (6. 27. 6). Astaspes, the satrap of Carmania,

COMMENTARY LXVII. 4

failed to anticipate Alexander's needs and was later executed on suspicion of a wish to revolt (Curt. 9. 10. 21, 29).

LXVII. *The Revel through Carmania. Alexander and Bagoas.*

1. ἀναλαβὼν . . . τὴν δύναμιν: At Pura; see Arr. 6. 27. 1; Curt. 9. 10. 18; Diod. 17. 106. 1. The stop was brief—Strabo 15. 2. 7.

κώμῳ χρώμενος: Curt. (9. 10. 24 ff.) gives an elaborate and rhetorical description of this celebration, which was said to be an imitation of Dionysus' triumphal procession after his victory over the Indians (see Strabo 15. 1. 6); Diod. 17. 106. 1 also mentions it. Arrian, however, states (6. 28. 1–3) that neither Ptolemy nor Aristobulus nor any reputable authority mentions this story and he expressly rejects it, setting it down as legend. Most modern writers agree, although Radet characteristically accepts it in a chapter entitled 'La Bacchanale de Carmanie' (pp. 337 ff.). Schachermeyr 385 accepts the fact of the κῶμος, but rejects the view that it was ordered by Alexander. Probably the legend arose from the festivities held in Carmania to mark the Indian victory and the safe passage of the army through the Gedrosian desert(!) (Arr. 6. 28. 3); for this view see Wilcken 201, Welles on Diod. 17. 106. 1. The celebration which followed shortly after when Nearchus joined Alexander in Carmania may also be responsible (*Ind.* 36. 3). The legend is often assigned to Cleitarchus, e.g. by Tarn 2. 46, Wilcken loc. cit.; but there is no certainty.

2. θυμέλης: Originally an altar, then particularly the altar of Dionysus in the theatre; hence a 'stage, platform'.

ἐν ὑψηλῷ . . . πλαισίῳ: 'on a lofty, conspicuous, oblong scaffold'.

4. ῥυτοῖς: drinking-cups or horns, running to a point, where there was a small hole through which the wine flowed in a thin stream. They were frequently made in elaborate shapes, e.g. elephant, trireme, dwarf; the plates at the end of vol. 5 of the Loeb Athenaeus show a rhyton in the shape of a horse's head—the wine would flow from its mouth. For more details see Athenaeus 11. 496 f–7 e.

θηρικλείοις: Athenaeus (11. 470 e–2 d—the *locus classicus*) tells us that these vessels were generally held to be named after their inventor Thericles, a Corinthian working at Athens in the time of Aristophanes. The alternative view, that they were so-called because they featured the skins of wild animals (θηρία) is now discounted. Athenaeus describes the vessels as kylikes with concave sides, and elsewhere (469 b) calls them expensive metal vessels. But he mentions a Thericlean krater and there were evidently several shapes in different materials. For modern views see *RE* 5A, 2367 f. (Nachod), Pfuhl, *Malerei u. Zeichnung der Griechen* (München, 1923), 1. 460.

κυαθίζοντες: Madvig's emendation seems necessary. The meaning 'draw wine by dipping cup into bowl' assigned to βαπτίζοντες by LSJ is not supported by Aristopho 14. 5, where the sense seems to be rather 'soused'. For κυαθίζειν in this sense see especially Polyb. 8. 6. 6, ταῖς μὲν ναυσὶν αὐτοῦ κυαθίζειν ἐκ θαλάττης Ἀρχιμήδη, and cf. *Marc.* 17. 2 (as emended).

7. τῆς Γεδρωσίας: 'Plutarch has by a mere slip written "Gedrosia" for "Carmania" ' (Badian, *CQ* N.s. 8 (1958), 151). Dacier's Καρμανίας is unjustified. For some examples of such arbitrary slips see Tarn 2. 341, n. 5.

λέγεται δέ κτλ.: For this incident cf. Athenaeus 13. 603 a–b, φιλόπαις δ᾽ ἦν ἐκμανῶς καὶ Ἀλέξανδρος ὁ βασιλεύς. Δικαίαρχος γοῦν ἐν τῷ περὶ τῆς ἐν ᾽Ιλίῳ θυσίας Βαγώου τοῦ εὐνούχου οὕτως αὐτόν φησιν ἡττᾶσθαι ὡς ἐν ὄψει θεάτρου ὅλου καταφιλεῖν αὐτὸν ἀνακλάσαντα, καὶ τῶν θεατῶν ἐπιφωνησάντων μετὰ κρότου οὐκ ἀπειθήσας πάλιν ἀνακλάσας ἐφίλησεν. Tarn (2. 320 ff.) argues that Dicaearchus has invented the whole story; but as he was a pupil of Aristotle and a contemporary of Alexander was he likely to have invented an incident whose refutation would expose him to ridicule? Tarn finds a motive in the fact that Dicaearchus was a Peripatetic and so might seek, in revenge for Callisthenes' execution, to defame Alexander by showing him as a homosexual. However, Badian has shown (op. cit., 150 ff.) that there is little or no evidence for a Peripatetic attack on Alexander such as Tarn envisages. Moreover, it appears that Dicaearchus differed with Theophrastus and with Aristotle himself; see frs. 25 ff. with commentary on pp. 50 ff. in F. Wehrli, *Dikaiarchos* (Basle, 1944). Badian rightly rejects Tarn's view that the location in Gedrosia instead of Carmania and the reference to a 'theatre' prove the anecdote a fiction. E. Mensching, *Historia* 12 (1963), 276 ff., also regards it as improbable that the Bagoas story was invented by Dicaearchus. In particular he rightly holds that Dicaearchus did not pass an unfavourable verdict on Alexander; the unfavourable attitude in Athenaeus is due to that writer or to an intermediary. Probably few contemporaries of Alexander would have been shocked by the story. Even if D. did invent it, this would not mean that he was actuated by malice. It is by no means certain that, as Badian maintains, Plutarch's account does not derive from Dicaearchus. He may be using the same source as Athenaeus if we allow for the different emphasis of the two authors; in Plutarch the emphasis is on drunkenness, in Athenaeus on homosexuality.

περιβαλών: 'embracing'. For this use LSJ cite only Xen. *An.* 4. 7. 25, but there are ten other instances of the verb in Plutarch. It usually occurs in the aorist participle and is, consequently, frequently confused with περιλαμβάνειν, but at *Ti. Gracch.* 12. 2 περιέβαλλεν is certain. At *Aem.* 10. 5 and *Ant.* 10. 9 the verb is also used with καταφιλεῖν. For this verb, 'kiss passionately', see Lucian *Am.* 13.

LXVIII. *The arrival of Nearchus. Alexander plans to circumnavigate Africa. Revolt and misgovernment in the Empire. Dispute between Cleopatra and Olympias. Alexander punishes Abulites and Oxyartes.*

1. **ἐνταῦθα**: In December 325 Nearchus landed in the district of Harmozeia (Hormuz) and met Alexander after a journey of five days inland; their meeting is vividly described at Arr. *Ind.* 33 ff., from Nearchus' own account. Diodorus (17. 106. 4) wrongly writes of a meeting in a sea-side town called Salmus.

ὥρμησεν αὐτός . . .: Various versions of Alexander's western plans are extant. Curtius (10. 1. 17–19—at the time of the meeting with Nearchus) relates that Alexander intended to attack Carthage *from Syria*, march through North Africa to the 'Pillars of Hercules' and return (? by sea) past the Alps and Italy to Greece. 'With this in view' Alexander ordered 700 *septiremes* to be built at Thapsus (on the Euphrates) and taken to Babylon. He does not explain how these ships could contribute to a western expedition. Arrian (7. 1. 2–3) relates, on the authority of 'some historians' (cf., however, 4. 7. 5, where he appears to give his own opinion) that Alexander planned to circumnavigate Arabia and Africa, sail into the Mediterranean and conquer Libya and Africa. Earlier, in his speech at the Hyphasis (Arr. 5. 26. 3), Alexander had outlined a similar plan. No prudent man, however, will place much reliance on Arrian's speeches (the geography in § 2 of this speech is not Alexander's; see 44. 1 n.), and it is clear that neither Ptolemy nor Aristobulus is the source of his information in Book 7. Some scholars, indeed, have found in their silence an argument in favour of the view that Alexander never entertained such plans, but there is no reason why they should have mentioned his future intentions. Nevertheless the source of the statements of Plutarch, Curtius, and Arrian is unknown. This applies whether we conceive of a single plan for circumnavigation and conquest (as given by Arrian), or of an (earlier) plan to circumnavigate Africa given up in favour of a direct attack on Carthage (given in part by Plutarch and in garbled form by Curtius); so Schachermeyr 445, 525, n. 276; id. *JOEAI* 137 f.

The chief support for the view that Alexander intended western conquests has been found in the Plans ('Hypomnemata') said by

Diodorus (18. 4. 2 ff.) to have been left behind by Alexander at his death and presented by Perdiccas to the army assembly for acceptance or rejection. Among the most important of these (τὰ μέγιστα καὶ μνήμης ἄξια) he lists a project to build 1,000 ships (larger than triremes) in Phoenicia, Syria, Cilicia, and Cyprus, for an expedition against Carthage and the maritime peoples of North Africa, against Spain and the coast as far as Sicily. The authenticity of these Plans has been much discussed (see the works cited at the end of this note), and only a few important points can be made here. Tarn (2. 379 f.) and Andreotti (134 f.) have maintained that the assembly was not competent to deal with such matters; but we know too little of the authority of the assembly to be sure of this and it can be argued, in any case, that the exceptional circumstances justified such a course. Formerly the authority of the well-informed and trustworthy Hieronymus of Cardia (see T. S. Brown, *AHR* 52 (1946/7), 684 ff.) was considered sufficient guarantee of the Plans' genuineness—despite Tarn's arguments (most recently 2. 380 f.), it is likely that he is Diodorus' source—but it is now conceded that acceptance or rejection must depend on their content.

The proposal to build six costly temples in Greece and Macedonia, where temples already existed, and that for an interchange of population between Europe and Asia may excite suspicion, but nothing can be proved either way. Nevertheless the Plans contain some surprising omissions; there is no mention of the Arabian expedition (see 76. 2 n.), or of the rebuilding of the temple of Bel at Babylon (see 73. 1 n.). It can be maintained that the Plans dealt only with future projects, but the force of this argument is much weakened by the inclusion of a plan to complete the memorial to Hephaestion (72. 5 n.), unless this is due to Alexander's concern for his friend's memory. Moreover the authenticity of the Plans is, in my opinion, rendered questionable by the statement (Diod. 18. 4. 6) that *all* the Plans were cancelled (ἔκριναν μηδὲν τῶν εἰρημένων συντελεῖν); for we know that the memorial to Hephaestion was certainly completed. But what absolutely forbids acceptance of the Plans as a whole is the proposal to erect a memorial to Philip (presumably at Aegae in Macedonia, as is often said, although Diodorus gives no indication of location) *in the same shape and of the same size as the largest of the Egyptian pyramids.* For if Alexander did intend to build a memorial of this nature (wherever it was to be) then he must have been not merely a megalomaniac but a raving lunatic. The falsity of this particular item need not, of course, involve the condemnation of *all* the Plans; but the project for western conquest must be regarded with suspicion, for it may be pure speculation about his intentions. Yet it would be rash to affirm that Alexander had no such plans; we may even agree with

Arrian (7. 1. 4) that Alexander would not have been satisfied even if he added Europe to Asia. It is true that a rational review of the military and economic situation would have ruled out projects of this magnitude, as Andreotti rightly stresses (139 f.). But Alexander's state of mind at this time was distinctly peculiar, if we may judge by the nature and cost of Hephaestion's memorial, by his letter to Cleomenes, and by his *request* for deification; see *CQ* N.s. 3 (1953), 156 f.

Bibliography: Schachermeyr 451 ff., and especially id. *JOEAI* 41 (1954), 118–40 (with full bibliography on pp. 118–19)—the best case for acceptance; against acceptance, Tarn 2. 378 ff., Hampl, *Studies* . . . *Robinson* 819 ff.; add to Schachermeyr's list Pearson, *Historia* 3 (1955), 451 ff. (the best short account, although too dependent on Tarn), and Andreotti, *Saeculum* 8 (1957), 133 ff. (both against).

3. ἡ δ' ἄνω στρατεία . . .: For the campaign in Bactria and India see ch. 57 ff., for Alexander's wound ch. 63. 2 ff., and for the losses in Gedrosia ch. 66. 4 n. For these same reasons for unrest see Arr. 7. 4. 2–3.

ἀπιστίᾳ τῆς σωτηρίας . . .: cf. Curt. 10. 1. 7, 'rex, cognita causa, pronuntiavit ab accusatoribus unum et id maximum crimen esse praeteritum, desperationem salutis suae'.

Various revolts had indeed taken place (see Arr. 6. 27. 3, 29. 3; Curt. 9. 10. 19 f.), but the satraps had, in general, remained loyal. Yet we know of the executions of three satraps, Astaspes, Orxines, and Autophradates (Berve nos. 173, 592, 189), apart from those of Abulites and Oxathres (see 68. 7). It is noteworthy that two of these were put to death 'on suspicion'. The excuse put forward by Arrian (7. 4. 3) and Curtius (10. 1. 39)—cf. *Alex.* 42. 3–4—that Alexander was too ready to listen to accusations is doubtless true, but it tends to obscure the king's fear of rebellion. At this time the four generals in Media—Cleander, Sitalces, Heracon, and Agathon—were summoned to court and three at least were executed (Arr. 6. 27. 3–4, Curt. 10. 1. 1–9), allegedly for plundering tombs and oppressing the inhabitants.

For a fully documented, critical examination of this important period see Badian, *JHS* 81 (1961), 16–43, who writes, justifiably, that 'It is clearly no exaggeration to speak of a reign of terror'. Note, in particular, his argument that Alexander's concern for good government (see Arr. 6. 27. 5) does not fully explain the execution of the generals, since Cleomenes, the satrap of Egypt (Berve no. 431), who remained unharmed, had committed crimes at least as great; for Alexander's letter to Cleomenes, see 72. 5 n. Badian's suggestion, that the king feared rebellion by this powerful group, carries conviction. I should, however, attach little importance to the retention of satraps at court; this need not, as Badian admits, have a sinister implication. In fact, no instance of 'detention' is known, since Stasanor (the instance given) was soon sent back to his satrapy (Arr. 6. 29. 1). See further § 7 below.

4. ὅπου . . . ὑπὸ γυναικός: On Olympias' relations with Antipater see ch. 39. 11. Plutarch seems to mean that this event took place in 324; in fact not later than 331 Olympias, worsted in her struggle with Antipater, retired to her native Epirus (Diod. 18. 49. 4). There her daughter Cleopatra had acted as regent since 334 when her husband Alexander left for South Italy. He was killed there late in 331 and Olympias was already in Epirus by the time his corpse arrived home (Livy 8. 24. 17). Plutarch's suggestion that Cleopatra and Olympias were leagued against Antipater is rejected by Berve (2. 212), who holds correctly that Cleopatra withdrew to Macedonia, doubtless after a struggle, to escape her formidable mother's domination. There is no evidence that Cleopatra sought to displace Antipater in Macedonia. She remained there and Olympias in Epirus until Alexander's death. Hypereides (*pro Euxippo* 25) refers to Olympias' claim to control Molossia, which meant in effect controlling Epirus at this date; see C. Klotzsch, *Epeirotische Geschichte* (Berlin, 1911). From there in 324 she demanded the surrender of Harpalus by the Athenians (Diod. 17. 108, 7).

Νέαρχον . . . ἔπεμψεν: Arr. 6. 28. 6, *Ind.* 36. 4–9; Diod. 17. 107. 1; Curt. 10. 1. 16. Nearchus was to sail up the Pasitigris and join Alexander at *Susa*—for his meeting with the king see Arr. *Ind.* 42. 7 f.; 7. 5. 6. Curtius and Diodorus wrongly think of a voyage up the Euphrates to Babylon. Plutarch (ch. 73. 1) follows the same source, presumably Cleitarchus.

ἐμπλῆσαι † πολεμίων: *Locus nondum sanatus.* Reiske's πόλεων is perhaps nearest the manuscript reading, but Alexander will hardly have been thinking of founding cities at this time—Arr. 7. 19. 5; 20. 2 refer to a later period. H. Erbse (*Rh. Mus.* 100 (1957), 285) proposes σταθμῶν, 'stations for ships', which gives good sense but seems hardly likely to have been corrupted into πολεμίων.

καταβαίνων: Alexander advanced inland to Pasargadae. Hence Reiske proposed ἀναβαίνων; but the error may be due to Plutarch's defective geography.

ἐκόλαζε τοὺς πονηρούς . . .: Plutarch includes the satraps; on the executions see above 68. 3 n.

7. Ἀβουλίτου: Abulites had administered Susiane under Darius III. He surrendered Susa and its treasures (see 36. 1 n.) to Alexander, who confirmed him in his satrapy (Arr. 3. 16. 7 ff., Curt. 5. 2. 8 ff., Diod. 17. 65. 5). His son Oxathres (Berve no. 585), whom Plutarch calls

Oxyartes by confusion with Roxane's father, had been pardoned with his father and subsequently was appointed satrap of Paraetacene (Arr. 3. 19. 2), perhaps under Abulites.

Tarn (2. 299) remarks that Alexander did not use a sarissa and regards the story as invented; but, although the sarissa may be a theatrical detail (so Berve 2. 291), the executions are confirmed by Arrian (7. 4. 1).

μηδὲν . . . παρασκευάσαντος: That Alexander sent a request for assistance to the satrap of distant Susiane is highly unlikely—for the evidence see 66. 7 n. Badian (CQ N.s. 8 (1958), 148; JHS 81 (1961), 21) is probably right to connect the executions with Alexander's need to find a scapegoat for his ill-planned march through Gedrosia. It hardly admits of doubt that Apollophanes, the satrap of Gedrosia (Berve no. 105), who was deposed by Alexander for failing to carry out his orders (Arr. 6. 27. 1), would have been executed, had he not been (unknown to Alexander) already killed in battle against the Oreitae (Arr. Ind. 23. 5).

LXIX. *Alexander pays the customary dues to the Persian women. He punishes the robber of Cyrus' tomb. Calanus' death.*

1–2. ἐν δὲ Πέρσαις . . .: At Pasargadae. The origin of this custom was related by Ctesias, whose account is preserved by Plutarch (*Mor.* 246 a, b), Nicolaus Damascenus (*F. Gr. Hist.* no. 90, fr. 66 at p. 369), Justin 1. 6. 13 ff., and Polyaenus 7. 45. 2. When Cyrus revolted from the Medes, the Persians were defeated by Astyages near Pasargadae and fled in disorder. The Persian women met them and shamed them into renewing the battle, in which they were victorious. As a reward Cyrus instituted this payment.

Plutarch is our only authority for the statement about Ochus (Artaxerxes III Ochus) who reigned from 358–338; his source is evidently an Alexander-historian, possibly Aristobulus. His statement is doubtful, since during his reign Ochus had a palace constructed on the terrace at Persepolis (Olmstead 489). On these sections see further Stadter 53 ff.

3. τὸν K. τάφον: The tomb of Cyrus the Elder was situated in the royal park at Pasargadae, the ancient capital of Persia. The task of restoration was entrusted to Aristobulus, who described the tomb both as he saw it intact in 330 and after it had been plundered; see Arr. 6. 29. 4–30. 2; Strabo 15. 3. 7 (730) = Aristobulus fr. 51 a, 51 b. Aristobulus' description agrees remarkably well with the extant remains of the Mešed mâder i Suleiman; see Herzfeld, *Klio* 8 (1908), 36–43. It is often reproduced, e.g. in *CAH* Plates 1. 312 b and

Schachermeyr Tafel XII. Onesicritus (fr. 34), on the other hand, made the tomb ten storeys high and in Ps.-Call. (2. 18. 1) it has 12 storeys!

3. Πουλαμάχος: Nothing further is known of this man (Berve no. 679). Plutarch's statement cannot be accepted in view of the evidence of Aristobulus (Arr. 6. 29. 11) that the Magi, the hereditary guardians of the tomb, even under torture did not incriminate themselves or anyone else. Curtius' statement (10. 1. 22 ff.) that Orxines, the satrap of Persia, was falsely charged with this crime by the eunuch Bagoas and executed is exposed to the same objection. Arrian (6. 30. 1–2) says only that Orxines was put to death for plundering royal tombs and temples and putting Persians to death without cause. See, however, Badian's arguments (*CQ* N.s. 8 (1958), 147 ff.) in favour of Curtius' version.

4. Ἑλληνικοῖς ὑποχαράξαι γράμμασιν: 'to inscribe underneath in Greek'. Aristobulus (fr. 51 a, b = Arr. 6. 29. 8, Strabo 15. 3. 7) says that the inscription was in Persian and ran thus: ὦ ἄνθρωπε, ἐγὼ Κῦρός εἰμι ὁ Καμβύσου ὁ τὴν ἀρχὴν Πέρσαις καταστησάμενος [κτησάμενος, Strabo] καὶ τῆς Ἀσίας βασιλεύσας [βασιλεύς, Strabo]. Μὴ οὖν φθονήσῃς μοι τοῦ μνήματος. He says nothing of a Greek version inscribed underneath, but the third-century writer Aristos of Salamis (*F. Gr. Hist.* no. 143, fr. 1), who mentions both a Greek and a Persian version, may support Plutarch's statement. Onesicritus (fr. 34 = Strabo loc. cit.) records a 'Greek inscription in Persian letters', but his account does not inspire confidence (see above).

6. ὁ δὲ Καλανός: Calanus fell ill at Pasargadae (Strabo 15. 717) and his funeral took place near the borders of Persia and Susiane (Diod. 17. 107. 1; Arr. 7. 3. 1), where Plutarch appears to place it. Aelian *VH* 5. 6 wrongly puts it in Babylon.

This incident made a deep impression on the onlookers and most writers on Alexander included it in their works; see Chares fr. 19, Onesicritus fr. 18, Nearchus fr. 4; Arrian is probably based on Ptolemy, who was entrusted with the erection of the pyre (Berve 2. 187). For the vogue of the story in antiquity see M. Hadas, *Hellenistic Culture* (New York, 1959), 178 f. Strabo loc. cit. stresses the lack of agreement in detail among writers; cf. Arr. 7. 3. 2.

7. ἐπευξάμενος ... ἀπαρξάμενος: The regular preliminaries to a sacrifice; see, e.g., Homer *Il.* 3. 273 ff. The cutting off of the hair is a symbolic act signifying the devotion of the whole body; for Indian parallels see Berve 2. 187, n. 2. For κατασπένδω = 'devote' cf. *Sert.* 14. 5 and Strabo 3. 4. 18 (both of the followers of Sertorius).

αὐτὸν δ' ἐκεῖνον κτλ.: Arrian (7. 18. 6) gives the story as a λόγος—no one paid any attention to Calanus' words until Alexander's death in Babylon recalled them. Cicero (*De div.* 1. 47) cites the utterance to show that even barbarians possess 'quiddam praesentiens atque divinans'; cf. Val. Max. 1. 8. ext. 10.

Ziegler (*Rh. Mus.* 84 (1935), 383) suggested reading κατόψεσθαι or transposing ἐν Βαβυλῶνι to precede χρόνον to avoid the hiatus; but Kronenberg (*Mnemos.* 5 (1937), 311) notes over twenty instances of hiatus after proper names.

8. κατακλιθεὶς καὶ συγκαλυψάμενος: Two versions of Calanus' conduct were current; Plutarch's account agrees with those of Arrian (7. 3. 5), οὕτω δὴ ἐπιβάντα τῇ πυρᾷ κατακλιθῆναι μὲν ἐν κόσμῳ, and Strabo 15. 717, γενομένης δὲ πυρᾶς καὶ τεθείσης ἐπ' αὐτῆς χρυσῆς κλίνης, κατακλιθέντα εἰς αὐτήν, ἐγκαλυψάμενον ἐμπρησθῆναι; cf. Aelian *VH* 5. 6, ἀτρέπτως εἱστήκει. In the rival version (Chares fr. 19 = Athenaeus 437 a, and Onesicritus fr. 18 = Lucian *De morte Peregrini* 25) Calanus is said to have *hurled* himself into the fire. As Onesicritus (ap. Strabo 15. 1. 65 ad fin.) writes that the Gymnosophist who commits suicide sits down on the pyre, orders it to be lighted and is consumed without moving (ἀκίνητον καίεσθαι), it is possible, in view of his dislike of Calanus (see Brown 77), that he has depicted him as failing to observe the traditional practice. Chares will have followed his version.

ἐκαλλιέρησεν ἑαυτόν: 'he sacrificed himself acceptably' (Perrin); lit. 'with good omens'.

τῷ πατρίῳ νόμῳ κτλ.: Onesicritus (fr. 17 a = Strabo 15. 1. 65) says that disease was regarded by the Gymnosophists as most disgraceful and that they committed suicide to avoid it. This is denied by Megasthenes (ap. Strabo 15. 1. 68), Μεγασθένης δ' ἐν τοῖς μὲν φιλοσόφοις οὐκ εἶναι δόγμα φησὶν ἑαυτοὺς ἐξάγειν. τοὺς δὲ ποιοῦντας τοῦτο νεανικοὺς κρίνεσθαι. But Zarmarus (see below) is said to have burned himself κατὰ τὰ πάτρια Ἰνδῶν ἔθη (Strabo 15. 720; cf. Cassius Dio 54. 9).

9. πολλοῖς ἔτεσιν ὕστερον: Among the many embassies which reached Augustus at Samos in the winter of 20 b.c. was one from an Indian king Porus (or Pandion; see Strabo 15. 686). The three surviving ambassadors were seen by Nicolaus Damascenus at Antioch and his account (*F. Gr. Hist.* no. 90, fr. 100) was used by Strabo and probably by Cassius Dio. He relates that with the embassy came a Gymnosophist, called by Strabo Zarmanochegas, by Cassius Dio Zarmarus. This man went to Athens, was initiated into the mysteries, and burnt himself there. His act was commemorated by an inscription on his tomb (Strabo loc. cit.).

LXX. *A fatal drinking contest. The Susa marriages. Payment of the soldiers' debts. Antigenes' fraud.*

1. ὁ δ' Ἀλέξανδρος: According to Athenaeus (437 a–b = Chares fr. 19 a) and Aelian *VH* 2. 41, Alexander first held a γυμνικὸν ἀγῶνα καὶ μουσικόν and added this drinking contest to honour Calanus and to gratify the Indian fondness for wine. Aelian says it was native to the Indians. The prize of a crown is confirmed by Aelian, ὁ δὲ τὰ νικητήρια ἀναδησάμενος ἐν αὐτοῖς ἦν Πρόμαχος. Nothing further is known of Promachus.

2. στέφανον ταλαντιαῖον: So Sintenis for the MSS. στέφανον τάλαντον. Both Athenaeus and Aelian say that the winner received a talent, with thirty minae and ten minae respectively for second and third. Less probable is Stephanus' suggestion, στέφανον καὶ τάλαντον.

Thirty-five died immediately and six a short time later in their tents (Athenaeus loc. cit.). Hence Reiske favoured πίνοντες, the reading of Λ—'inter potandum ipso in triclinio exspirabant'. But Athenaeus writes τῶν οὖν πιόντων . . . παραχρῆμα ἐτελεύτησαν.

3. τῶν δ' ἑταίρων γάμον: The festivities, which lasted for five days in April 324, were described in detail by Chares, the Royal Chamberlain, who was doubtless an eyewitness. His account is preserved (in part) by Athenaeus (538 b–539 a = fr. 4) and, less fully, by Aelian *VH* 8. 7; it is to be preferred to Arr. 7. 4. 4 ff., even if this derives from Ptolemy (so Tarn 2. 333, n. 1; *contra* Strasburger 46); see also Diod. 17. 107. 6 and Curt. 10. 3. 11–12.

Alexander's object was not to 'celebrate the conquest of the Persian empire', as Tarn 1. 110 maintains; it symbolized rather 'the intermingling of the Macedonians with the Persians . . . and with the Medes their kinsmen and the other Iranians' (Wilcken 208—the best account). Hampl, *La Nouvelle Clio* 6 (1954), 118 f., rightly stresses that this 'policy of fusion' has nothing to do with a conception aiming at a union of peoples and continents, as asserted by Tarn loc. cit., Radet 342, and others, who wrongly think of mass marriages on an enormous scale (see below). Hampl, loc. cit., regards the marriages as an attempt to settle the differences between the Macedonians and the Persians, which made Alexander's position as 'King of the Persian Empire' very difficult. Schachermeyr 398 ff. emphasises the 'titanic' quality of Alexander who was able to 'persuade' (ἔπεισε, Diod. loc. cit.) ninety of his leading followers to take Persian wives, of whom almost all rid themselves after Alexander's death.

Not all writers welcomed the marriages as enthusiastically as Plutarch did in the *Moralia* (329 e, f); e.g. Justin (12. 10. 10) says that Alexander weds the noble Asiatics to the Macedonians 'ut communi facto *crimen* regis levaretur'. It is noteworthy that in the *Life* Plutarch conspicuously fails to register enthusiasm for the marriages. Elsewhere (*Mor.* 338 d) he himself comments on the political advantages of the marriages.

C. M. Robertson, *JRS* 45 (1955), 58 ff., suggests that the Susa marriages are portrayed on the Boscoreale paintings.

Στάτειραν: The eldest daughter of Darius is uniformly called Stateira, perhaps by confusion with her mother, except by Arr. 7. 4. 4 who in his list of weddings gives the official (correct) name, Barsine (see Tarn 2. 334, n. 4, and ch. 21 above). On her death at the hands of Roxane see ch. 77. 6. Aristobulus (ap. Arr. loc. cit.) relates that Alexander married Parysatis, the younger daughter of Ochus, as well as Stateira; if this is true, Alexander will have intended to link himself with *both* the royal houses of Persia.

διανέμων κτλ.: 92 of Alexander's Companions married Persian women. This is the figure given by Chares in Athenaeus; Aelian has 90 (a round number) and Plutarch at *Mor.* 329 e gives 100, probably a rounding-up of Chares' figure. His source there (and doubtless here) is probably Chares rather than Onesicritus, as suggested by Jacoby *F. Gr. Hist.* 2D. 434 on Chares fr. 4. Arrian loc. cit. puts the number at 80.

τῶν ἤδη προγεγαμηκότων: Arrian (7. 4. 8) confirms that many Macedonian soldiers had *previously* married Asian women. He puts the number at 10,000, and states that Alexander had their names registered and gave them gifts. This has nothing to do with the 'policy of fusion'.

[καλόν]: 'Prorsus est delendum, ut vitiose iteratum e γάμον' (Reiske).

διαλύσας: The text is probably sound; for the structure of the sentence, τά τ' ἄλλα+participle, see Arr. 7. 12. 2. If a finite verb is required, διελύσατο is a more probable correction than the anonymous διέλυσε, since -το may easily have fallen out before the following τοῦ. The middle is supported also by διελύετο (*Mor.* 339 c) and διαλέλυμαι (Arr. 7. 10. 3), both of the same incident. Reiske thought that ἀπέδωκεν, or something similar, had fallen out after δανείσασιν, but at *Mor.* 339 c Plutarch writes διελύετο τοῖς δανείσασιν ὑπὲρ πάντων, precisely the same construction.

τὰ χρέα . . . διαλύσας: Arr. 7. 5. 1–3; Diod. 17. 109. 1–2; Curt. 10. 2. 9–11; Justin 12. 11. 1–3.

All our sources agree that the incident took place at Susa, before the arrival of the 30,000 young Persians (see ch. 71. 1). As far as the sum paid out is concerned, Curtius gives the same figure as Plutarch,

9,870 talents, as presumably does Diodorus, 'a little less than 10,000'; Arrian and Justin both have 20,000.

Plutarch says nothing of the significance of the incident, that the Macedonians, suspecting that Alexander wished to find out who had been extravagant, refused to register as debtors and Alexander paid the debts on the mere production of a bond. This is symptomatic of the lack of sympathy between Alexander and his men at this time (see ch. 71. 1).

4. Ἀντιγένης ὁ ἑτερόφθαλμος: At *Mor.* 339 b Antigenes (Berve no. 84) is called ὁ *Πελληναῖος* and coupled with Tarrias (Atarrias) and Philotas as men invincible in battle but slaves to women and gold; there Tarrias plays the role attributed here to Antigenes.

Tarn (2. 314, n. 1), pointing to the confusion of Antigenes and Antigonus at Diod. 18. 39. 6, asserts that Antigonus the One-Eyed is meant here. But on the commonly accepted dating for Antigonus— all the sources, including Hieronymus, put his birth between 387 and 380 (see Berve 2. 43; Beloch 4. 2. 133)—he could scarcely be described as ἔτι νέος ὤν, perhaps about 20, at the siege of Perinthus in 340. However, Beloch (loc. cit.) has argued that Antigonus was born about 365, chiefly on the ground that he was the friend of Eumenes (born 362) and that his elder son, Demetrius, was not born before 336. We may add that Antigonus is said by Suidas to have been the brother (more correctly the half-brother) of the Macedonian historian, Marsyas, who was born about 360 (see Berve no. 489). This dating is attractive since, as Antigonus was a native of Pella, *Πελληναῖος* in the *Moralia* could be emended to *Πελλαῖος* (as Berve tentatively suggests), and we should have the occasion, otherwise unknown, on which Antigonus lost his eye. It might also be argued that the odds against there being two men called Antigenes and Antigonus who had both lost an eye are high, but, as Professor Welles reminds me, there must have been many one-eyed men in the ancient world. Against Beloch's dating may be set the definite statement of Hieronymus that Antigonus was 81 years at his death in 301, and the remark of Demetrius (*ap.* Justin 16. 1. 12) that his father had served with Philip. Perhaps also Plutarch's narrative suggests a soldier of inferior rank to Antigonus.

ἀπέτεισε: The manuscript reading involves an awkward change of subject, since the subject of ἀπέτεισε can only be Alexander. Zonaras' reading (p. 302), τὸ ἀργύριον λαβών, suggests that he had in his text of Plutarch not ἀπέτεισε, but ἀπετείσατο, 'he (Antigonus) had the money paid to him'. The -το of ἀπετείσατο might easily be lost before τὸ ἀργύριον and the change of -α to -ε would inevitably follow.

5. Φιλίππου . . . Πέρινθον: Summer 340; see Diod. 16. 74. 2–76. 4, and on the exact date Philochorus, *F. Gr. Hist.* no. 328, fr. 54 (with Jacoby's note in 3B Supplement, 331).

6. βαρυθυμίας: 'depression, despondency'; again coupled with λύπη at Mar. 40. 8, ταῦτ' ἀκούσαντα τὸν Μάριον ὑπὸ λύπης καὶ βαρυθυμίας ἀπορία λόγων ἔσχεν. Cf. *Pyrrh.* 26. 18 (with ὀργή); *Sert.* 10. 5.

LXXI. *The arrival of the 30,000 young Persians and the mutiny at Opis. Discharge of the veterans.*

1. τῶν δὲ παίδων . . .: On the date of the formation of this force see ch. 47. 6. On their arrival at Susa see Arr. 7. 6. 1 ; Diod. 17. 108. 1–3 ; Justin 12. 11. 4.

εὐχέρειαν . . . ἐπιδειξαμένων: 'displaying remarkable skill and agility'. For εὐχέρεια (often confused with εὐχειρία) see *Per.* 13. 4, 'deftness' (of an artist), and especially Polyb. 15. 13. 1 (with τόλμη). For κουφότης = 'agility, fitness', see *Ages.* 34. 7 (τοῦ σώματος) ; οἱ κουφότατοι often occurs in Arrian in this sense—see 24. 12 n.

τοῖς δὲ Μακεδόσι κτλ.: The grief and annoyance of the Macedonians is confirmed by Arrian 7. 6. 2–5 (cf. 7. 8. 2), who mentions a number of other grievances—Alexander's adoption of Persian dress, the Susa marriages, Alexander's approval of Peucestas' adoption of Persian dress and language, and especially the incorporation of Persian troops in the Hipparchies. On this last see especially P. A. Brunt, *JHS* 83 (1963), 43, who argues that this was very recent, and G. T. Griffith ibid. 68 ff., who would date it to 328 ; cf. Badian, *JHS* 85 (1965), 160 f., who points out that the passages in Arrian are *alternative* versions of the grievances. Arrian concludes (7. 6. 5), ταῦτα πάντα ἐλύπει τοὺς Μακεδόνας, ὡς πάντη δὴ βαρβαρίζοντος τῇ γνώμῃ Ἀλεξάνδρου, τὰ δὲ Μακεδονικὰ νόμιμά τε καὶ αὐτοὺς Μακεδόνας ἐν ἀτίμῳ χώρᾳ ἄγοντος.

2. διὸ καὶ τοὺς ἀσθενεῖς: So Arr. 7. 8. 1–2, especially 2. The Macedonians were angry with Alexander ὡς ὑπερορώμενοί τε ἤδη πρὸς Ἀλεξάνδρου καὶ ἀχρεῖοι πάντη ἐς τὰ πολέμια νομιζόμενοι. . . . According to Curtius (10. 2. 12) the soldiers demanded to be sent home because they were afraid that Alexander intended to establish his permanent capital in Asia. A completely different motive is given by Justin (12. 11. 5), who attributes the mutiny to the desire of the younger 'veterans' to be sent home ; the merits of this view are argued by C. A. Robinson, *AHR* 62 (1957), 343, n. 97.

Plutarch places the mutiny at *Susa*, as do the vulgate writers (Diod., Justin locc. citt., Curt. 10. 2. 12–4. 3). Arr. 7. 8. 1–12. 3 correctly says it took place at Opis.

3. τοὺς . . . πυρριχιστάς: No other author mentions the young Persians in this connection; both Arr. 7. 8. 3 and Justin 12. 11. 6 state that the mutineers bade Alexander campaign with the help of his 'father', meaning Ammon, a remark which aroused Alexander to fury. πυρριχισταί are dancers of the πυρρίχη, a war dance probably called after its inventor Pyrrichus (Strabo 10. 3. 8, 4. 16); less likely is Aristotle's explanation (fr. 519 R³) that it gets its name from being danced at the funeral-pyre (πυρά) of Patroclus.

4. πρὸς ταῦτα κτλ.: Plutarch's account differs considerably from Arrian's. (*a*) he says nothing of the arrest and execution of the thirteen ringleaders; (*b*) Arrian and Diodorus (17. 109. 3) both say that Alexander gave commands in the army to leading Persians, but only Justin (12. 12. 4) mentions the Persian attendants; (*c*) according to Arrian (7. 11. 4 f.), Alexander remained in his palace for two days and on the third day assigned commands to the Persians. When the repentant Macedonians came to the palace Alexander came out immediately—contrast Plutarch § 8; (*d*) Plutarch says nothing of the banquet or of Alexander's prayer for ὁμόνοιά τε καὶ κοινωνία τῆς ἀρχῆς between Macedonians and Persians (Arr. 7. 11. 8 f.).

Plutarch alludes only briefly (§ 4, πολλὰ μὲν ἐλοιδόρησεν αὐτοὺς πρὸς ὀργήν) to the long and passionate speech delivered by Alexander to the Macedonians (Arr. 7. 9–10; Curt. 10. 2. 15–29).

5. διδόντες λόγον: ἑαυτοῖς (proposed by Reiske and certainly necessary for the sense) may be understood from the following αὐτούς; Plutarch would probably not have repeated the word within so short a distance. For λόγον ἑαυτοῖς διδόναι = 'deliberate' see LSJ s.v. λόγος VI. 3 and δίδωμι 5. The anonymous διαδόντες λόγον could only mean 'spreading a report'. But Reiske's transposition and change of word order are violent and uncalled for. The passage may be translated: 'The Macedonians began to be humbled (ἐταπεινοῦντο is inceptive); they thought the matter over and found that they had been almost maddened by rage and jealousy. Then they came to their senses. . . .'

6. συμφρονήσαντες: 'coming to their senses'; so taken by Perrin, Langhorne, Ax, and Ruegg. Reiske translates 'omnesque *unanimi consensu*; so essentially North, Stewart. Perhaps Plutarch has both meanings in mind. For the various meanings of the word see ch. 9. 14 n.

ἄνοπλοι καὶ μονοχίτωνες: In Arrian (7. 11. 4) the mutineers throw down their arms in front of the palace door in token of surrender. Here their appearance in a single garment has the same significance. So the soldiers of Fimbria surrender to Sulla μονοχίτωνες ἐκ τοῦ στρατοπέδου προϊόντες (*Sull.* 25. 1). The word is common in this sense; see the examples collected in Holden's edition, ad loc.

8. τοὺς ἀχρήστους: About 10,000 (Arr. 7. 12. 1; Diod. 17. 109. 1).

δωρησάμενος μεγαλοπρεπῶς: Alexander paid them for the time of their journey home, and gave each a talent as gratuity. Craterus was appointed to lead them (Arr. 7. 12. 4); see further 74. 2.

γράψας πρὸς Ἀντίπατρον: This is not mentioned elsewhere, but the letter may be genuine. Certainly it does not contradict Arr. 7. 12. 4, as Pearson (*Hist.* 3 (1954–5), 446, n. 73) maintains; see further *PACA* 4 (1961), 18.

προεδρίαν: The privilege of sitting in the front seats at public games, in theatres, and in public assemblies, bestowed on distinguished foreigners (as, e.g., Delphi honours Nearchus and his descendants—*GHI* 2. 182), on ambassadors, and distinguished citizens. For the frequency of the honour see the index to *SIG*.

LXXII. *The Death of Hephaestion. Alexander's immoderate grief.*

1. εἰς Ἐκβάτανα: Late summer 324. Ecbatana is the modern Hamadan, the ancient capital and treasury of the Medes, to which Darius had fled after Gaugamela. It became the summer residence of the Parthian kings; see Strabo 11. 13. 1.

τὰ κατεπείγοντα: 'pressing matters'. For the verb see ch. 32. 2.

ἦν ἐν θεάτροις: 'he was busy with theatrical productions', not 'theatres' (as Perrin). These were accompanied by drinking bouts (Arr. 7. 14. 1; Diod. 17. 110. 7, πότους συνεχεῖς). It was probably at this time that the satyr-drama *Agen* (see 8. 3 n.) was performed; see Beloch 4. 2. 434 ff.

τρισχιλίων . . . τεχνιτῶν: The τεχνῖται doubtless included both athletes and actors, since Arrian (7. 14. 10) relates that Alexander provided 3,000 performers for an athletic and literary contest in honour of Hephaestion after his death. Arrian remarks that they performed shortly after at Alexander's own funeral. On these performers in general see Berve 1. 73 ff.; he appears, however, to regard these 3,000 as actors.

2. Γλαῦκον: called Glaucias (Berve no. 228) by Arrian; see below.

ψυκτῆρα μέγαν κτλ.: 'finishing off (ἐκπιών) a great wine-cooler full of wine'. The *psykter* which Alcibiades and Socrates emptied in Plato's *Symposium* (213 e) held more than 8 κοτυλαί, about half a gallon.

3. οὐδενὶ λογισμῷ: For Hephaestion's relations to Alexander see ch. 47. 9. Arrian (7. 14. 2) remarks that all writers agreed that Alexander's grief was great; he points out that their accounts varied greatly according to their attitude to Hephaestion or Alexander. We have scanty fragments of one monograph by Ephippus, *On the deaths of Alexander and Hephaestion* (*F. Gr. Hist.* no. 126); see Tarn 2. 4 for this literature.

ἵππους τε κεῖραι κτλ.: Only Plutarch mentions the clipping of the horses; see also *Pel.* 34. 2. It was not without precedent, since Plutarch relates that the Thessalians clipped their horses and cut their own hair on hearing of the death of Pelopidas (*Pel.* 33. 3); cf. Eur. *Alc.* 425 ff. This was also a Persian practice; see Herod. 9. 24. Arrian (7. 14. 4) records that some writers related that Alexander cut his hair (cf. Aelian *VH* 7. 8); he regards the story as probable because of Alexander's desire to rival Achilles. The dismantling of the battlements is attested by Plutarch at *Pel.* 34. 2, and Aelian loc. cit. Aelian calls the action 'barbaric', and Plutarch is also strongly critical. For other evidence of Alexander's grief see Arr. 7. 14. 8 ff. and Diod. 17. 114. 4. This extravagant grief agrees with other actions at this period of Alexander's life; see *CQ* N.S. 3 (1953), 151 ff.

τὸν δ' ἄθλιον ἰατρόν κτλ.: Some writers said that Glaucias was hanged for giving Hephaestion a wrong dose, others said for not stopping him drinking (Arr. 7. 14. 4). Berve (2. 112) suggests with some probability that this was the official version, designed to exculpate the king.

ἕως ἐξ Ἄμμωνος: Diod. (17. 115. 6) writes that Hephaestion was honoured as a *god* in accordance with Ammon's response, and he is probably supported by Justin (12. 12. 12), 'eum post mortem ut *deum* coli iussit' (Alex.), although he does not mention Ammon. But Arrian confirms that an embassy was sent to Siwah (7. 14. 7) and that 'Ammon said that it was lawful to sacrifice to Hephaestion as a *hero*' (7. 23. 6). Moreover, when Hypereides (*Epit.* 21) writes (spring 322) that the Athenians were compelled to look on at sacrifices made to men καὶ τοὺς τούτων οἰκέτας ὥσπερ ἥρωας τιμᾶν, it seems impossible in the context to resist the conclusion that he is referring to Alexander and Hephaestion, and the passage has generally been taken in this way (so, e.g., E. Bickerman, *Athenaeum* 41 (1963), 71). P. M. Fraser (*CR* N.S. 8 (1958), 153 f.) doubts whether 'anyone would understand οἰκέτας, which means servants or slaves, as applying to Hephaestion, *even if* there was a direct reference to Alexander in the passage'. But may not Hypereides be hinting, that, since Alexander was king of Persia, his Grand Vizier was his slave in true Persian fashion? We may perhaps compare Demosthenes' description of Philip's deputies

(? Antipater or Parmenio) as δοῦλοι (*Phil*. 3. 32). According to Lucian (*Cal.* 17) Hephaestion received temples and precincts in the cities, his name was used in the most solemn oaths, and he received sacrifice as a πάρεδρος καὶ ἀλεξίκακος θεός; cf. Diod. (loc. cit.), Alexander decreed that Hephaestion should receive sacrifice as a θεὸς πρόεδρος (generally emended to πάρεδρος). What this evidence amounts to is far from clear, but it cannot in any case be accepted against the explicit statements of Plutarch and Arrian; see further Bickerman op. cit. 81 ff., and Fraser (loc. cit.), who rightly reject the thesis of C. Habicht (*Gottmenschentum und griechische Städte* (München, 1956) 28 ff., that, by introducing the worship of Hephaestion, Alexander was paving the way for his own deification.

4. τοῦ δὲ πένθους: The Cossaeans were a tribe of brigands living in the rugged mountains of Luristan, south-west of Ecbatana. They had preserved their independence against the Persians, from whose kings they exacted tribute. Normally they abandoned their village strongholds when attacked, but Alexander prevented this by the speed of his attack in the winter when they least expected it. Within forty days he had utterly defeated them, and many of the Cossaeans were killed or captured, though only Plutarch mentions a massacre. Subsequently A. founded cities, so that they should become settled and peaceful cultivators of the soil. See Arr. 7. 15. 1–3, *Ind.* 40. 6–8; Diod. 17. 111. 4–6; Strabo 11. 13. 6.

ἐναγισμός: Properly of sacrifice to a hero (as here), as opposed to sacrifice to a god, θεός.

For a similar expression see *Pyrrh*. 31. 1, ὁ δὲ Πύρρος ὥσπερ ἐναγισμόν τινα τῷ παιδὶ τελέσας καὶ λαμπρὸν ἐπιτάφιον ἀγωνισάμενος, καὶ πολὺ τῆς λύπης ἐν τῷ πρὸς τοὺς πολεμίους ἀφεὶς θυμῷ, προῆγεν ἐπὶ τὸ Ἄργος.

5. τύμβον δὲ καί κτλ.: Hephaestion's body was to be taken to Babylon by Perdiccas and the pyre was to be erected there (Diod. 17. 110. 8; Arr. 7. 14. 8). Although among the projects in the Plans which were cancelled after Alexander's death was one for the completion of Hephaestion's 'pyre' (Diod. 18. 4. 2), there is no doubt that the work was completed, since Diod. 17. 115. 2–4 describes the finished monument. Its shape was influenced by the Babylonian *ziggurats* (Wilcken 234 f., Schachermeyr 423, id. *JOEAI* 41 (1954), 127 f.). Arrian (loc. cit.) agrees with Plutarch that it cost 10,000 talents; Diod. 17. 115. 5 and Justin 12. 12. 12 say 12,000 talents. Alexander wrote to Cleomenes, the satrap of Egypt, promising him pardon for his past *and future* crimes if he erected ἡρῷα for Hephaestion at Alexandria and Pharos; on the authenticity of this letter (Arr. 7. 23. 8) see *CQ* n.s. 3 (1953), 157.

ἀπὸ μυρίων ταλάντων: The same expression in Arrian (loc. cit.).

Although LSJ (III. 2) cite only one example (a Coan inscription) of ἀπό+genitive to express cost, the construction is not uncommon in Plutarch; see, e.g., *Luc.* 13. 4, 24. 1, 29. 10.

τῶν τεχνιτῶν: 'architects'; as in § 8.

Στασικράτην: In the *Moralia* (335 c–e) also Plutarch calls him Stasicrates, but it is certain that the architect was Deinocrates (Berve no. 249); see Vitruvius 2, pr. 2, 3 and Strabo 14. 1. 23 (641). Berve (s.v. Στασικράτης, no. 720) inclines to the view that Stasicrates was one of Deinocrates' subordinates, but the slip—it is no more than that—is probably due to Plutarch writing from memory.

μεγαλουργίαν τινά κτλ.: 'because in his innovations there was always promise of great magnificence, boldness and ostentation' (Perrin); cf. *Mor.* 335 c. Berve (2. 130) points to the tendency of the Rhodian school towards enormous works, as evinced by the famous Colossus of Rhodes.

6. πρότερον ἐντυχών: Presumably in 332/1, when Deinocrates was entrusted by Alexander with the task of laying out Alexandria; see Vitruvius loc. cit., Pliny *NH* 5. 62, and the other references in *RE* 1, 1380 ff. (Puchstein).

τὸν Θρᾴκιον Ἄθων: The most easterly of the three peninsulas running out from Chalcidice into the North Aegean. Xerxes in his invasion of Greece cut a canal through the peninsula, to which Alexander refers at *Mor.* 335 e.

7. ἂν οὖν κελεύῃ: See especially *Mor.* loc. cit. (more detailed); Strabo loc. cit.; Vitruvius loc. cit.; Lucian *Pro Imag.* 9.

8. ταῦτα μὲν οὖν κτλ.: In the *Moralia* Alexander remarks that it is enough for Athos to be a memorial to the *hubris* of one king; the Caucasus, Tanais, and the Caspian Sea will reflect *his* deeds.

LXXIII. *Various events depress Alexander.*

1. εἰς δὲ Βαβυλῶνα προάγοντος: In the spring of 323. For a description of Babylon see Herodotus 1. 178; Strabo 16. 1. 5—a plan in *RE* 2, 2696. According to Diod. (17. 112. 3) the Chaldaeans met Nearchus (? in Babylon) when Alexander was encamped about forty miles from the city. In Arrian the Chaldaeans spoke to Alexander himself (7. 16. 5).

ἀφίκετο γὰρ αὖθις . . .: Plutarch seems to follow the same tradition as Diodorus and Curtius. They report that in the previous year Nearchus was to sail to the Euphrates, while Arrian gives his destination as Susa—see ch. 68. 6. Nearchus had recently arrived with his fleet at

Babylon, apparently for the first time, according to Arrian (7. 19. 3).
ἀφῖκτο (Coraes) is probable; he compares *Caes.* 41. 4.

Χαλδαίους: Astrologers, who were accustomed to predict future
events by a method based on age-old observations of the heavenly
bodies (Diod. 17. 112. 2; cf. Strabo 16. 1. 6); see Cumont 152 ff.
παραινοῦντας ἀπέχεσθαι Βαβυλῶνος: They had an oracle from Bel
(Arr. 7. 16. 5) or had heard of the king's approaching death by study
of the stars (Diod. loc. cit.). Alexander had a suspicion that their
advice was designed to keep to themselves the revenues of the temple
of Bel (Marduk), which they would lose when the rebuilding ordered
by Alexander was completed (Arr. 3. 16. 4; 7. 17. 1–4—from Aristobulus). Diodorus oddly remarks that the Chaldaeans said that
Alexander could escape danger if he re-erected the temple of Bel. Both
writers agree that Alexander attempted to take the Chaldaeans' advice, but eventually had to enter Babylon.

2. διαφερομένους: 'flying about' (Perrin). For this sense of the verb see
ch. 43. 1. But the common meaning, 'quarrel, fight with', is more
appropriate; so Ax, Ruegg.

The fighting of birds had long been regarded as a sign of disaster to
come; see Homer *Od.* 2. 150 ff., where the doom of the suitors is
prophesied by the seer Halitherses, and cf. Soph. *Ant.* 999 ff. (Teire-
sias), Aesch. *PV* 492 ff.

3. ἔπειτα μηνύσεως κτλ.: 'Plut. *Alex.* 73 abbreviates the story so
severely that it reflects credit on no one' (Pearson *LHA* 182, n. 167).
For the full version see Arrian 7. 18. 1–4 = Aristobulus fr. 54, who
got his information from Pythagoras (Peithagoras) himself; cf. App.
BCiv. 2. 639 f.—probably also from Aristobulus; see G. Wirth,
Historia 13 (1964), 209 ff.

Jacoby (*F. Gr. Hist.* 2D. 523, 10) points out that Aristobulus cannot
be Plutarch's source here, since according to Plutarch information
was laid *against* Apollodorus while in Arrian (and Appian) Apollodorus informs Alexander.

ὡς εἴη . . . τεθυμένος: lit. 'that he had caused a victim to be sacrificed',
i.e. had consulted the gods.

4. τὸ ἧπαρ ἦν ἄλοβον: Cf. for the same omen *Pyrrh.* 30. 5, *Ages.* 9. 5,
Xen. *Hell.* 3. 4. 15, and especially Eur. *El.* 827 f., καὶ λοβὸς μὲν οὐ
προσῆν | σπλάγχνοις, with Keene's note; 'the lobe would normally
cover and conceal the portal vein and the gall-bladder'. The shape
and colour of these was significant, but the absence of the lobe was
the gravest portent; see Cicero *De div.* 2. 32; App. loc. cit. τὰ ὕστατα
λέγει; Arr. loc. cit. μέγα εἰπεῖν εἶναι χαλεπόν.

5. τὸν Π. οὐδὲν ἠδίκησεν: In fact Alexander praised him for his out-spokenness (παρρησία). Peithagoras survived to prophesy the deaths of Perdiccas in 321 and Antigonus at Ipsus in 301 (Arr. 7. 18. 5).

τὰ πολλὰ . . . διέτριβε: See Arr. 7. 21–2 = Arist. fr. 55, and Strabo 16. 1. 9–11 (740–1) = Arist. fr. 56.

ἀποδυσαμένου δέ κτλ.: In Diod. 17. 116. 2–4 Alexander has taken off his clothes to be rubbed with oil, but there is no mention of ball playing. Aristobulus (fr. 58, ap. Arr. 7. 24. 1–3) has quite a different setting: when Alexander was drafting fresh troops into the army he left his throne unattended. He says nothing about Alexander taking off his clothes.

Welles (Diodorus, Loeb ed., 462, n. 2) points out that it was 'capital' for anyone to sit on the throne of the king of Persia. Berve (on Διονύσιος no. 278) thinks, however, that this incident may be connected with the Sacae festival, described by Dio Chr. 4. 66 (cf. *RE* IA, 1769 f.), at which a condemned criminal acted as king for a period before his execution; for this practice see J. G. Frazer, 'The Dying God' (= *The Golden Bough*³, vol. 2) 113 ff. Cf. Pearson *LHA* 158, n. 50.

7. οἱ νεανίσκοι οἱ ⟨συ⟩σφαιρίζοντες: On the ball-players see ch. 39. 5.

8. συμφρονήσας: 'coming to his senses'.

Διονύσιος: not otherwise known. 'one of the natives' (Diod.); 'some quite obscure person' (Arr.).

9. τὸν Σάραπιν: See on ch. 76. 9. Diodorus says that the prisoner's chains were spontaneously loosed, but he has no mention of Sarapis. In Arrian's version the prisoner was under open arrest.

LXXIV. *Cassander angers Alexander. His subsequent fear of the king.*

1. τὸν μὲν ἄνθρωπον κτλ.: Diodorus (17. 116. 4) also says that Alexander put the man to death in accordance with the advice of the seers, in order that the trouble forecast might light upon the man's head. Tarn (2. 77 f.) argues that this shows that the man was regarded as a scapegoat and that, since the important point is that a scapegoat should live to bear other people's guilt, it is impossible that he should have been put to death. In fact, scapegoats *were* put to death; see Suidas, s.v. φαρμακός, and the numerous examples collected by Frazer, 'The Scapegoat' (= *The Golden Bough*³, vol. 6), 252 ff. Aristobulus (Arr. loc. cit.) says he was tortured to reveal the truth, but says nothing of his fate; Pearson *LHA* 159, goes beyond the evidence in talking of his release.

δύσελπις . . . ὕποπτος: 'distrustful now of the favour of the gods and suspicious of his friends'. For δύσελπις cf. *Ages*. 6. 11, γεγονὼς δύσελπις διὰ τὸν οἰωνόν; *Nic*. 2. 5 (with ἀθαρσής). For the active sense of ὕποπτος see *Mor*. 728 a, and especially 976 d, ὕποπτος οὖσα καὶ πεφυλαγμένη πρὸς τὰς ἐπιθέσεις.

2. Ἀντίπατρον ἐφοβεῖτο: Tarn (i. 112) holds that there was 'complete mutual loyalty' between Alexander and Antipater and that suggestions of discord are later propaganda; Alexander aimed at securing unity in Greece, and 'a new policy required a new man'; cf. Wilcken 222. Although this view is based on too favourable a judgement of the Exiles' Decree (see, e.g., Badian *JHS* 81 (1961), 28 ff.), which was certainly not 'a wise and statesmanlike measure', Antipater was hated by the Greeks and it could be argued that his replacement was due to this. However, Tarn's view is vigorously disputed by Badian (36 f.), who points to Antipater's negotiations with the Aetolians (see 49. 14 n.). He argues that Alexander felt that Antipater's strong position in Macedonia—continually emphasized by Olympias (for her relations with Antipater, see 39. 11 n.)—constituted a serious threat and had decided to get rid of him; cf. Beloch 4. 1. 45. Antipater, for his part, warned by the punishments meted out to other leaders (see 68. 3 n.), must have been aware what fate awaited him if he obeyed Alexander's order to take out reinforcements to Asia. Badian points out that, although Craterus had been sent (?) in August 324 to replace Antipater, at Alexander's death (June 323) he had not advanced beyond Cilicia and Antipater was still in Macedonia. How are we to explain the long delay, if not by Antipater's fears of Alexander? G. T. Griffith, who contests Badian's view of the relationship of Antipater and Alexander (*PACA* 1965, 12–17), suggests that, in view of the discontent aroused in Greece by the Exiles' Decree and trouble in Thrace, Antipater was convinced that this was not the moment to send reinforcements to Asia. Craterus, he suggests (less plausibly), had orders from Alexander not to enter Macedonia until Antipater had left so that the disgruntled veterans led by him might not meet the new recruits. Griffith's strongest (but not altogether decisive) point undoubtedly is that it is difficult to believe that had Antipater felt himself seriously menaced by Alexander he would have placed Cassander (as well as Iolaos) in his power.

Ἰόλας: see ch. 77. 2.

Κάσανδρος: The eldest son of Antipater, born *c*. 355 (Berve no. 414). He seems to have remained with his father until he was sent out to Babylon towards the end of 324; Diod. 17. 17. 4 appears to place him in charge of Thracians and Paeonians in 334, but Κάσανδρον should probably be emended to Ἀσάνδρον (Beloch 3. 2. 325). It is generally held (e.g. by Tarn 1. 120, Glotz–Cohen 1. 179, Berve 2. 202) that he was sent to answer accusations against his father, but it is more likely that his mission was connected with the order for Antipater's supersession (Badian *JHS* 81 (1961), 37; cf. Schachermeyr 427). Griffith, op. cit. 14, suggests that his mission was to explain to Alexander the situation in Greece.

ἐγέλασε προπετέστερον: It is difficult to believe that Cassander acted in this tactless manner when, on any view, he was engaged on a delicate mission and when, one would think, it was important to make a good impression on Alexander. The story is suspect, since both Polyperchon (Curt. 8. 5. 21 ff.) and Leonnatos (Arr. 4. 12. 2) are said to have acted in a similar manner in Bactra. Tarn (2. 299) regards the falsity of the accounts of Plutarch and Curtius as patent; the truth, he considers, is given by Arrian since Leonnatus 'suffered nothing thereby', whereas Polyperchon was kept in custody for a long time. This is quite arbitrary, especially as Arrian reports his version as a λόγος, but the check to Leonnatus' career (see 21. 2 n.) tends to support Arrian's account.

For another clash between Cassander and Alexander see *Mor.* 180 f. Whatever the truth of these stories, it is certain that Cassander's reception was unfriendly. His hatred of Alexander's house is a fact; see Curt. 10. 10. 19; Diod. 17. 118. 2, 19. 49–51, 53.

4. τοὺς κατηγοροῦντας: These complainants are said by Tarn (1. 120) and Glotz–Cohen (1. 179) to have been Thracians and Illyrians. They were more probably Greeks; see Berve 2. 202, Schachermeyr 427, Badian op. cit. 34 f.

5. τῶν Ἀριστοτέλους: 'of the disciples of Aristotle', i.e. Antipater and his circle. Castiglioni (*Gnomon* 13 (1937), 142) suggested τῶν ⟨ἀπ'⟩ Ἀριστοτέλους, with the same meaning. For this construction cf. *Brut.* 2. 2, and the examples cited by Tarn 2. 427, n. 1.

οἰμωξομένων: 'who will suffer for it'.

6. δευσοποιόν: lit. 'deeply-dyed'. Hence 'became so rooted in the mind of Cassander' (Stewart), 'made so lasting an impression' (Langhorne).

ἤδη Μακεδόνων βασιλεύοντα: Cassander, Lysimachus, and Ptolemy all took the royal title in 305 in answer to Antigonus, who had assumed it in 306 following the great naval victory of his son Demetrius off Salamis in Cyprus (Diod. 20. 53. 4; *Demetr.* 17–18). Plutarch's statement (*Demetr.* 18. 4) that Cassander did not assume the title is refuted by inscriptions (*SIG* 332) and coins (Head 228).

See in general *CAH* 6. 499, Glotz–Cohen 1. 333, Beloch 4. 1. 156.

κρατοῦντα τῆς Ἑλλάδος: It is difficult to assign a date to this incident, which is not mentioned elsewhere. It must lie between the assumption of the royal title in 305 and the end of summer in 304 when Demetrius gained possession of all central Greece. This he retained until his recall to Asia at the end of 302, and from then until his death in 298 Cassander could only loosely be said to be in control of Greece. Tarn (2. 339) thinks that Plutarch must have got the story of Cassander's visit from the temple records. This is possible, but if they did record the visit they certainly did not relate this anecdote, and it is difficult to believe that he heard it from the priests. Much more probably Plutarch came across it in the course of his reading.

LXXV. *Alexander gives way to superstition. He contracts a fever and dies.*

1. δ' οὖν: Plutarch resumes the narrative from the end of 74. 1. The remainder of ch. 74 is a digression introduced by the words πρὸς τοὺς φίλους ὕποπτος.

ἐνέδωκε τότε πρὸς τὰ θεῖα: 'Alexander, then, since he had become sensitive to indications of the divine will' (Perrin); although ἐνέδωκε perhaps means rather 'surrendered, gave way to'—cf. *Num.* 22. 12, εἰς δεισιδαιμονίαν ἐνέδωκεν and see the examples cited by Holden on *Sull.* 28. 7. τὰ θεῖα has the same sense as τὰ θεῖα in § 2 and τὸ θεῖον in 74. 1, although it is equivalent in the context to 'superstition'.

μαντευόντων: Reiske denies that μαντεύειν is used in the active and adds 'et si fuisset, numini conveniret, non hominibus'; but at Arr. *Ind.* 11. 4 f. the active and middle are used indiscriminately of the Indian wise men.

⟨καὶ ἀναπληρούντων κτλ.⟩: Ziegler adopts Reiske's brilliant transposition. This clause is out of place in § 2, where Plutarch makes a general reflection on the evils of atheism and superstition.

ἀβελτερίας: Aristotle's ideal ruler (*Pol.* 1315 a) must be δεισιδαίμων (here in a good sense = 'with religious scruples'), δεῖ δ' ἄνευ ἀβελτερίας φαίνεσθαι τοιοῦτον.

2. περιφρόνησις: 'contempt'. Plutarch prefers this form to the classical καταφρόνησις; cf. *Pomp.* 57. 6, *Per.* 5. 3, and especially *Cam.* 6. 6, ἀλλὰ τοῖς τοιούτοις (revelations of the divine will) καὶ τὸ πιστεύειν σφόδρα καὶ τὸ λίαν ἀπιστεῖν ἐπισφαλές ἐστι διὰ τὴν ἀνθρωπίνην ἀσθένειαν, ὅρον οὐκ ἔχουσαν οὐδὲ κρατοῦσαν αὑτῆς, ἀλλ' ἐκφερομένην ὅπου μὲν εἰς δεισιδαιμονίαν καὶ τῦφον, ὅπου δ' εἰς ὀλιγωρίαν τῶν θείων καὶ περιφρόνησιν· ἡ δ' εὐλάβεια καὶ τὸ μηδὲν ἄγαν ἄριστον.

ἡ δεισιδαιμονία: On the meaning of δεισιδαιμονία in earlier writers, where it sometimes has a favourable sense, see especially Nilsson 1.

796 ff., with the literature cited there. For its meaning in Plutarch see Nilsson 2. 392 f., and add H. Erbse, *Hermes* 80 (1952), 296 ff. What Plutarch meant by δεισιδαιμονία can be seen in his youthful essay, *De Superstitione* (*Mor.* 164 e–171 f), and most clearly in *Cam.* 6. 6 (quoted above). In the *De Superstitione* Plutarch had vigorously attacked δεισιδαιμονία, regarding it as even worse than its opposite, ἀθεότης. His attitude to both is consistently hostile throughout his writings; see, e.g., *Mor.* 355 d (with Babbitt's note in the Loeb ed.) and the examples from the *Lives* cited by Erbse op. cit., 300 ff. In religion, as in much else, Plutarch was essentially a middle-of-the-road man—τὸ μηδὲν ἄγαν ἄριστον. At the end of the *De Superstitione* he writes 'some trying to escape superstition rush into atheism, thus overleaping true religion (εὐσέβεια), which lies in the middle'.

3. χρησμῶν . . . κομισθέντων: From Ammon; see ch. 72. 3.

4. ἐστιάσας . . . Νέαρχον: cf. Arr. 7. 24. 4, τεθυκὼς τοῖς θεοῖς τάς τε νομιζομένας θυσίας ἐπὶ ξυμφοραῖς ἀγαθαῖς καί τινας καὶ ἐκ μαντείας (i.e. in accordance with Ammon's advice) εὐωχεῖτο ἅμα τοῖς φίλοις καὶ ἔπινε πόρρω τῶν νυκτῶν. The sacrifice ἐπὶ ξυμφοραῖς ἀγαθαῖς refers to Nearchus' forthcoming expedition; ἐπί means 'with a view to', not 'in thanks for', as several translators understand it.

Μηδίου δεηθέντος: Arr. loc. cit.; Diod. 17. 117. 1; Justin 12. 13. 6 ff. Medius (Berve no. 521), a Thessalian from Larisa, had apparently accompanied Alexander as a personal friend, for, although he had been a trierarch on the voyage down the Hydaspes, there is no record of his having held a military command. In 323 he evidently enjoyed Alexander's favour, and by his enemies was called the leader of the flatterers; see *Mor.* 65 d, cited on ch. 23. 7. However, he was subsequently accused of having had a hand in the king's murder (Arr. 7. 27. 2), and may have written his memoirs (a single fragment in *F. Gr. Hist.* no. 129) partly in order to defend himself against the charge of complicity. For details see Pearson *LHA* 68–70; *F. Gr. Hist.* 2D. 442.

5. ὅλην τὴν . . . ἡμέραν: The feast with Nearchus took place on the 16th of Daisios, the first κῶμος with Medius on the night 16th/17th. It is clear from the Diary (Ephemerides) used by Arrian (7. 25. 1) that there was an interval between the two κῶμοι with Medius, during which Alexander slept and dined; the drinking then went on far into the night (17th/18th). For an apparently authentic list of the guests (? on the second occasion) see Ps.-Call. 3. 31 with Berve's note (2. 261, n. 4).

σκύφον Ἡρακλέους: Plutarch here attacks the dramatic version of Alexander's illness given by Cleitarchus. According to Diodorus (17.

117. 1–2) Alexander drank vast quantities of unmixed wine in commemoration of the death of Hercules; the annual festival on Mt. Oeta would be familiar to Medius, as a Thessalian (see Welles' note, p. 466 Loeb ed.). Then Diodorus continues μέγα ποτήριον πληρώσας ἐξέπιεν. ἄφνω δὲ ὥσπερ ὑπό τινος πληγῆς ἰσχυρᾶς πεπληγμένος ἀνεστέναξε μέγα βοήσας; cf. Justin 12. 13. 8, 'accepto poculo media potione repente velut telo confixus ingemuit'; Ps.-Call. 3. 31, καὶ πιὼν ἐξαίφνης ἀνεβόησεν ὥσπερ τόξῳ πεπληγμένος διὰ τοῦ ἥπατος. Arr. 7. 27. 2 rejects the version of some writers that ὀδύνην τε αὐτῷ (sc. Ἀλεξάνδρῳ) ἐπὶ τῇ κύλικι γενέσθαι ὀξεῖαν.
The skyphos was particularly associated with Hercules; see Macrobius Sat. 5. 21. 16 ff., 'scyphus Herculis poculum est ita ut Liberi patris cantharus'; Suidas s.v. σκύφος; Seneca Ep. 83. 23 '(Alexandrum) intemperantia bibendi et ille Herculaneus ac fatalis scyphus condidit'. See, in general, Athenaeus 11. 469 c ff.

τινες . . . πλάσαντες: 'some thought it their duty to write as if they were creating the tragic and heart-rending finale of some great drama'.
For ἐξόδιον cf. Pel. 34. 1, τὴν Διονυσίου ταφὴν, οἷον τραγῳδίας μεγάλης τῆς τυραννίδος ἐξόδιον θεατρικὸν γενομένην and Crassus 33. 7, εἰς τοιοῦτόν φασιν ἐξόδιον τὴν Κράσσου στρατηγίαν ὥσπερ τραγῳδίαν (? -ίας) τελευτῆσαι, although in the latter passage Long (Bohn trans.) and Langhorne may be correct in holding that ἐξόδιον has the sense of the Latin exodium, a farce after a tragedy.
Phillip de Lacy, 'Biography and Tragedy in Plutarch', AJP 73 (1952), 159–71, points out that 'tragic', 'dramatic', and 'theatrical' are normally terms of censure in Plutarch's writings, and that 'Plutarch often links the tragic and theatrical with the mythical and false, in contrast to the historical and true'. Doubtless πλάσαντες is purposely used here.

6. Ἀριστόβουλος δέ . . .: F. Gr. Hist. no. 139, fr. 59. Aristobulus is combating the view that Alexander's death was due to excessive drinking, as maintained by Ephippus (F. Gr. Hist. no. 126, fr. 3) and Nicobule (F. Gr. Hist. no. 127, fr. 1, where ἀνεπαύετο = 'died' (so Jacoby 2D. 440; contra Pearson LHA 67, n. 26)). Tarn (2. 41, n. 5) appears justified in rejecting Jacoby's view that all the last part of this chapter, from ἑστιάσας δὲ λαμπρῶς, is Aristobulus. More debatable is his contention that Aristobulus' view is supported by the Diary, which officially records his fever on 18th Daisios. This means, according to Tarn, that 'on the 17th Alexander felt the shivering and malaise of the oncoming malaria . . . and drank hard to try to check it'.

τριακάδι Δαισίου μηνός: On the calendar see ch. 25. 2. In ch. 76. 9 Plutarch, quoting the Diary, gives τῇ τρίτῃ φθίνοντος, i.e. the 28th

Daisios, as the date of Alexander's death, while here Aristobulus says that he died on the last day of Daisios. The apparent discrepancy is best resolved by the assumption that the month was a 'hollow' one of 29 days, and that Aristobulus, following Greek practice, reckoned the evening as the beginning of the next day (the 29th), while the Diary, following a different system which did not begin a new day in the evening, gave the date as the 28th; for this solution see Beloch 4. 2. 27, who considers that, since Aristobulus could not be mistaken about this, the last day of Daisios passed as the official date of Alexander's death.

In Ps.-Call. 3. 35 Alexander is related to have died on the 4th of the Egyptian month Pharmouthi, and the corresponding date in the Julian calendar, 13 June (on the equation see Unger, *Phil.* 39 (1880), 494), has been universally accepted as the equivalent of 29 Daisios. This is incorrect. In 1955 there was published a tablet of a Babylonian astronomical diary in which the entry 'month II, Babylonian day 29 (= 10/11 June), king died' occurs. As this entry is contemporary, it is to be preferred to the evidence of Ps.-Call. and the date of Alexander's death should be altered to 10 June. On all this see A. E. Samuel *Ptolemaic Chronology* (München, 1962), 46 f.

LXXVI–LXXVII. 1. *The official account of Alexander's last days.*

1. ἐν δὲ ταῖς ἐφημερίσιν: Arrian (7. 25. 1–26. 3) also gives a version of the Royal Diary (αἱ βασίλειοι ἐφημερίδες) dealing with the events leading to Alexander's death. This agrees substantially with Plutarch's version, but begins with the night of 16th/17th Daisios and differs in a number of details; see Pearson, *Historia* 3 (1954/5), 432 f. The two versions are set out in parallel columns by Jacoby, *F. Gr. Hist.* 2B. 619–22, and C. A. Robinson *The Ephemerides of Alexander's expedition* (Providence, 1932), 64–8; they are translated by Robinson *HA* 32 ff. The version given by Aelian *VH* 3. 23 (*F. Gr. Hist.* 117, fr. 2 a), which he attributes to Eumenes, bears little resemblance to either.

It has been almost universally held (see Pearson, op. cit. 435, n. 28) that Arrian derived his version from Ptolemy, who had access to the original Diary. But Pearson (429 ff.) has advanced decisive arguments against this view; he maintains that none of the extant fragments can be considered authentic. He points out that (*a*) the Diary (in both versions) contains a glaring anachronism, the mention of Sarapis—but see below, on § 9; (*b*) Arrian seems to mention the Diary as 'a familiar literary work', separate from Ptolemy and Aristobulus, whose accounts contained nothing further (οὐ πόρρω = nihil praeterea), but were not necessarily identical with it; (*c*) it is surprising, if Ptolemy used the Diary, that he failed to mention his use of so reliable a source; (*d*) the other references to the Diary do not suggest an official document. Pearson's conclusion (436 ff.) is that the version used by Arrian was probably composed by a Hellenistic writer calling himself 'Strattis of Olynthus' (see *F. Gr. Hist.* no. 118), who wrote 'Five Books of Diaries on the Exploits of Alexander', based on Ptolemy and Aristobulus. Plutarch's version will be derived (? ultimately) from the same source; (so, independently, Schachermeyr 526, n. 289). This is closer to the original than Arrian's version (see 77. 1 n.); where they differ Pearson holds that Arrian has corrected 'Strattis' by reference to Ptolemy and Aristobulus.

On the Ephemerides see also 23. 4 n.

ἐν τῷ λουτρῶνι: so Arr. 7. 25. 1, *καθεύδειν αὐτοῦ* (i.e. in the bath-house), *ὅτι ἤδη ἐπύρεσσε.*

2. καὶ τὰ ἱερὰ . . . ἐπιθείς: I should prefer to adopt the suggestion of Eugen Plew (*Jahrbüch. für Klass. Philol.* 103 (1871), 533 ff.) that, in view of the similarity of the accounts of Plutarch and Arrian, and especially since on every day the sacrifice takes place in the morning, this phrase should follow the preceding *λουσάμενος.* The repetition of *λουσάμενος* easily accounts for the misplacing of the phrase.

3. τοῖς περὶ Νέαρχον ἐσχόλαζε: Here *τοῖς περὶ Νέαρχον* is probably a genuine plural, since Arrian (7. 25. 4) writes 'N. and the other officers'. Wilcken, *Phil.* 53 (1894), 88, translates *ἐσχόλαζε* as 'gave audience', citing *Demetr.* 3; add *Demetr.* 43. Nevertheless 'gave audience to' is probably too formal; 'devoted himself to' is more what Plutarch means.

ἀκροώμενος . . . θάλατταν: i.e. hearing about Nearchus' voyage from India. Arrian's account (7. 25. 2) is completely different; he writes that on the 20th Daisios Alexander explained to Nearchus and the other officers about the voyage and how it was to be conducted three days hence, and on the following days also he is greatly concerned with Nearchus' *forthcoming* voyage. Berve (2. 271; cf. *RE* s.v. Nearchos (3), 2134) accepts Plutarch's version without comment; but more probably Plutarch has misunderstood his source.

4. ταὐτὰ ποιήσας: i.e. he bathed, sacrificed, and conversed with Nearchus.

5. τὴν μεγάλην κολυμβήθραν: 'the large swimming-pool', implying the existence of several (Wilcken op. cit. 113).

τοῖς ἡγεμόσι διελέχθη . . .: According to Arrian, Alexander again discussed the forthcoming voyage on this day (the 22nd) and on the 23rd, which Plutarch omits.

6. ταξιάρχους: χιλιάρχας (Arr.), 'colonels, battalion commanders'. For the use of titles based on numbers see Berve 1. 202 f.

7. τὰ πέραν βασίλεια: i.e. back over the Euphrates, ἐκ τοῦ παραδείσου ἐς τὰ βασίλεια (Arr. 7. 25. 6). He has already mentioned that Alexander was carried from the royal palace of Nebuchadnezzar on the west bank to the royal gardens.

8. τοῖς M. ἔδοξε τεθνάναι: Arrian (7. 26. 1) conjectures, probably rightly, that the rank and file suspected the officers of concealing Alexander's death from them.

ἐν τοῖς χιτῶσι: i.e. without arms or armour; cf. ch. 71. 6.

9. οἱ περὶ Πύθωνα καὶ Σέλευκον: P. (the son of Krateuas, Berve no. 621) is more correctly called Peithon by Arrian. He commanded a ship on the voyage down the Hydaspes in 326 and in the following year was a Bodyguard (Arr. 6. 28. 4). Shortly before this he attended the party given by Medius (Ps.-Call. 3. 31), and his part in the negotiations after Alexander's death, when he supported Perdiccas, suggests that he was an important personage. Subsequently he was satrap of Media, first backing Perdiccas, then Antigonus, by whom he was put to death in 316. Hieronymus of Cardia (Diod. 18. 36. 4) described him as 'second to none for valour and reputation'.

On Seleucus see ch. 42. 1. Arrian (7. 26. 2) mentions also Attalus, Peucestas, and Menidas, and the seers Demophon and Cleomenes; they kept an all-night vigil in the temple of Sarapis.

εἰς τὸ Σεραπεῖον: The vexed question of the institution of the Sarapis cult is discussed most recently by C. B. Welles, *Historia* 11 (1962), 271–98, with an extensive, though necessarily selective, bibliography at 271, n. 1. A fair statement of current opinion is given by Tarn, *Hellenistic Civilisation* 3rd ed. (London, 1952), 356; 'Egyptians at Memphis had worshipped Osiris in his Apis form as Osiris-Hapi, to the Greeks Osorapis; Ptolemy I, or those about him, combined this deity with Greek elements and therefrom made what was in effect a new god, Sarapis'; cf. Nilsson 2. 147, Wilcken 276, 307.

About the Egyptian origin there is no longer any dispute; see Welles loc. cit., Cumont 70 ff., 231 ff. Few too would disagree about the second part of Tarn's statement; see Welles op. cit. 288, n. 83. Welles, however, thinks it mistaken; he argues vigorously that Alexander already found a cult of Sarapis at Rhacotis (Alexandria), and carried it with him to the East. He points (283–5) to the local Alexandrian tradition (Ps.-Call. 3. 33. 9–13, supported by two later writers), which attributes to Alexander the foundation of a temple to Sarapis (for the (indecisive) archaeological evidence see Welles 296–8); to the mention by Plutarch (39. 3) of a boy Serapion and (73. 4) of the god

Sarapis himself; and especially to the present passage. This would be decisive, if it could be shown that the original Ephemerides referred to a Serapeion in Babylon in 323. Even if Ptolemy did not substitute Sarapis for the original Bel (Marduk) as propaganda for his own national god (so originally Wilcken *UPZ* 82; cf. Tarn 2. 300 and many others; but against this 'crude falsification' Welles 289, n. 91, Pearson *Historia* 3 (1955), 438 and n. 40), the extant Diary is probably a late production (see 76. 1 n.), and the mention of Sarapis may not be original.

Finally, Welles (290 ff.) adds a new, and in his view decisive, piece of evidence, an inscription found in Hyrcania in 1959. This is a manumission in the form of a dedication to Sarapis and dates from 263–261 B.C. Welles stresses the remoteness of the area and the poor relations (political and commercial) between Ptolemies and Seleucids, which (he suggests) make it unlikely that the foundation of a temple was the work of a trader or traveller. 'Every probability', he concludes, 'favors the assumption that the temple goes back to Alexander's day'. But probability it remains, and the undeniable tendency to connect Alexander with Sarapis (cf. the early third century story of Diogenes the Cynic (Diog. Laert. 6. 63), on which see now J. Servais, *Ant. Class.* 28 (1959), 98 ff.) may be due to the desire to attribute everything to Alexander rather than to an actual connection between him and Sarapis.

On the other hand, the positive evidence for the institution of the cult by Ptolemy I is scanty; see Roeder *RE* IA. 2401 f. Tacitus *Hist.* 4. 83 f and Plutarch *Mor.* 361 f–362 b (cf. 984 b) relate the story of a mission sent by Ptolemy to bring back a cult-statue, but, even if it is true, it is not evidence that Ptolemy instituted the cult; as Welles (295 f.) points out, Tacitus refers to a 'sacellum Serapidi atque Isidi antiquitus sacratum'. The lack of early inscriptional evidence is indecisive.

τῇ δὲ τρίτῃ φθίνοντος: 10 June 323. See ch. 75. 6.

77. 1. τὰ πλεῖστα κατὰ λέξιν: For the view that Plutarch reproduces the original more closely than Arrian see especially Wilcken, *Phil.* 53 (1894), 113; cf. Strasburger 48.

LXXVII. 2 ff. *Plutarch discounts the story that Alexander was poisoned. Roxane murders Stateira, aided by Perdiccas, who controls the weak-witted Arrhidaeus.*

77. 2. φαρμακείας δ': All translators take Plutarch to mean that no one had any suspicion of poisoning immediately; but he may equally well mean that no one, i.e. no particular person, *incurred* suspicion of having poisoned Alexander; for this sense of the phrase see LSJ and ch. 48. 3.

Some historians, however, *did* relate that the rumour that Alexander was poisoned by Antipater and his sons was current immediately; see Diod. 17. 117. 5–118. 2 and Curt. 10. 10. 14–19. Jacoby (*F. Gr. Hist.* 2D. 479, *RE* 11, 635) considers their authority to have been Cleitarchus; if so, he can only have given the poisoning story as an interesting account and not as the real cause; in Diodorus and Curtius Alexander's death is caused by the 'cup of Hercules'.

Arrian (7. 27) and Plutarch categorically reject the idea that Alexander was poisoned, while Diod. and Curt. clearly do not believe it; only Justin (12. 13. 10–14. 9) and the writers of the Romance (Ps.-Call. 3. 31, Iul. Val. 3. 56, Epit. Mett. 88, 89, 96–8, 110) accept it. For a full discussion see Mederer 140 ff.

The falsity of the story cannot be *proved*, but the probability that it was a slander started by Olympias is high. Its ready acceptance is easily explained by Antipater's known dislike of Alexander's policies (whatever the state of their personal relationship—see 75. 2 n.) and by his supersession by Craterus, together with the fact that Cassander had lately gone from Macedonia to Babylon and Iolaos, as cupbearer, had ample opportunity to administer the poison. Stories of poisoning were, of course, frequent in antiquity when the state of medicine did not enable the cause of a sudden death to be readily ascertained. Even old men, such as Augustus and Tiberius, were alleged to have been poisoned; see, e.g., Tac *Ann.* 1. 5. 1; Suet. *Tib.* 73. 2.

πολλοὺς μὲν ἀνελεῖν: Philip Arrhidaeus, his wife Eurydice (who was forced to commit suicide) and 100 noble Macedonians, friends of Cassander (Diod. 19. 11. 8; cf. Pausanias 1. 11. 4, 8. 7. 7). For the situation see Tarn in *CAH* 6. 480 f., Glotz–Cohen 1. 294 ff., Beloch 4. 1. 107 ff.

ἐκρῖψαι τὰ λείψανα: Cassander took an appropriate revenge when in 316 he had Olympias murdered and her body thrown out unburied; see Diod. 17. 118. 2, and for the events leading up to her capture id. 19. 49–51.

'Ιόλας or, better, 'Ιόλαος (Berve no. 386) was the younger brother of Cassander. Except for his presence on a mission to Perdiccas in 322 nothing further is known of him; he must, of course, have been dead by 317. The statement at *Mor.* 849 f (not by Plutarch) that Hypereides proposed honours for him for administering the poison to Alexander is unsupported.

3. οἱ δ' Ἀριστοτέλην: Arrian (7. 27. 1) relates this story without indication of authorship; cf. Pliny *NH* 30. 149. In the versions of Diodorus, Curtius, and Justin there is no mention of Aristotle; his association with the plot is evidently a later invention (see Mederer 150).

Nothing is known of Hagnothemis. Antigonus took the royal title in 306 (see ch. 74. 6), but we need not suppose that Hagnothemis got his information after this date; he may have had it before Antigonus became king, if indeed he did not invent it.

4. τὸ δὲ φάρμακον . . . : The poison is frequently said to have been a draught of water from the R. Styx; see Curt. 10. 10. 17, Pausanias 8. 17. 6, Vitruvius 8. 3. 16; Pliny 30. 149, Theophrastus ap. Antig. Carystium, *Hist. Mir.* 158 (174); cf. Seneca *Q.N* 3. 25. 1–2; it could only be carried in the hoof of a mule, or an ass, or a horse (to the above refs. add Arr. 7. 27. 1, Justin 12. 14). Nonacris (ruined in Pausanias' day) and the water of Styx, which runs into the R. Crathis, lay west of Pheneus (the modern Phonia) in North Arcadia (Pausanias 8. 17. 6; cf. Herod. 6. 74). The valley of the Styx is illustrated in the Loeb Pausanias vol. 5, p. 144; see also the description by Frazer, *Pausanias* loc. cit.

The water is not poisonous, though very cold (coming from the snow-fields of Mt. Chelmus, 8,000 ft. high), but the antiquity of the belief in its deadly nature is shown by the fact that oaths were taken by it (Herod. 6. 74). Homer (*Il.* 2. 751 ff.) shows that the belief was much older than the fifth century; 'he is only transferring to heaven a practice which has long been customary on earth' (Frazer).

The general sense of the passage is clear, but the text is certainly corrupt; see Ziegler's discussion in *Rh. Mus.* 84 (1935), 385–387. The text of Zonaras is identical, except that he has ὃ δρόσον ὥσπερ λεπτήν for Plutarch's ἦν ὥσπερ δρόσον λεπτήν. This is unexceptionable, since there is no objection to hiatus after proper names; see Kronenberg *Mnemos.* (1937), 311. But, as Ziegler remarks, the change would be palaeographically improbable. The most recent discussion is that of H. Erbse in *Rh. Mus.* 100 (1957), 285 f., who reads ἀπὸ πηγῆς τινὸς ἐν Νωνάκρι ῥεούσης, an improvement on Ziegler and Kronenberg but not compelling. It is difficult to see how the feminine relative can stand, since it is not the dew which is stored in the hoof but the water, ὕδωρ.

5. τεκμήριον αὐτοῖς κτλ.: Curtius (10. 10. 9–13) records a report that the corpse lay in its coffin for seven days without suffering any decay or even discoloration; he does not believe it himself. In Aelian *VH* 12. 64 thirty days passed before the corpse was attended to and then only because of a vision experienced by Aristander!

τῶν ἡγεμόνων στασιασάντων: For the events after Alexander's death see Arr. *Succ.* (= *F. Gr. Hist.* no. 156) fr. 1. 1 ff.; Diod. 18. 2. 1 ff. The generals supported by the cavalry wished Roxane's unborn child to succeed Alexander, if it proved to be a boy; the infantry, led by

Meleager, πόθῳ τοῦ Φιλιππείου γένους (App. *Syr.* 52), chose Arrhidaeus (see § 7) to rule as Philip III. The matter came near to civil war before a compromise was reached by which the throne was to be shared by Philip III and Roxane's child, if a boy. It is possible, however, that the child was designated Philip's successor; see Badian *Gnomon* 34 (1962), 382. For modern accounts see Bengtson 359 ff. and, in detail, M. J. Fontana, *Le lotte per la successione* . . . (Palermo, 1960) with Badian's comments, op. cit. 381 ff.

6. ἡ δὲ Ῥωξάνη κτλ.: Roxane was seven months pregnant (so Justin 13. 2. 5; Curt. (10. 6. 9) less probably gives 5 months) and gave birth in August to a son who was proclaimed Alexander; cf. Ps.-Call. 3. 33. 11, Iul. Val. 3. 58.

δυσζήλως δ' ἔχουσα: On Stateira see ch. 70. 3. Her younger sister, Drypetis (Berve no. 290), had been captured after Issus and had married Hephaestion at Susa. Reiske (ad loc.) oddly thinks that τῆς ἀδελφῆς refers to Roxane's sister; τοὺς νεκρούς is proof of the contrary.

εἰδότος ταῦτα Περδίκκου: Perdiccas (Berve no. 627) had strongly supported the claims of Roxane's child in the negotiations at Babylon (Curt. and Justin, locc. citt.). He was a Macedonian of noble descent, perhaps connected with the royal house, who had served with Alexander from his accession. He commanded an infantry brigade in the three great battles, by 330 he was a Bodyguard and in India a hipparch. But his rapid rise began in the last few months of Alexander's life. After the death of Hephaestion and the departure of Craterus he succeeded to the command of the leading hipparchy of the Companion cavalry and acted as unofficial Vizier (Chiliarch). He received from Alexander on his death-bed his ring and royal seal and subsequently became Chiliarch officially (Arr. *Succ.* 3). The difficult question of his relation to Craterus cannot be discussed in detail here. It has often been held (see, e.g., Beloch 4. 1. 65) that Craterus was appointed to a position superior to Perdiccas, which gave him charge of the person of Philip III and made him regent of the whole Empire; but for trenchant criticism of this view see Badian op. cit. 383 f. Whatever the situation may have been in theory, it is clear that in practice Perdiccas was in supreme control in Asia, and retained control of Philip since Craterus was on his way to Macedonia (see on 71. 8) and was later detained in Greece by the Lamian War.

7. τὸν Ἀρριδαῖον: Berve no. 781. He was perhaps about thirty years old, but nothing (apart from the events in ch. 10) is known of him during Alexander's reign. His mother Philinna was a native of Larisa (refs. in Berve 2. 385, n. 4), and is sometimes called 'saltatrix' (Athenaeus 578 a, Justin 9. 8. 2), sometimes 'scortum' (Justin 13. 2.

11). This evidence is worth little. The facts that Arrhidaeus was brought up at court (see ch. 10), and that he was chosen by the infantry as Alexander's successor show that he was recognized as a prince of the royal blood. Alexander's description of him as τὸν νόθον (10. 2) is merely a term of abuse. Nevertheless, his weakness of mind is well attested (see esp. Diod. 18. 2. 2, ψυχικοῖς δὲ πάθεσι συνεχόμενον ἀνιάτοις (from Hieronymus); cf. Mor. 337 d; Justin 13. 2. 11, 14. 5. 2; App. Syr. 52; Porphyr. Tyr. fr. 2 (F. Gr. Hist. 2B. 1198)), and Fontana's attempt to attribute this to the malice of Hieronymus is misconceived; see Badian op. cit. 382.

ὥσπερ δορυφόρημα . . . ἐφελκόμενος: All English translators conceive δορυφόρημα to mean a bodyguard, e.g. Perrin renders it 'to safeguard, as it were, the royal power'; but Ax and Ruegg correctly connect the simile with the stage—Perdiccas took Arrhidaeus round with him 'gleichsam als Statisten ('supernumerary') der königlichen Macht' (Ruegg), 'den er sozusagen die stumme Rolle des Königs spielen ließ' (Ax).

δορυφόρημα is used of the κωφὰ πρόσωπα or mute characters on the stage; hence of Arrhidaeus, as at Mor. 791 e, ὁ δέ, ὥσπερ ἐπὶ σκηνῆς δορυφόρημα κωφόν, ἦν ὄνομα βασιλείας καὶ πρόσωπον ὑπὸ τῶν ἀεὶ κρατούντων παροινούμενον (I give the manuscript text; Pohlenz in vol. v. 1 of the Teubner Moralia (1957) praef. ix–x, suggests transferring καὶ πρόσωπον to between δορυφόρημα and κωφόν, where there is a lacuna in some manuscripts, and altering βασιλείας to βασιλέως), and Mor. 337 d, ἀγωνιστῇ γὰρ ἡγεμονίας ὑποκριτὴν ἐπεισήγαγε, μᾶλλον δ' ὡς ἐπὶ σκηνῆς τὸ διάδημα κωφὸν διεξῆλθε τῆς οἰκουμένης, where Pohlenz's emendation of τὸ διάδημα to δορυφόρημα is very probable.

9. ὑπ' Ὀλυμπιάδος κακωθέντα: There is no other evidence of Olympias' guilt. It may well be due to Cassander's propaganda; see Tarn 2. 116, n. 2.

Niebuhr saw long ago that the beginning of the Caesar was missing, owing to the loss of a leaf or leaves of the archetype. Ziegler (Rh. Mus. 84 (1935), 387–90) has advanced strong arguments to show that this loss involved the end of the Alexander. By a comparison with the end of other Lives he makes it probable that Plutarch is unlikely to have concluded with a relatively detailed account of Arrhidaeus and to have failed to mention the fate of Roxane and Olympias.

ADDENDA

p. 22 (7. 5). Alexander's πόθος has been discussed at length by H. Montgomery, *Gedanke und Tat* (Lund, 1965), 191 ff. He seems to me to disprove Ehrenberg's contention that the word was used by Alexander.

p. 55 (21. 9). S. L. Radt (*Mnemosyne* 1967, 122 f.) holds that the words καλῆς καὶ γενναίας γυναικός mean that Parmenio advised Alexander to marry *any* beautiful and noble woman, not necessarily Barsone. Hence Aristobulus need not be supposed to have confused Memnon's widow and Darius' daughter.

p. 98 (37. 6). Badian (*Hermes* 95 (1967), 186) accepts Plutarch's figure of four months, although he would put Alexander's arrival and departure about a month earlier (see, however, 38. 1 n.). In his view Alexander waited at Persepolis for news of the outcome of the rising in Greece, of which he had heard on the way to Susa late in November.

p. 100 (38. 8). Badian argues (loc. cit.) that Alexander, who could not afford to wait any longer at Persepolis, set fire to the palace deliberately, to remind the Greeks and his own Macedonians that he had not forgotten the homeland, that he was not, after all, the Great King. S. K. Eddy, *The King is Dead* (1961), 110 ff., suggests that Alexander delayed in order to fire the palace at the time of the Akitu New Year festival, as a piece of deliberate propaganda.

p. 145 (52. 4). Radt (op. cit., 123 ff.) argues convincingly that τῶν συνήθων is neuter in the phrase ὀλιγωρίας τῶν συνήθων, 'Anaxarchus had gained a reputation for despising convention'.

p. 188 (68. 1). On the 'Hypomnemata' see now Badian's discussion in *Harv. Stud.* 72 (1968), 183 ff. While agreeing with Schachermeyr that they are not a late forgery, he holds that the content of Alexander's Plans is irrecoverable, since Perdiccas, in order to ensure their rejection, added the plan for the completion of Hephaestion's memorial and probably touched up the remainder. The 'pyramid' plan still seems to me difficult to accept in any form (see, however, Badian, op. cit., 195), unless Dr. Green should be correct in suggesting (by letter) that Alexander referred simply to 'my father', and that someone inserted 'Philip' by way of misguided explanation. What Alexander intended was the restoration of the great ziggurat of Bel-Marduk, whom he regarded as his 'father'. For the ziggurat see 72. 5 n.; Strabo (16. 1. 5 (738)) describes it as a πυραμίς.

p. 204 (73. 7). For two different explanations of this incident see Eddy, op. cit., 109 ff., and Ph.-J. Derchain and J. Hubaux, 'Le Fantôme de Babylone', *L'Antiquité classique* 19 (1950), 367 ff.

INDEXES

I. AUTHORS AND PASSAGES

The figures in bold type indicate the pages of this book

Hypereides, **214**.
  Adv. Dem. 32. 4, **34–5**.
  Epit. 21, **200**.
  Pro Euxippo 25, **190**.

Idomeneus, **xlviii n. 5**.
Inscriptions,
  GHI 1. 19, **92**; 1. 21, **92**; 2. 157, **8**;
  2. 173, **3**; 2. 182, **26**, **199**; 2. 184–5,
  37; 2. 187, **liii**.
  IG 2². 358B, **103**; 2². 2325, **45**.
  SIG 251 H, **34**; 252 N, **65**; 282, **110**;
  312, **74**, **138**; 314, **100**; 332, **206**;
  829 a, **xv**, **xvi**; 835 b, **xvi**.
Isocrates, *Ep.* 4, **22**; *Ep.* 5, **17**.
Ister (*F. Gr. Hist.* 334), **124–5**.

Justin, 1. 6. 13 ff., **191**; 7. 6. 10 ff., **3**;
  11. 5. 5, **37**; 11. 6. 12, **42**; 11. 12.
  1 ff., **77–8**; 11. 15. 5, **114**; 12. 10.
  10, **194–5**; 12. 11. 5, **197**; 12. 13. 8,
  209; 15. 3. 3 ff., **157**; 15. 4. 16,
  175; 15. 4. 20, **173**.

Livy, 9. 17–19, **lxi**.
Lucan, 10. 20 ff., **lxi**.
Lucian, *Cal. non tem. cred.* 17, **201**.
  De morte Peregrini 25, **193**.
  Hist. conscr. 40, **126**.
  Pro Imag. 9, **202**.
Lydus, *De Mens.* 4. 77, **149**.

Marsyas of Pella (*F. Gr. Hist.* 135–6),
  196.
  fr. 2, **130**.
Megasthenes (*F. Gr. Hist.* 715), **172–3**,
  179, **193**.
Metz Epitome, ch. 70, **129**; chs. 79–84,
  179; ch. 97, **127**.

Nearchus (*F. Gr. Hist.* 133), 26, **179**,
  181, **185**, **190**, **199**, **202**, **208**, **211**;
  relations with Onesicritus, **183**;
  meeting with A., **187**.
Nicobule (*F. Gr. Hist.* 127), fr. 1, **209**;
  fr. 2, **144**.
Nicolaus Damascenus (*F. Gr. Hist.* 90),
  fr. 66, **191**; fr. 100, **193**.

Onesicritus (*F. Gr. Hist.* 134), **l**, **lvi–
vii**, 14, 26, 66, **124**, **162**, **170**; date
of book, **126–7**; visits Gymnosophists, **179–81**; source of *De
Alex. fort.*, **xxxi**; relations with
Nearchus, **183**.

Papyrus, *Berlin* 13044, **179**.
Pausanias, 9. 40. 10, **23**; 10. 24. 6, **38**.
Philip of Chalcis, **125**.
Philip of Theangela (*F. Gr. Hist.* 471),
  125.
Philon of Thebes, **125**.
Philostratus, *Vit. Apoll.* 2. 43, **174**.
Phylarchus (*F. Gr. Hist.* 81), **xlvii n. 4**,
  106.
Pindar, *Olympians* 8. 21 ff., **146**.
  fr. 106 (Bowra), **31**.
Plato, **xxv**, **xxix**; *Republic* and *Laws*,
  xxiv, **xxxi**; Plutarch's use of, **xix**,
  xlvii n. 2 (letters).
  Menex. 238 a, **159**.
  Rep. 528 c, **104**.
Pliny the Elder, **xliii–iv**.
  NH 2. 235, **94**; 6. 36, **117**; 6. 60, **182**;
  6. 62, **163**, **175**; 8. 154, **15**.
Pliny the Younger, *Ep.* 3. 5, **xliv**.
Plutarch, family and career, **xiii–xvii**;
  knowledge of Latin, **xv**; interest in
  science, **95–6**; ruler-cult, **73**; philosophy, **xix–xxi**; view of passions,
  xxi; interest in physiognomy, **9**;
  hostility to sophists, **xxi–iii**; to
  superstition, **208**; to theatre, **209**;
  careless of terminology, **37**.
Parallel Lives, chronology of, **xxxiv–
vii**; selection of material, **xl–xli**;
  arrangement of material, **xxxix–
xl**, **138**, **148**, **163**; aims and
  methods, **xxxvii–xlix**; errors in,
  xliv; digressions in, **95**; use of
  monuments, etc., **xlix**; choice of
  heroes, **xxxiii–iv**; cross-references
  in, **xxxv–vi**; *synkriseis*, **xxxiv**.
Alexander, authors cited in, **xlix**;
  Apophthegmata, **xliv**; *De Alexandri
fortuna*, summary and analysis,
  xxiii–xxxiii; *De Romanorum fortuna*, **xxx**; *Mulierum virtutes*, **xlv–vi**;
  sources, 14, 31, 38, 45, 54, 63, **87**,
  95, **106**, **125**, **131**, **139**, **142**, **143**,
  145, **149**, **152**, **162**, **176–7**, **180**,
  186, **191**, **195**, **203**.
Moralia, 40 c–41 e, **xxiii**; 42 d, **lxvii
n. 2**; 53 c, **10**; 65 d, **60**, **147**; 65 f,
  57–8; 105 a, **9**; 180 a, **13**; 246 a–b,
  191; 259 d–260 d, **31–2**; 292 e, **35**;
  330 a, **121**; 332 f, **114**; 334 d–e, **76**;
  335 a–c, **9–10**; 335 c–e, **202**; 337 d,
  217; 337 e, **59**; 338 d, **129**; 339 b,
  196; 339 d–f, **133**; 339 f, **lxiii n. 3**,

II. GREEK

III. GENERAL

Figures in parentheses refer to persons listed in Berve's second volume.

Q

PRINTED IN GREAT BRITAIN
AT THE UNIVERSITY PRESS, OXFORD
BY VIVIAN RIDLER
PRINTER TO THE UNIVERSITY